S0-BCT-655

WITHDRAWN

GROWING UP LATINO

Growing Up Latino

MEMOIRS AND STORIES

Edited with an Introduction by
Harold Augenbraum
and Ilan Stavans

Foreword by
Ilan Stavans

A Marc Jaffe Book
HOUGHTON MIFFLIN COMPANY
Boston   New York   1993

Copyright © 1993 by Harold Augenbraum and Ilan Stavans
All rights reserved

No part of this work may be reproduced or transmitted in any form or by any means, electronic or mechanical, including photocopying and recording, or by any information storage or retrieval system without the prior written permission of the copyright owner unless such copying is expressly permitted by federal copyright law. With the exception of nonprofit transcription in Braille, Houghton Mifflin is not authorized to grant permission for further uses of copyrighted selections reprinted in this book without the permission of their owners. Permission must be obtained from the individual copyright owners as identified herein. Address requests for permission to make copies of Houghton Mifflin material to Permissions, Houghton Mifflin Company, 215 Park Avenue South, New York, New York 10003.

Library of Congress Cataloging-in-Publication Data

Growing up Latino : memoirs and stories / edited by Harold Augenbraum and Ilan Stavans.

p.   cm.

"A Marc Jaffe book."

Includes bibliographical references.

ISBN 0-395-66124-2 (pbk.)   ISBN 0-395-62231-X

1. American fiction — Hispanic American authors.   2. Hispanic American youth — Fiction.   3. Hispanic Americans — Biography. 4. Short stories, American.   5. Autobiography.   I. Augenbraum, Harold.   II. Stavans, Ilan.

PS647.H58G76   1993   92-32624

813'.54080868 — dc20   CIP

PRINTED IN THE UNITED STATES OF AMERICA

AGM 10 9 8 7 6 5 4 3 2 1

"Daughter of Invention," from *How the García Girls Lost Their Accents* by Julia Alvarez. Copyright © 1991 by Julia Alvarez. Reprinted by permission of Susan Bergholz Literary Services, New York.

"The Mambo Kings Play Songs of Love," from *The Mambo Kings Play Songs of Love* by Oscar Hijuelos. Copyright © 1989 by Oscar Hijuelos. Reprinted by permission of Farrar, Straus & Giroux, Inc.

"Silent Dancing," from *Silent Dancing: A Partial Remembrance of a Puerto Rican Childhood* by Judith Ortiz-Cofer. Reprinted by permission of Arte Público Press, University of Houston.

"The Moths," from *The Moths and Other Stories* by Helena María Viramontes. Reprinted by permission of Arte Público Press, University of Houston.

"Un Hijo del Sol" by Genaro Gonzalez. Reprinted by permission of Arte Público Press, University of Houston.

"An Apology to the Moon Furies," from *Casualty Report* by Ed Vega. Reprinted by permission of Arte Público Press, University of Houston.

"The Ruins," from *Days of Plenty, Days of Want* by Patricia Preciado Martin. Copyright © 1988 by Bilingual Press/Editorial Bilingüe, Arizona State University, Tempe, Arizona.

"The Closet," from *The Last of the Menu Girls* by Denise Chávez. Reprinted by permission of Arte Público Press, University of Houston.

"Alien Turf," from *Down These Mean Streets* by Piri Thomas. Copyright © 1967 by Piri Thomas. Reprinted by permission of Alfred A. Knopf, Inc.

"The Day the Cisco Kid Shot John Wayne," from *The Day the Cisco Kid Shot John Wayne* by Nash Candelaria. Copyright © 1988 by Bilingual Press/Editorial Bilingüe, Arizona State University, Tempe, Arizona.

"Mr. Mendelsohn," from *El Bronx Remembered: A Novella and Stories* by Nicholasa Mohr. Copyright © 1975 by Nicholasa Mohr. Reprinted by permission of HarperCollins Publishers.

"On the Road to Texas: Pete Fonseca" by Tomás Rivera. Reprinted by permission of Arte Público Press, University of Houston.

"Kipling and I," from *A Puerto Rican in New York* by Jesús Colón. Reprinted by permission of International Publishers.

"The Hammon and the Beans" by Américo Paredes. First published in *The Texas Observer* (April 18, 1963). Reprinted by permission of the author.

"Pocho," from *Pocho* by José Antonio Villareal. Copyright © 1959 by José Antonio Villareal. Used by permission of Doubleday, a division of Bantam Doubleday Dell Publishing Group, Inc.

"The Autobiography of a Brown Buffalo," from *The Autobiography of a Brown Buffalo* by Oscar "Zeta" Acosta. Copyright © 1972 by Oscar "Zeta" Acosta. Reprinted by permission of Vintage Books, a division of Random House, Inc.

"First Communion," from *Family Installments: Memories of Growing Up Hispanic* by Edward Rivera. Copyright © 1982 by Edward Rivera. Reprinted by permission of William Morrow & Company, Inc.

"Brother Imás," from *Klail City* by Rolando Hinojosa-Smith. Reprinted by permission of Arte Público Press, University of Houston.

"Golden Glass" by Alma Villanueva. Copyright © 1982 by Bilingual Press/Editorial Bilingüe, Arizona State University, Tempe, Arizona. Reprinted from *Hispanics in the U.S.: An Anthology of Creative Literature*, edited by Francisco Jimenez and Gary D. Keller, by permission of Bilingual Press.

"My Father's Flag" by J. L. Torres. Reprinted from *The Americas Review*, Vol 14, No.2 (Summer), by permission of Arte Público Press, University of Houston.

"Being Mean," from *Living up the Street* by Gary Soto. Copyright © 1985 by Gary Soto. Used by permission of Strawberry Hill Press, Portland, Oregon.

"People Should Not Die in June in South Texas" by Gloria Anzaldúa. Reprinted by permission of the author.

"The Monkey Garden," from *The House on Mango Street* by Sandra Cisneros. Copyright © 1989 by Sandra Cisneros. Reprinted by permission of Susan Bergholz Literary Services, New York.

"The Apple Orchard" by Rudolfo A. Anaya. Copyright © 1979 by Rudolfo Anaya. Used by permission of the author.

"Aria," from *Hunger of Memory* by Richard Rodriguez. Copyright © 1982 by Richard Rodriguez. Reprinted by permission of David R. Godine, Publishers.

Carla and Audrey, Alison and Joshua
beloved

CONTENTS

FOREWORD

UNNAVIGABLE, flowing some 1,880 miles from southwest Colorado to the Gulf of Mexico, the Rio Grande, known in Spanish as *el Río Bravo del Norte* and in English as the Tortilla Curtain, is the dividing line, the end and the beginning, of the United States and Hispanic America. The river not only separates the twin cities of El Paso and Ciudad Juárez, Brownsville and Matamoros, but also and more essentially is an abyss, a wound marking distinctive idiosyncracies. To the north, a triumphant culture with its eyes to the future, the product of Puritan British pilgrims convinced they were the New Israel, a chosen people destined to inhabit the Eden across the Atlantic. To the south, a stumbling civilization fixated on the past, the illegitimate child of Iberian *conquistadores*, thirsty for gold and power, and Indian mothers raped while the crucifix stood as witness.

Language is useful in contrasting both worldviews. Spanish, labyrinthine in nature, has at least four conjugations to address the past; the lone future tense is hardly used. One can portray a past event in multiple ways, but when it comes to one of tomorrow, a speaker in Buenos Aires, Lima, Mexico City, and Caracas has little choice. The fact is symptomatic: Hispanics, unable to recover from history, are obsessed with memory. English, on the other hand, is exact, matter-of-fact — in Jorge Luis Borges's words, "mathematical," a tongue with plenty of room for conditionals, ready to seize destiny.

Spanish makes objects female and male, while in English the same things lack gender. As if one were not enough, Spanish has two verbs for *to be:* one used to describe permanence, another to refer to location and temporality. Thus, a single sentence, say Hamlet's famous dilemma, *To be, or not to be,* is inhabited in Spanish by a double, never self-negating, clear-cut meaning: to be or not to be alive; to be or not to be here. English simplifies: to be, period — here and now. Again, Spanish has two verbs for *to know:* one used to characterize knowledge through experience, the other to designate memorized information. To know Prague is not the same as to know the content of the Declaration of Independence. Much less baroque, English refuses complication.

Linguistic reveries such as these highlight the psychological abyss. Octavio Paz, the 1990 Nobel Prize winner, claims Hispanics are introverted and ought to be seen as extraordinary actors. The owners of a huge collection of selves, they hide behind a different one depending on the occasion. Their talent to pretend, to escape, is magnificent: reality for them is an infinite theater, their whole life a stage. Anglos, on the other hand, are reward-oriented, straightforward and moralistic in their earthly transactions. It is puzzling to consider why the Almighty placed the two cultures face to face — distant neighbors divided by what seems a capricious separation.

And yet, and yet . . . there is a bridge across the abyss. Frontier dwellers, neither here nor there, dreaming in Spanish and living in English, U.S. Hispanics are the symbol of an encounter — citizens with a polarized identity. The book in hand is a display of their self-portraits, a sum of masks, a game of mirrors: the south inhabiting the language and reality of the north, one worldview infiltrating the other. English-speaking Nuyorican, Chicano, and Cuban writers know two verbs for *to be* and *to know,* and are obsessed with the past. But they communicate with Anglos and other minorities, therefore adapting, reshaping, reinventing their innermost experience. Although diverse in backgrounds and nationalities, their collective identity is one. And indeed this volume, the result of twenty-five different pens, despite its variety of styles and subjects, has an amazing autobiographical homogeneity, as if one supreme creator, a writer of writers, were responsible for every one of its pages.

The legend goes that without enough power to undo military and political invasions by the United States, Latin America opted for a silent revolution — the so-called Moctezuma's Revenge. The goal has been to slowly invade the blood and bones of the aggressor's body, to transform from within, to remain stubbornly loyal to folklore and ancient traditions, and, sooner or later, to unmask the true Hispanic — the conqueror. The memoirs and stories included here are a laboratory in which a new collective self is being forged. They detail the Hispanic journey from darkness to light, from rejection to assimilation, from silence to voice . . . from Spanish into English. But the evolution is unconventional at best, at times abnormal and explosive. Instead of integrating, U.S. Hispanics decode and renew: the Empire State Building as a pyramid in Teotihuacán. The future *es nuestro*. Rather sooner than later, this bridge across the abyss, these frontier dwellers, will prove that the Rio Grande is pure fiction, a commodity, a governmental invention. The south shall cohabit the north — Latin America *in* the United States. Not a futuristic scene for those acquainted with present-day Los Angeles, New York City, and Miami. A time may come when the English verb *to be* proves insufficient, when the ubiquitous Spanish becomes an official tongue, when *el Río Bravo del Norte* becomes navigable. This anthology is a preview.

ILAN STAVANS

INTRODUCTION

Soldier of the Culture Wars

As one gets older, childhood years are often conveniently consolidated into one perfect summer's afternoon. The events can be projected on a light blue screen; the hurtful parts can be edited out, and the moments of joy brought in sharp focus to the foreground. It is our show. But with all that on the cutting room floor, what remains to tell?
— JUDITH ORTÍZ-COFER, *Silent Dancing*

T RY TO IMAGINE THE FOLLOWING: at all the borders and points of entry to the United States there are signs that read, "Welcome to the United States of America. You are entering a culture-war zone. Proceed with caution. P.S.: We like culture wars, or why else would we have them so often?"

The United States is a country of migrants, a moving stage populated by large groups of people whose uprooting from other countries brings with it individual and collective joy and sorrow. Conflicts are inevitable. Dominators claim to be superior; the dominated seek cultural parity and political and personal power. Arguments erupt over the relative importance of assimilation and cultural retention. The dominant, Anglo-American culture rationalizes the former, "minority" cultures the latter. Everyone generates a high moral tone.

Today, at the center of the conflict is the Hispanic, the man, woman, or child who speaks Castilian Spanish as his or her mother tongue, or whose ancestors did so. We in the United States often perceive Hispanics as a monolithic or amorphous group. They have divided loyalties, we say, and live between two cultures and two languages. But this is a narrow definition, a figment that Americans have created to fill our need to make these diverse peoples into a single one that we can then understand. On the other hand, some Hispanics also perpetuate the fiction of unanimity, which they see as the fastest road to national political power.

From such a bubbling cauldron, the Hispanic writer has recently emerged as a cultural interpreter. He or she (many of the most distinctive voices are female) has begun to construct coherence from cultural variations, through autobiographical narrative, memoir, and fiction. Much of the work may represent an early stage in the development of an "ethnic" tradition of Hispanic letters written in English. *Growing Up Latino: Memoirs and Stories* explores that stage, highlights those writers who have played a role in it, and presents some of the best coming-of-age stories by Hispanics in the United States.

At the risk of promoting a tyranny of numbers, for the purposes of this introduction we will divide the different national populations that we have come to call Hispanic into five major groups: Chicanos, or those of Mexican origin (13.3 million souls, according to the 1990 Census); Central Americans (2.6 million), Puerto Ricans (2.2 million), Cubans (1 million); and other nationalities from the Caribbean, the largest of which is Dominican (about 1.4 million). In addition, former nationals and exiles from many South American countries reside in the United States.

Those of Mexican descent live mainly in Texas, New Mexico, Arizona, California, and Illinois. With the exception of the last of these, they live on land that was sold in 1848 to the White House by Generalísimo Santa Anna for $15 million as part of the Treaty of Guadalupe Hidalgo. Along with Native Americans, with whom they have had a long history of intermarriage, promoted originally by the conquering Castilian rulers of the sixteenth and seventeenth centuries, Mexicans are the oldest inhabitants of this part of America. They call their region Aztlán, a mythical homeland where the Aztecs, a nomadic tribe, first lived before the 1325 founding of Tenochtitlán, the capital of their empire (on the site of present-day Mexico City). Mexican-Americans — they are also called Chicanos, Xicanos, Pochos, La Raza, Spaniards, Texas Mexicans, or, simply, Mexicanos — have a strong sense of belonging to that part of the earth, an element that is central to the region's folklore and literature.

Chicano history in Aztlán predates the Declaration of Independence by more than four centuries. As a result of this long history and the consequent development of social institutions, literary production by Mexican-Americans is rich in poetry, drama, the novel, and the popular ballad known as *corrido*. That production is massive and boasts four or five times the output of any other Latino national group. In recent times Mexican-American literature in English took early themes from *corrido* and developed short stories about conflicts along the border. The early short fiction of Américo Paredes, written in the 1930s and 1940s, focused on these conflicts. In 1959 José Antonio Villareal published *Pocho*, which most critics consider the first Chicano novel.

By the 1970s, Chicano prose had blossomed. Tomás Rivera's lyrical *And the Earth Did Not Part* (1971), set in agricultural south Texas, and Rudolfo Anaya's astonishing *Bless Me, Ultima* (1972), the first part of a New Mexico trilogy that later included *Heart of Aztlán* (1976) and *Tortuga* (1979), oscillated between rural and urban scenes. Oscar "Zeta" Acosta, a lawyer by profession who had been involved in the militant Chicano movement in the late 1960s, but who disappeared in 1974, wrote two personal accounts of his political experiences. In *The Autobiography of a Brown Buffalo* (1972) he portrays himself as a Robin Hood of sorts, and in *The Revolt of the Cockroach People* (1973) he becomes the legal defender of Chicanos accused of rioting. Acosta's anarchic, dazzling literary voice has recently reached a wider readership with the reissuing of his books by a mainstream publisher.

The parade of Chicano literature continued with Ron Arias's bookish *The Road to Tamazunchale* (1975); Arturo Islas's controlled

The Rain God (1983) and *Migrant Souls* (1989); Rolando Hinojosa's polished re-creations of an imaginary town in Texas, in the Klail City Death Trip series of novels; the mordant stories of Sandra Cisneros in *Woman Hollering Creek* (1991); and Victor Villaseñor's epic autobiography of his family, *Rain of Gold* (1991). Although literary critics have not always included them as "ethnic" literature, such works as John Rechy's *City of Night* (1963), about the underground world of homosexuality, and Thomas Sanchez's *Mile Zero* (1989) also helped shape a sense of ethnic identity and togetherness.

The presence of Cubans in the United States dates back to the nineteenth century, but the first great wave of immigrants left Cuba in 1959 and the early 1960s rather than live under Fidel Castro's revolution. They settled mainly in Florida and metropolitan New York City. Most of these Cubans, called *gusanos* ("worms") or exiled reactionaries by Castro's supporters, were mainly well-educated middle-class citizens who were able to rise quickly, both socially and economically. A second wave, comprising lower-income and less urban groups, fled to Miami in 1980 in the Mariel boatlift, named for the Cuban port from which they embarked. The Marielitos are often denigrated in this country because the boatlift included convicted criminals released from Cuban jails, but it also included blue-collar workers seeking a better life in the United States and people whose families were separated by the revolution.

Cuban-American literature also has a long tradition, though it consists mostly of works in Spanish. José Martí, one of the leading voices of the *modernista* movement that shook Latin America from 1885 to 1915, wrote his Spanish-language poetry in Key West and New York City. He had heard Walt Whitman read from *Leaves of Grass* and was profoundly influenced. Recent Cuban-American literature is characterized by an air of nostalgia and an almost destructive political pathos. Reinaldo Arenas, the author of *Farewell to the Sea* (1973), *The Ill-Fated Peregrinations of Fray Servando* (1974), and *The Palace of the White Skunks* (1990), wrote the latter part of his oeuvre in Manhattan, and even blamed Castro for his contracting AIDS.

Puerto Rico has suffered from foreign intervention, by Spain and the United States, since 1493. Compared with other Hispanics in the United States, Puerto Ricans have the lowest standard of living. Migration to New York and other cities on the East Coast began in large numbers in the 1940s and generally consisted of people seeking economic betterment. That Puerto Ricans were the first "immigrants" to be able to return easily to their country of origin — a commonwealth filled with unease over U.S. influence and often with a collective fear of being swallowed up by an American culture its people do not share — complicates this migration in various ways.

Poetry and drama dominate Puerto Rican literature in English. In fact, despite the high quality of their stirring memoirs and autobiographical fiction about living in the United States, Puerto Ricans have published only about thirty prose fiction or autobiographical works in English. They are important landmarks, however, among them Jesús Colón's *A Puerto Rican in New York and Other Sketches* (1961), Piri Thomas's *Down These Mean Streets* (1967), and Nicholasa Mohr's *El Bronx Remembered* (1975). In recent years, Edward Rivera's *Family Installments* (1983), Ed Vega's *The Comeback* (1985) and *Mendoza's Dreams* (1987), and Yvonne Sapia's *Valentino's Hair* (1991) represent a blossoming of talent in the Puerto Rican community of prose writers.

Since the early 1980s literature by another group has emerged, works of other Hispanics, including the Guatemalan Victor Perera's *Rites* (1983), the Dominican Julia Alvarez's *How the García Girls Lost Their Accents* (1991), and the Colombian Jaime Manrique's *Latin Moon in Manhattan* (1992).

Americans love memoirs and autobiographical fiction. A sense of self, place, and history pervades our literature, from the writings of Benjamin Franklin to those of Harold Brodkey. Within this tradition, ethnic and immigrant writing plays an important role, as members of ethnic groups have sought a well-grounded sense of self in a mobile society.

The U.S. ethnic memoir goes back at least 150 years, when books like *Narrative of the Life of Frederick Douglass, an American Slave, Written by Himself* laid the groundwork for an African-American literature. Later reactions to such narratives, first by Booker T. Washington (*Up from Slavery*) and then W. E. B. Du Bois (*The Souls of Black Folk*), set the tone for a burgeoning literature, influenced by the experience of slavery, through which writers would explore new segments of African-American society and its relationship to white Anglo-Saxon culture.

African-American autobiographical narrative, especially in the growing-up story, played an important role in the development of African-American literature between the formative years of 1930 and 1960, when writers struggled for acceptance into the canon. This politico-literary struggle is particularly relevant to current efforts by Hispanic writers, and comparisons can be made between Richard Wright's *Native Son* and James Baldwin's *Go Tell It on the Mountain*, for example, and several novels about adolescence by U.S. Hispanics of the past thirty years.

Early Jewish-American writers also created stirring ethnic stories in their memoirs and autobiographical fiction, in their case focusing on the immigrant experience and the dissolution of the strong Eastern European patriarchy. The immigrant experience became an imaginative construct, and stories of growing up dominated much of Jewish-American fiction in the first three decades of this century. Such works as Mary Antin's *The Promised Land* and Abraham Cahan's *The Rise of David Levinsky* cleared a path for later writers — Henry Roth, Saul Bellow, Philip Roth, Cynthia Ozick — who could move on to different themes during their writing careers.

The emergence of these literary traditions was fueled by the individual writer's need to assimilate the confusion and anger that often results from growing up *and* being ethnic in a country in which ethnicity is not always prized. The ethnic culture is explored, celebrated, denigrated, and often rejected. In the process of analyzing one's own place within the two cultures, the writer creates a new literature and, generally, a third path.

This is not to say that coming-of-age fiction and memoir is a necessary step for the individual writer of any ethnic group, Hispanic or otherwise. We can again cite Rechy, Hinojosa, Vega, and Cecile Pineda as examples of Hispanic writers whose work is not wholly autobiographical. Ed Vega once stated, "I started thinking about publishing a book. Then it hit me. I was going to be expected to write one of those great American immigrant stories like *Studs Lonigan, Call It Sleep,* or . . . *Manchild in the Promised Land.* I suppose I could do it if forced to, but I can't imagine writing a great autobiographical novel about being an immigrant. In fact, I don't like ethnic literature all that much except when the language is so good that you forget about the immigrant writing it."

The watershed event in the development of the Latino coming-of-age story was the 1959 publication of José Antonio Villareal's novel *Pocho* (a *pocho* is an Americanized Mexican, a person who has left much of his heritage behind and taken on characteristics of the Anglo). In this story of a young boy growing up among farm laborers in California, Villareal explores feelings engendered by the main character's ambivalence about the two cultures in which he has to live. Richard Rubio ("Richard Blond"), the protagonist, questions the values of both cultures and rejects his parents' blind acceptance of Hispanic customs and beliefs, including religion and childhood education. As the novelist Julia Alvarez recently said about her own writing, Villareal also is "exploring his hyphen." Villareal, who was born in the United States, has since renounced his citizenship and lives in Mexico City.

The second major event in the development of the Latino tradition of growing-up stories was the 1961 publication of a collection of essays and reminiscences by a labor organizer and newspaper columnist, Jesús Colón, called *A Puerto Rican in New York and Other Sketches.* Colón had emigrated from Puerto Rico when he was seventeen years old, and his book documents the brutal existence of the young Puerto Rican immigrant in New York City. Although Villareal and Colón lived a continent apart, the publication of their books marked the birth of the Latino English-language prose literature tradition.

In the next few years, Hispanic coming-of-age stories, novels, and memoirs erupted around the country. In New York, Thomas's *Down These Mean Streets,* Mohr's *El Bronx Remembered,* and Edward Rivera's *Family Installments* depicted the unceasing difficulties of Hispanic life in the city. In California and the Southwest,

Anaya's *Bless Me, Ultima*, Ernesto Galarza's *Barrio Boy*, and Richard Rodriguez's *Hunger of Memory* painted three quite different portraits of growing up Mexican-American. As Cubans and Dominicans surged into the United States to escape the political upheavals of their countries, they, too, began to produce rich work.

These writers have written widely diverse accounts of childhood and adolescence. Accordingly, in placing writers of many Latino cultures and sensibilities together, we must confront the terms "Hispanic," which is preferred by the United States government, and "Latino," often preferred by practitioners of the arts. The vague concept of "Hispanicity" depends on an often-unarticulated agreement among users of the terms that different Hispanic national cultures share experiences, which is not always the case. We *do* believe that there exists a limited, shared Hispanic or Latino experience, consisting of linguistic background (Castilian Spanish), cultural mythography (Catholicism and pre-Columbian folklore), and political disaffection (discrimination and disempowerment). Until recently, however, literary criticism has focused on the separate major national groups in the United States, as if these shared experiences did not exist. Our idea in compiling this anthology is to highlight commonality, but at the same time to appreciate cultural divergence.

When one thinks of Hispanics in the United States, it is often in terms of their great communities: East Los Angeles, El Barrio and Washington Heights in New York City, Little Havana in Miami, and the Rio Grande valley. Yet, even though Americans often call these communities Hispanic, they remain national ghettos defined by country of origin — that is, Chicano, Puerto Rican, Dominican, Cuban, or Colombian barrios. Communities are further divided between those who have come for a temporary stay, who will return home after their working lives are over, and those who have set down roots, whose families may have lived in the United States since before there even *was* a United States. Assimilation, championed by such political conservatives as Linda Chavez, is in contrast with cultural autonomy.

Whether presently spoken or as part of a familial past, the

Spanish language unifies Hispanics. However, the extent to which Hispanic writers use Spanish in their writing varies widely. Some writers, such as Tomás Rivera and Aristeo Brito, have chosen to write in Spanish, while others create solely in English; still others use both English and Spanish, and a few write in something that Rolando Hinojosa has called *un caló pachuco* (loosely translated, "a zoot-suit patois") — Spanglish, a hybrid, a middle ground.

Choice of language plays a significant role in the development of the Hispanic writer's voice and message. "I lack language," wrote the novelist and editor Cherríe Moraga, author of *Loving in the War Years: lo que nunca pasó por sus labios* (*what has never passed her lips*). The use of two languages in the title itself expresses the difficulty of narrating personal experiences in one language when they have been lived in another. (Do some types of experiences occur in English and others in Spanish? Do they overlap?) Oscar Hijuelos, a Cuban-American novelist, enjoys recalling how, at the age of four, he became dangerously ill and was taken to a Connecticut hospital. He entered speaking Spanish and left speaking English, because the Anglo nurse taking care of him would answer his pleas only when she was addressed "with recognizable words." The Spanish writer Felipe Alfau, resident in the United States for seventy years, makes the linguistic dilemma the subject of his novel-within-a-novel, *Chromos*. "The moment one learns English," reads the opening paragraph, "complications set in." Knowing that one's characters speak one tongue, and the reader another, can create an overwhelming paradox. Its resolution carries political overtones: if written in English, the text is largely directed to Anglos and attacked by the Spanish-speaking community as a sellout to the establishment. But since the Spanish-speaking population in the United States has much lower literacy rates than its English-speaking counterpart, a book in Spanish would be meant for a readership in the writer's country of origin or for a handful of enthusiastic academic colleagues and friends.

During the sixteenth and seventeenth centuries, Iberian *conquistadores* and missionaries used Catholicism as a vehicle to spread their so-called superior culture, to "civilize" the "savage" indigenous population. The encounter between Spaniards and indigenes resulted in a new theological product, part polytheistic, part Roman Catholic, with its own icons. Latinos share many aspects of this hybrid religion, the result of centuries of syncretism.

Jesus Christ lies at the center of this hybrid faith, but the Virgin Mary — and her Mexican incarnation, the Virgin of Guadalupe — is the true source of idolatry. The abundance of saints, the *santería*, with the power to bring rain, keep evil spirits away, and restrain the individual from sinful behavior, contributed greatly to the development of a shadow religion, which emerged to satisfy the people's need to maintain their own religious practices (generally, and reductively, referred to as folk religions). Unofficial, noninstitutional shamans — like the *yerbero* (or *botánico*), who provides herbs to cure maladies, and the *santero*, who battles demons — continue to flourish alongside a more traditional European-style Catholicism and have been transferred to Hispanic culture in the United States. These figures appear in works by such prose writers as Rudolfo Anaya and Judith Ortíz-Cofer. A questioning of received Catholic beliefs also imbues much Latino literature, including the work of Oscar Acosta, Edward Rivera, and José Antonio Villareal.

Finally, political disaffection from the Anglo ruling class has helped form a shared experience. In order to gain a measure of political power for Chicanos, during the 1960s César Chávez, of the United Farm Workers, and Jaime ("Corky") Rodríguez orchestrated a movement of intellectual and social self-definition, political activism, and a collective search for identity. But their drive toward political power has been hampered by the changing nature of the Chicano population, because of a continuing immigration from Mexico, most of which is made up of illiterate or semiliterate people. Puerto Ricans, centered in New York City, still search for cohesive political power, with their loyalties divided by a movement for the independence of the island of Puerto Rico. Many Cuban-Americans face a similar problem. They fully expect to return to Cuba when the Castro regime falls, and refuse to pledge full allegiance to the United States. In other words, limited political power, along with negative stereotypes, has become the Hispanic commonality.

* * *

One of the problems U.S. Hispanic writers have had is the constant critical comparisons to the magic realists of Latin America, such masterly writers as Jorge Luis Borges and Gabriel García Márquez, who were introduced to English-language readers in the 1970s and early 1980s during a period that became known as El Boom. When first published in 1967, García Márquez's *One Hundred Years of Solitude* not only became an immediate classic but influenced many writers worldwide, including Salman Rushdie, Isabel Allende, and the Palestinian exile Anton Shammas. Unintentionally, the novel, set in Macondo, a fictitious coastal town in the Caribbean populated by forgotten army generals, powerful matrons, and corrupt politicians, created an image for readers in Europe and North America of the banana republics across the Rio Grande and in the Caribbean, which strongly influenced U.S. views of the Hispanic. Thanks to García Márquez, Borges, Mario Vargas Llosa, and others whose art suggests a link between fiction and reality, dreams and everyday life, magic realism has become a kind of Latin American trademark. Lumped together with Latin American writers and often expected to produce an art along this same stylistic line, writers of Hispanic origin across the United States have suffered from this massive explosion of exoticism. Expectations run high, and they are frequently asked to invent magic realities full of butterflies and forgotten colonels.

Another group against whose writing and image-making Hispanic writers have had to struggle has been Anglo fiction writers whose principal characters are Hispanic. There are generally two types of these writers, the sympathetic stereotypists and the unsympathetic ones.

As far back as the nineteenth century, in the works of James Fenimore Cooper and the popular dime novels of the time, Hispanic stereotypes were the rule rather than the exception. In 1884 Helen Hunt Jackson, who was an acquaintance of Henry James, a friend of Emily Dickinson, and a passionate defender of the rights of American Indians during the latter part of the century, wrote *Ramona*, a powerful naturalistic novel about the adventures of a young woman. Set in old California and describing the fading Spanish order, the novel has a lively and engaging, but annoyingly wooden, Hispanic cast of characters. After close to three hundred editions at home and numerous translations abroad, the text has managed to help make its views of post–Civil War ethnicity prevail. Much like the writing of Harriet Beecher Stowe and, later, Gertrude Atherton, Jackson's conception of the native was based on pity, compassion, and romance, but is not a three-dimensional portrait based on an intimate understanding of the culture. Narrative accounts of the same period written by other voices, indigenous ones, are relatively unknown, at least to the general public. History is written by the winner. No proud member of that fading Spanish order, albeit fluent in English, could ever describe the other side of the story and get the kind of attention given to *Ramona*.

A Stephen Crane short story, "A Man and Some Others," published in 1897, also portrays Hispanics simplistically. It centers around the life and times of a group of outlaws in southwestern Texas and along the Mexican border, tracing their violent struggle against the Anglos. John Steinbeck's *Tortilla Flat* tried to celebrate the Mexican-American view of work, yet ultimately leaves the reader with an image of Mexican-Americans as lazy, bumbling drunkards. The literary parade continues with Willa Cather, John Reed, Katherine Anne Porter, Dashiell Hammett, Raymond Chandler, Ernest Hemingway, and Jack Kerouac. Unfortunately, these writers' sympathies toward Hispanics and their cultures worked against themselves, resulting in negative images of Latinos. The production — and reproduction — of these stereotypes arose from the writer's often limited understanding of Hispanic culture. It also stemmed from an overestimation of readers' understanding of Latino culture, or their willingness to understand.

Unsympathetic Hispanic characters abound in popular literature, especially in the Dime Novels published by Erastus Beadle in the nineteenth century and their literary successors, pulp detective novels of the twentieth. In post–World War II America, movies and television continued this representation. In recent years the tide has begun to turn, with sympathetic fiction about Hispanics by such Anglos as John Nichols (*The Milagro Beanfield War*), Christine Bell (*The Perez Family*), and John Sayles (*Los Gusanos*).

Another kind of writer is the "unreal realist," our name for the impostor, the Anglo who takes a Hispanic name and pretends to write realistic accounts of growing up Hispanic. Although we could cite several of these (for example, "Amado Muro," whose real name was Chester Seltzer), perhaps the most outrageous was the case of "Danny Santiago."

When Santiago's first novel, *Famous All Over Town*, appeared in 1983, reviewers praised it as wonderful and hilarious. Chato Medina, its courageous hero, was a denizen of an unlivable barrio in East Los Angeles, the product of a disintegrating family who had a bunch of disoriented friends. The novel received the Richard and Hinda Rosenthal Foundation Award of the American Academy and Institute of Arts and Letters, and was described as a stunning debut about adolescent initiation among Hispanics. The author's bio on the back cover, which appeared without a photograph, stated that he had been raised in California and that many of his stories had appeared in national magazines. The arrival of a talented writer was universally acclaimed. Nevertheless, success turned sour. A journalist and ex-friend of Santiago, motivated by personal revenge, announced his true identity in a piece published in the *New York Review of Books*. Daniel James, the author's real name, was not a young Chicano but a septuagenarian Anglo educated at Andover and Yale. A lyricist of Broadway musicals and a screenwriter of Hollywood monster movies, he had joined the Communist Party during the 1930s and was blacklisted during the McCarthy era. From low-budget films to darling of U.S. Hispanic literature — an interesting career move.

In compiling this anthology, we used three criteria: the authors had to be Hispanic, the plots about growing up, and the prose powerful and engaging. We were struck by the quality and sincerity of current Latino writing. The selection process was difficult, and because of space and structural limitations, we were forced to omit such names as Arturo Islas, Roberta Fernández, Roberto Fernández, Ron Arias, and Cherríe Moraga. We were constantly aware that every anthology necessarily creates its own double: a volume of those stories left out.

Most of the entries are stories originally published in magazines, although at times — in the case of Oscar "Zeta" Acosta's *The Autobiography of a Brown Buffalo*, Rolando Hinojosa's piece "Brother Imás" from *Klail City*, and Oscar Hijuelos's *The Mambo Kings Play Songs of Love* — we have chosen excerpts from novels or longer narratives that can be read independently. In addition, the border between fiction and nonfiction is in most cases difficult to define — that, to be sure, is the intention of almost all of the twenty-five writers included: one person's reality is someone else's fiction, and vice versa.

We found that the selections easily fell into one of three subject areas, though some could have been placed in at least two. The volume begins with "Imagining the Family," a collection of literary snapshots and memorabilia detailing domestic manners in the Latino community here and abroad. The place called home, more than a reality, appears to be an invention of memory, and these tales are a map of a certain existential geography in the collective mind. The first entry is by Julia Alvarez, the only Dominican represented here (and the only Dominican who has published fiction in English). Her cast of characters shoot forward into the exuberance of American culture by taking as a model the egotism of "the good, grey poet" Walt Whitman. The patriarchy of the world the protagonist thinks she is leaving behind reels her back in, but Alvarez leaves us with the impression that her heroine is living in a new world where even the old obstacles of culture can be overcome.

Next we move to "Gringolandia," the Hispanic in Anglo territory, with the well-known story of Nuyorican Piri Thomas facing the onslaughts of Italian-Americans in New York. This section, where the issues inherent in encounters between Latinos and Anglos in matters political and social, from the early twentieth century until today, are vividly described, also includes the bittersweet fictional memories of Nicholasa Mohr, the explosive prose of "Zeta" Acosta, and a tantalizing segment of the novel *Pocho* by José Antonio Villareal.

We end with "Songs of Self-Discovery," a title clearly inspired by Whitman. This section finds young women alone, facing death and eternity. It also deals with the anxious and comical aspects of growing up Catholic: Ed Rivera's hero, Santos Malangués, receives his First Communion only to have the Eucharist break across the bridge of his nose after his behavior unnerves the priest. The volume ends with Richard Rodriguez's "Aria," about writing and language, and what it means to live within the Latino family. This long piece, the opening chapter of the author's book-length memoir *Hunger of Memory*, finds him torn, ripped apart, by having to choose between two languages and two cultures. For him there is no middle ground: to accept one is to reject the other.

In *Down These Mean Streets*, Piri Thomas writes: "Wanna know how many times I've stood up on a rooftop and yelled out to anybody: 'Hey, World, here I am. Hallo, World — this is Piri. That's me. I wanna tell ya I'm here . . . and I want recognition." The construction of narrative, the art of memoir or autobiographical fiction, represents to these writers an opportunity to search for meaning in a world without coherence. Hispanics in the United States are uprooted from one culture and expected to participate fully in another, or live in both simultaneously. They grow up in the midst of the American culture wars. Life here can seem conflicted and chaotic, but it gives them much to construct and explore.

HAROLD AUGENBRAUM
ILAN STAVANS

Imagining the Family

JULIA ALVAREZ

Daughter of Invention

F OR A PERIOD after they arrived in this country, Laura García tried to invent something. Her ideas always came after the sightseeing visits she took with her daughters to department stores to see the wonders of this new country. On his free Sundays, Carlos carted the girls off to the Statue of Liberty or the Brooklyn Bridge or Rockefeller Center, but as far as Laura was concerned, these were men's wonders. Down in housewares were the true treasures women were after.

Laura and her daughters would take the escalator, marveling at the moving staircase, she teasing them that this might be the ladder Jacob saw with angels moving up and down to heaven. The moment they lingered by a display, a perky saleslady approached, no doubt thinking a young mother with four girls in tow fit the perfect profile for the new refrigerator with automatic defrost or the heavy-duty washing machine with the prewash soak cycle. Laura paid close attention during the demonstrations, asking intelligent questions, but at the last minute saying she would talk it over with her husband. On the drive home, try as they might, her daughters could not engage their mother in conversation, for inspired by what she had just seen, Laura had begun inventing.

She never put anything actual on paper until she had settled her house down at night. On his side of the bed her husband would be conked out for an hour already, his Spanish newspapers draped over his chest, his glasses propped up on his bedside table, looking out eerily at the darkened room like a disembodied bodyguard. In her lighted corner, pillows propped behind her, Laura sat up inventing. On her lap lay one of those innumerable pads of paper her husband brought home from his office, compliments of some pharmaceutical company, advertising tranquilizers or antibiotics or skin cream. She would be working on a sketch of something familiar but drawn at such close range, so she could attach a special nozzle or handier handle, the thing looked peculiar. Her daughters would giggle over the odd doodles they found in kitchen drawers or on the back shelf of the downstairs toilet. Once Yoyo was sure her mother had drawn a picture of a man's you-know-what; she showed her sisters her find, and with coy, posed faces they inquired of their mother what she was up to. Ay, that was one of her failures, she explained to them, a child's double-compartment drinking glass with an outsized, built-in straw.

Her daughters would seek her out at night when she seemed to have a moment to talk to them: they were having trouble at school or they wanted her to persuade their father to give them permission to go into the city or to a shopping mall or a movie — in broad daylight, Mami! Laura would wave them out of her room. "The problem with you girls . . ." The problem boiled down to the fact that they wanted to become Americans and their father — and their mother, too, at first — would have none of it.

"You girls are going to drive me crazy!" she threatened, if they kept nagging. "When I end up in Bellevue, you'll be safely sorry!"

She spoke in English when she argued with them. And her English was a mishmash of mixed-up idioms and sayings that showed she was "green behind the ears," as she called it.

If her husband insisted she speak in Spanish to the girls so they wouldn't forget their native tongue, she'd snap, "When in Rome, do unto the Romans."

Yoyo, the Big Mouth, had become the spokesman for her sisters, and she stood her ground in that bedroom. "We're not going to that school anymore, Mami!"

"You have to." Her eyes would widen with worry. "In this country, it is against the law not to go to school. You want us to get thrown out?"

"You want us to get killed? Those kids were throwing stones today!"

"Sticks and stones don't break bones," she chanted. Yoyo could tell, though, by the look on her face, it was as if one of those stones the kids had aimed at her daughters had hit her. But she always pretended they were at fault. "What did you do to provoke them? It takes two to tangle, you know."

"Thanks, thanks a lot, Mom!" Yoyo stormed out of that room and into her own. Her daughters never called her Mom except when they wanted her to feel how much she had failed them in this country. She was a good enough Mami, fussing and scolding and giving advice, but a terrible girlfriend parent, a real failure of a mom.

Back she went to her pencil and pad, scribbling and tsking and tearing off sheets, finally giving up, and taking up her *New York Times*. Some nights, though, if she got a good idea, she rushed into Yoyo's room, a flushed look on her face, her tablet of paper in her hand, a cursory knock on the door she'd just thrown open. "Do I have something to show you, Cuquita!"

This was Yoyo's time to herself, after she finished her homework, while her sisters were still downstairs watching TV in the basement. Hunched over her small desk, the overhead light turned off, her desk lamp poignantly lighting only her paper, the rest of the room in warm, soft, uncreated darkness, she wrote her secret poems in her new language.

"You're going to ruin your eyes!" Laura began, snapping on the overly bright overhead light, scaring off whatever shy passion Yoyo, with the blue thread of her writing, had just begun coaxing out of a labyrinth of feelings.

"Oh, Mami!" Yoyo cried out, her eyes blinking up at her mother. "I'm writing."

"Ay, Cuquita." That was her communal pet name for whoever was in her favor. "Cuquita, when I make a million, I'll buy you your very own typewriter." (Yoyo had been nagging her mother for one just like the one her father had bought to do his order forms at home.) "Gravy on the turkey" was what she called it when someone was buttering her up. She buttered and poured. "I'll hire you your very own typist."

Down she plopped on the bed and held out her pad. "Take a guess, Cuquita." Yoyo studied the rough sketch a moment. Soap sprayed from the nozzle head of a shower when you turned the knob a certain way? Instant coffee with creamer already mixed in? Time-released water capsules for your potted plants when you were away? A keychain with a timer that would go off when your parking meter was about to expire? (The ticking would help you find your keys easily if you mislaid them.) The famous one, famous only in hindsight, was the stick person dragging a square by a rope — a suitcase with wheels? "Oh, of course," Yoyo said, humoring her. "What every household needs: a shower like a car wash, keys ticking like a bomb, luggage on a leash!" By now, it had become something of a family joke, their Thomas Edison Mami, their Benjamin Franklin Mom.

Her face fell. "Come on now! Use your head." One more wrong guess and she'd show Yoyo, pointing with her pencil to the different highlights of this incredible new wonder. "Remember that time we took the car to Bear Mountain, and we re-ah-lized that we had forgotten to pack an opener with our pick-a-nick?" (Her daughters kept correcting her, but she insisted this was how it should be said.) "When we were ready to eat we didn't have any way to open the refreshments cans?" (This before flip-top lids, which she claimed had crossed her mind.) "You know what this is now?" Yoyo shook her head. "Is a car bumper, but see this part is a removable can opener. So simple and yet so necessary, eh?"

"Yeah, Mami. You should patent it." Yoyo shrugged as her mother tore off the scratch paper and folded it carefully, corner to corner, as if she were going to save it. But then she tossed it in the wastebasket on her way out of the room and gave a little laugh like a disclaimer. "It's half of one or two dozen of another."

None of her daughters was very encouraging. They resented her spending time on those dumb inventions. Here they were, trying to fit in America among Americans; they needed help figuring out who they were, why the Irish kids whose grandparents had been micks were calling them spics. Why had they come to this country in the first place? Important, crucial, final things, and here was their own mother, who didn't have a second to help them puzzle any of this out, inventing gadgets to make life easier for the American moms.

Sometimes Yoyo challenged her. "Why, Mami? Why do it? You're never going to make money. The Americans have already thought of everything, you know that."

"Maybe not. Maybe, just maybe, there's something they've missed that's important. With patience and calm, even a burro can climb a palm." This last was one of her many Dominican sayings she had imported into her scrambled English.

"But what's the point?" Yoyo persisted.

"Point, point, does everything need a point? Why do you write poems?"

Yoyo had to admit it was her mother who had the point there. Still, in the hierarchy of things, a poem seemed much more important than a potty that played music when a toilet-training toddler went in its bowl.

They talked about it among themselves, the four girls, as they often did now about the many puzzling things in this new country.

"Better she reinvents the wheel than be on our cases all the time," the oldest, Carla, observed. In the close quarters of an American nuclear family, their mother's prodigious energy was becoming a real drain on their self-determination. Let her have a project. What harm could she do, and besides, she needed that acknowledgment. It had come to her automatically in the old country from being a de la Torre. "Garcia de la Torre," Laura would enunciate carefully, giving her maiden as well as married name when they first arrived. But the blank smiles had never heard of her name. She would show them. She would prove to these Americans what a smart woman could do with a pencil and pad.

She had a near miss once. Every night, she liked to read the *New York Times* in bed before turning off her light, to see what the Americans were up to. One night she let out a yelp to wake up her husband beside her. He sat bolt upright, reaching for his glasses, which in his haste he knocked across the room. "¿Qué pasa? ¿Qué pasa?" What is wrong? There was terror in his voice, the same fear she'd heard in the Dominican Republic before they left. They had been watched there; he was followed. They could not talk, of course, though they had whispered to each other in fear at night in the dark bed. Now in America, he was safe, a success even; his Centro de Medicina in the Bronx was thronged with the sick and the homesick yearning to go home again. But in dreams he went back to those awful days and long nights, and his wife's screams confirmed his secret fear: they had not gotten away after all; the SIM had come for them at last.

"Ay, Cuco! Remember how I showed you that suitcase with little wheels so we should not have to carry those heavy bags when we traveled? Someone stole my idea and made a million!" She shook the paper in his face. "See, see! This man was no bobo! He didn't put all his pokers on a back burner. I kept telling you, one of these days my ship would pass me by in the night!" She wagged her finger at her husband and daughters, laughing all the while, one of those eerie laughs crazy people in movies laugh. The four girls had congregated in her room. They eyed their mother and each other. Perhaps they were all thinking the same thing: wouldn't it be weird and sad if Mami did end up in Bellevue?

"¡Ya, ya!" She waved them out of her room at last. "There is no use trying to drink spilt milk, that's for sure."

It was the suitcase rollers that stopped Laura's hand; she had weathervaned a minor brainstorm. And yet, this plagiarist had gotten all the credit, and the money. What use was it trying to compete with the Americans: they would always have the head start. It was their country, after all. Best stick close to home. She cast her sights about — her daughters ducked — and found her husband's office in need. Several days a week, dressed profession-ally in a white smock with a little name tag pinned on the lapel, a shopping bag full of cleaning materials and rags, she rode with her husband in his car to the Bronx. On the way, she organized the glove compartment or took off the address stickers from the maga-zines for the waiting room because she had read somewhere how by means of these stickers drug addict patients found out where doctors lived and burglarized their homes looking for syringes. At night, she did the books, filling in columns with how much money they had made that day. Who had time to be inventing silly things!

She did take up her pencil and pad one last time. But it was to help one of her daughters out. In ninth grade, Yoyo was chosen by her English teacher, Sister Mary Joseph, to deliver the Teachers' Day address at the school assembly. Back in the Dominican Republic growing up, Yoyo had been a terrible student. No one could ever get her to sit down to a book. But in New York she needed to settle somewhere, and since the natives were unfriendly and the country inhospitable, she took root in the language. By high school, the nuns were reading her stories and compositions out loud in English class.

But the specter of delivering a speech brown-nosing the teachers jammed her imagination. At first she didn't want to and then she couldn't seem to write that speech. She should have thought of it as "a great honor," as her father called it. But she was mortified. She still had a slight accent, and she did not like to speak in public, subjecting herself to her classmates' ridicule. It also took no great figuring to see that to deliver a eulogy for a convent full of crazy, old, overweight nuns was no way to endear herself to her peers.

But she didn't know how to get out of it. Night after night she sat at her desk, hoping to polish off some quick, noncommittal little speech. But she couldn't get anything down.

The weekend before the assembly Monday morning, Yoyo went into a panic. Her mother would just have to call in tomorrow and say Yoyo was in the hospital, in a coma.

Laura tried to calm her down. "Just remember how Mister Lincoln couldn't think of anything to say at the Gettysburg, but then, bang! *Four score and once upon a time ago,*" she began reciting. "Something is going to come if you just relax. You'll see, like the Americans say, *Necessity is the daughter of invention.* I'll help you."

That weekend, her mother turned all her energy toward helping Yoyo write her speech. "Please, Mami, just leave me alone, please," Yoyo pleaded with her. But Yoyo would get rid of the goose only to have to contend with the gander. Her father kept poking his head in the door just to see if Yoyo had "fulfilled your obligations," a phrase he had used when the girls were younger and he'd check to see whether they had gone to the bathroom before a car trip. Several times that weekend around the supper table, he recited his own high school valedictorian speech. He gave Yoyo pointers on delivery, notes on the great orators and their tricks. (Humbleness and praise and falling silent with great emotion were his favorites.)

Laura sat across the table, the only one who seemed to be listening to him. Yoyo and her sisters were forgetting a lot of their Spanish, and their father's formal, florid diction was hard to understand. But Laura smiled softly to herself and turned the lazy Susan at the center of the table around and around as if it were the prime mover, the first gear of her attention.

That Sunday evening, Yoyo was reading some poetry to get herself inspired: Whitman's poems in an old book with an engraved cover her father had picked up in a thrift shop next to his office. *I celebrate myself and sing myself . . . He most honors my style who learns under it to destroy the teacher.* The poet's words shocked and thrilled her. She had gotten used to the nuns, a literature of appropriate sentiments, poems with a message, expurgated texts. But here was a flesh-and-blood man, belching and laughing and sweating in poems. *Who touches this book touches a man.*

That night, at last, she started to write, recklessly, three, five pages, looking up once only to see her father passing by the hall on tiptoe. When Yoyo was done, she read over her words and her eyes filled. She finally sounded like herself in English!

As soon as she had finished that first draft, she called her mother to her room. Laura listened attentively while Yoyo read the speech out loud, and in the end her eyes were glistening too. Her face was soft and warm and proud. "Ay, Yoyo, you are going to be the one to bring our name to the headlights in this country! That is a beautiful, beautiful speech. I want for your father to hear it before he goes to sleep. Then I will type it for you, all right?"

Down the hall they went, mother and daughter, faces flushed with accomplishment. Into the master bedroom where Carlos was propped up on his pillows, still awake, reading the Dominican papers, already days old. Now that the dictatorship had been toppled, he had become interested in his country's fate again. The interim government was going to hold the first free elections in thirty years. History was in the making, freedom and hope were in the air again! There was still some question in his mind whether or not he might move his family back. But Laura had gotten used to the life here. She did not want to go back to the old country, where, de la Torre or not, she was only a wife and a mother (and a failed one at that, since she had never provided the required son). Better an independent nobody than a high-class house slave. She did not come straight out and disagree with her husband's plans. Instead, she fussed with him about reading the papers in bed, soiling their sheets with those poorly printed, foreign tabloids. "The *Times* is not that bad!" she'd claim if her husband tried to humor her by saying they shared the same dirty habit.

The minute Carlos saw his wife and daughter filing in, he put his paper down and his face brightened, as if at long last his wife had delivered the son and that was the news she was bringing him. His teeth were already grinning from the glass of water next to his bedside lamp, so he lisped when he said, "Eh-speech, eh-speech!"

"It is so beautiful, Cuco," Laura coached him, turning the sound on his TV off. She sat down at the foot of the bed. Yoyo stood before both of them, blocking their view of the soldiers in helicopters landing amid silenced gun reports and explosions. A few weeks ago it had been the shores of the Dominican Republic. Now it was the jungles of Southeast Asia they were saving. Her mother gave her the nod to begin reading.

Yoyo didn't need much encouragement. She put her nose to the fire, as her mother would have said, and read from start to finish without looking up. When she concluded, she was a little embarrassed at the pride she took in her own words. She pretended to quibble with a phrase or two, then looked questioningly to her mother. Laura's face was radiant. Yoyo turned to share her pride with her father.

The expression on his face shocked both mother and daughter. Carlos's toothless mouth had collapsed into a dark zero. His eyes bored into Yoyo, then shifted to Laura. In barely audible Spanish, as if secret microphones or informers were all about, he whispered to his wife, "You will permit her to read *that*?"

Laura's eyebrows shot up, her mouth fell open. In the old country, any whisper of a challenge to authority could bring the secret police in their black VWs. But this was America. People could say what they thought. "What is wrong with her speech?" Laura questioned him.

"What ees wrrrong with her eh-speech?" Carlos wagged his head at her. His anger was always more frightening in his broken English. As if he had mutilated the language in his fury — and now there was nothing to stand between them and his raw, dumb anger. "What is wrong? I will tell you what is wrong. It show no gratitude. It is boastful. *I celebrate myself? The best student learns to destroy the teacher?*" He mocked Yoyo's plagiarized words. "That is insubordinate. It is improper. It is disrespecting of her teachers —" In his anger he had forgotten his fear of lurking spies: each wrong he voiced was a decibel higher than the last outrage. Finally, he shouted at Yoyo, "As your father, I forbid you to make that eh-speech!"

Laura leapt to her feet, a sign that *she* was about to deliver her own speech. She was a small woman, and she spoke all her pronouncements standing up, either for more projection or as a carryover from her girlhood in convent schools where one asked for, and literally took, the floor in order to speak. She stood by Yoyo's side, shoulder to shoulder. They looked down at Carlos. "That is no tone of voice —" she began.

But now Carlos was truly furious. It was bad enough that his daughter was rebelling, but here was his own wife joining forces with her. Soon he would be surrounded by a houseful of independent American women. He too leapt from the bed, throwing off his covers. The Spanish newspapers flew across the room. He snatched the speech out of Yoyo's hands, held it before the girl's wide eyes, a vengeful, mad look in his own, and then once, twice, three, four, countless times, he tore the speech into shreds.

"Are you crazy?" Laura lunged at him. "Have you gone mad? That is her speech for tomorrow you have torn up!"

"Have *you* gone mad?" He shook her away. "You were going to let her read that . . . that insult to her teachers?"

"Insult to her teachers!" Laura's face had crumpled up like a piece of paper. On it was written a love note to her husband, an unhappy, haunted man. "This is America, Papi, America! You are not in a savage country anymore!"

Meanwhile, Yoyo was on her knees, weeping wildly, collecting all the little pieces of her speech, hoping that she could put it back together before the assembly tomorrow morning. But not even a sibyl could have made sense of those tiny scraps of paper. All hope was lost. "He broke it, he broke it," Yoyo moaned as she picked up a handful of pieces.

Probably, if she had thought a moment about it, she would not have done what she did next. She would have realized her father had lost brothers and friends to the dictator Trujillo. For the rest of his life, he would be haunted by blood in the streets and late night disappearances. Even after all these years, he cringed if a black Volkswagen passed him on the street. He feared anyone in uniform: the meter maid giving out parking tickets, a museum guard approaching to tell him not to get too close to his favorite Goya.

On her knees, Yoyo thought of the worst thing she could say to her father. She gathered a handful of scraps, stood up, and hurled them in his face. In a low, ugly whisper, she pronounced Trujillo's hated nickname: "Chapita! You're just another Chapita!"

It took Yoyo's father only a moment to register the loathsome nickname before he came after her. Down the halls they raced, but Yoyo was quicker than he and made it into her room just in time to lock the door as her father threw his weight against it. He called down curses on her head, ordered her on his authority as her father to open that door! He throttled the doorknob, but all to no avail. Her mother's love of gadgets saved Yoyo's hide that night. Laura had hired a locksmith to install good locks on all the bedroom doors after the house had been broken into once while they were away. Now if burglars broke in again, and the family was at home, there would be a second round of locks for the thieves to contend with.

"Lolo," she said, trying to calm him down. "Don't you ruin my new locks."

Finally he did calm down, his anger spent. Yoyo heard their footsteps retreating down the hall. Their door clicked shut. Then muffled voices, her mother's rising in anger, in persuasion, her father's deeper murmurs of explanation and self-defense. The house fell silent a moment, before Yoyo heard, far off, the gun blasts and explosions, the serious, self-important voices of newscasters reporting their TV war.

A little while later there was a quiet knock at Yoyo's door, followed by a tentative attempt at the doorknob. "Cuquita?" her mother whispered. "Open up, Cuquita."

"Go away," Yoyo wailed, but they both knew she was glad her mother was there, and needed only a moment's protest to save face.

Together they concocted a speech: two brief pages of stale compliments and the polite commonplaces on teachers, a speech wrought by necessity and without much invention by mother and daughter late into the night on one of the pads of paper Laura had once used for her own inventions. After it was drafted, Laura typed it up while Yoyo stood by, correcting her mother's misnomers and mis-sayings.

Yoyo came home the next day with the success story of the assembly. The nuns had been flattered, the audience had stood up and given "our devoted teachers a standing ovation" — what Laura had suggested they do at the end of the speech.

She clapped her hands together as Yoyo recreated the moment. "I stole that from your father's speech, remember? Remember how he put that in at the end?" She quoted him in Spanish, then translated for Yoyo into English.

That night, Yoyo watched him from the upstairs hall window, where she'd retreated the minute she heard his car pull up in front of the house. Slowly, her father came up the driveway, a grim expression on his face as he grappled with a large, heavy cardboard box. At the front door he set the package down carefully and patted all his pockets for his house keys. (If only he'd had Laura's ticking keychain!) Yoyo heard the snapping open of locks downstairs. She listened as he struggled to maneuver the box through the narrow doorway. He called her name several times, but she did not answer him.

"My daughter, your father, he love you very much," he explained from the bottom of the stairs. "He just want to protect you." Finally, her mother came up and pleaded with Yoyo to go down and reconcile with him. "Your father did not mean to harm. You must pardon him. Always it is better to let bygones be forgotten, no?"

Downstairs, Yoyo found her father setting up a brand-new electric typewriter on the kitchen table. It was even better than her mother's. He had outdone himself with all the extra features: a plastic carrying case with Yoyo's initials decaled below the handle, a brace to lift the paper upright while she typed, an erase cartridge, an automatic margin tab, a plastic hood like a toaster cover to keep the dust away. Not even her mother could have invented such a machine!

But Laura's inventing days were over, just as Yoyo's were starting up with her school-wide success. Rather than the rolling suitcase everyone else in the family remembers, Yoyo thinks of the speech her mother wrote as her last invention. It was as if, after that, her mother had passed on to Yoyo her pencil and pad and said, "Okay, Cuquita, here's the buck. You give it a shot."

OSCAR HIJUELOS

The Mambo Kings Play
Songs of Love

I T WAS A Saturday afternoon on La Salle Street, years and years
ago when I was a little kid, and around three o'clock Mrs.
Shannon, the heavy Irish woman in her perpetually soup-stained
dress, opened her back window and shouted out into the courtyard, "Hey, Cesar, yoo-hoo, I think you're on television, I swear it's
you!" When I heard the opening strains of the *I Love Lucy* show
I got excited because I knew she was referring to an item of
eternity, that episode in which my dead father and my Uncle Cesar
had appeared, playing Ricky Ricardo's singing cousins fresh off the
farm in Oriente Province, Cuba, and north in New York for an
engagement at Ricky's nightclub, the Tropicana.

This was close enough to the truth about their real lives — they
were musicians and songwriters who had left Havana for New
York in 1949, the year they formed the Mambo Kings, an orchestra
that packed clubs, dance halls, and theaters around the East
Coast — and, excitement of excitements, they even made a fabled
journey in a flamingo-pink bus out to Sweet's Ballroom in San
Francisco, playing on an all-star mambo night, a beautiful night of
glory, beyond death, beyond pain, beyond all stillness.

Desi Arnaz had caught their act one night in a supper club on
the West Side, and because they had perhaps already known each

other from Havana or Oriente Province, where Arnaz, like the brothers, was born, it was natural that he ask them to sing on his show. He liked one of their songs in particular, a romantic bolero written by them, "Beautiful María of My Soul."

Some months later (I don't know how many, I wasn't five years old yet) they began to rehearse for the immortal appearance of my father on this show. For me, my father's gentle rapping on Ricky Ricardo's door has always been a call from the beyond, as in Dracula films, or films of the walking dead, in which spirits ooze out from behind tombstones and through the cracked windows and rotted floors of gloomy antique halls: Lucille Ball, the lovely red-headed actress and comedienne who played Ricky's wife, was housecleaning when she heard the rapping of my father's knuckles against that door.

"I'm commmmmming," in her singsong voice.

Standing in her entrance, two men in white silk suits and butter-fly-looking lace bow ties, black instrument cases by their side and black-brimmed white hats in their hands — my father, Nestor Castillo, thin and broad-shouldered, and Uncle Cesar, thickset and immense.

My uncle: "Mrs. Ricardo? My name is Alfonso and this is my brother Manny . . ."

And her face lights up and she says, "Oh, yes, the fellows from Cuba. Ricky told me all about you."

Then, just like that, they're sitting on the couch when Ricky Ricardo walks in and says something like, "Manny, Alfonso! Gee, it's really swell that you fellas could make it up here from Havana for the show."

That's when my father smiled. The first time I saw a rerun of this, I could remember other things about him — his lifting me up, his smell of cologne, his patting my head, his handing me a dime, his touching my face, his whistling, his taking me and my little sister, Leticia, for a walk in the park, and so many other moments happening in my thoughts simultaneously that it was like watching something momentous, say the Resurrection, as if Christ had stepped out of his sepulcher, flooding the world with light — what we were taught in the local church with the big red doors —

because my father was now newly alive and could take off his hat and sit down on the couch in Ricky's living room, resting his black instrument case on his lap. He could play the trumpet, move his head, blink his eyes, nod, walk across the room, and say "Thank you" when offered a cup of coffee. For me, the room was suddenly bursting with a silvery radiance. And now I knew that we could see it again. Mrs. Shannon had called out into the courtyard alerting my uncle: I was already in his apartment.

With my heart racing, I turned on the big black-and-white television set in his living room and tried to wake him. My uncle had fallen asleep in the kitchen — having worked really late the night before, some job in a Bronx social club, singing and playing the horn with a pickup group of musicians. He was snoring, his shirt was open, a few buttons had popped out on his belly. Between the delicate-looking index and forefingers of his right hand, a Chesterfield cigarette burning down to the filter, that hand still holding a half glass of rye whiskey, which he used to drink like crazy because in recent years he had been suffering from bad dreams, saw apparitions, felt cursed, and, despite all the women he took to bed, found his life of bachelorhood solitary and wearisome. But I didn't know this at the time, I thought he was sleeping because he had worked so hard the night before, singing and playing the trumpet for seven or eight hours. I'm talking about a wedding party in a crowded, smoke-filled room (with bolted-shut fire doors), lasting from nine at night to four, five o'clock in the morning, the band playing one-, two-hour sets. I thought he just needed the rest. How could I have known that he would come home and, in the name of unwinding, throw back a glass of rye, then a second, and then a third, and so on, until he'd plant his elbow on the table and use it to steady his chin, as he couldn't hold his head up otherwise. But that day I ran into the kitchen to wake him up so that he could see the episode, too, shaking him gently and tugging at his elbow, which was a mistake, because it was as if I had pulled loose the support columns of a five-hundred-year-old church: he simply fell over and crashed to the floor.

A commercial was running on the television, and so, as I knew I wouldn't have much time, I began to slap his face, pull on his burning red-hot ears, tugging on them until he finally opened one eye. In the act of focusing he apparently did not recognize me, because he asked, "Nestor, what are you doing here?"

"It's me, Uncle, it's Eugenio."

I said this in a really earnest tone of voice, just like that kid who hangs out with Spencer Tracy in the movie of *The Old Man and the Sea*, really believing in my uncle and clinging on to his every word in life, his every touch like nourishment from a realm of great beauty, far beyond me, his heart. I tugged at him again, and he opened his eyes. This time he recognized me.

He said, "You?"

"Yes, Uncle, get up! Please get up! You're on television again. Come on."

One thing I have to say about my Uncle Cesar, there was very little he wouldn't do for me in those days, and so he nodded, tried to push himself off the floor, got to his knees, had trouble balancing, and then fell backwards. His head must have hurt: his face was a wince of pain. Then he seemed to be sleeping again. From the living room came the voice of Ricky's wife, plotting as usual with her neighbor Ethel Mertz about how to get a part on Ricky's show at the Tropicana, and I knew that the brothers had already been to the apartment — that's when Mrs. Shannon had called out into the courtyard — that in about five more minutes my father and uncle would be standing on the stage of the Tropicana, ready to perform that song again. Ricky would take hold of the microphone and say, "Well, folks, and now I have a real treat for you. Ladies and gentlemen, Alfonso and Manny Reyes, let's hear it!" And soon my father and uncle would be standing side by side, living, breathing beings, for all the world to see, harmonizing in a duet of that *canción*.

As I shook my uncle, he opened his eyes and gave me his hand, hard and calloused from his other job in those days, as superintendent, and he said, "Eugenio, help me. Help me."

I tugged with all my strength, but it was hopeless. Still he tried: with great effort he made it to one knee, and then, with his hand braced on the floor, he started to push himself up again. As I gave him another tug, he began miraculously to rise. Then he pushed my hand away and said, "I'll be okay, kid."

With one hand on the table and the other on the steam pipe,

he pulled himself to his feet. For a moment he towered over me, wobbling as if powerful winds were rushing through the apartment. Happily I led him down the hallway and into the living room, but he fell over again by the door — not fell over, but rushed forward as if the floor had abruptly tilted, as if he had been shot out of a cannon, and, wham, he hit the bookcase in the hall. He kept piles of records there, among them a number of the black and brittle 78s he had recorded with my father and their group, the Mambo Kings. These came crashing down, the bookcase's glass doors jerking open, the records shooting out and spinning like flying saucers in the movies and splintering into pieces. Then the bookcase followed, slamming into the floor beside him: the songs "Bésame Mucho," "Acércate Más," "Juventud," "Twilight in Havana," "Mambo Nine," "Mambo Number Eight," "Mambo for a Hot Night," and their fine version of "Beautiful María of My Soul" — all these were smashed up. This crash had a sobering effect on my uncle. Suddenly he got to one knee by himself, and then the other, stood, leaned against the wall, and shook his head.

"Bueno," he said.

He followed me into the living room and plopped down on the couch behind me. I sat on a big stuffed chair that we'd hauled up out of the basement. He squinted at the screen, watching himself and his younger brother, whom, despite their troubles, he loved very much. He seemed to be dreaming.

"Well, folks," Ricky Ricardo said, "and now I have a real treat for you . . ."

The two musicians in white silk suits and big butterfly-looking lace bow ties, marching toward the microphone, my uncle holding a guitar, my father a trumpet.

"Thank you, thank you. And now a little number that we composed . . ." And Cesar started to strum the guitar and my father lifted his trumpet to his lips, playing the opening of "Beautiful María of My Soul," a lovely, soaring melody line filling the room.

They were singing the song as it had been written — in Spanish. With the Ricky Ricardo Orchestra behind them, they came into a turnaround and began harmonizing a line that translates roughly into English as: "What delicious pain love has brought to me in the form of a woman."

My father . . . He looked so alive!

"Uncle!"

Uncle Cesar had lit a cigarette and fallen asleep. His cigarette had slid out of his fingers and was now burning into the starched cuff of his white shirt. I put the cigarette out, and then my uncle, opening his eyes again, smiled. "Eugenio, do me a favor. Get me a drink."

"But, Uncle, don't you want to watch the show?"

He tried really hard to pay attention, to focus on it.

"Look, it's you and Poppy."

"Coño, sí . . ."

My father's face with his horsey grin, arching eyebrows, big fleshy ears — a family trait — that slight look of pain, his quivering vocal cords, how beautiful it all seemed to me then . . .

And so I rushed into the kitchen and came back with a glass of rye whiskey, charging as fast as I could without spilling it. Ricky had joined the brothers onstage. He was definitely pleased with their performance and showed it, because as the last note sounded he whipped up his hand and shouted "Olé!," a big lock of his thick black hair falling over his brows. Then they bowed and the audience applauded.

The show continued on its course. A few gags followed: a costumed bull with flowers wrapped around its horns came out dancing an Irish jig, its horn poking into Ricky's bottom and so exasperating him that his eyes bugged out, he slapped his forehead and started speaking a-thousand-words-a-second Spanish. But at that point it made no difference to me, the miracle had passed, the resurrection of a man, Our Lord's promise which I then believed, with its release from pain, release from the troubles of this world.

JUDITH ORTÍZ-COFER

Silent Dancing

W*e have a home movie of this party. Several times my mother and I have watched it together, and I have asked questions about the silent revelers coming in and out of focus. It is grainy and of short duration but a great visual aid to my first memory of life in Paterson at that time. And it is in color — the only complete scene in color I can recall from those years.*

We lived in Puerto Rico until my brother was born in 1954. Soon after, because of economic pressures on our growing family, my father joined the United States Navy. He was assigned to duty on a ship in Brooklyn Yard, New York City — a place of cement and steel that was to be his home base in the States until his retirement more than twenty years later. He left the Island first, tracking down his uncle who lived with his family across the Hudson River, in Paterson, New Jersey. There he found a tiny apartment in a huge apartment building that had once housed Jewish families and was just being transformed into a tenement by Puerto Ricans overflowing from New York City. In 1955 he sent for us. My mother was only twenty years old, I was not quite three, and my brother was a toddler when we arrived at El Building, as the place had been christened by its new residents.

My memories of life in Paterson during those first few years are in shades of gray. Maybe I was too young to absorb vivid colors and details, or to discriminate between the slate blue of the winter sky and the darker hues of the snow-bearing clouds, but the single color washes over the whole period. The building we lived in was gray, the streets were gray with slush the first few months of my life there, the coat my father had bought for me was dark in color and too big. It sat heavily on my thin frame.

I do remember the way the heater pipes banged and rattled, startling all of us out of sleep until we got so used to the sound that we automatically either shut it out or raised our voices above the racket. The hiss from the valve punctuated my sleep, which has always been fitful, like a nonhuman presence in the room — the dragon sleeping at the entrance of my childhood. But the pipes were a connection to all the other lives being lived around us. Having come from a house made for a single family back in Puerto Rico — my mother's extended-family home — it was curious to know that strangers lived under our floor and above our heads, and that the heater pipe went through everyone's apartment. (My first spanking in Paterson came as a result of playing tunes on the pipes in my room to see if there would be an answer.) My mother was as new to this concept of beehive life as I was, but had been given strict orders by my father to keep the doors locked, the noise down, ourselves to ourselves.

It seems that Father had learned some painful lessons about prejudice while searching for an apartment in Paterson. Not until years later did I hear how much resistance he had encountered with landlords who were panicking at the influx of Latinos into a neighborhood that had been Jewish for a couple of generations. But it was the American phenomenon of ethnic turnover that was changing the urban core of Paterson, and the human flood could not be held back with an accusing finger.

"You Cuban?" the man had asked my father, pointing a finger at his name tag on the navy uniform — even though my father had the fair skin and light brown hair of his northern Spanish family background and our name is as common in Puerto Rico as Johnson is in the United States.

"No," my father had answered, looking past the finger into his adversary's angry eyes. "I'm Puerto Rican."

"Same shit." And the door closed. My father could have passed as European, but we couldn't. My brother and I both have our mother's black hair and olive skin, and so we lived in El Building and visited our great-uncle and his fair children on the next block. It was their private joke that they were the German branch of the family. Not many years later that area too would be mainly Puerto Rican. It was as if the heart of the city map were being gradually colored in brown — *café con leche* brown. Our color.

The movie opens with a sweep of the living room. It is "typical" immigrant Puerto Rican decor for the time: the sofa and chairs are square and hard-looking, upholstered in bright colors (blue and yellow in this instance, and covered in the transparent plastic) that furniture salesmen then were adept at making women buy. The linoleum on the floor is light blue, and if it was subjected to the spike heels as it was in most places, there were dime-sized indentations all over it that cannot be seen in this movie. The room is full of people dressed in mainly two colors: dark suits for the men, red dresses for the women. I have asked my mother why most of the women are in red that night, and she shrugs, "I don't remember. Just a coincidence." She doesn't have my obsession for assigning symbolism to everything.

The three women in red sitting on the couch are my mother, my eighteen-year-old cousin, and her brother's girlfriend. The "novia" is just up from the Island, which is apparent in her body language. She sits up formally, and her dress is carefully pulled over her knees. She is a pretty girl but her posture makes her look insecure, lost in her full-skirted red dress which she has carefully tucked around her to make room for my gorgeous cousin, her future sister-in-law. My cousin has grown up in Paterson and is in her last year of high school. She doesn't have a trace of what Puerto Ricans call "la mancha" (literally, the stain: the mark of the new immigrant — something about the posture, the voice, or the humble demeanor making it obvious to everyone that that person has just arrived on the mainland, has not yet acquired the polished look of the city dweller). My cousin is wearing a tight red-sequined cocktail dress. Her brown hair has been lightened with peroxide around the bangs, and she is holding a cigarette very expertly between her fingers, bringing it up to her mouth in a sensuous arc of her arm as she talks animatedly with my mother, who has come up to sit between the two women, both only a few years younger than herself. My mother is somewhere halfway between the poles they represent in our culture.

It became my father's obsession to get out of the barrio, and thus we were never permitted to form bonds with the place or with the people who lived there. Yet the building was a comfort to my mother, who never got over yearning for *la isla*. She felt surrounded by her language: the walls were thin, and voices speaking and arguing in Spanish could be heard all day. *Salsas* blasted out of radios turned on early in the morning and left on for company. Women seemed to cook rice and beans perpetually — the strong aroma of red kidney beans boiling permeated the hallways.

Though Father preferred that we do our grocery shopping at the supermarket when he came home on weekend leaves, my mother insisted that she could cook only with products whose labels she could read, and so, during the week, I accompanied her and my little brother to La Bodega — a hole-in-the-wall grocery store across the street from El Building. There we squeezed down three narrow aisles jammed with various products. Goya and Libby's — those were the trademarks trusted by her Mamá, and so my mother bought cans of Goya beans, soups, and condiments. She bought little cans of Libby's fruit juices for us. And she bought Colgate toothpaste and Palmolive soap. (The final *e* is pronounced in both those products in Spanish, and for many years I believed that they were manufactured on the Island. I remember my surprise at first hearing a commercial on television for the toothpaste in which Colgate rhymed with "ate.") We would linger at La Bodega, for it was there that mother breathed best, taking in the familiar aromas of the foods she knew from Mamá's kitchen, and it was also there that she got to speak to the other women of El Building without violating outright Father's dictates against fraternizing with our neighbors.

But he did his best to make our "assimilation" painless. I can still see him carrying a Christmas tree up several flights of stairs to our apartment, leaving a trail of aromatic pine. He carried it formally, as if it were a flag in a parade. We were the only ones in El Building that I knew of who got presents on both Christmas Day and on *Día de Reyes*, the day when the Three Kings brought gifts to Christ and to Hispanic children.

Our greatest luxury in El Building was having our own television set. It must have been a result of Father's guilty feelings over the isolation he had imposed on us, but we were one of the first families in the barrio to have one. My brother quickly became an avid watcher of Captain Kangaroo and Jungle Jim. I loved all the family series, and by the time I started first grade in school, I could have drawn a map of middle America as exemplified by the lives of characters in *Father Knows Best, The Donna Reed Show, Leave It to Beaver, My Three Sons*, and (my favorite) *Bachelor Father*, where John Forsythe treated his adopted teenage daughter like a princess because he was rich and had a Chinese houseboy to do everything for him. Compared to our neighbors in El Building, we were rich. My father's navy check provided us with financial security and a standard of living that the factory workers envied. The only thing his money could not buy us was a place to live away from the barrio — his greatest wish and Mother's greatest fear.

In the home movie the men are shown next, sitting around a card table set up in one corner of the living room, playing dominoes. The clack of the ivory pieces is a sound familiar. I heard it in many houses on the Island and in many apartments in Paterson. In Leave It to Beaver, *the Cleavers played bridge in every other episode; in my childhood, the men started every social occasion with a hotly debated round of dominoes. The women would sit around and watch, but they never participated in the games.*

Here and there you can see a small child. Children were always brought to parties and, whenever they got sleepy, put to bed in the host's bedrooms. Babysitting was a concept unrecognized by the Puerto Rican women I knew: a responsible mother did not leave her children with any stranger. And in a culture where children are not considered intrusive, there is no need to leave the children at home. We went where our mother went.

Of my preschool years I have only impressions: the sharp bite of the wind in December as we walked with our parents toward the brightly lit stores downtown, how I felt like a stuffed doll in my heavy coat, boots and mittens; how good it was to walk into the five-and-dime and sit at the counter drinking hot chocolate.

On Saturdays our whole family would walk downtown to shop

at the big department stores on Broadway. Mother bought all our clothes at Penney's and Sears, and she liked to buy her dresses at the women's specialty shops like Lerner's and Diana's. At some point we would go into Woolworth's and sit at the soda fountain to eat.

We never ran into other Latinos at these stores or eating out, and it became clear to me only years later that the women from El Building shopped mainly at other places — stores owned either by other Puerto Ricans or by Jewish merchants who had philosophically accepted our presence in the city and decided to make us their good customers, if not neighbors and friends. These establishments were located not downtown but in the blocks around our street, and they were referred to generically as La Tienda, El Bazar, La Bodega, La Botánica. Everyone knew what was meant. These were the stores where your face did not turn a clerk to stone, where your money was as green as anyone else's.

On New Year's Eve we were dressed up like child models in the Sears catalogue — my brother in a miniature man's suit and bow tie, and I in black patent leather shoes and a frilly dress with several layers of crinolines underneath. My mother wore a bright red dress that night, I remember, and spike heels; her long black hair hung to her waist. Father, who usually wore his navy uniform during his short visits home, had put on a dark civilian suit for the occasion: we had been invited to his uncle's house for a big celebration. Everyone was excited because my mother's brother, Hernán — a bachelor who could indulge himself in such luxuries — had bought a movie camera which he would be trying out that night.

Even the home movie cannot fill in the sensory details such a gathering left imprinted in a child's brain. The thick sweetness of women's perfume mixing with the ever-present smells of food cooking in the kitchen: meat and plantain *pasteles*, the ubiquitous rice dish made special with pigeon peas — *gandules* — and seasoned with the precious *sofrito* sent up from the Island by somebody's mother or smuggled in by a recent traveler. *Sofrito* was one of the items that women hoarded, since it was hardly ever in stock at La Bodega. It was the flavor of Puerto Rico.

The men drank Palo Viejo rum and some of the younger ones

got weepy. The first time I saw a grown man cry was at a New Year's Eve party. He had been reminded of his mother by the smells in the kitchen. But what I remember most were the boiled *pasteles* — plantain or yucca rectangles stuffed with corned beef or other meats, olives, and many other savory ingredients, all wrapped in banana leaves. Everyone had to fish one out with a fork. There was always a "trick" *pastel* — one without stuffing — and whoever got that one was the "New Year's Fool."

There was also the music. Long-playing albums were treated like precious china in these homes. Mexican recordings were popular, but the songs that brought tears to my mother's eyes were sung by the melancholic Daniel Santos, whose life as a drug addict was the stuff of legend. Felipe Rodríguez was a particular favorite of couples. He sang about faithless women and broken-hearted men. There is a snatch of a lyric that has stuck in my mind like a needle on a worn groove: "De piedra ha de ser mi cama, de piedra la cabecera . . . la mujer que a mí me quiera . . . ha de quererme de veras. Ay, ay, corazón, ¿por qué no amas . . . ?" I must have heard it a thousand times since the idea of a bed made of stone, and its connection to love, first troubled me with its disturbing images.

The five-minute home movie ends with people dancing in a circle. The creative filmmaker must have asked them to do that so that they could file past him. It is both comical and sad to watch silent dancing. Since there is no justification for the absurd movements that music provides for some of us, people appear frantic, their faces embarrassingly intense. It's as if you were watching sex. Yet for years, I've had dreams in the form of this home movie. In a recurring scene, familiar faces push themselves forward into my mind's eye, plastering their features into distorted close-ups. And I'm asking them: "Who is she? Who is the woman I don't recognize? Is she an aunt? Somebody's wife? Tell me who she is. Tell me who these people are."

"See the beauty mark on her cheek as big as a hill on the lunar landscape of her face — well, that runs in the family. The women on your father's side of the family wrinkle early; it's the price they pay for that fair skin. The young girl with the green stain on her wedding dress is *la novia* — just up from the Island. See, she lowers her eyes as she approaches the camera like she's supposed to. Decent girls never look you directly in the face. *Humilde*, humble, a girl should express humility in all her actions. She will make a good wife for your cousin. He should consider himself lucky to have met her only weeks after she arrived here. If he married her quickly, she will make him a good Puerto Rican–style wife; but if he waits too long, she will be corrupted by the city, just like your cousin there."

"She means me. I do what I want. This is not some primitive island I live on. Do they expect me to wear a black mantilla on my head and go to mass every day? Not me. I'm an American woman and I will do as I please. I can type faster than anyone in my senior class at Central High, and I'm going to be a secretary to a lawyer when I graduate. I can pass for an American girl anywhere — I've tried it — at least for Italian, anyway. I never speak Spanish in public. I hate these parties, but I wanted the dress. I look better than any of these humildes here. My life is going to be different. I have an American boyfriend. He is older and has a car. My parents don't know it, but I sneak out of the house late at night sometimes to be with him. If I marry him, even my name will be American. I hate rice and beans. It's what makes these women fat."

"Your prima is pregnant by that man she's been sneaking around with. Would I lie to you? I'm your great-uncle's common-law wife — the one he abandoned on the Island to marry your cousin's mother. I was not invited to this party, but I came anyway. I came to tell you that story about your cousin that you've always wanted to hear. Remember that comment your mother made to a neighbor that has always haunted you? The only thing you heard was your cousin's name and then you saw your mother pick up your doll from the couch and say: 'It was as big as this doll when they flushed it down the toilet.' This image has bothered you for years, hasn't it? You had nightmares about babies being flushed down the toilet, and you wondered why anyone would do such a horrible thing. You didn't dare ask your mother about it. She would only tell you that you had not heard her right and yell at you for listening to adult conversations. But later, when you were old enough to know about abortions, you suspected. I am here to tell you that you were right. Your cousin was growing an Americanito in her belly when this movie was made. Soon after she put something long and pointy into her pretty self, thinking maybe she could get rid of the problem before breakfast and still make it to her first class at the high school. Well, niña, her screams could be heard downtown. Your aunt, her Mamá, who had been a midwife on the Island, managed to pull the little thing out. Yes, they probably flushed it down the toilet, what else could they do with it — give it a Christian burial in a little white casket with blue bows and ribbons? Nobody wanted that baby — least of all the father, a teacher at her school with a house in West Paterson that he was filling with real children, and a wife who was a natural blond.

"Girl, the scandal sent your uncle back to the bottle. And guess where you cousin ended up? Irony of ironies. She was sent to a village in Puerto Rico to live with a relative on her mother's side: a place so far away from civilization that you have to ride a mule to reach it. A real change in scenery. She found a man there. Women like that cannot live without male company. But believe me, the men in Puerto Rico know how to put a saddle on a woman like her. La Gringa, they call her, ha, ha, ha. La Gringa is what she always wanted to be . . ."

The old woman's mouth becomes a cavernous black hole I fall into. And as I fall, I can feel the reverberations of her laughter. I hear the echoes of her last mocking words: *La Gringa, La Gringa!* And the conga line keeps moving silently past me. There is no music in my dream for the dancers.

When Odysseus visits Hades, asking to see the spirit of his mother, he makes an offering of sacrificial blood, but since all of the souls crave an audience with the living, he has to listen to many of them before he can ask questions. I, too, have to hear the dead and the forgotten speak in my dream. Those who are still part of my life remain silent, going around and around in their dance. The others keep pressing their faces forward to say things about the past.

My father's uncle is last in line. He is dying of alcoholism, shrunken and shriveled like a monkey. His face is a mass of wrinkles and broken arteries. As he comes closer, I realize that in his features I can see my whole family. If you were to stretch that rubbery flesh, you could find my father's face, and deep within *that* face — mine. I don't want to look into those eyes ringed in purple. In a few years he will retreat into silence, and take a long, long time to die. *Move back, Tío,* I tell him. *I don't want to hear what you have to say. Give the dancers room to move, soon it will be midnight. Who is the New Year's Fool this time?*

HELENA MARÍA VIRAMONTES

The Moths

I WAS fourteen years old when Abuelita requested my help. And it seemed only fair. Abuelita had pulled me through the rages of scarlet fever by placing, removing, and replacing potato slices on my temples; she had seen me through several whippings, an arm broken by a dare jump off Tío Enrique's toolshed, puberty, and my first lie. Really, I told Amá, it was only fair.

Not that I was her favorite granddaughter or anything special. I wasn't even pretty or nice like my older sisters and I just couldn't do the girl things they could do. My hands were too big to handle the fineries of crocheting or embroidery and I always pricked my fingers or knotted my colored threads time and time again while my sisters laughed and called me Bull Hands with their cute water-like voices. So I began keeping a piece of jagged brick in my sock to bash my sisters or anyone who called me Bull Hands. Once, while we all sat in the bedroom, I hit Teresa on the forehead, right above her eyebrow, and she ran to Amá with her mouth open, her hand over her eye while blood seeped between her fingers. I was used to the whippings by then.

I wasn't respectful either. I even went so far as to doubt the power of Abuelita's slices, the slices she said absorbed my fever. "You're still alive, aren't you?" Abuelita snapped back, her pasty gray eye beaming at me and burning holes in my suspicions. Regretful that I had let secret questions drop out of my mouth, I couldn't look into her eyes. My hands began to fan out, grow like a liar's nose until they hung by my side like low weights. Abuelita made a balm out of dried moth wings and Vicks and rubbed my hands, shaped them back to size, and it was the strangest feeling. Like bones melting. Like sun shining through the darkness of your eyelids. I didn't mind helping Abuelita after that, so Amá would always send me over to her.

In the early afternoon Amá would push her hair back, hand me my sweater and shoes, and tell me to go to Mama Luna's. This was to avoid another fight and another whipping, I knew. I would deliver one last direct shot on Marisela's arm and jump out of our house, the slam of the screen door burying her cries of anger, and I'd gladly go help Abuelita plant her wild lilies or jasmine or heliotrope or cilantro or hierbabuena in red Hills Brothers coffee cans. Abuelita would wait for me at the top step of her porch, holding a hammer and nail and empty coffee cans. And although we hardly spoke, hardly looked at each other as we worked over root transplants, I always felt her gray eye on me. It made me feel, in a strange sort of way, safe and guarded and not alone. Like God was supposed to make you feel.

On Abuelita's porch, I would puncture holes in the bottom of the coffee cans with a nail and a precise hit of a hammer. This completed, my job was to fill them with red clay mud from beneath her rosebushes, packing it softly, then making a perfect hole, four fingers round, to nest a sprouting avocado pit, or the spidery sweet potatoes that Abuelita rooted in mayonnaise jars with toothpicks and daily water, or prickly chayotes that produced vines that twisted and wound all over her porch pillars, crawling to the roof, up and over the roof, and down the other side, making her small brick house look like it was cradled within the vines that grew pear-shaped squashes ready for the pick, ready to be steamed with onions and cheese and butter. The roots would burst out of the rusted coffee cans and search for a place to connect. I would then feed the seedlings with water.

But this was a different kind of help, Amá said, because Abuelita was dying. Looking into her gray eye, then into her brown one, the doctor said it was just a matter of days. And so it seemed only fair that these hands she had melted and formed found use in rubbing her caving body with alcohol and marijuana, rubbing her arms and legs, turning her face to the window so that she could watch the bird of paradise blooming or smell the scent of clove in the air. I toweled her face frequently and held her hand for hours. Her gray wiry hair hung over the mattress. For as long as I could remember, she'd kept her long hair in braids. Her mouth was vacant, and when she slept her eyelids never closed all the way. Up close, you could see her gray eye beaming out the window, staring hard as if to remember everything. I never kissed her. I left the window open when I went to the market.

Across the street from Jay's Market there was a chapel. I never knew its denomination, but I went in just the same to search for candles. There were none, so I sat down on one of the pews. After I cleaned my fingernails, I looked up at the high ceiling. I had forgotten the vastness of these places, the coolness of the marble pillars and the frozen statues with blank eyes. I was alone. I knew why I had never returned.

That was one of Apá's biggest complaints. He would pound his hands on the table, rocking the sugar dish or spilling a cup of coffee, and scream that if I didn't go to mass every Sunday to save my goddamn sinning soul, then I had no reason to go out of the house, period. *Punto final.* He would grab my arm and dig his nails into me to make sure I understood the importance of catechism. Did he make himself clear? Then he strategically directed his anger at Amá for her lousy ways of bringing up daughters, being disrespectful and unbelieving, and my older sisters would pull me aside and tell me if I didn't get to mass right this minute, they were all going to kick the holy shit out of me. Why am I so selfish? Can't you see what it's doing to Amá, you idiot? So I would wash my feet and stuff them in my black Easter shoes that shone with Vaseline, grab a missal and veil, and wave goodbye to Amá.

I would walk slowly down Lorena to First to Evergreen, counting the cracks on the cement. On Evergreen I would turn left and walk to Abuelita's. I liked her porch because it was shielded by the vines of the chayotes and I could get a good look at the people and car traffic on Evergreen without them knowing. I would jump up the porch steps, knock on the screen door as I wiped my feet, and call, Abuelita? Mi Abuelita? As I opened the door and stuck my head in, I would catch the gagging scent of toasting chile on the *placa*. When I entered the *sala*, she would greet me from the kitchen, wringing her hands in her apron. I'd sit at the corner of the table to keep from being in her way. The chiles made my eyes water. Am I crying? No, Mama Luna, I'm sure not crying. I don't like going to mass, but my eyes watered anyway, the tears dropping on the tablecloth like candle wax. Abuelita lifted the burnt chiles from the fire and sprinkled water on them until the skins began to separate. Placing them in front of me, she turned to check the menudo. I peeled the skins off and put the flimsy, limp-looking green and yellow chiles in the *molcajete* and began to crush and crush and twist and crush the heart out of the tomato, the clove of garlic, the stupid chiles that made me cry, crushed them until they turned into liquid under my bull hand. With a wooden spoon, I scraped hard to destroy the guilt, and my tears were gone. I put the bowl of chile next to a vase filled with freshly cut roses. Abuelita touched my hand and pointed to the bowl of menudo that steamed in front of me. I spooned some chile into the menudo and rolled a corn tortilla thin with the palms of my hands. As I ate, a fine Sunday breeze entered the kitchen and a rose petal calmly feathered down to the table.

I left the chapel without blessing myself and walked to Jay's. Most of the time Jay didn't have much of anything. The tomatoes were always soft and the cans of Campbell soup had rust spots on them. There was dust on the tops of cereal boxes. I picked up what I needed: rubbing alcohol, five cans of chicken broth, a big bottle of Pine Sol. At first Jay got mad because I thought I had forgotten the money. But it was there all the time, in my back pocket.

When I returned from the market, I heard Amá crying in Abuelita's kitchen. She looked up at me with puffy eyes. I placed the bags of groceries on the table and began putting the cans of soup away. Amá sobbed quietly. I never kissed her. After a while, I patted her on the back for comfort. Finally: "¿Y mi Amá?" she asked in a whisper, then choked again and cried into her apron.

Abuelita fell off the bed twice yesterday, I said, knowing that I shouldn't have said it and wondering why I wanted to say it because it only made Amá cry harder. I guess I became angry and just so tired of the quarrels and beatings and unanswered prayers and my hands just there hanging helplessly by my side. Amá looked at me again, confused, angry, and her eyes were filled with sorrow. I went outside and sat on the porch swing and watched the people pass. I sat there until she left. I dozed off repeating the words to myself like rosary prayers: when do you stop giving when do you start giving when do you . . . and when my hands fell from my lap, I awoke to catch them. The sun was setting, an orange glow, and I knew Abuelita was hungry.

There comes a time when the sun is defiant. Just about the time when moods change, inevitable seasons of a day, transitions from one color to another, that hour or minute or second when the sun is finally defeated, finally sinks into the realization that it cannot, with all its power to heal or burn, exist forever, there comes an illumination where the sun and earth meet, a final burst of burning red-orange fury reminding us that although endings are inevitable, they are necessary for rebirths, and when that time came, just when I switched on the light in the kitchen to open Abuelita's can of soup, it was probably then that she died.

The room smelled of Pine Sol and vomit, and Abuelita had defecated the remains of her cancerous stomach. She had turned to the window and tried to speak, but her mouth remained open and speechless. I heard you, Abuelita, I said, stroking her cheek, I heard you. I opened the windows of the house and let the soup simmer and overboil on the stove. I turned the stove off and poured the soup down the sink. From the cabinet I got a tin basin, filled it with lukewarm water, and carried it carefully to the room. I went to the linen closet and took out some modest bleached white towels. With the sacredness of a priest preparing his vestments, I unfolded the towels one by one on my shoulders. I removed the sheets and blankets from her bed and peeled off her thick flannel nightgown. I toweled her puzzled face, stretching out the wrinkles, removing the coils of her neck, toweled her shoulders and breasts. Then I changed the water. I returned to towel the creases of her stretch-marked stomach, her sporadic vaginal hairs, and her sagging thighs. I removed the lint from between her toes and noticed a mapped birthmark on the fold of her buttock. The scars on her back, which were as thin as the lifelines on the palms of her hands, made me realize how little I really knew of Abuelita. I covered her with a thin blanket and went into the bathroom. I washed my hands, turned on the tub faucets, and watched the water pour into the tub with vitality and steam. When it was full, I turned off the water and undressed. Then, I went to get Abuelita.

She was not as heavy as I thought, and when I carried her in my arms, her body fell into a V, and yet my legs were tired, shaky, and I felt as if the distance between the bedroom and bathroom was miles and years away. Amá, where are you?

I stepped into the bathtub, one leg first, then the other. I bent my knees to descend into the water, slowly, so I wouldn't scald her skin. There, there, Abuelita, I said, cradling her, smoothing her as we descended, I heard you. Her hair fell back and spread across the water like eagle's wings. The water in the tub overflowed and poured onto the tile of the floor. Then the moths came. Small, gray ones that came from her soul and out through her mouth fluttering to light, circling the single dull light bulb of the bathroom. Dying is lonely and I wanted to go to where the moths were, stay with her and plant chayotes whose vines would crawl up her fingers and into the clouds; I wanted to rest my head on her chest with her stroking my hair, telling me about the moths that lay within the soul and slowly eat the spirit up; I wanted to return to the waters of the womb with her so that we would never be alone again. I wanted. I wanted my Amá. I removed a few strands of hair from Abuelita's face and held her small light head within the hollow of my neck. The bathroom was filled with moths, and for the first time in a long time I cried, rocking us, crying for her, for me, for Amá, the sobs emerging from the depths of anguish, the misery of feeling half born, sobbing until finally the sobs rippled into circles and circles of sadness and relief. There, there, I said to Abuelita, rocking us gently, there, there.

GENARO GONZALEZ

Un Hijo del Sol

NACER: AL AMANECER

A DÁN as a child had an ability to remain unnoticed. Not withdrawn: he merely accommodated himself to the campesino environment to become a part of it. While his *jefitos* harvested a stranger's crops, Adán milled through the fields, scroungy, chocolate. A misplaced Mexican mirage in the backroads of Michigan, a boy-creature shimmering in heat. He picked the harvest only when it betrayed a strain of overabundance, a cow whose swollen teats *must* be milked. He spent his nights in El Norte smearing firefly glow on his body or sometimes in an abandoned car feeling up a little girl his own age whose name he never knew or later forgot. When playing *las escondidas* behind tents and trucks, someone inevitably glimpsed a woman in white or heard a whistling *lechuza*, and that was enough to break up the games for the night. Bedding on the floor, veiled by a surplus-store mosquito net, Adán often pretended to be a spider waiting behind its web for insects, although he wouldn't have known what to do after actually catching one, being that spiders were very mysterious about this. Adán did not consciously regard his life as free and happy; he lived it out of a continuous necessity. Today his only real appreciation of that life comes from remembering that he used to lie on a cotton-filled truck bed and gaze at an imposing sky while his parents drove through a temperatureless night. Adán hoisted himself up the side of a wooden panel, to be thrust back by the wind onto a sinking sea of silent cotton, impossible to walk on. Just stretch out and breathe in the smells, covered up snugly by a huge cotton body-muff. Not warm, just unable to conceive of differences such as heat or cold.

Adán went back to McAllen to begin the process of growing up, of growing old. He discovered freedom (natural, not the castrate freedom of societies) by having it taken away. Attendance in kindergarten forced and sporadic, fiasco. Assignment: Acculturation Process, Lesson 1. Stand up in front of the class and deliver a mutilated version of simple songs in English. Adán swaggers through "Aquí está el águila negra." Someone missed the boat! No, no, Adán. You must sing in English now. So he just stopped attending kindergarten.

CIRCOS Y SELVAS

Adán could recall having seen a robin in El Valle only once during his entire childhood. Robins and other northern birds supposedly migrated southward in search of warmth, but to Adán's knowledge, only shriveled snowbirds roosted here in winter. The snowbirds, or *turistas*, were valued more than whooping cranes for the golden eggs they laid unto other capitalist birds of prey; they were protected under the auspices of the local chamber of commerce. (In spite of the traffic problems their cumbersome vehicles caused in winter, the *turistas* were repaid in kind: the summer months saw families of Valle migrants in El Norte, temporarily invading the land — an appropriate cultural exchange program to rival the best of colleges.)

The South is known for its whitewashed "southern hospitality." But the hospitality-handout is a phenomenon peculiar to El Valle, wherein wintering snowbirds strew crumbs among the natives. Apparently the tourist trade, regarded as a sacred sort of foreign aid to El Valle's poor, cannot be stressed strongly enough. In school

Adán would be led to believe it was a symbiotic ass-kiss-ass process (i.e., "They buy more oranges, thus creating more jobs for orange pickers"), but for him their lives crossed only when the *turistas* slummed through the barrios ("Here but for the grace of God live I") or lost their way, in the utmost arrogance honking to break up and glide through interrupted street games. Their bewildered stares at the surrounding motley *bandidos* only broadened the vacuum between the simple sweltering streets and their elaborate world. The car/tomb. Antiseptic. Shielding. Plush in its doctor's office chill. One day Prieto had enough and hurled a stone at a black Cadillac (to him they all drove Cadillacs). Not as an act of chosen insurrection but as the natural way to destroy an antithesis. The glass screams, a gust of cold sterile air escapes from within, giving Adán a pee-chill. Too lifeless, too unlike the surrounding heat he knew. The withered mummies inside startle from their death, the opened tomb vomits a cold, foreign air onto the torrid barrio streets. *Las viejitas* — the caked putrid faces, sexless, haunted at themselves. No life: anti-sensual. They come here to die. El Valle: an elephant graveyard hidden from the outside world. An empty nightmare that recurs.

LABORES

That school vacations were during summer seemed no accident: *how else* could the cotton be gleaned and the ripe tomatoes raped from the vines, if not for the *jefitas* with their miniature children-hordes marching across the jungle fields of El Valle? A few of the more fortunate families would leave for El Norte and return with tales of a campesino Cibola, where one merely rustled the cherry-laden limbs for the fruit to fall heavily onto his hands. Best of all, they said, the *patrones* are considerate and "understand us." Adán could not figure out how it was possible for a *patrón* to "understand" his workers and remain their *patrón*. Adán tried to recall his life, his *other* life in El Norte, but could only remember having known *things* — air, trees, soil, streams — not people (maybe people as *objects* that blended into the soil).

Instead Adán would find himself in El Valle, transported at odd intervals to a new *"campo,"* there to spend his time, keep out of trouble and even make some money. Besides, no *vatos* stayed on the streets during the day, they all put in *their* time somewhere. Cover up, "no te vayas a poner prieto." Decked out in faded shirt and jeans (the cotton-picker jumpsuit), the shirt several sizes too small and belonging to another era, sleeves through vanity rolled up two and a half times, but otherwise ideal for *la pisca*.

Sunrise. *Vamos a piscar.* Cool morning with cotton moisture-heavy. Straddled over plants — jean legs wet with dew — alarm clock for rabbits and snakes. Showdowns of cotton boll battles trusting no one within fifty feet, old women ducking stray shots, screaming some philosophy about might-as-well-throw-away-money. "La cagan, rucas," Adán philosophized back. Eventually Don Ernesto, the sweat-patched truck driver, came to squelch the free-for-all, warning the "bastardos huevones" that he had but to contact some border patrolmen on his truck telephone (an old disintestined radio). These officers, he explained, were his intimate friends and had agreed to deport any troublemakers from his camp; then an old man who flirted with girls replied that Don Ernesto did indeed attract special attention from *la migra:* whenever patrolmen checked the camp for wetbacks, they always corralled Don Ernesto first due to his suspicious, outlaw looks. Finally Don Ernesto flatly threatened to leave the *chavalos* in the field to walk back home if they kept fighting. His peculiar diplomacy won.

Adán moves on, dragging his sack like a huge, stuffed albino serpent. He inspects his hands, smudged with leaf stains and squashed caterpillars, perfumed with pesticide. He stands up, sees his shadow almost gone. *Hora de comer*, or just about . . . Adán hammocks his sack under the trailer; he reclines Roman-style, feasting on *tacos de frijoles y papas*, lukewarm pale red Kool-Aid, and sometimes a soft splotchy banana almost turned to pudding. Over such cuisine he discusses the day's work with an elite group of young goldbrickers who have retired for brunch. The *patrón* drops by in his pickup, a pained, crowsfeet expression around the eyes, a snarl around the mouth, a bulge around his belt. He climbs up the trailer. Taking a sample of picked cotton in one hand, he stares at the *piscadores*, scans the field in utter disgust, as if seeking whoever picked *that* particular handful of shitty cotton. And liquid, bedroom eyes lazily looked out from the pickup: the *patrón's* teenage daughter smiles in Cleopatra lust from her Nile River pickup-barge. *Los vatos*, their theories on *gavacha* promiscuity rekindled, mutter back and huddle around the pickup. What his friends saw in the plump, slackmouth girl — necklaced in prickly heat rash — was beyond Adán; it seemed not so much lust as a method to hit the *patrón* through his daughter. (Christ, those *chicanitos calientes* would proposition any girl outside their immediate family!; *los bordos*, levees outside McAllen notorious as makeout places for their older brothers, were already legendary in their conversations.)

Again the drag of *pisca . pisca . . pisca . . .* Daydreams border on sunfed hallucinations, eyes and hands automatically discriminate whiteness of cotton from field of vision. *Pisca, pisca.* A girl removes her picking sack and walks off to a deserted patch in the field. Her head bobs down, body bends, she squats, disappears. Macho heads young and old bob up, bodies unbend, they stretch, dissimulate silence of mutual hard-on. Then back to . . . *pisca . pisca.* Sweat and pesticide — nostril nausea. Sweat salt burns his eyes. (For some time Adán thought the sickening odor was a natural by-product of the plants. Only much later did he correlate the airplane dusters with the nausea, that being when a duster once sprayed a field where Adán had wandered chasing a rabbit.) . . . Goddamn, not *one* cloud to cool things off.

TIRED. DEAD. Stand fixedly on a burning dying afternoon. Feel not just a dull backache but *being tired* with: the motionless soil, the meaningless horizons, the lightyear-distant truck — all suffocated and weak in this french-fried heat. Having scorned all movement and murdered all time. Staring achingly at the penitents in the plastic Purgatorio, bent upon their work, eyes and minds as one, only the dangling carrot/mirage of the American cornucopia (Let them eat cotton); expecting in his favor to see them *all* stand up, gaze contentedly at the bullfight passes of a far-off airplane duster; then agonized, remove the heavy yoke of the albatross picking sack from their necks and . . . as One . . . walk away proud. (Adán yanks off a yet-green cotton boll, an act tabooed by the *pinche patrón.* He fingers the boll-juicy flesh inside, unnatural in its pallor. Because of me, Adán reasons, it will never serve its purpose. Adán then shreds the compact fibers and throws the ravaged, undeveloped cotton boll away. He turns in the lazy heat to look at Sylvia, her bent body straining her tight full ass. Nude Woman Picking Cotton, 1959 . . . Then (Lubbock, Tejas . . . A crude sign: white cotton boll. The sentence: "No niggers, dogs or meskins allowed."))

LA RAÍZ

As man reversing to child to seed to ancestors. And then beyond. Querétaro, México. Dawn through greenglass of bus, past primitive nonyears. Adán, unable to sleep all night, now sees the soft countryside with somnambulist eyes, with slowmotion mind where images bisect and burst in time-war explosions; images breathe in dull luster of confrontation with senses where artificial levels — time, maps — dissolve to yield unique experience. Marineblue sky he never would have thought possible. Land and low clouds in serape color and design. Transparent beauty. Coupled with invisible *indio* presence hangs in revolution atmosphere leaps in galvanic-genetic stimulus within Adán. Lucio, seated in the next row, likewise hypnotized by some kinetic kinship with the peopled land.

Adán continues to stare out. A hunched, burdened figure streaks by in the opposite direction and Adán looks back. Outside the detached bubble of the bus a man dressed in black — his age undetermined — carries a small coffin upon his back. The coffin of a child, deceptively simple — brown and smooth — as the simplicity of a child's life. His gaze downcast, he strides carefully over rough, plowed ground. Clouds mountains valleys fields provide a sharp immobile background to the plodding man; they seem at once respectfully silent and aloofly indifferent. The man walks slowly, whether because of the coffin's weight or the terrain or perhaps his sorrow, Adán doesn't know. He watches until the man and the coffin fuse into a single blur . . .

Then walking through downtown México, D.F. Trying to merge

yet always separate, as oil film on water. Prodigal son transfigured through time and travel, now unrecognized by his family. As Adán seeks a country's life-source he is blitzed by props of lopsided miniskirts, effeminate superheroes, "*clases de inglés.*" People en masse running crawling in the opposite direction, the lost look of lemmings toward cliffs of USA-emulation.

Further down into barrios with street soccer games religiously played on every block. *Chavalas bien chulas* walk by, baptized by the sprinkling of rain. Children's voices in rhythmic mimicry of barrio slang. *Los locos* under the shelter of awnings, red dreaming eyes entertained by crazy raindrops shooting down like crystal bb's on non-hips. Other *locos* drift with extrovert smile out onto the street among *chavalitos*. *Ojos grifos*, mostly slits in sunlight, now bloom with the cool fascination of single raindrops tapping on their person, wide-eyed that something falling from So High doesn't hurt at all; each raindrop comes as a surprise, like suddenly crashing through chunks of fog in the night. They lift their faces to the sky, perhaps to lingering Aztec spirits of rain and yerba; they offer their minds in sweet sacrifice to herbs. Eyes become rain magnets become the very rain . . .

El sol. An old woman wrinkled within the folds of her shawl sells religious tokens in the name of Christ. Passersby give her looks of disgust for her unchristian hunger. She seems somewhat grateful for the patrons and shade of a cathedral which hangs huge in its background irony. In partial balance a young man of *indio* features pores with brown eyes over something simply entitled *El Che*. Adán notes that the *indio* sits on a bench in the sunlight, away from the shadow of the church. He seems not at all to shy from the steeple's shadow in vampire fright, but is perhaps annoyed that the church is itself a shadow.

It begins to rain again. Lucio walks alone. Adán walks alone. Alone in the company of outsiders and other outlaws. For the moment there is nothing more in his head worth saying aloud. Adán walks in silence through gauze curtains of rain, his face very much alive as cool raindrops burst upon animal warmth then evaporate into *** (He remembers fadedly feels vibrantly as multiple episodes superimpose on his mind. Stained snapshots: a dark boy running from the nowhere heat of smoldered afternoons,

slapped softly by wet sheets flapping on laundry lines, hot chocolate chest licked cool by moisture of dampsmelling towels. Simultaneously, he hurries across a scorching street — asphalt brands
urgent tingles on bare feet, shock runs up behind his neck and
cascades in warm pools of liquid eyes; a whiff of nostril blood, body
trembles in heat shivers, he leaps under the neutral shade of a
mesquite, his feet become concrete cool become dry-ice cold for
an instant; the hot rush from his face sinks to his lungs to his legs
out from his toes in total release, as warm shudders of a bursting
pee on powder dirt; he stands quietly alone in his triumph over
pain, ready to conquer the streets.) He stands quietly alone —

EL MESTIZO Y SU MISTERIO: SIN FIN

A feeling of abysses, of canyons, of losing someone to the hungers
of time and the universe. Houses — their windows X'd with
boards — hung out in El Valle, paralyzed in iron lungs. This feeling
within Adán, as of losing someone and finding his own sense of self
that much more. Eternity of ghost-town streets, emptiness sweeps
a vacuum. Something part air, part fire, and part death surrounds
him. Adán breathes the air to live; the fire — burning in his
mind — to act; the other stagnates into history and afterthought.

Yet the heat in the fields and barrios of El Valle had fused. A
fire had sparked. For Adán, his life proved more demanding, more
insistent: it forced him to live with this fire or burn out. A harsher
sun enveloped El Valle. Before, it had drowsed Adán, had drained
his commitment and his *raza's* life through centuries of evapora-
tion. Today the sun can not wither Adán; it exposes, it reveals. He
can no longer ignore that the sun feeds him fire. *El sol.* Burning
timepiece of a burning mestizo. The sun being time. The time
being Now.

"Sale a dar la vuelta," suggests 'Milio. "Cirol, 'ta bien agüitado."
Roaming the town with the magnetism of Mexico's border towns
clutching their minds harder. They decide to give McAllen one last
look. *El drive-in. Muerto. El parque. Muerto. El centro. Muerto.*
Walking by a store, something catches Adán's attention.

A large wall mirror faces him. He tries to look at the mirror with
detached inspection, but his gaze immediately locks him *into* the

mirror. His eyes seem fascinated with themselves, with their mad prophet reflection, at seeing themselves through themselves. In doing so, his eyes alternately become beholder and beheld, beheld and beholder. As if they can only see and know themselves by being *other* eyes, ouside eyes which likewise must be seen by what they see. Adán stared . . . stared back . . . stared . . . stared back. Two pairs of eyes — those of himself and of his reflection — mesmerized each other and met at some *distance between* the mirror and Adán. He felt himself as being someplace *outside* his body. Where am *I?* he thought. Space. Spaced out. *Estoy afuera. Yo soy . . . Adán nadA. Adán nadA. Adán nada . . .*

His mind had no recourse but to accept this rebellion, this extreme awareness taking place. Adán realizes that he is paradoxically *more* than himself, that something *within* him is also beyond him. He is beyond his own understanding.

Later, they decide to go to a rock dance. They enter the building. The heavy bass thumps deep inside their chests like a second heartbeat. Sauntering with almost staged ease toward the musicians' platform, they slip through crevices of crushed teenagers. Adán notices a group of Chicanas. Next to them, a large cluster of *gavachas* with characteristic plump-ass-pants / tiny-*chiches*-shirt had attracted the attention of a few older, foppishly dressed Chicanos, who in turn had attracted the attention of some heavyset *gavachos*. 'Milio was noticeably pissed at the *reglaje* behavior of the older Chicanos, adding that they probably called themselves Spanish-American to boot.

Slowly at first, then steadily, the *gavachos* trickle toward the mismatched crowd of *gringas* and Chicanos, prepared to defend the already torn-down bastion of white female virginity. A scuffle — one of the well-dressed Chicanos falls, bleeding. Adán and several others rush to the small circle. More people, fighting, pushing, running away. Adán looks at the Chicano on the floor; a hard fist is thumped onto his kidneys. Adán moves away, reaches for his knife, turns back to see a shock of blond hair and eyes crying . . . Adán suspends the knife in final decision, weighing the victim versus the act . . . An obsidian blade traces a quick arc of instinct — somewhere in time an angry comet flares, a sleeping mountain crupts, an Aztec sun explodes in birth***

ED VEGA

An Apology to the Moon Furies

L AST YEAR, on one of those damp gray afternoons in late fall
when remembrances of lost youth flail at the spirit like the
broken-winged agony of a fallen bird, Dan Cartagena, standing
under an umbrella, the sickly smell of flowers burning his nostrils
and the soft rain mixing with his tears as they fell to the ground,
watched friends and relatives move in the foglike drizzle, each
person shrouded in his own pain and much as the shadows they
were themselves destined to become, dutifully performed the
empty rituals which helped him lay his brother Raymond to rest.

The chill opaque light struggling to find its way through the
evergreens, the dark clothing of mourning, the tactful heaviness of
the minister's words, the whispered regrets and averted looks,
seemed, rather than funereal, a somber if mocking celebration of
the haunting sadness which had always clouded his brother's life.

As the expensive coffin was lowered into the earth, memories,
like guests who've overstayed and materialize at inopportune times
to break the established rhythm of a household, flitted in and out
of Cartagena's consciousness. While flowers and clods of softened
clay were tossed into the grave, he recollected events and tried
matching them to family photographs. Primarily, however, his
mind appeared obsessed with his brother's first painting, the sole
reality which still held him as if in bondage to Raymond. The

family photos, curled, yellowed by time, their images dated and out of place, lay in an old but remarkably well-preserved cigar box in the bottom right-hand drawer of his father's desk. Nearly six feet in length, the desk was a massive, intricately carved, nine-drawer antique with pewter handles rather than knobs. The first genuine family heirloom, it was the seat of family power and the place from which his father had conducted business. Cartagena had inherited the desk and all its incumbent responsibilities seemingly years before his father's death.

In contrast to the desk, which he had accepted as a requisite yoke for his advancement, his brother's painting had always been a more significant symbol and one which he had never deciphered. Like a physical deformity which makes others uncomfortable, the painting hung in the living room of Cartagena's Manhattan apartment, clashing, his ex-wife had always insisted, with its decor. Still garishly brilliant in color, bordered the past twelve years by a gilded frame, it seemed alive and demanding of constant attention while transforming itself with time into a reminder of distance and loneliness but mostly of longing — each day, rather than becoming an answer to his relationship to Raymond, folding back into itself like darkly violet dreamwaves to further complicate unanswered questions about him.

Complying with his mother's wishes to have Raymond buried next to his father in New York, Cartagena had flown to California for his body. Ilse had seemed relieved. Cartagena could never bring himself to call her Raymond's wife. In spite of his legal training, his mind rebelled against the common-law equality. Similarly, the words *friend, lady*, and *woman* proved as inadequate. One of those passive, kind, inoffensive women who manage to adapt themselves to their mate's needs, Ilse had been, in Cartagena's assessment, merely an attendant to Raymond's misery.

Austere, reserved, removing himself objectively from the aura of pathos surrounding the situation, Cartagena made no moral judgment about her apparent lack of grief and polite refusal to fly back to New York for the funeral. Granting the living the prerogative of amends, he rationalized her actions by telling himself that Ilse had been the one to personally endure his brother's pain the past ten years. His suicide, while not an easy matter for the family to accept, had been predictable given his life prior to knowing her. The Beat Generation, peyote Jell-O, Kerouac's credo, West Coast jazz, and early morning Venice Beach wine and pot parties. And yet her Scandinavian coldness, her almost Oriental resignation to his death, didn't sit well with him. Cartagena found himself needing to ask what had finally driven Raymond to his death. Sensing that any explanation she offered would only multiply his confusion, Cartagena held back and, as he had done for as long as he could recall, carried out his responsibilities diplomatically, efficiently. Legal briefs, after all, were intended to state facts, not create drama. The touch of creativity emerged in compiling information, not in making it entertaining.

To avoid the post-funeral chatter and inevitable family invitations to dinner and commiseration, Cartagena excused himself and sought out his cousin Peter. A member of the other Cartagenas, the ones his own family, excepting Raymond, had treated so distantly, Peter was the perfect listener. Educated, sophisticated, and seemingly content with his life in spite of a broken marriage, Peter had developed into the only one of their generation who had managed to overcome the stigma of being an immigrant's child.

They got into Peter's car, rode slowly out of the cemetery, and once on the highway with Peter handling the Mercedes effortlessly, Cartagena began opening up. As if his heart could no longer carry the weight of worrying about Raymond since he had left home over twenty years before, Cartagena confessed that he had never truly known Raymond. "I guess people thought we were close," he said. Peter Cartagena listened. He did not comment or offer explanations for the tragedy. Instead, he concentrated on the road, slick now from the steady downpour.

Growing up, Cartagena's perception of his brother had always been distorted. He was more like a father than a brother. Unhappily, he was one of those itinerant fathers who drift in and out of a child's life, to leave voids which can only be filled by fantasy. Raymond was rarely home in those days. Being away contributed to Cartagena's awe. When Raymond did show up, Cartagena listened religiously to his every word and imitated his brashness and quick wit among his own friends. Understandably, they laughed and told him he was trying to act grown-up. When he was with him, no matter how much he tried preventing it, he appeared, even to himself, hypnotized by Raymond.

"I couldn't believe the things he did, Pete. Or for that matter what the hell was going on with him. I couldn't even tell if he liked me half the time. All I wanted was for him to pay attention to me. And he did, but it was like there was something which held his interest more. I suppose I was jealous. With other people he'd go a little nuts, you know. It was confusing as hell. Even as a kid I could tell something was wrong. It was like he was going out of his way to be misunderstood. Whenever he got into it with family or friends, he seemed to be asking, in some crazy, complicated way, to be injured. It got so I started hating normal conversations."

Social intrigue, however, held little interest for Cartagena back then. Every waking moment not spent thinking about Raymond was consumed by his passion for the Brooklyn Dodgers. Hoping they finished on top to play the hated Yankees, he followed their every move by filling notebooks with photos, box scores, press stories, and ticket stubs of Ebbets Field games.

"Ironically, the year Ray went into the service I experienced enough hatred for a lifetime. It was during the Korean War, I guess. Between the North Koreans, the Chinese, and the New York Giants, my world turned completely dark."

While in the service and later in college, Raymond's visits to the Cartagena house (he never felt it was *his* house) became milestones of unhappiness for the family. During those rare visits, daily activities came to a standstill. Letters went unanswered; important telephone calls ignored; television schedules scrambled to fit his taste; shopping dates carefully planned by Cartagena's sisters canceled; and meals, the one enterprise which punctuated the natural flow of the day, invariably late. The household, unusually calm in Raymond's absence, became a confusing aggregation of seething tempers, threats, and injured feelings.

Initially everyone laughed about his effect on them. With each visit, however, the situation worsened. Each time he came home on leave, he left deeper wounds in all of them. After the war it became apparent that no one could talk to him for longer than a few minutes without coming away scarred. If it wasn't his mother's idiosyncratic attention to housekeeping detail, it was his father's energetic drive in his law practice, or his sisters' concern with fashion and popular music. His arguments varied only in content, never in intensity. But the worst times were those when, out of a sense of what Cartagena now surmised was Raymond's idea of personal responsibility, his brother introduced questions of a philosophical nature. Within ever narrowing frameworks of ideas, he challenged everyone with the expanding universe, the origins of the human species, and the relationship between time and space, subjects which in spite of their apparent importance had no immediate relevance to people attempting to meet car payments, worrying over mortgages, advancing themselves at whatever they were doing, and above all forgetting the *Marine Tiger*, that real and oftentimes metaphorical ship which brought thousands of their people to New York.

Raymond's attacks on his father, it had seemed to Cartagena earlier, as he listened to the minister offer a prayer for his brother's soul, had been the most unjustified of all. The four of them — Raymond, Angie, Fran, and himself — had been the recipients of his father's hard work and relative financial success, a reality preferable to Raymond's world of unformed ideals and painful experiences. It was a world, as much as Raymond may have disliked its plastic and somewhat shallow aspects, which provided the family with a spacious two-story house in Rockaway, music lessons (ballet for Angie and Fran), summers away from the city, and an almost paradisiac existence compared to what they heard about or read in newspapers concerning other Puerto Rican families.

As if time possessed a quality not measured in minutes, Raymond would spend hours, sometimes days, belaboring a point. Like a skilled boxer, he dodged, jabbed, and hooked words into others, waiting patiently for signs of fatigue, injury, or loss of concentration. Without mercy, unconscious of his emotional killer instinct, he'd deliver his knockout punch: a line from an obscure play, the name of an equally obscure Dutch painter, the lowest ERA of a pitcher with a last-place club, or the migratory habits of the Canada goose. It didn't matter. Engaging all comers in a fierce battle over the most insignificant of points, and with only the slightest provocation, Raymond expounded on politics, music, books, science, religion, and any other subject anyone had the audacity to mention in passing while he was present.

During these exhibitions of mental agility, Cartagena stood very still and watched Raymond wave his long arms, frowning one minute, laughing sarcastically the next, driven, Cartagena imagined in later years, by intellectual demons. Possessed, his brother would pace the floor, pleading his case as if it were of supreme importance that things were seen his way. More often than not, people gave up and granted him the point, leaving him to grow dark and morose once more.

"I mean, watching Raymond operate was like watching the Dodgers play. The score never told you what the other team had gone through, the humiliation. He would have been a great lawyer. That's what the old man used to say, anyhow."

And yet, like the Dodgers of the fifties, thought Cartagena as his cousin turned the car onto the Long Island Expressway, there was something tragic and quite frail about Raymond Cartagena, almost as if he were too good to be true, and whatever held him together was quite tenuous.

"There was a difference of seven years between us, Pete. It seemed like twenty-seven, he was so far out sometimes. I was never one of his targets, and to this day I can't figure out why. I guess it was my awe of the guy. He was like a magician. I couldn't wait for him to come home. You can't imagine what it was like living out there. Never mind that we were the only P.R.s for miles around. Everything became boring very quickly. I used to think Rockaway was the place where fads came to die. All the kids were crazy about the Dodgers. We all collected baseball cards, and whenever we weren't involved in flipping them or trading them, we'd sit around talking about how much we hated girls and how dumb our teachers were."

Raymond's seemingly tough manner and his vast knowledge easily made him the most complex person Cartagena knew at the time. And yet in spite of the burden he'd had to carry the past twenty years, he could recall the kindness which always came through. Of all the memories these were the most difficult to accept. When Raymond was away, Cartagena spent long hours recalling his visits, wishing for his return so that in the spur of the moment, oblivious of time or schedules, he'd ask Cartagena if he wanted to go for a walk and they'd end up in the Bronx Zoo after riding the subway for nearly two hours. Or he'd take him to visit his friends, all of whom were strange and exotic in their long beards and sandals even in winter, their women so pale and spacy and sweet. Or they'd just walk, and speaking very softly he'd tell him, in precise detail, of the places he'd visited, how the people dressed, what they ate and the language they spoke.

There was always a sadness to his voice then. A sadness produced by not being able to recapture all he had experienced in his travels. Unlike most people who accept this fact as one of the failings of being human, Raymond Cartagena fought against it, punishing himself because he couldn't recall the exact colors of the boat which carried him from Pireefs to Mikonos; not being content that he described the chalk-white chapels etched, almost carved, against the metallic blue sky, the brilliant sunlight ringing the whiteness so that even Cartagena as a child heard the color.

Softly, always softly, talking about greens and blues when he told about the waters of the Aegean, so that his words compelled Cartagena to look below the shimmering surface of the sea and in his mind's eye capture each stone and sea urchin. And then Raymond, racking his poor tortured soul, would begin to grow dark and angry because he couldn't recall the colors of the boat and couldn't lie about it.

"Even then he didn't turn against me, Pete. Can you understand that? It was like he was protecting me. The thing would only last a few seconds with me and then he was back to himself and talking quietly again. I mean, I really believe the other stuff was a front. You know, defenses."

He was a great storyteller, and without much effort Cartagena was transported to far-off places; Raymond's mesmerizing voice weaving incredible tales set in bazaars in North Africa; his language fluid and rich, filled with foreign words which Cartagena was certain were being pronounced exactly as they were meant to be, this later proven by listening to him speak a dozen languages fluently. When Raymond spoke, Cartagena was there. Rabat, Sidi Slimane, Casablanca, Tripoli — all of them air force bases from which Raymond explored the world — *minaret, caliph, bedouin;* painting camel caravans miles long as they wend their way ribbon-like across a desert sunset; the sound of his words lingering so that there were tones between them . . . "That was a *muezzin* calling the faithful to worship from the *minaret,*" he'd say, and Cartagena was spellbound by the whining sounds; and he'd tell of drums and belly dancers so that alone at night Cartagena still found himself, at the age of thirty-eight, haunted by the sensuous flesh of a dancer, her feet bare and her finger cymbals never fading until he fell asleep; stopping at times, his dear departed brother whom he hardly knew, to gaze into the distance of his mind as if on the shore of an immense river deep in the Amazon jungle; pausing to reflect on some inner sorrow before continuing his painful journey; whisking him away, this time to landing on the South Pole during a snowstorm, stressing, so that Cartagena never forgot, that only on that pole, not on its opposite, were penguins to be found.

"He tried to teach me Morse code a couple of times. That's what he did on the plane. He was a radio operator. I never caught on but it never bothered him. I guess he knew I enjoyed his company. I'm willing to bet he enjoyed playing big brother to me and that was all there was to it. But God help me, Pete. I feel used by him. The times I saw him as an adult he was always kind and encouraging, but it was like he knew something about me that I'd never be able to understand. I don't know. Maybe I'm just angry at the waste."

Raymond spent four years in the air force, was discharged and returned home for a couple of months before leaving again for California to attend college on the GI Bill, refusing his father's offer of financial help. One evening when Raymond had been home barely a week, there was a violent argument between him and his father over Raymond's statement that he'd never get married because he disliked children, adding that women were only good for one thing and it wasn't for having children. Cartagena hadn't understood Raymond's side of the argument but never asked anyone about it, fearing that a discovery of his ignorance would destroy their alliance. Cartagena had been deeply wounded by the remark. For weeks, feeling betrayed, he avoided Raymond. Eventually Raymond became aware of the silence, and without asking him what had caused his withdrawal told him that it hadn't been his intention to hurt his feelings. "I guess I was thinking of myself as a kid," he'd said. "I wasn't very good at it, Danny," he'd added, smiling sadly, awkwardly. "I stunk at everything. Sports, school, girls, friendship. Everything seemed senseless. The only thing I could do well was remember stuff nobody else did."

His father had been quite angry, a rarity for him. He ended up telling Raymond that being logical was only good up to a point. Raymond made a gesture of disgust and, muttering something about ignorance and stupidity, walked out of his father's study. Head down, Raymond came upstairs to draw. Although he generally spent his time sketching nature, whenever any unpleasantness took place between him and his father, Raymond attempted to draw people. As if whatever was hurting him were literally spilling out through his fingers and onto his drawing pad, he created ugly people, whose faces, disfigured by pain, their bodies twisted grotesquely and their hands gnarled, struggled to free themselves from the paper.

They were similar to Goya's sketches of war, except that they had a quality of their own. The eyes of the people were especially tragic. In Goya one saw the horror in the people's eyes, but in Raymond's sketches there was more. In his drawings the horror was obvious, but beyond it there was a profound awareness, a self-consciousness, a watching of their own humanity crumbling before them without their being able to check the process.

Four months before Raymond Cartagena swallowed a bottle of pills and was found dying at the bottom of a cliff below his house in Big Sur, *The Western Review of the Arts* called him one of the most promising artists of the decade. This after a number of successful shows in the San Francisco area. His paintings were selling well and little seemed to be standing in his way. And yet it hadn't been enough to sustain him. Ilse's letters to Angie, with whom she had established an odd bond considering the difference in the two women, were always filled with melancholic apology: "Yesterday we had friends over for rum punch and fruitcake. We decorated the Christmas tree and watched the sun set. A warm breeze was blowing from the south and Ray said it smelled like snow. Lorne told him his nose was drunk because the radio said it was sixty-seven degrees. Ray went up into his studio and stayed there the rest of the evening." It was as if she were responsible for Raymond's unhappiness, a trait Cartagena often thought she must have acquired from him, who, as his life drew to a close, spent more and more of his time absorbing everyone else's pain. The assassinations, the farm workers, the Soledad Brothers, war resisters, and the Vietnam War had all taken their toll on his brother.

At the funeral his mother had cried and told Angie that Raymond should've married Ilse. "What's going to become of her and the children?" she'd asked of no one, lost and alone in her sorrow, recalling perhaps the time Lorne and Melissa had spent with her two years before. Ilse and Raymond had gone off to Rhodes for six months, and when they returned the twins were chattering away in Spanish as if born to it. Their transformation had pleased Raymond, but within a week he was back into one of his dark moods, ranting and raving about the Greek dictatorship. Toward the end he no longer argued with anyone but would sit for hours, pensive, troubled, the area around him laden with tension.

Raymond, guessed Cartagena, was a genius who had somehow become aware that it wasn't enough to be able to see. He seemed driven by a need to prove himself far greater than anyone he'd known. No one, as far as he knew, least of all Cartagena himself, had ever been able to figure out the standards by which Raymond measured himself. Cartagena was certain, however, that whenever his brother approached the perfection he sought, he found flaws in himself undetectable by anyone else.

Gifted as Raymond proved to be, his father was not far behind. He was a hard worker and unlike Raymond had no need for self-scrutiny, limiting his power of discernment to his legal practice. A master of the compromise, he never lost his temper beyond the point where a situation could not be immediately repaired. Although he never talked about himself or his background to his children, their mother filled in the details of his life, creating for them a hero whom Raymond, Cartagena often imagined, could never surpass or, worse yet, equal.

"Papa ran away from home at the age of sixteen," his mother had once said to them. "There were nine other children in the family. They worked at picking coffee and tobacco in the hills around Cacimar, in the center of the island. Even though we were both from the area, my family never knew any of his relatives until we got married. My family lived in the town and his lived in the country. He was a country boy. A *jíbaro*. Very smart and serious, but very suspicious like all of his people. And always polite. Anyway, he left home, made his way to the capital, and worked around the docks. When he had enough money he paid his way on board a ship bound for New York. That was around 1929 or '30 and things weren't too good anywhere."

His mother's eyes had become misted with remembering and she had then told them about Juan Cartagena working in a factory, studying English and going to school at night. Eventually, he graduated from City College. In his junior year, working as an accountant for the factory which had originally hired him, he met and married Teresa Beltrán. Driven, Cartagena often imagined, much like Raymond but in a more conventional manner, his father continued to work as an accountant and began law school. Six years later he finished his law studies and passed the bar examination. Raymond was already eight when his father opened his first office in downtown Brooklyn. In the family photo album there was still a picture of Juan Cartagena in cap and gown, his wife and two of his children, the eldest, Raymond and Angela, in front of them. Ray is wearing a double-breasted suit and a wide tie. Frances had been three or four at the time and too young to take to the graduation. Cartagena himself had arrived — almost as an afterthought, he had often been told — the previous year.

It was conceivable that, gifted with a remarkable memory, Raymond had stored every injury ever received during those years, each emotional setback, each minor disappointment, adding to his misery and confusion about himself.

As his cousin slowed down to enter the Grand Central Parkway, now bumper to bumper and moving carefully because of the driving rain, Cartagena recalled how once in a while Raymond would talk to him about living in a walkup apartment in El Barrio, to this day a foreign country to him. When he talked about those days, his voice became almost inaudible, his manner totally subdued.

"One time he took me to the building where he had lived with my parents, Pete. I guess it was his first recollection of a home."

The neighborhood was like nothing Cartagena had ever seen. He had been frightened by the harshness of the people, the squalor, the garbage in the empty lots, and the incredible summer din of the street. The colors, smells, and sounds seemed strangely forbidden. Like invisible ocean waves they attacked his senses relentlessly. Cartagena had shaken his head violently when Raymond had pulled him over to a store in whose window there rested shining and wrinkled pig ears, tails, snouts, and what Raymond later explained were pig's intestines filled with a mixture of rice, spices, and pig's blood. The black woman had appeared to recognize Raymond. They had spoken in Spanish for a few minutes but Cartagena hadn't understood their çoded language. Years later, when friends talked about people talking Puerto Rican, Cartagena had been angry. He insisted, and as best as he could tried to explain, that Puerto Ricans spoke Spanish. Privately, however, he had to admit that although the language was Spanish, it was ciphered and sifted through the common experience of harried people to protect them from outsiders; the language twisting and turning uncomfortably, the words five, six, seven times removed from their original meaning so that when they were spoken, one could tell immediately whether the person was friend or foe — never knowing whether one's very own presented a threat except through the language.

Cartagena's eyes had behaved as if they had a will of their own when confronted with the dazzling carnage of what had once been an animal. His eyes darted from the woman's thick, greasy fingers to the black-brown sausage. But Raymond had been very gentle and spoke about being a little boy. Carefully, Cartagena chose a codfish fritter, a *bacalaíto*, bit gingerly into the crisp batter and liked it. Raymond had then asked him if he'd like to go for a boat ride, and they'd walked west to the park. After he'd paid for the boat rental and they were walking toward the edge of the lake, he'd spoken about how he and his father and mother would come to Central Park and rent a boat every Sunday afternoon in the summertime. "I cried when we moved away," he'd said once they were in the boat and he'd begun rowing. "It was safer then. I don't mean it was really safe, because there were fights and fires, but I felt safe. The same thing in Brooklyn. We'd go to Prospect Park or to Coney Island and walking home in late afternoon I'd feel tired but good. When we got to the house I was glad at first but then I don't know what happened. I didn't miss the apartment in Brooklyn but kept thinking about the one here in El Barrio. I missed walking up the five flights after school. There was an old man who flew pigeons from the roof. *Don Zoilo. Don Zoilo el de las palomas*, people called him. He had hundreds of them and he'd let me feed them. You would've liked it here, Danny."

And then he said something which Cartagena only lately began to understand and which haunted him almost as much as what took place before Raymond left for California the first time. They were out in the middle of the lake when Raymond suddenly stopped rowing. For a few minutes the boat drifted lazily in the afternoon breeze and Cartagena could feel the sun on his arms. "We grow up too fast, Danny. All of us. We leave our memories behind. Mama and Papa in P.R. and me here, in some dark hall or alley, some backyard full of broken glass and junk. I don't remember where I left mine so I keep coming back." Cartagena had watched Raymond's long delicate hand trail in the water, the fingers rippling the surface ever so slightly. "I guess it can't be helped," he'd said. "We leave them behind like old shoes, Danny. We get caught up in getting ahead and we forget our memories and where we came from. And then we hurt and we don't know why."

The night of the argument with his father, his mother came into Raymond's room to say good night and asked him why he argued so much. Thrown off balance by her concern, Raymond shrugged his shoulders like a little boy. Confronted directly, he was reduced to his simplest self. But his explanations then hardly went beyond a shrug. This time, mustering up a defense, he quickly explained that he enjoyed arguing. "I don't believe in anything, Mama," he'd said proudly. "I can take either side and do all right. I guess I'm lucky."

Cartagena didn't understand much of what Raymond argued about. He recalled asking his sisters on numerous occasions about the nature of the disputes. The only information ever provided by them came in the form of warnings, stressing above all that his wisest course was to stay away from Raymond, at all costs never repeat any of his crazy ideas, and always believe in God.

It was apparent to Cartagena even then that his sisters lived in mortal fear of Raymond's words. Although strong, spirited girls possessing their brother's stubborn streak, they individually lacked his stamina. Only when they joined forces and employed some exotic feminine ruse, such as crying and exaggerating their emotional injury, did they succeed in stalemating him. Generally, they steered clear of him. If he happened to come into a room and found them talking, they immediately busied themselves with dusting figurines, straightening picture frames, or closing or opening drapes.

He always knew what they were up to and laughed at them. The day after the argument with his father, Raymond surprised Angie and Fran in the dining room while they were setting the table for supper. They were talking about Angie's engagement to Kevin Monahan. She and Kevin had met at Brooklyn College, and even though Angie was just in her first year they had decided to get married. Raymond told them that marriage wasn't for getting a new house and clothes and a car like they did in the movies. He told them that it was all they ever thought about, and didn't they have anything inside their heads other than pictures from magazines showing the perfect American housewife in her perfect American home? Angie told him that she didn't know what he was talking about since he wasn't ever going to get married, so it wasn't any of his business what they talked about.

Momentarily stymied, Raymond recuperated and informed

them that precisely because he saw what empty-headed things women were, he had decided not to get married. It wasn't much of a retort but the forcefulness of his voice was enough to quiet them. In the four years Raymond was away his sisters had grown to tolerate him, much in the same fashion as his mother. Rather than caving in and becoming emotional as they had done in the past, they now indulged his every whim without paying much attention to his words. Although still rattled, they were able to maintain some semblance of composure. "We're not that bad, are we, Ray? Well . . . maybe you're right," Angie'd said. "Have you had anything to eat? Supper's almost done if you'd like to sit down. We're having spaghetti."

Their attitude angered Raymond, and disregarding their newly found sophistication concerning the management of the unruly male of the species, he battered relentlessly at their defenses. Within ten minutes he had once again reduced them to chronic hysteria and the only thing which saved him from physical attack was the fact that Angie and Fran had developed into beautiful young women and spent a great deal of time out of the house on picnics, dates, shopping trips into Manhattan (which like everyone else around them they called The City), and school. Their schedule did not allow for protracted battles. On that day, they were due at a baby shower for one of Angie's girlfriends. This time, however, unable to withstand another minute of Raymond's sarcasm, they rose against him and, screaming, forced him to retreat up the stairs, laughing as he went. "You're nuts, Ray!" screamed Angie, going four or five steps after him. "Nuts! That's what you are." Fran, not daring to go any higher than the bottom step, added that Raymond should be locked up and the key thrown away. No one thought much about the incident.

Something, however, had happened to Raymond in the interchange. For the next twenty-four hours he remained in his room. Then he emerged, unshaven, his lanky body stooped over and his hair nestlike. As if attempting to blind himself, he kept pressing his eyes into his head. When his mother asked him what was the matter, he told her he'd been working on a painting. He began rummaging through the refrigerator and piling bread, cheese, ham, pickles, the mustard jar, and a pitcher of orange juice on a big platter, then returned to his room. When he came down the next morning he looked worse than before.

"He smelled so badly that Mom told him to go upstairs and take a bath, Pete. Without a word, he nodded, told her she was right, and like a little kid went up, took a bath, and went to sleep for the next thirty-six hours."

The next time the Cartagena family saw Raymond he was dressed in brown penny loafers, a pair of gray slacks, a button-down shirt with an Ivy League tie, and one of the Harris Tweed jackets he'd purchased in Scotland while on a stopover. He had shaved, combed his hair, and looked like every mother's dream. It was Sunday morning and Raymond accompanied the family to church. Juan Cartagena, seizing opportunity where he found it, although not a man given to religious sentiment, had joined the Lutheran Church. The move had allowed him to retain some of the trappings of the Catholic faith of his youth and incorporate the Protestantism of the country which had so readily adopted him. The pastor, Dr. Ewing, was so shocked to see Raymond that he spent a full ten minutes in a rather convoluted digression from his sermon and spoke about the "prodigal son," a concept which Cartagena had not yet understood nor cared to.

"I thought it meant insane," said Cartagena as his cousin approached the Triborough Bridge. "Really, in my mind the word had distinct connotations of mental imbalance. I suppose the inference back then was that Ray was wasting his life."

When the family returned home from church, everyone seemed relaxed and in a pleasant mood. Angie and Fran had chosen to forget about their run-in with Raymond and were back to being solicitous and charming. This lasted for the better part of the afternoon and evening. After supper Raymond informed the family that he had a surprise. With a naiveté which far exceeded her contrived lack of intelligence, Angie asked if it was something which he had brought back from Morocco and had not yet shown them. "No, nothing like that," Raymond had said, smiling in his strange way so that his sisters didn't know whether he was being friendly or mocking them. "It's a portrait of the two of you." Angie then asked if that's what he had been doing up in his room all that time. Raymond nodded sheepishly and Fran turned to her mother and said, "Isn't that sweet, Mama?"

Their mother nodded politely and looked at her husband, who, it seemed to Cartagena, had known all along what Raymond was up to. With this, Raymond went bounding up the stairs. When he returned he was carrying his easel. There appeared to be a painting on the easel but he had draped a sheet over them both. He set the easel down in the middle of the living room and with great theatrical gestures removed the sheet to reveal his first actual oil painting.

"It was fantastic, Pete. I mean both ways. Really great and totally far out. I mean, you've seen it."

In the foreground of the large canvas a young man was racing headlong, the lines of motion of his naked body so beautifully outlined, so perfect, his flight so desperate that it appeared as if in the next second he would plunge out of the painting and into their midst. As in Raymond's ink drawings, the face was etched with indescribable agony, the fear in the young man's eyes calling out desperately. He was being pursued by two women dressed in evening gowns, one white, the other yellow. The faces of the two women were television screens, each with a miniature painting on them. With their arms outstretched they seemed about to dig their talonlike scarlet fingernails into the young man's back. In the background, across a desolate violet and blue horizon, twelve moons delicately hued in golden light drifted over desert mountains.

The more Cartagena stared at the painting, the more convinced he became that something terrible was about to happen. No one spoke and the eerie light of the painting, the yellow moons, the long blood-filled claws, seemed to glow. Way out, beyond the consciousness of the moment, Cartagena heard the water pounding the beach, the sound growing solidly until it became a steady hum inside him. His father was the first to speak but he hadn't understood him. It had seemed more as if their father were uttering a prayer. For years Cartagena regretted his intrusion into the silence to praise his brother's creation, believing the praise should have come from someone else. "It looks like what you told me about the Sahara," he'd said.

Raymond had smiled and nodded his approval. Angie and Fran said not a word. They remained in their seats, glancing at the painting and then at each other and at their mother for what seemed too long. The spell was finally broken when the phone rang. Fran jumped up and announced it was for her. She raced out of the living room and upstairs. With perhaps a bit more decorum but with the same intent, Angie followed her. Raymond continued to smile until his father shook his head despairingly and Raymond draped the sheet over the painting. "I knew everyone would like it," he'd said, and hoisting the easel over his head, marched upstairs.

By this time his mother and sisters were convinced that Raymond had gone off the deep end. He became more argumentative and very slowly household activities began once more to revolve around his erratic behavior and schedule. He would come and go at all hours of the night, and on more than one occasion brought home objects which inspired the family to believe that somewhere along the line they had mistreated Raymond and he was now paying them back. One evening, after informing them that he was going out in search of the truth, he returned with an enormous piece of driftwood, bleached almost white by exposure to salt and sun and polished smooth by the sand. It was nearly ten o'clock at night, but he managed to hold everyone's attention until midnight. He pointed out faces, shapes of countries, letters which formed words, which in turn, after involved logical sequences, spelled out messages. There were animals disguised as flowers and flowers disguised as jewels and on and on until everyone drifted away from him, making excuses as they left. That night Angie had a nightmare.

It was shortly after this that his mother and sisters decided that Raymond's trouble was lack of female companionship. In spite of his opposition they arranged for him to meet Annie Pardo. Annie was Miguel Pardo's daughter. Don Miguel, as his father addressed him, was one of his clients. He owned an import-export company specializing in tropical foods, a moving company, twenty-five buildings in East Harlem and the South Bronx, several houses along Rockaway Beach, and part interest in a hotel in Miami Beach.

Raymond, when he wanted to, had impeccable manners and a charm so delicate that he could disarm most women with his helplessness. For more than a week after he found that Annie was coming to dinner, he behaved with infinite restraint in everything he did. Each word had the kind of caring and affection which amazed even his sisters. That Sunday he again went to church with the family. Dressed and well scrubbed, he listened attentively to Dr. Ewing's sermon, something which on previous occasions he had been unable to do, choosing instead to keep up a whispered and sarcastic commentary on everything uttered by the silver-haired minister.

Around four that afternoon, a limousine delivered Annie Pardo from Jamaica Estates, and after some preliminary chitchat during which Raymond easily won Annie over and relieved Angie's last remnants of anxiety over his possible behavior, the family sat down to dinner. Raymond was seated at one end of the table and his father at the other. Next to his father, on his left, sat his mother. Cartagena was on his father's right with Fran next to him. Angie sat on Raymond's left and Annie on his right.

Cartagena didn't like Annie Pardo, then or now, and his view of what took place had always been colored by his antipathy. She hadn't changed much in twenty years, so that at the time she could best be described as she was today, a snob. In her second year at Barnard College, wealthy, quite beautiful Annie Pardo was the Puerto Rican's answer to the Jewish-American Princess, a PRAP — blond hair and blue eyes, two genetic traits which impressed even Cartagena's parents, who as far as he could recall had never suffered from undue emphasis upon physical characteristics as a requisite for acceptance, being the two of them quite attractive in their own right and having produced, in their olive-skinned, black-haired offspring, four equally attractive specimens.

The incident with Annie Pardo began quite innocently with a discussion of art, a subject which, on a superficial level, she had apparently mastered. The family had gone through the meal, en-joying Doña Teresa's fine cooking: an enormous roast beef, mashed potatoes, peas and carrots and salad. She had just brought two freshly baked apple pies to the table and was on her way back to the kitchen for the ice cream when Raymond slapped his forehead in disbelief.

"What? What did you say?" he suddenly said to Annie.

During a spirited discussion on fashions, Annie had recounted her experiences in Europe the previous summer, extrapolating, in what must have seemed to her infinite mental agility, trends in dress to the subject of art, and painting in particular, coming to rest, more out of lack of breath than any derived conclusion, at her stay in Rome. Up to that point Raymond hadn't said much. When he didn't get the required response to his question, he informed Annie that Rome was a decadent city and that it hadn't produced any decent art in hundreds of years. In the light from the candles along the middle of the table, Raymond resembled a tiger, the feral tone of his voice making what he said more powerful than its content.

"Have you been there?" asked Annie, smiling, her head tilted coyly to one side and her eyes ready to tear into Raymond.

"Yes, several times," he replied, his own gaze boring into Annie's.

There was at those moments a quality to his voice which warned others not to trespass into his domain. Some, unschooled in this phenomenon of animal dynamics, went ahead and argued only to find themselves ridiculed by Raymond's counterarguments. Annie, exposed as she had been to some measure of good breeding and waspish cattiness among her schoolmates, began backing off, seeking refuge in the safest possible area, common experience, hoping, Cartagena had imagined later, that Raymond, thus far behaving like a gentleman, would see that she recognized her blunder and spare her.

"Then you must have visited the Sistine Chapel," she said brightly. "How did you like Michelangelo's work?" She had pronounced the name in Italian. Years later Cartagena understood her fascination for the Italian language and culture, since it became clear that she viewed herself as descended from northern Italian nobility, by which path he never ascertained.

"Michelangelo was a tool of the state, a puppet of the ruling class and the pope," shot back Raymond angrily.

He could have said anything because Annie's reaction was instantaneous. She blushed bright red, coughed twice into the back of her hand, and answered him.

"Are you an authority on Italian art?" she asked haughtily, her chin raised defiantly and her eyes attempting to pierce his.

"No, I'm not," Raymond said calmly. "I am an artist."

Annie laughed.

It was by no means derisive laughter, but it might as well have been. Cartagena's suspicion had always been that she was shocked. Even after having Angie and Fran mention Raymond's drawing, she never imagined he would be so bold as to declare himself an artist. The scene became almost comical after that.

"You?" Annie'd sputtered, unable to contain her laughter.

"Yes, me," Raymond had said, pounding the table so that his desert plate rose several inches and clattered noisily against Annie's glass. "I am an artist. And you, blondie, are a phony. A little spic phony masquerading as an upper-class debutante, when all you are is a petit-bourgeois nitwit."

Cartagena recalled laughing at the entire thing until his brother said "petit bourgeois." He was suddenly convinced that Raymond had directed an ancient curse, learned from a Berber tribe, at Annie Pardo and that within seconds she would turn into a camel and begin braying. His father put a hand on Cartagena's arm and he immediately understood the gravity of the situation.

Annie Pardo was gasping for air and trying to get up from the table. Angie, Fran, and their mother immediately went to her and escorted her upstairs to the bathroom. Once there, she angrily disposed of her dinner, was washed and then taken to Fran's room, where she proceeded to faint. Raymond got up from the table, put on his coat, and left the house. He was gone four days.

"When he came back he looked awful, Pete. His eyes were red from smoking grass and drinking and he hadn't shaved. I guess that's when he started growing a beard. He told me he'd stayed at his friend Albert's house in the Village. He looked just like one of his drawings."

Cartagena had just come in from school and Raymond smiled as if to tell him he was sorry. When he came downstairs that night, Raymond was clean-shaven and looked better, but the worry lines on his forehead were etched deeper and he couldn't look his father in the eye. He offered no explanation for his behavior toward Annie Pardo and none was elicited from him. Angie and Fran lowered their heads when they saw him. His mother, looking extremely troubled, remained, as was her manner, impassive in the face of a crisis. Cartagena's father had had enough of his son's theatrics and remained in his study, refusing to join the family at supper.

Two days later at the supper table, Raymond announced that he was leaving for California to attend school. The announcement threw everyone into a panic. Angie was engaged to be married and the entire family, bound by tradition, had assumed, perhaps with some trepidation, that Raymond would remain in New York until June and, if not serve as an usher, at least attend the ceremony and reception.

Another terrible argument ensued and Raymond informed the family that he had far more important things to do than attend a wedding, especially in a church. Cartagena's father told him that it was a shame that he did not feel enough love for his sister to remain home for a few more months.

"Maybe that's why I'm leaving," Raymond had said, and turned away to go upstairs.

"Wait a minute," said his father.

"No, Dad," he said, turning. "I've waited long enough."

His father watched him go upstairs and stood looking sadly after him. Cartagena guessed that Raymond meant to say that he loved Angie, but it didn't seem that way. As the years passed and Angie's marriage ended in divorce, leaving her with two children to support, one of whom, Jamie, had to have periodic treatment on a kidney machine, Raymond's love for her became more apparent as he contributed to the medical expenses. But then, it all seemed complicated and strange, and the very next day Raymond went out to say goodbye to his friends. He came back to the house and began packing, taking very few clothes but making sure he took all of his art books and paints. He strapped the easel to the largest of his suitcases and placed them in the hall outside his room.

That afternoon, before supper, Raymond asked him if he wanted to go for a walk. Cartagena was torn by the invitation, wishing to spend time with Raymond but not wanting it to be for the purposes of saying goodbye.

"How about it, Danny," he'd said, tousling his hair.

"Sure," Cartagena'd replied and shrugged his shoulders as if it didn't matter one way or the other. A big, lumpy, dry feeling took over his throat and his chest became tight. "I guess I don't mind. Let me get my jacket."

He ran upstairs and before he got to his room he felt the tears. In the bathroom he pounded his head to make the tears stop and then splashed cold water on his face. When he was sure he wouldn't start crying again, he put on his jacket and ran back down. He had made up his mind to ask Raymond to take him along.

"Mama, Ray and I are going out for a walk," he said loudly as he reached the bottom of the stairs. He needed, if only for a brief moment, to cement the bond between himself and Raymond, perhaps threatening with his words his own independence and instigating, if not worry, disquietude, that like Raymond he too would drift out of their lives and return transformed.

Outside, the sun had begun setting and the streetlights were on along the row of neat houses with manicured lawns. The air was crisp and clear, and a faint fragrance of salt water and flowers drifted in the spring breezes. They walked quietly down to the beach and then to the edge of the water to watch the horizon and the lights where the beach turned out to the point.

"Do you know why I have to go away?" Raymond asked after a while.

"No," Cartagena replied. "I guess you don't want Angie to marry Kevin."

Shrugging his shoulders, Raymond began walking parallel to the water.

"I don't care if she marries him," he'd said. "He's a nice guy. I just think she's going to be unhappy as hell in a few years. She's not a stupid woman, you know."

Cartagena had wanted to tell him that Angie was not a woman, that she was their sister, a girl. He followed Raymond as he went on talking very softly and sadly with the sun going down and night beginning to cover them, the lights out on the point like stars millions of years into time.

"I love Angie and Fran and you and Mom and Dad, but I don't

know how to show it the right way. Not like everyone else, anyway. I can't even say it too well because then I'd have to do certain things, and if I didn't I'd feel like a hypocrite. You know, like I was lying."

Cartagena hadn't quite understood what Raymond was talking about, but knew that something terrible was eating away at his brother and that he was sorry to be leaving. After a while Raymond was quiet and they just walked and walked until they were almost to the point. On their way back Raymond seemed to be feeling better. Cartagena asked him if he would write from California and Raymond said he would if Cartagena wrote and told him exactly everything he did in his baseball games. Cartagena said he would and then Raymond stopped, turned to watch the water, and sat down on the sand. Cartagena sat next to him. Raymond then lay back and stretched his arms and legs so that he looked like a giant gingerbread man.

"Did you really like my painting?" he'd asked, sounding to Cartagena like his friend, Joey Goldstein, who was always worried that people didn't like the things he wore, or what he said, or his birthday parties.

"Sure," Cartagena'd answered. "It was just like you told me about the Sahara. You know, blue and gold and the moon shining down on the pyramids, except you didn't have any pyramids. The women were horrible, though. I mean, you drew them good but they were . . . you know, scary. Were they supposed to be Angie and Fran?"

"Cut it out," he'd said, laughing. "That was a joke."

"Yeah, some joke."

"What do you mean?"

Raymond had been genuinely surprised.

"I think it scared them."

"Well, yeah. Some jokes are like that," Raymond had said somberly. "I guess that's why I have to go. Everybody's too grown-up around here."

"Like Angie and Fran?"

"Sure, like them. But it's everybody else. I don't mean you. You'll always be a kid like me. Everybody's got a little kid and a grown-up inside of them. Everybody. One day the grown-up joins the crowd and starts telling the kid to shut up so he can take over and run the show. I guess that's why I said I didn't want to have kids that time. I don't want to be the one to help them shut up. I can't even tell the kid inside of me to shut up. You know, tell him to behave. I guess I never will. But you like it, huh?"

"I really did, Ray," Cartagena'd said, and almost choked with emotion, then and now, because Raymond asked him if he wanted it.

"To keep?" he'd asked.

"Of course to keep. I'll frame it for you."

"Really?"

"Yeah, sure," Raymond said. He turned over and they'd wrestled in the sand and Cartagena had laughed and laughed until his face hurt. When they stopped laughing and were lying exhausted on the sand, Cartagena asked his brother if he could go to California with him. Raymond didn't answer him, and when Cartagena asked him again, he shook his head.

"It wouldn't work out, Danny," he'd said. "You have to go to school, and with me around that would never happen. Even if you were older, it wouldn't work out. I have to do this alone. It's like when you're playing ball. Nobody can bat for you. You know that."

Raymond had helped him up and they had walked back to the house. His mother made them hot chocolate and said nothing about sand on the carpets. Raymond spent the rest of the evening making a frame for the painting and signing it down in the right-hand corner, his script hand so neat that it looked as if the name, *Cartagena*, had been stamped on.

"It's called *An Apology to the Moon Furies*," he'd said when he was finished and was cleaning out the thin, needlelike brush. "Will you remember? It doesn't mean anything. Just a joke between one kid and another."

Cartagena said he would remember and Raymond nodded several times, his eyes sad like in his drawings, veiled and moist as if it were his turn to cry. He had turned to the wall and hung the painting, taking an unusually long time to line it up. He then sat on Cartagena's bed, looked as if he were about to say something, got up, and went to his own room.

"He was gone ten years except for a couple of times he came to New York when he was in school. When he came back after the ten years, he had Ilse and the twins," Cartagena said as his cousin stopped in front of Cartagena's Riverside Drive building. "Thanks for listening, Pete," he said, patting Peter's knee. As he got out of the car he thought of telling Peter to give him a call sometime but knew it would be awkward when they met again. Peter was like all of the Cartagena men, private and enigmatic. Cartagena didn't want to bury any more of them.

The rain had slackened but still fell in its originally hazy drizzle. The streetlights in the park had come on, and feeling suddenly old, Cartagena went into the building, into the elevator, and up to his apartment. Tired, he turned on the lights in the living room, went to the kitchen, pulled out a tray of ice from the refrigerator, and with a bottle of Scotch sat in his soft reclining chair and stared at Raymond's painting.

After the third drink he decided he hated the painting and had displayed it these many years as a matter of loyalty. He had never understood why his brother had wanted him to have it and why he derived so much enjoyment whenever he'd seen it on his visits to New York. Cartagena poured himself another drink and tried to fathom what was troubling him. An immense sorrow now enveloped him and his mourning felt much too personal.

He recalled hearing Raymond, late that last night, moving his suitcases down the stairs and his father starting up the car to drive him to the airport. He had wanted it to be a dream but when he got up the next morning Raymond was gone. Feigning illness, he had refused to go to school and toward late afternoon left the house and walked alone on the beach. The sky had turned dark and the sea angry, the waves racing up on the shore to punish the pilings of the old pier. A few seagulls floated in the wind offshore but slowly drifted inland to seek refuge. Cartagena had sat down in the sand feeling the storm coming, the air growing thicker and the colors changing, the sand itself becoming gray and the water lead-colored, and knew only now that it was his last day as a child.

PATRICIA PRECIADO MARTIN

The Ruins

I T WAS GETTING so that almost every day Alma was going to the
ruins on the riverbank. Not that her mother knew, of course.
She was expressly forbidden to go there. It was a place, her mother
Mercedes warned, that winos went on occasion, and young lovers,
frequently. One never knew what kind of mischief or carnal
knowledge one might come upon or witness. When Señora Romero spoke like this — of the proximity of temptation or occasions of sin — she would finger the large gold medallion of the
Sagrado Corazón that she wore around her neck and invoke protection for her oldest daughter from the phalanx of saints with
which she was on a first-name basis. The image of the Sagrado
Corazón was fortified on the reverse side with an engraving of the
Virgen de Guadalupe, and Señora Romero wore the medal like the
medieval armor of a crusader prepared to do battle with the infidel.
It was a pose Alma saw her mother strike with frequency —
inspired by the worldliness promoted by newspapers, television,
popular music, *protestantes* and errant in-laws.

(She was not being disrespectful, Alma had convinced herself,
when her mother would begin her pious sermons, to imagine Doña
Mercedes, a fury on a rearing stallion — lance raised, mail clanking,
banners aloft — routing unbelievers and sinners from the *cantinas*

and alleyways of south Tucson, until they knelt trembling and repentant at the vestibule of Santa Cruz Church. Señora Romero mistook Alma's dreamy unwavering stare for attentiveness, and so these periodic encounters left all parties satisfied. In reality, Señora Romero never behaved in any manner that would have called attention to herself: decorum, simplicity and moderation were the measures by which she lived her life and by which she ruled her family.)

It was easy enough for Alma to keep her afternoon sojourns secret from her mother. The excuses were varied and plentiful: extra homework in the library, a dance committee, an after-school game or conference with a teacher. In truth, there was never anything or anyone at school that attracted Alma's attention or detained her there. She was a solitary and thoughtful girl — dutiful in her studies, retiring in her behavior, guarded in her conversation — and so she went unnoticed by her teachers and ignored by the giggling groups of friends that gathered in animated knots in the halls, in the cafeteria and on the school grounds.

(Alma seemed plain to the casual observer. Her dress was modest, almost dowdy, created from cheap fabric by the nimble fingers of her mother on her Singer treadle sewing machine. She wore no makeup or jewelry, in contrast to her peers at school: with their brightly colored clothes and lips, patterned stockings and flashy plastic accessories, they swarmed through the halls like flocks of rainbow-hued wingless birds. But it could be said that Alma had a certain beauty: she was slim and muscular and lithe, with dark, serious eyes and coppery brown curly hair that obeyed no comb or brush or stylistic whim of her mother. Señora Romero had long ago given up trying to tame Alma's unruly locks with ribbons and barrettes, abandoning these efforts to dedicate herself to other pursuits that were more pliable to her will.)

Alma always made sure that she arrived home from school at a reasonable hour — in time to help with supper chores or to babysit her younger siblings if needed. Señora Romero never questioned her tardiness or investigated, satisfied that the delay of an hour, or sometimes two, was taken up with school activities. A growing family, household duties and spiritual obligations kept Señora

Romero busy enough. It contented her that there were no calls from the principal or teachers, and Alma's excellent grades were testament enough to her industriousness and trustworthiness. All was well.

Señora Romero prided herself on the fact that her household ran so smoothly, and she credited the personal intervention of the Sagrado Corazón de Jesús for her good fortune. She was a dedicated and energetic woman who scrubbed, polished, cooked, washed, ironed, sewed and prayed with great fervor. Her humble home was spotless, her children orderly, her marriage stable, if predictable. Her soul was as spotless as her house, and it was the former that preoccupied her the most — but never (and she was scrupulous on this issue) to the neglect of her domestic duties. Nonetheless, during the week there always seemed to be a funeral, *bautismo* or *velorio* to attend; a vigil to keep; a *manda* to complete; a novena or rosary to recite; a *visita* to deliver; an altar cloth to iron and mend. And she was grateful for Alma's good-natured helpfulness around the house.

In addition to her weekly obligations, on Sunday mornings Señora Romero arose faithfully at 5 A.M. to go to the Santa Cruz parish hall to help make menudo with the Guadalupanas to sell after all the masses. It was recompense enough for her that, thanks in part to her pious efforts and sacrifices, the ancient pastor and his ancient barrio church were solvent. She always made sure, however, that she was home by nine o'clock to marshal her immaculate family to church in time to sit in the front pew at the ten o'clock mass. Her energy in matters spiritual seemed boundless, and she was admired, and at times envied, by the other matrons of the south-side parish for the sanctity and punctuality demonstrated by her family.

Alma's father, Señor José Romero, was a patient and thoughtful man who complied with his wife's spiritual and devotional exigencies without complaining. He had a strong faith, in a manner of speaking, although it had developed more out of philosophical musings and awe of the universe than out of any adherence to theological doctrines. Nonetheless, he faithfully attended church when it was required or politic to do so, and he willingly helped out with repairs at the crumbling church and rectory whenever he could find the time.

Señor Romero was a good provider whose dependability as a mason for the Estes Homes Construction Company kept his family modestly housed, clothed and fed. He moonlighted at a Whiting Brothers gas station for the extras — music lessons, the yearly trip to California, gifts for special occasions. He himself had few material wants, and, having no interest in money matters, he handed over his paycheck to his thrifty and capable wife, who wrought miracles not only with saints but with his weekly stipend.

Señor Romero did, however, always manage to set aside a few dollars for himself from his overtime earnings which he lavished on his one passion — books. Whenever he could, he would browse among the stacks in the Carnegie Public Library by the park, and he would often check out as many as a dozen books at a time. But Señor Romero loved most of all wandering among the dusty aisles of the dimly lit used bookstore in the old section of downtown. He would spend hours, when possible, leafing through the musty yellowed volumes, studying the tables of contents and illustrations, fingering the cracked leather bindings embossed with gold lettering. The proprietor, a laconic, prematurely gray-haired man confined to a wheelchair due to a childhood illness, didn't seem to mind. They never spoke except in greeting, yet in an indefinable way they were the most intimate of companions. Whenever Señor Romero had accumulated enough savings, he would buy an antique volume or two, and his book collection had grown to the point that it occupied every available shelf and tabletop in their small home. He had taken to caching his books in cardboard boxes under the beds — as long as he kept them neatly stored his orderly wife did not complain.

Señor Romero read voraciously — in Spanish as well as in English. He seemed to have no literary preferences — poetry, philosophy, history, the natural sciences, fiction, biography — all he consumed with equal fervor. Night after night, he would read in his easy chair after the house had turned quiet — the younger children tucked in bed with prayer, his saintly wife occupied with her evening devotions. Alma would study her father through the doorway while doing her homework at the kitchen table. At times he would pause in his reading and close his book, a finger keeping his place. He would shut his eyes in meditation, his head in a halo of light and smoke, his patrician face composed. Alma alone knew about the tiny flame that burned in the hidden hearth of his soul, and she understood that the flame would flicker with meaningless chatter. He, in turn, sensed in his favorite daughter the very same embers glowing unattended. There was an unspoken pact between them, and thus they kept their silence.

Alma cut west across the football field, as had become her custom. Her backpack dangled loosely on her shoulders — she had left her books behind in her locker, having finished her homework during the lunch hour. Across the field she could see jostling groups of students heading east — crossing at the light on South Twelfth Avenue to play video games in the shopping mall or to hang out with Cokes and cigarettes at the Circle K. The less fortunate who had to ride the school buses were crowding and shoving in lines as they embarked. The bus driver, an angular man with a long-suffering face, whose request for a transfer was still sitting on the principal's desk, hunched over the steering wheel in resignation. Alma could see arms flailing out the windows in greeting, or directing paper missiles, and she could hear the muffled shouts and catcalls of the students who were good-naturedly elbowing one another for seats.

There was a cut in the chainlink fence by the bleachers at the far end of the field. It had been repaired many times, but it never stayed mended, this section of the fence being the most accessible and least detected place for those students wanting free entry to the football games. Alma stepped through the break in the fence and headed north, parallel with the dry riverbed that cut a wide swath between the highway and the school grounds. There was a faint path, but since it was seldom used, except by her, it was overgrown, and the ankle-high weeds and seeds scratched her legs and embedded themselves in her socks.

She hurried now, because the late November days were getting shorter, and her mother told time by the proximity of the sun to the horizon. It was not cold, but the weakening sun looked hazy and gave an illusion of winter. A gust of wind portending a change in the weather blew unexpectedly out of the south. Alma shivered and wrapped her ill-fitting cardigan more tightly around herself. The path narrowed gradually as she continued north, angling now slightly west toward the slope where she would descend into the riverbed in order to cross to the opposite bank. A few hundred yards farther and she could see across the river to the old mission orchard on the other side — a tangle of denuded trees — peach, apricot, pomegranate, fig and lemon, leafless now and overgrown with wild grape and the vines of the morning glory and the buffalo gourd. On the periphery of the abandoned orchard, the silhouettes of two dead cottonwoods thrust their giant trunks into the sky as if in failed supplication for water. By now Alma could see the decaying walls of the ancient adobe *convento*, and she could discern the elusive wisp of smoke that arose from somewhere amid the ruins. Far to the southeast, in the direction of the Santa Rita Mountains, she could now see dark clouds dragging their heavy burden over the mountain peaks. If the wind quickened, the storm would be here before dusk.

Alma walked faster now, scrambling down one side of the dry river's eroded bank and up the other, artfully sidestepping the litter of flash-flood debris, the broken glass and shiny aluminum of beer busts, discarded construction material and abandoned furniture and car parts. When she had reached the other side of the bank, she brushed her way through a stand of scraggly carrizo and walked over a plank suspended over a narrow, ragged cut where the river had meandered decades ago. At last she reached the neglected and overgrown orchard that had become her musing and, lately, her observation place. The trees were gnarled with age and barren now, but even in the spring they boasted few leaves, having to depend on the sparse and unpredictable desert rains for their irrigation. It was nothing short of a wonder that they were still alive: each season seemed to be their last, but now the native shrubs and vines had so intertwined themselves with their sorrowful hosts that they seemed perennially, unnaturally, green.

It was here within view of the ruins that Alma had chosen her secret hiding place: here she would sit day after day on a discarded car seat with broken springs that she had laboriously hauled up from the riverbed. It was from this vantage point that she would observe the comings and goings of the strange old woman who had taken up residence in the crumbling site. They had never spoken, but Alma was sure that the old woman was aware of her presence, and at times she thrilled with the sure knowledge that she, also, was being watched at a distance. It was just a matter of time before their eyes would meet and they would speak. She was sure of it, and her daily watchful ritual was enacted because of the possibility, nay the inevitability, of that encounter.

Doña Luz had squatted at the old ruin since the death of her mother three years before. Although the matriarch of the Martínez family was ninety-seven years old at the time of her death, she had been of robust health and keen of mind and spirit until shortly before her death. When her ancestral family adobe had been bulldozed with the blessing of a progressive city council to make way for a multilevel parking garage in the inner city, she had died — some said of a broken heart — within a month of relocation to public housing on the city's far south side. (The urban renewal project had continued on schedule in spite of the fact that Doña Luz — always a spirited and independent woman — had, in a last desperate show of defiance, thrown herself down in front of the wrecking ball. This had resulted in a rash of negative publicity and a spate of sympathetic letters that had proved embarrassing to the city fathers. The furor died down within a few weeks, however, as the populace's short-lived attention turned to more pressing matters like the World Series.)

Within a week of her mother's death, Doña Luz moved out of their one-bedroom apartment at La Reforma. The family heirlooms had been sold over the years to get through the hard times and to supplement Doña Luz's meager earnings as a folder and stacker at Haskell Linen Supply. Doña Luz's remaining tattered possessions — clothing, bedding, an antique trunk, a wood-burning stove, and a few pieces of weather-beaten furniture — had somehow mysteriously and miraculously reappeared in the one section of the abandoned *convento* ruins that still had a portion of its roof intact. The city fathers, who had annexed the site, chose to look the other way. It was considered an eyesore, used by some as a dump, and did not have potential for development in the forseeable future. They preferred to concentrate their energies and attentions on other, more potentially lucrative and respectable areas of the city.

(Doña Luz had been well known to officials before her celebrated encounter with the wrecking ball. She had been, in her more youthful and vigorous days, a thorn in the side of several generations of bureaucrats and attorneys, having laid claim, with faded documents and dog-eared deeds, to several acres of land where the multistory government complexes now stood in the heart of the city. Needless to say, the Martínez claims proved fruitless in spite of years of wrangling in the courts, their case weakened by the passing of time, the mists of history, a dearth of witnesses and a maze of legal and bureaucratic entanglements.)

Thus the weary city fathers were only too happy to ignore Doña Luz's latest display of obstreperousness, satisfied that age, infirmity and time had taken their toll on her senses. They were wrong, of course, having no way of knowing that Doña Luz's senses were intact, she having abandoned the fleeting awards of politics and protest for what she considered to be more sublime and spiritual matters. Nevertheless, her ghostly comings and goings at the ruins disturbed no one, threatened nothing, and they had received no complaints.

Mi casa es su casa.

Alma hunkered down into the torn plastic of the car seat, closing her eyes and concentrating her thoughts, trying to stay warm. For the air had turned suddenly colder now, and the clouds, gathering speed, had slammed over the weakening sun like a curtain being drawn. Like a room with its candles snuffed out, the orchard and the ruins lay suddenly in shadows. The clouds, blackened and tinged with purple, scudded across the blank sky like so many tall ships in a tempestuous sea.

When Alma at last opened her eyes, she was startled to see

Doña Luz standing before her, extending a veined hand to help her rise. Doña Luz had made her way across the bramble- and branch-strewn field soundlessly, like a ghostly dark cat on padded feet. The old woman's hair was completely white — long and wispy like spun sugar candy. It blew about her face like smoke that threatened to disappear with the quickening wind. She was dressed completely in black: her long dress of coarse homespun cloth hung down to her ankles. The style of the skirt and bodice was reminiscent of those Alma had seen worn by the stern-faced women in the treasured antique photographs of her mother. On her feet Doña Luz wore a pair of old-fashioned high-tops with no laces. She wore on her shoulders a threadbare fringed and embroidered shawl of the finest woven silk — the only surviving heirloom of her family's more exalted and prosperous days. Her face was brown, fine-boned and high-cheeked, wrinkled with age and weathered with adversity. Her eyes, set deeply and far apart, were small and bright, and so dark that they seemed to have no pupils. In the sudden obscurity that had come unnaturally with the storm, Doña Luz's luminous eyes were the only beacons in the darkened fields.

"Ven, mi hija. Ya es la hora." Doña Luz addressed Alma in Spanish in an urgent, musical voice. In the many weeks of her vigil, Alma had prepared herself for this moment, and she was not frightened by the sudden apparition of Doña Luz. She grasped Doña Luz's bony arm to steady herself as she arose from her seat; she was surprised at its strength in spite of its weightless fragility. She walked with her silently across the fallow autumn fields to her dwelling place in the *convento*. The wind was roaring now, whipping the delicate and brittle branches of the fruit trees. The branches, threatening to snap, made a rasping, protesting sound that rivaled the din of the wind itself. Before they were halfway across the field, the promised moisture came, not in the usual rain but in unexpected, silent flakes of snow that fell so thickly that everything in the orchard was blurred as though seen through a cataract-veiled lens. By the time they reached the adobe shelter of Doña Luz, Alma was shivering with the wind and the blowing snow. Doña Luz pushed open the heavy hewn door of her shelter, and in the smoldering half-light of ancient kerosene lamps Alma saw what she thought were hundreds of giant tattered white moths pinned to the ceiling and the rafters and the walls, covering the sparse furniture or fallen, ankle deep, flightless and abject, on the floor.

"Tú estás encargada de todo esto," Doña Luz whispered to Alma with a dramatic sweep of her hand.

Outside, the snow gathered at the curtainless windows like gauze . . .

When Alma's eyes had focused and become accustomed to the smoky room, she distinguished through the haze, not moths, but shreds of paper on which notes had been carefully and laboriously written in a spidery scrawl.

Doña Luz continued to explain in a whisper: "This is the history of our people which I have gathered — the land grants and the homesteads and the property transfers; the place names of the mountains and the rivers and the valleys and the pueblos; the families and their names and their issue; the deeds, honorable and dishonorable; the baptisms, the weddings, the funerals; the prayers and the processions and the santos to whom they are directed; the fiestas, religious and secular; the milagros and the superstitions. She droned on in a cadence, and as she spoke, Alma, still grasping her bony hand and surveying with wonder the testament of Doña Luz, felt the warmth of that hand flow into her being like water being poured. "The recipes, the herbs and the cures; the music and the songs and the dances; the prose and the poems, the sorrows, the joys; the gain and the loss. This is my legacy. But I am old and failing. I entrust it to you lest it be lost and forgotten."

The wind continued to howl and the snow veiled the windows in white lace . . .

Alma stopped to pick up several pieces of the tattered scraps that lay at her feet, each veined with the faint tracings of Doña Luz's careful script. Squinting in the opaque half-light she read: "On February 10, 1897, Don Jesús María Figueroa perfected the title of his three sections of land under the Homestead Act. He and his family settled in the fertile canyon of the Madrona Draw of the mountain range we call Los Rincones. He named it Rancho de Los Alizos because of the great trees that grew there. He built his home, corrales and a chapel. There three generations of Figueroas prospered, cultivating grain, vegetables and fruit, and raising livestock. In 1939 the United States Department of the Interior, claiming eminent domain, expropriated the land. Before he left for town, the grandson of Don Jesús María Figueroa burned the buildings and the two thousand dollars he received in payment . . ."

Alma read a second note, her eyes straining in the ever-darkening room: "The feast day of San Isidro, the patron saint of farmers, is May 15th. A little statue of the saint is carried through the fields, the farmers and their families singing alabanzas, offering their humble crops and praying that this year's planting might be successful. This is his prayer:

Señor San Isidro
De Dios tan querido
Pues en la labor
Tu seáis mi padrino

Fuiste a la labor
Comenzaste a arriar
Junto con los hombres
Que iban a sembrar.

Porque sois de Dios amado
Y adornado de esplandor
Bendecid nuestro sembrado
San Isidro Labrador . . ."

And the thickening snow smothered the windows and the ruins like a shroud.

Alma continued to read with a mounting sense of urgency now: "Here is written the corrido of the ill-fated race when Don Antonio Valenzuela lost all he possessed when his superior and beautiful horse El Merino lost to El Pochi at Los Reales in 1888.

¿Qué hubo, Merino mentado?
¿Qué siente tu corazón?
¿Por qué estás apachangado
Cuando eres tú en el Tucsón
El caballo acreditado
Dueño de la situación . . .?"

The unfinished song flew from Alma's hands when suddenly, and without warning, a tornadolike gust blew open the unlocked door of Doña Luz's hovel. The airborne flakes blasted in with a ferociousness, and then Alma saw, helpless and aghast, that the shreds of precious paper, in an avalanche of blinding whiteness, had metamorphosed into giant white moths again. They quickened with life and took to the air in a dizzying funnel of flight. Blowing snow mingled with blowing paper and rose and fell and then eddied into a blizzard of memories. And then the memories and the spirit of Doña Luz fluttered out the open door in a thousand swirling fragments in the direction of the south wind somewhere west of Aztlán.

DENISE CHÁVEZ

The Closet

I

WHEN I CLOSE my eyes I can see Christ's eyes in the darkness. It's an early summer afternoon, and I should be sleeping. Instead, I'm standing in the silence of my mother's closet
holding a luminescent sliding picture of the Shroud of Turin. One
image reveals Christ as he might look fleshed out; the other shows
shadows of skin pressed against white cloth. A slant of light filters
through the closed door.

"It's my turn! Let me in! I want to see!" Mercy whispers impa-
tiently from behind the door. In the half-tone darkness my eyes
travel from the wedding photograph at the back of the closet to
the reality of my mother's other life. Shoes crowd the floor,
teacher's shoes, long comfortable plastic loafers, sandals and open-
toed pumps in blue and black, the sides stretched to ease the
bunions' pressure. They are the shoes of a woman with big feet,
tired legs, furious bitter hopes. They are the shoes of someone who
has stood all her life in line waiting for better things to come.

"Mother! Mother!" I yelled one day across the downtown shoe
store. "Is size ten too small?" She answered with an impatient
pinching under-the-sweater look reserved for nasty children who

have the audacity to perform obscenities in public. She scowled across the crowded room, "No! And don't yell, your voice carries!"

Mother was married at age thirty-two to a man who bathed twice a day. Juan Luz Contreras was very clean. He was the town's best catch, a descendant of the Contreras family of west Texas. Head 'em up. Round 'em up. Ride 'em out. Dead. Juan Luz was poisoned by an unscrupulous druggist — oh, unwittingly. He was forced to drink acid. Someone poured it down his throat, but why? He had a wife and a child but three days old. His wife was my mother. For many years I wondered who the man in the wedding photograph was. He wasn't my father. My father still lived with us at that time, but he wasn't home much. Who was the man in the photograph if he wasn't my father? Later I found out he was Juan Luz, my mother's first husband. Ronelia's father.

When my father finally left our home, it was Juan Luz's face in the crowded closet who comforted me. From all accounts he was a perfect man.

Standing in the closet I can smell mother, all of her, forty-eight years old in her flowered bathrobes and suits of gradually increasing girth. It is the soft, pungent woman smell of a fading mother of three girls, one of them the daughter of the unfortunate Juan Luz.

In the darkness there is the smell of my mother's loneliness. Next to me the portrait of my mother and Juan Luz is hidden behind piles of clothes which are crowded into the house's largest closet. All those memories are now suffocated in cloth. So whoever comes, whatever man comes, and only *one* could, he would not feel alarm. But would my father come, being gone so long?

I remember the nights my father was home, sitting in his favorite red chair, reading the evening newspaper and later telling stories to Mercy and me.

"A is for Aardvark and in the Name of the Father and the Son and Little Lulu and Iggy went to the store . . . and what did you learn today, baby?"

Sometimes, alone on the armchair or on his lap, I recounted tales of Dick and Jane and little blond-haired Sally.

"Please, Daddy, tell me the story of the two giant brothers, Hilo and Milo."

*   *   *

When I open my eyes I return to the darkness of the closet. With small feet I stand on my mother's shoes. I could never fill them even if I tried.

If I didn't hold the body of Christ in my hands and if there wasn't anything to glow in the dark and then to disappear, I could still see faces in the closet and hear people talking and feel alone. I'm afraid in the middle of the day. Me, supposed to be taking a nap in August and it being the hottest month to be born in and with a crying baby sister outside the door yell-whispering, "Come on, it's *my* turn!"

And there I'd be, holding on to the brass-colored knob with one hand, and Mercy yanking with both, and the Shroud of Turin in my left hand getting crumpled and there I'd be, whispering, "Shut up, shut up! She'll hear you and so I'm looking, okay? It's *my* turn! Okay?" The boxes are open and soon scarves and hats will be all over the floor and I'll have to get a chair and put them up on the top rack and while I'm up there I'll look at the cloth flowers and feathers and I might want to play dress up with the hats.

"We'll listen to the records on the top shelf, Mercy. 'The Naughty Lady of Shady Lane' and 'Fascination.' We'll dance like we like to dance."

"We'll be floating ballerinas meeting each other halfway under the tropical-bird light fixture. You can practice your diving while I count the flowers, arranging them in rows and humming, 'Let me go, let me go, let me go, lover,' while you rest from your long swim."

"It's my turn, Rocío. You get to look at the Christ eyes all the time!"

"There's no eyes. Only sockets."

"If I squint Chinesey, I can see eyes."

"Yeah?"

"So let me have the thing, it's my turn. You always look too long."

"You might get scared, baby."

"Me, no — you *promised*."

"Baby, Baby, Baby! There's no eyes, only sockets!"

"Open that door, you promised!"

"Go ahead, baby, come inside, here's the light!"

I turn the light on Christ and Juan Luz and my mother and all my dark secret young girl thoughts, and face my little Sally sister with her baby limp hair.

"Go ahead Mercy Baby! Take the stupid thing. But let me look one more time." I yank on the old pink and chartreuse belt that has become my mother's light cord, and go back inside the closet for one last look. I stumble across the gift box, full of vinyl wallets and heart-shaped handkerchiefs and a plastic container of car- and animal-shaped soap. The gift box is regularly replenished by my mother's elementary school students' Christmas and birthday gifts: "Merry Christmas, love Sammy. To Teacher from Mary. You are nice, Mrs. Esquibel, I'll never forget you. Bennie Roybal. 1956."

I turn off all the lights and close the door as tight as I can. I look at the glow-in-the-dark Jesus card and slide it back and forth. The skeleton color of yellow-white bone is electrified, and I can feel and see the Christ eyes in the almost total darkness.

"So here it is, Baby! Leave me alone. I'm going to lie down on the bed and rest. Don't bother me, and remember, this is the invisible line — your side, and mine. Don't cross over like you do, with those rubbery hairy spidery legs of yours. Here, see this pillow? Gosh, if we had a yardstick it would be good, but anyway, this pillow divides me from you, my side from yours, okay, Baby? I want the side by the wall and the pictures. So that when I'm drifting off to sleep, I can look at Ronelia in her wedding dress when she was seventeen years old and just married. She wore Mother's dress and Mother's veil — well, maybe not the veil, but the little plastic pillbox crown with wax flower buds. Maybe you and I will someday wear that dress, Mercy, okay? Okay? What do you think?"

"Oh, leave me alone!" she says.

As I lay in bed, Mamá Consuelo and her husband stare at me from across the room. Their faces are superimposed on wood. It's more than a photograph. It's a carved picture of two people, one of them a stranger. I don't ever know what to call my grandfather. I never called him and he never called me. So he doesn't have a name. He's my grandfather. He was strong. He was good. He worked hard during the Depression. He was better off than most.

He died in his sleep from a blood clot or brain hemorrhage. All I know is that he had a headache, leaped over my sleeping grandmother in the middle of the night to take an aspirin and then went back to sleep and never woke up. About Mamá Consuelo I know more.

"Oh Mercy, sleeping in the afternoons makes me tired. Without something to do or think about I'll really fall asleep. I might as well get the crown of thorns down from the crucifix and try them on."

"Are you sure, Rocío, shouldn't you leave them alone?"

Over mother's bed there's a crucifix, and on the crucifix there's a crown of thorns. Real thorns, like the ones Christ was crowned with, only these are very small and they cover just the center of my head, the baby spot. It doesn't matter that they're baby-sized, because when I push them down I feel what Christ felt. Oh, they hurt, but not too much. I never pushed them down all the way. But I can imagine what they feel like. They have long waxy spikes with sharp tips. I can imagine the rest. I've been stabbed by pencils in both my palms. The one on my right looks like the stigmata.

Naps. I hate naps because there's so much to do and think and feel, especially in August. If I have to sleep, I like it to be quick and over with before I know it, or long and happy with a visit to the Gray Room.

The Gray Room is a place I visit when I'm alone. The Gray Room was before my littleness, before my fear of cloth shadows from clothes on chairs, and of the dark animals the shadows made.

It began when I was a little girl. I was never afraid. Every day I visited a world which the others knew nothing about. Not Ronelia, not my mother, not my father, not even Mercy.

No one knew I lived in the Gray Room or that I flew through air and time. I entered the Gray Room late at night when the house was quiet and I was alone. I'd crawl through the hall closet and into the concrete passageway that was our house's foundation. Down I would go, into the enormous basement, inching my way into the awesome darkness, alone, unhampered, guided more or less by a voice that pulled and drew me, further, further, into the concrete maze. The space became larger, a room of immense proportions, a high room, an altar room, a sanctuary where I was the only Devout. Higher, higher, I climbed, past the attic, to the labyrinth that was the Gray Room. This world was my refuge — this world unknown to all!

One day I began to live two separate lives. One magical, the other fearful. I'd wake up screaming, "The animals! The animals!" I heard the foggy mist of concerned voices. "But even you don't understand, Mercy! You always say, 'The closet! There's nothing under our house, no rooms, no space for you to crawl through. There's no house above or underneath our house. There's no huge room without a ceiling!'

"But Mercy, I've *been* there. I've spoken to the Keeper of the Room. He's an animal and brown. He wanted to make the room smaller, but I said no. 'There's no space for you, go away.' Now the room is white and blue and mine, alone.

"All this came to me in dreams. I felt presences and heard voices and the sound of breathing and music far away, then near. There was smoke in my room. I couldn't breathe. The animals crowded into corners. I woke up in the middle of the night trying to run away. Mother turned on the hall light to check in on me and gave me a baby aspirin. I drifted off again. 'Walking in your sleep,' mother called it.

"Mercy, would you believe me if I told you that I was born in a closet?"

"Rocío, you're crazy!"

Mother was forty years old. She'd been a widow nine years. A table was brought into the room, but the legs were removed because the doorway was too small. When I was born, Mother and I came crashing down. I shot into a closet full of shoes, old clothes. It was 4:48 A.M. on a hot August day. Ronelia hung outside the door. She was ten years old, too young to see such things.

Later, I imagined the wood, the splinters, the darkness and the shoes. And yet, on playing back the tape, Mercy, I always play back love. The things that we imagine support us never do. The world takes us quickly, handles us harshly, splinters us, casts us down and sends us forward to more pain. And yet, when I play back the tape, Mercy, I always play back love, much love.

I hear voices that say: "We are the formless who take form, briefly, in rooms, and then wander on. We are the grandmothers, aunts, sisters. We are the women who love you."

"Oh my God, Mercy, do you understand these things?"

No amount of tears will ever wash the pain or translate the joy. Over and over, it's the same, then as now. Birth and Death. There's me, in the Grey Room, or in the closet with the shoes.

"Mercy, remember the closets, remember them?"

II

The bathroom closet was full of ointments, medicines, potions to make us softer, more beautiful, less afraid. It held vials to relieve us, deceive us. It was the mysterious healing place, place of bandages, Mercurochrome and cotton balls. The center part contained the "good" towels, used only for company. They sat in their special pile, waiting for the occasional party, the welcome stranger, the annual holiday. Below this were kept the special blankets and the sheets, all folded tidily. They waited for that overnight guest or beloved family member, for nights of rearranged beds and noise and laughter. On the higher shelf were filmy containers of generic aspirin that were consumed candylike by Mother, for headaches, backaches, heartaches. In the corner was an unused snakebite kit, with its rubber hand pump and arm tie. We fantasized this ordeal and practiced what to do if that time should ever come. The *one* time presented itself, but we were in Texas, on the way to the Big Bend National Park. The two of us had gotten off the crowded car to stretch. We heard the sound of a rattler and there we were, kitless, three hundred miles from home!

After I talked to that snake, what did you do, Mercy? I ran, wildly, madly, all the way back to the car. I knew we could have died. One of us at least. It would have been me, for I was closest to the snake and saw him first. We drove on, the boy cousins up front, the girl cousins in the back. I know it would have been me.

The snakebite kit is still there, next to a greasy baby oil bottle. We never had suntan lotion until we were older, as we never had artichokes to eat, or eggplant or okra. We had summer dreams of swimming all day long, until our eyes were red, our toes and fingers pruney and our crotches white and soft and surrounded by tanned skin. Earlier we'd taken a shortcut near the Marking-Off Tree. The shortcut led to a world of water games: splish-splash, tag, dibble-dabble. You were the swimmer, Mercy, and I the observer. In my dreams I was always just surfacing to air, having swum from an almost fatal underwater voyage. Later I stood in the darkened shade of the small blue and white bathroom, peeling off my bathing suit like a second layer of skin. My body was ice-cold and excited, slightly damp.

I stripped to summer clothes, shorts and cotton tops, and thongs. My hair was wet, in strips, my lips red, my cheeks browned, my eyes wild and smaller than normal size. My wet, slithering body found solace in cloth. I felt a great and immense hunger, as swimmers do, especially children. I took a towel from the closet, the white ones bordered in black that we were allowed to use, and saw from the corner of my eye a "miniature," placed there by my dad, who was always hiding them. I found his bottles everywhere, in his chest of drawers, under his bed. The bathroom smelled of my cool flesh, of Vicks and liquor, of old prescriptions for ever-present maladies.

In the closet were remedies for women's ailments, hardened waxy suppositories, blood pressure tablets, weight pills, sulfa drugs, cough medicines, and aspirins of all sizes and shapes. There were medications for the head, the rectum, the stomach, the bladder, the eyes, the heart. The old shaving lotion was a reminder that we lived in a house of women.

An enema bag, salmon-colored and slightly cracked, the nozzle head black and foreboding, was poised and ready to be used. The last time Mother gave me an enema I was twelve, not yet a woman, but old enough to be embarrassed. I was sick, too tired to fight. Vicks and the smell of my discomfort all intermingled.

At age sixteen I sucked in the hot, pleasant, forbidden cigarette smoke and blew it out of the wire screens, hoping it would disappear. The butts were dispatched of in the usual two ways — flushed away or wrapped in Kleenex. I lit matches hoping the sulphur smell would mask my sins. But Mother knew. Mother took her aspirin not to worry about me while I smoked nude on the toilet, blowing out smoke through the meshed wire.

The bathroom was a closet. It held sexual adolescent dreams. It was full of necessities and bodily functions. Everyone hid there. Some letters from lost lovers, others, old used diaphragms.

III

I smelled Johnny. Johnny again. Johnny's blue sweatshirt jacket that he accidentally left in the living room over Christmas vacation. It was mine for three long weeks. I hung it in my closet, along with my clothes. When I closed the door I smelled Johnny, the indefinable sweetness of his young masculinity.

"Oh God, Rocío, you are so gross, you are the grossest woman I know!"

"Oh, settle down, just settle down, Mercy, will you?"

The smells of the closet are lusty and broad: the smells of a young woman's body odors and special juices and the memory of slithering afterbirths. This was where I slid — into the closet full of shoes. The closet smelled of summer and long nights and red lips and drying-out burnt bobby socks. I washed them every night and dried them on the floor. They were my one and only pair. One day they were burned beyond hope. I took them up to the attic to be hidden. My passions and fantasies were lost in time that way — stuffed into dark corners. And yet, the truth I speak is not an awkward truth. I treasured the smells and touches and the darkness of those closets. All were receptacles for a me I always wanted to be, was.

IV

The TV room closet was Ronelia's. Her old strapless prom dresses were there, her evening gowns of tulle with their spaghetti straps. The closet was immense and covered the entire side of the wall. It was built by Regino Suárez. The wooden doors never opened without a struggle but got stuck midway, so that you had to push one way and then the other to get inside. In this closet were stored long dresses, costumes and party shawls, with Mother's notations: "Summer Long. Ronelia's Party. Wedding Dress, Nieves'." Alongside were her initials and the date: "Ronelia FHA Queen, 1955, Yellow Tulle, N.E."

The long cardboard boxes were crammed onto the top shelf, below them in pink and blue clothing bags were the furs, the beaver Tío Frutoso trapped himself, the suede with the fur neckpiece, the imitation beige fur coat Mercy wore, and Mamá Consuelo's muff. The closet smelled of old petticoats and musty fur. Its contents included two wedding dresses, a new one and an old one. The new one Mother picked up at a sale for five dollars. The old one she wore when she married Juan Luz. Ronelia and Mercy later wore that dress, but at that time it was carefully sealed in plastic at the very bottom of the top shelf. Anything to do with him — photographs, articles of clothing, papers — were sacred and off-limits. To me, they were the Ark of the Covenant — deep and full of mysterious untouchability. I was ignorant of the past and the relationship of my mother to this man, long since dead.

Children assign mystery to small objects and create whole worlds from lost objects, pieces of cloth. This closet, then, was a glistening world of dances and proms and handsome dates. It was Ronelia's wedding at the age when most of us are still children. The closet meant dancing life to me. It contained my Zandunga costume, the dress I wore when I danced with Mercy as my "male" partner for bazaars and fiestas.

"Ay Zandunga, Zandunga, mamá, por dios . . . Ay Zandunga . . . Zandunga . . ."

This closet was Nieves at her best, her finest, and Mercy in imitation beige fur with a silk lining. The closet held two brides, one eternally wedded, the other husbandless. This closet was time and fantasy and dreams — and it was Regino's — ill made.

V

The living room closet held the house umbrella in rainbow colors. For many years there was but this one umbrella, large, sturdy, friendly. It came out late summer afternoons when we played outside in the rain. It welcomed and dispatched guests, friends who had come to visit. It protected us in early fall rainstorms. It shielded us in the early evening times when the fierce wildness of unleashed summer tensions rose and fell. This closet was rain, the hope of rain. To desert souls, rain is the blessed sex of God. It cleanses and refreshes. It is still the best mother, the finest lover.

The rainbow umbrella emerged, unhooked from its long nail, and was opened outside. It dried on the porch, each time a little grayer. One day it was replaced in black, by one of its funereal sisters.

This closet was the "guest" closet. It held all coats except Johnny's, which had found a dearer resting place. The overflowing "good" clothes, from the fancy-dress coat closet, were placed there too. In it Christmas and birthday gifts were hidden along with the gift box. Later, paper bags full of rummage and used clothing were placed inside, on their way south. This closet was a clearing-house — the "outgoing" closet, the last stop before dispersal — to needy families, young marrieds, senior citizens who used the hand-sewn lap rugs Nieves made. It was a closet full of seasonal smells: summer rain, dark winter clothes, the faint odor of Avon perfume like dried autumn flowers, the spring smell of soap and freshness. The closet smelled of luggage and time, of faded newspapers and old passports. Behind the door were dated check stubs and unused prayer books. The door smelled too, of wood and fingerprints. The ceiling had a trap door that led to the Gray Room. This closet was but another valve leading to the many chambers of the house's heart — where inside beat my other life.

VI

Nieves's closet was her life, her artery of hope. Those corners were hers, unviolated. In the back, on the right, behind her clothes, was her wedding photograph. She and Juan Luz, both slim, with bright, serious faces, stared out to the photographer. Behind them, leading to vast spacious rooms, was a stairway, a mirror on each side. From one wall hung the lasso, symbol of marriage. Nieves clutched a white glove in her left hand, her right arm was at a ninety-degree angle. Nieves stood next to Juan Luz and both of them faced right. Her hair was short, in the style of the twenties, with soft loose curls, not as she later wore it, in a bun, austere. Juan Luz was handsome, with a full head of hair that on second glance seemed subject to thinning, if not localized baldness. His hand was tightly clenched, as hers was relaxed. They gazed forward, loving, bright-eyed, with hand-painted pink cheeks. They were sealed in time — a photograph on their happiest day.

One year later Juan Luz was dead, Nieves was a widow, Ronelia was born, and Mercy and I were still in limbo.

Moving back and up, Nieves's world was full of old records, "The Singing Nun," Augustín Lara, mementos of her teaching days, her work with children. Hers was a closet packed with scarves, new shoes, old photograph albums, a chipped statue of San Martín de Porres, tapes of the Living Bible and charismatic church revivals, as well as home movies of us as children standing by the willow tree.

The closet floor is strewn with paper, boxes. When Mercy and I stand in there, with the Christ eyes, we have to be careful.

"Leave me alone! It's my turn!"

"Give me the Christ eyes, Rocío!"

"Oh, go lay down, Baby."

"Don't pull that knob. Mother's gonna find out and get mad. You made me knock something over."

"Okay, okay, let me find the cord. There, see. That didn't take so long. Hey, Mercy, if you crouch down like this, it's better. That way, you feel darker."

I crouch in the closet wanting to know what it is like to feel crucified, to carry the sins of the world. I feel as if I'd already earned my crown of thorns. I imagine the splinters, the wood.

Each step into a closet was a step forward into that other world, the world of concrete corridors, the endless labyrinths, a soundless foray into the maze of faceless forms, living spirits. Up there, down there, in there, they were all the same, they lead into the heart and spirit of the house. When the spirit was sick, the nocturnal journey was long, the gasping for air at the bottom of an endless summer pool. When the spirit was pure, the long rope flew down from the sky and I was beamed up on an umbilical cord of light. I flew beyond the Gray Room into the Blue Room and farther up, into the great vast No Room of the living sky. Up beyond worlds, I flew into a universe of change, to the No Place of dreamers who do not dream.

"And *how* did it happen, Rocío?" I wanted Mercy to say when I told her about the Gray Room.

"Do you think it has something to do with seeing the house's bones, I mean, its skeleton? The wood, the house frame, the concrete slabs?"

"Maybe it had something to do with seeing the sliced-away mountain," I said. "Remember that mountain? All my life I thought mountains were soft inside."

"You're kidding!"

"Seeing that mountain changed my life! It was one of the five most important things that ever happened to me; the discovery of perspective in the fourth grade was three."

"What are two, four and five, Rocío?"

"I can't tell you that, Mercy."

"Tell me, tell me," she begged.

"God bless, do I have to tell you *everything*?"

"Look, I'll tell you about the Gray Room. Will you be quiet, then?" I'm in the hallway closet. I see Grandpa's death mask wrapped in white satin. I see the box of paper dolls we got on Christmas. I see your crown from elementary school, when you were Bazaar Queen. Why did you cry? I wouldn't have cried, but then, I wasn't Queen. I move aside the belt cord from Mother's green bathrobe. I uncover the box of Christmas cards. I move the old rubber rainshoes and plastic raincoats. I make room for myself and step inside. I glide past everybody. I am far away now, past the color and the noise, past the cloth shadows. I am past everyone. Alone. Alone without noise. I don't need to turn on the light.

"Oh, but Rocío, aren't you afraid of the dark?" Mercy said at last, trying on the crown of thorns and then putting them on her side of the bed. "Aren't you afraid of the Christ eyes?"

"Not of the Christ eyes," I said, "but the brown animals scare me and I don't want to be afraid."

"Tell me about the Blue Room," she said after a long pause. "It sounds *so* beautiful."

"It is," I said, lying down to rest on the bed, not bothering to tell her she was on my side again. "It's a beautiful enormous room and it's blue. But you know, the other day I went in there and it was all white and the floor was like dry ice."

"You mean it changes?" Mercy said with surprise. "Tell me about it before it changed," she said drowsily.

"The Blue Room is my favorite room. It's the most magnificent, incredible room you'd ever hope to see, Mercy. It has a round ceiling that goes up forever. It's so big that I have to fly back and forth to get around. It's a beautiful room and it's mine. It's all mine!"

"Golly," Mercy said, yawning.

"Watch it! You almost made me turn over on the thorns. Put them up, would you?"

"Rocío, Rocío, if that's *your* room, what's *mine?*"

"I don't know, Mercy, everybody has their *own* room, their *own* house."

"They do?" she said with a faraway voice.

"Gaaa, Mercy, do I have to tell you *everything?*"

Gringolandia

PIRI THOMAS

Alien Turf

Sometimes you don't fit in. Like if you're a Puerto Rican on an Italian block. After my new baby brother, Ricardo, died of some kind of germs, Poppa moved us from 111th Street to Italian turf on 114th Street between Second and Third Avenue. I guess Poppa wanted to get Momma away from the hard memories of the old pad.

I sure missed 111th Street, where everybody acted, walked, and talked like me. But on 114th Street everything went all right for a while. There were a few dirty looks from the spaghetti-an'-sauce cats, but no big sweat. Till that one day I was on my way home from school and almost had reached my stoop when someone called: "Hey, you dirty fuckin' spic."

The words hit my ears and almost made me curse Poppa at the same time. I turned around real slow and found my face pushing in the finger of an Italian kid about my age. He had five or six of his friends with him.

"Hey, you," he said. "What nationality are ya?"

I looked at him and wondered which nationality to pick. And one of his friends said, "Ah, Rocky, he's black enuff to be a nigger. Ain't that what you is, kid?"

My voice was almost shy in its anger. "I'm Puerto Rican," I said.

"I was born here." I wanted to shout it, but it came out like a whisper.

"Right here inna street?" Rocky sneered. "Ya mean right here inna middle of da street?"

They all laughed.

I hated them. I shook my head slowly from side to side. "Uh-uh," I said softly. "I was born inna hospital — inna bed."

"Umm, paisan — born inna bed," Rocky said.

I didn't like Rocky Italiano's voice. "Inna hospital," I whispered, and all the time my eyes were trying to cut down the long distance from this trouble to my stoop. But it was no good; I was hemmed in by Rocky's friends. I couldn't help thinking about kids getting wasted for moving into a block belonging to other people.

"What hospital, paisan?" Bad Rocky pushed.

"Harlem Hospital," I answered, wishing like all hell that it was five o'clock instead of just three o'clock, 'cause Poppa came home at five. I looked around for some friendly faces belonging to grown-up people, but the elders were all busy yakking away in Italian. I couldn't help thinking how much like Spanish it sounded. Shit, that should make us something like relatives.

"Harlem Hospital?" said a voice. "I knew he was a nigger."

"Yeah," said another voice from an expert on color. "That's the hospital where all them black bastards get born at."

I dug three Italian elders looking at us from across the street, and I felt saved. But that went out the window when they just smiled and went on talking. I couldn't decide whether they had smiled because this new whatever-he-was was gonna get his ass kicked or because they were pleased that their kids were welcoming a new kid to their country. An older man nodded his head at Rocky, who smiled back. I wondered if that was a signal for my funeral to begin.

"Ain't that right, kid?" Rocky pressed. "Ain't that where all black people get born?"

I dug some of Rocky's boys grinding and pushing and punching closed fists against open hands. I figured they were looking to shake me up, so I straightened up my humble voice and made like proud. "There's all kinds of people born there. Colored people, Puerto Ricans like me, an' — even spaghetti-benders like you."

"That's a dirty fuckin' lie" — *bash*, I felt Rocky's fist smack into my mouth — "you dirty fuckin' spic."

I got dizzy and then more dizzy when fists started to fly from everywhere and only toward me. I swung back, *splat, bish* — my fist hit some face and I wished it hadn't, 'cause then I started getting kicked.

I heard people yelling in Italian and English and I wondered if maybe it was 'cause I hadn't fought fair in having hit that one guy. But it wasn't. The voices were trying to help me.

"Whas'sa matta, you no-good kids, leeva da kid alone," a man said. I looked through a swelling eye and dug some Italians pushing their kids off me with slaps. One even kicked a kid in the ass. I could have loved them if I didn't hate them so fuckin' much.

"You all right, kiddo?" asked the man.

"Where you live, boy?" said another one.

"Is the bambino hurt?" asked a woman.

I didn't look at any of them. I felt dizzy. I didn't want to open my mouth to talk, 'cause I was fighting to keep from puking up. I just hoped my face was cool looking. I walked away from that group of strangers. I reached my stoop and started to climb the steps.

"Hey, spic," came a shout from across the street. I started to turn to the voice and changed my mind. "Spic" wasn't my name. I knew that voice, though. It was Rocky's. "We'll see ya again, spic," he said.

I wanted to do something tough, like spitting in their direction. But you gotta have spit in your mouth in order to spit, and my mouth was hurt dry. I just stood there with my back to them.

"Hey, your old man just better be the janitor in that fuckin' building."

Another voice added, "Hey, you got any pretty sisters? We might let ya stay onna block."

Another voice mocked, "Aw, fer Chrissake, where ya ever hear of one of them black broads being pretty?"

I heard the laughter. I turned around and looked at them. Rocky made some kind of dirty sign by putting his left hand in the crook of his right arm while twisting his closed fist in the air.

Another voice said, "Fuck it, we'll just cover the bitch's face with the flag an' fuck 'er for Old Glory."

All I could think of was how I'd like to kill each of them two or three times. I found some spit in my mouth and splattered it in their direction and went inside.

Momma was cooking, and the smell of rice and beans was beating the smell of Parmesan cheese from the other apartments. I let myself into our new pad. I tried to walk fast past Momma so I could wash up, but she saw me.

"My God, Piri, what happened?" she cried.

"Just a little fight in school, Momma. You know how it is, Momma. I'm new in school an' . . ." I made myself laugh. Then I made myself say, "But Moms, I whipped the living —— outta two guys, an' one was bigger'n me."

"Bendito, Piri, I raise this family in Christian way. Not to fight. Christ says to turn the other cheek."

"Sure, Momma." I smiled and went and showered, feeling sore at Poppa for bringing us into spaghetti country. I felt my face with easy fingers and thought about all the running back and forth from school that was in store for me.

I sat down to dinner and listened to Momma talk about Christian living without really hearing her. All I could think of was that I hadda go out in that street again. I made up my mind to go out right after I finished eating. I had to, shook up or not; cats like me had to show heart.

"Be back, Moms," I said after dinner. "I'm going out on the stoop." I got halfway to the stoop and turned and went back to our apartment. I knocked.

"Who is it?" Momma asked.

"Me, Momma."

She opened the door. "Qué pasa?" she asked.

"Nothing, Momma, I just forgot something," I said. I went into the bedroom and fiddled around and finally copped a funny book and walked out the door again. But this time I made sure the switch on the lock was open, just in case I had to get back real quick. I walked out on that stoop as cool as could be, feeling braver with the lock open.

There was no sign of Rocky and his killers. After a while I saw Poppa coming down the street. He walked like beat tired. Poppa hated his pick-and-shovel job with the WPA. He couldn't even hear the name WPA without getting a fever. *Funny*, I thought, *Poppa's the same like me, a stone Puerto Rican, and nobody in this block even pays him a mind. Maybe older people get along better'n us kids.*

Poppa was climbing the stoop. "Hi, Poppa," I said.

"How's it going, son? Hey, you sure look a little lumped up. What happened?"

I looked at Poppa and started to talk it outta me all at once and stopped, 'cause I heard my voice start to sound scared, and that was no good.

"Slow down, son," Poppa said. "Take it easy." He sat down on the stoop and made a motion for me to do the same. He listened and I talked. I gained confidence. I went from a tone of being shook up by the Italians to a tone of being a better fighter than Joe Louis and Pedro Montanez lumped together, with Kid Chocolate thrown in for extra.

"So that's what happened," I concluded. "And it looks like only the beginning. Man, I ain't scared, Poppa, but like there's nothin' but Italianos on this block and there's no me's like me except me an' our family."

Poppa looked tight. He shook his head from side to side and mumbled something about another Puerto Rican family that lived a coupla doors down from us.

I thought, *What good would that do me, unless they prayed over my dead body in Spanish?* But I said, "Man! That's great. Before ya know it, there'll be a whole bunch of us moving in, huh?"

Poppa grunted something and got up. "Staying out here, son?"

"Yeah, Poppa, for a little while longer."

From that day on I grew eyes all over my head. Anytime I hit that street for anything, I looked straight ahead, behind me, and from side to side all at the same time. Sometimes I ran into Rocky and his boys — that cat was never without his boys — but they never made a move to snag me. They just grinned at me like a bunch of hungry alley cats that could get to their mouse anytime they wanted. That's what they made me feel like — a mouse. Not like a smart house mouse but like a white house pet that ain't got no business in the middle of cat country but don't know better 'cause he grew up thinking he was a cat — which wasn't far from wrong 'cause he'd end up as part of the inside of some cat.

Rocky and his fellas got to playing a way-out game with me called one-finger-across-the-neck-inna-slicing-motion, followed by such gentle words as "It won't be long, spico." I just looked at them blank and made it to wherever I was going.

I kept wishing those cats went to the same school I went to, a school that was on the border between their country and mine, and I had *amigos* there — and there I could count on them. But I couldn't ask two or three *amigos* to break into Rocky's block and help me mess up his boys. I knew 'cause I had asked them already. They had turned me down fast, and I couldn't blame them. It would have been murder, and I guess they figured one murder would be better than four.

I got through the days trying to play it cool and walk on by Rocky and his boys like they weren't there. One day I passed them and nothing was said. I started to let out my breath. I felt great; I hadn't been seen. Then someone yelled in a high, girlish voice, "Yoo-hoo . . . Hey, paisan . . . we see yoo . . ." And right behind that voice came a can of evaporated milk — whoosh, clatter. I walked cool for ten steps, then started running like mad.

This crap kept up for a month. They tried to shake me up. Every time they threw something at me, it was just to see me jump. I decided that the next fucking time they threw something at me I was gonna play bad-o and not run. That next time came about a week later. Momma sent me off the stoop to the Italian market on 115th Street and First Avenue, deep in Italian country. Man, that was stompin' territory. But I went, walking in the style which I had copped from the colored cats I had seen, a swinging and stepping down hard at every step. Those cats were so down and cool that just walking made a way-out sound.

Ten minutes later I was on my way back with Momma's stuff. I got to the corner of First Avenue and 114th Street and crushed myself right into Rocky and his fellas.

"Well-l, fellas," Rocky said. "Lookee who's here."

I didn't like the sounds coming out of Rocky's fat mouth. And

I didn't like the sameness of the shitty grins spreading all over the boys' faces. But I thought, *No more! No more! I ain't gonna run no more.* Even so, I looked around, like for some kind of Jesus miracle to happen. I was always looking for miracles to happen.

"Say, paisan," one guy said, "you even buying from us paisans, eh? Man, you must wantta be Italian."

Before I could bite that dopey tongue of mine, I said, "I wouldn't be a guinea on a motherfucking bet."

"Wha-at?" said Rocky, really surprised. I didn't blame him; I was surprised myself. His finger began digging a hole in his ear, like he hadn't heard me right. "Wha-at? Say that again?"

I could feel a thin hot wetness cutting itself down my leg. I had been so ashamed of being so damned scared that I had peed on myself. And then I wasn't scared anymore; I felt a fuck-it-all atti- tude. I looked real bad at Rocky and said, "Ya heard me. I wouldn't be a guinea on a bet."

"Ya little sonavabitch, we'll kick the shit outta ya," said one guy, Tony, who had made a habit of asking me if I had any sen-your- ritas for sisters.

"Kick the shit outta me yourself if you got any heart, you motherfuckin' fucker," I screamed at him. I felt kind of happy, the kind of feeling that you get only when you got heart.

Big mouth Tony just swung out, and I swung back and heard all of Momma's stuff plopping all over the street. My fist hit Tony smack dead in the mouth. He was so mad he threw a fist at me from about three feet away. I faked and jabbed and did fancy dance steps. Big-mouth put a stop to all that with a punch in my mouth. I heard the home cheers of "Yea, yea, bust that spic wide open!" Then I bloodied Tony's nose. He blinked and sniffed without putting his hands to his nose, and I remembered Poppa telling me, "Son, if you're ever fighting somebody an' you punch him in the nose, and he just blinks an' sniffs without holding his nose, you can do one of two things: fight like hell or run like hell — 'cause that cat's a fighter."

Big-mouth came at me and we grabbed each other and pushed and pulled and shoved. *Poppa*, I thought, *I ain't gonna cop out. I'm a fighter, too.* I pulled away from Tony and blew my fist into his belly. He puffed and butted my nose with his head. I sniffed back. *Poppa, I didn't put my hands to my nose.* I hit Tony again in that same weak spot. He bent over in the middle and went down to his knees.

Big-mouth got up as fast as he could, and I was thinking how much heart he had. But I ran toward him like my life depended on it; I wanted to cool him. Too late, I saw his hand grab a fistful of ground asphalt which had been piled nearby to fix a pothole in the street. I tried to duck; I should have closed my eyes instead. The shitty-gritty stuff hit my face, and I felt the scrappy pain make itself a part of my eyes. I screamed and grabbed for two eyes with one hand, while the other I beat some kind of helpless tune on air that just couldn't be hurt. I heard Rocky's voice shouting, "Ya scum bag, ya didn't have to fight the spic dirty; you could've fucked him up fair and square!" I couldn't see. I heard a fist hit a face, then Big-mouth's voice: "Whatta ya hittin' me for?" and then Rocky's voice: "Putana! I ought ta knock all your fuckin' teeth out."

I felt hands grabbing at me between my screams. I punched out. *I'm gonna get killed,* I thought. Then I heard many voices: "Hold it, kid." "We ain't gonna hurt ya." "Je-*sus*, don't rub your eyes." "Ooooohhhh, shit, his eyes is fulla that shit."

You're fuckin' right, I thought, *and it hurts like coño.*

I heard a woman's voice now: "Take him to a hospital." And an old man asked: "How did it happen?"

"Momma, Momma," I cried.

'Comon, kid," Rocky said, taking my hand. "Lemme take ya home." I fought for the right to rub my eyes. "Grab his other hand, Vincent," Rocky said. I tried to rub my eyes with my eyelids. I could feel hurt tears cutting down my cheeks. "Come on, kid, we ain't gonna hurt ya," Rocky tried to assure me. "Swear to our mudder. We just wanna take ya home."

I made myself believe him, and trying not to make pain noises, I let myself be led home. I wondered if I was gonna be blind like Mr. Silva, who went around from door to door selling dish towels and brooms, his son leading him around.

"You okay, kid?" Rocky asked.

"Yeah," what was left of me said.

"A-huh," mumbled Big-mouth.

"He got much heart for a nigger," somebody else said.

A spic, I thought.

"For anybody," Rocky said. "Here we are, kid," he added. "Watch your step."

I was like carried up the steps. "What's your apartment number?" Rocky asked.

"One-B — inna back — ground floor," I said, and I was led there. Somebody knocked on Momma's door. Then I heard running feet and Rocky's voice yelling back, "Don't rat, huh, kid?" And I was alone.

I heard the door open and Momma say, "Bueno, Piri, come in." I didn't move. I couldn't. There was a long pause; I could hear Momma's fright. "My God," she said finally. "What's happened?" Then she took a closer look. "Ai-eeee," she screamed. "Dios mío!"

"I was playing with some kids, Momma," I said, "an' I got some dirt in my eyes." I tried to make my voice come out without the pain, like a man.

"Dios eterno — your eyes!"

"What's the matter? What's the matter?" Poppa called from the bedroom.

"Está ciego!" Momma screamed. "He is blind!"

I heard Poppa knocking things over as he came running. Sis began to cry. Blind, hurting tears were jumping out of my eyes. "Whattya mean, he's blind?" Poppa said as he stormed into the kitchen. "What happened?" Poppa's voice was both scared and mad.

"Playing, Poppa."

"Whatta ya mean, 'playing'?" Poppa's English sounded different when he got warm.

"Just playing, Poppa."

"Playing? Playing got all that dirt in your eyes? I bet my ass. Them damn Ee-ta-liano kids ganged up on you again." Poppa squeezed my head between the fingers of one hand. "That settles it — we're moving outta this damn section, outta this damn block, outta this damn shit."

Shit, I thought, *Poppa's sure cursin' up a storm*. I could hear him slapping the side of his leg, like he always did when he got real mad.

"Son," he said, "you're gonna point them out to me."

"Point who out, Poppa? I was playin' an' — "

"Stop talkin' to him and take him to the hospital!" Momma screamed.

"Pobrecito, poor Piri," cooed my little sister.

"You sure, son?" Poppa asked. "You was only playing?"

"Shit, Poppa, I said I was."

Smack — Poppa was so scared and mad, he let it out in a slap to the side of my face.

"Bestia! Ani-*mul!*" Momma cried. "He's blind, and you hit him!"

"I'm sorry, son, I'm sorry," Poppa said in a voice like almost crying. I heard him running back into the bedroom, yelling, "Where's my pants?"

Momma grabbed away fingers that were trying to wipe away the hurt in my eyes. "Caramba, no rub, no rub," she said, kissing me. She told Sis to get a rag and wet it with cold water.

Poppa came running back into the kitchen. "Let's go, son, let's go. Jesus! I didn't mean to smack ya, I really didn't," he said, his big hand rubbing and grabbing my hair gently.

"Here's the rag, Momma," said Sis.

"What's that for?" asked Poppa.

"To put on his eyes," Momma said.

I heard the smack of a wet rag, *blapt*, against the kitchen wall. "We can't put nothing on his eyes. It might make them worse. Come on, son," Poppa said nervously, lifting me up in his big arms. I felt like a little baby, like I didn't hurt so bad. I wanted to stay there, but I said, "Let me down, Poppa, I ain't no kid."

"Shut up," Poppa said softly. "I know you ain't, but it's faster this way."

"Which hospeetal are you taking him to?" Momma asked.

"Nearest one," Poppa answered as we went out the door. He carried me through the hall and out into the street, where the bright sunlight made a red hurting color through the crap in my eyes. I heard voices on the stoop and on the sidewalk: "Is that the boy?"

"A-huh. He's probably blinded."

"We'll get a cab, son," Poppa said. His voice loved me. I heard

Rocky yelling from across the street, "We're pulling for ya, kid. Remember what we . . ." The rest was lost to Poppa's long legs running down to the corner of Third Avenue. He hailed a taxi and we zoomed off toward Harlem Hospital. I felt the cab make all kinds of sudden stops and turns.

"How do you feel, hijo?" Poppa asked.

"It burns like hell."

"You'll be okay," he said, and as an afterthought added, "Don't curse, son."

I heard cars honking and the Third Avenue el roaring above us. I knew we were in Puerto Rican turf, 'cause I could hear our language.

"Son."

"Yeah, Poppa."

"Don't rub your eyes, fer Christ sake." He held my skinny wrists in his one hand, and everything got quiet between us.

The cab got to Harlem Hospital. I heard change being handled and the door opening and Poppa thanking the cabbie for getting here fast. "Hope the kid'll be okay," the driver said.

I will be, I thought. *I ain't gonna be like Mr. Silva.*

Poppa took me in his arms again and started running. "Where's emergency, mister?" he asked someone.

"To your left and straightaway," said a voice.

"Thanks a lot," Poppa said, and we were running again. "Emergency?" Poppa said when we stopped.

"Yes, sir," said a girl's voice. "What's the matter?"

"My boy's got his eyes full of ground-up tar an' —"

"What's the matter?" said a man's voice.

"Youngster with ground tar in his eyes, doctor."

"We'll take him, mister. You just put him down here and go with the nurse. She'll take down the information. Uh, you the father?"

"That's right, doctor."

"Okay, just put him down here."

"Poppa, don't leave me," I cried.

"Sh, son, I ain't leaving you. I'm just going to fill out some papers, an' I'll be right back."

I nodded my head up and down and was wheeled away. When

the rolling stretcher stopped, somebody stuck a needle in me and I got sleepy and started thinking about Rocky and his boys, and Poppa's slap, and how great Poppa was, and how my eyes didn't hurt no more . . .

I woke up in a room blind with darkness. The only lights were the ones inside my head. I put my fingers to my eyes and felt bandages. "Let them be, sonny," said a woman's voice.

I wanted to ask the voice if they had taken my eyes out, but I didn't. I was afraid the voice would say yes.

"Let them be, sonny," the nurse said, pulling my hand away from the bandages. "You're all right. The doctor put the bandages on to keep the light out. They'll be off real soon. Don't you worry none, sonny."

I wished she would stop calling me sonny. "Where's Poppa?" I asked cool-like.

"He's outside, sonny. Would you like me to send him in?"

I nodded. "Yeah." I heard walking-away shoes, a door opening, a whisper, and shoes walking back toward me. "How do you feel, hijo?" Poppa asked.

"It hurts like shit, Poppa."

"It's just for a while, son, and then off come the bandages. Everything's gonna be all right."

I thought, *Poppa didn't tell me to stop cursing.*

"And son, I thought I told you to stop cursing," he added.

I smiled. Poppa hadn't forgotten. Suddenly I realized that all I had on was a hospital gown. "Poppa, where's my clothes?" I asked.

"I got them. I'm taking them home an' —"

"Whatta ya mean, Poppa?" I said, like scared. "You ain't leavin' me here? I'll be damned if I stay." I was already sitting up and feeling my way outta bed. Poppa grabbed me and pushed me back. His voice wasn't mad or scared anymore. It was happy and soft, like Momma's.

"Hey," he said, "get your ass back in bed or they'll have to put a bandage there too."

"Poppa," I pleaded. "I don't care, wallop me as much as you want, just take me home."

"Hey, I thought you said you wasn't no kid. Hell, you ain't scared of being alone?"

Inside my head there was a running of *Yeah, yeah, yeah,* but I answered, "Naw, Poppa, it's just that Momma's gonna worry and she'll get sick an' everything, and —"

"Won't work, son," Poppa broke in with a laugh.

I kept quiet.

"It's only for a couple days. We'll come and see you an' every-body'll bring you things."

I got interested but played it smooth. "What kinda things, Poppa?"

Poppa shrugged his shoulders and spread his big arms apart and answered me like he was surprised that I should ask. "Uh . . . fruits and . . . candy and ice cream. And Momma will probably bring you chicken soup."

I shook my head sadly. "Poppa, you know I don't like chicken soup."

"So we won't bring chicken soup. We'll bring what you like. Goddammit, whatta ya like?"

"I'd like the first things you talked about, Poppa," I said softly. "But instead of soup I'd like" — I held my breath back, then shot it out — "some roller skates!"

Poppa let out a whistle. Roller skates were about $1.50, and that was rice and beans for more than a few days. Then he said, "All right, son, soon as you get home, you got 'em."

But he had agreed too quickly. I shook my head from side to side. Shit, I was gonna push all the way for the roller skates. It wasn't every day you'd get hurt bad enough to ask for something so little like a pair of roller skates. I wanted them right away.

"Fer Christ sakes," Poppa protested, "you can't use 'em in here. Why, some kid will probably steal 'em on you." But Poppa's voice died out slowly in a "you win" tone as I just kept shaking my head from side to side. "Bring 'em tomorrow," he finally mumbled, "but that's it."

"Thanks, Poppa."

"Don't ask for no more."

My eyes were starting to hurt like mad again. The fun was starting to go outta the game between Poppa and me. I made a face.

"Does it hurt, son?"

"Naw, Poppa. I can take it." I thought how I was like a cat in a movie about Indians, taking it like a champ, tied to a stake and getting like burned toast.

Poppa sounded relieved. "Yeah, it's only at first it hurts." His hand touched my foot. "Well, I'll be going now . . ." Poppa rubbed my foot gently and then slapped me the same gentle way on the side of my leg. "Be good, son," he said and walked away. I heard the door open and the nurse telling him about how they were gonna move me to the ward 'cause I was out of danger. "Son," Poppa called back, "you're un hombre."

I felt proud as hell.

"Poppa."

"Yeah, son?"

"You won't forget to bring the roller skates, huh?"

Poppa laughed. "Yeah, son."

I heard the door close.

NASH CANDELARIA

The Day the Cisco Kid
Shot John Wayne

J UST BEFORE I started the first grade we moved from Los Rafas
into town. It created a family uproar that left hard feelings for
a long time.

"You think you're too good for us," Uncle Luis shouted at Papa
in Spanish, "just because you finished high school and have a job
in town! My God! We grew up in the country. Our parents and
grandparents grew up in the country. If New Mexico country was
good enough for them —"

Papa stood with his cup and saucer held tightly in his hands, his
knuckles bleached by the vicious grip as if all the blood had been
squeezed up to his bright red face. But even when angry, he was
polite to his older brother.

"I'll be much closer to work, and Josie can have the car to shop
once in a while. We'll still come out on weekends. It's only five
miles."

Uncle Luis looked around in disbelief. My aunt tried not to look
at either him or Papa, while Grandma sat on her rocking chair
smoking a hand-rolled cigarette. She was blind and couldn't see the
anger on the men's faces, but she wasn't deaf. Her chair started to
rock faster, and I knew that in a moment she was going to scream
at them both.

"It's much closer to work," Papa repeated.

Before Uncle Luis could shout again, Grandma blew out a puff of cigarette smoke in exasperation. "He's a grown man, Luis. With a wife and children. He can live anywhere he wants."

"But what about the —"

He was going to say orchard next to Grandma's house. It belonged to Papa and everyone expected him to build a house there someday. Grandma cut Uncle short: "Enough!"

As we bumped along the dirt of Rafas Road toward home in the slightly used Ford we were all so proud of, Papa and Mama talked some more. It wasn't just being nearer to work, Papa said, but he couldn't tell the family because they wouldn't understand. It was time for Junior — that was me — to use English as his main language. He would get much better schooling in town than in the little country school where all the grades were in just two rooms.

"Times have changed," Papa said. "He'll have to live in the English-speaking world."

It surprised me. I was, it turned out, the real reason we were moving into town, and I felt a little unworthy. I also felt apprehensive about a new house, a new neighborhood, and my first year in school. Nevertheless, the third week in August we moved into the small house on Fruit Avenue, not far from Immaculate Heart Parochial School.

I barely had time to acquaint myself with the neighborhood before school began. It was just as well. It was not like the country. Sidewalks were new to me, and I vowed to ask Santa Claus for roller skates at Christmas like those that city kids had. All of the streets were paved, not just the main highway like in the country. At night streetlights blazed into life so you could see what was happening outside. It wasn't much. And the lights bothered me. I missed the secret warm darkness with its silence punctuated only by the night sounds of owls and crickets and frogs and distant dogs barking. Somehow the country dark had always been a friend, like a warm bed and being tucked in and being hugged and kissed good night.

There were no neighbors my age. The most interesting parts of the neighborhood were the vacant house next door and the vacant lot across the street. But then the rush to school left me no time to think or worry about neighbors.

I suppose I was a little smug, a little superior, marching off that first day. My little sister and brother stood beside Aunt Tillie and watched anxiously through the front window, blocking their wide-eyed views with their steaming hot breaths. I shook off Mama's hand and shifted my new metal lunchbox to that side so she wouldn't try again.

Mama wanted to walk me into the classroom, but I wouldn't let her, even though I was frightened. On the steps in front of the old brick school building a melee of high voices said goodbye to mothers, interrupted by the occasional tearful face or clinging hand that refused to let go. At the corner of the entrance, leaning jauntily against the bricks, leered a brown-faced tough whose half-closed eyes singled me out. Even his wet, combed hair, scrubbed face, and neatly patched clothes did not disguise his true nature.

He stuck out a foot to trip me as I walked past. Like with my boy cousins in the country, I stepped on it good and hard without giving him even so much as a glance.

Sister Mary Margaret welcomed us to class. "You are here," she said, "as good Catholic children to learn your lessons well so you can better worship and glorify God." Ominous words in Anglo that I understood too well. I knew that cleanliness was next to godliness, but I never knew that learning your school lessons was — until then.

The students stirred restlessly, and during the turmoil I took a quick look around. It reminded me of a chocolate sundae. All the pale-faced Anglos were the vanilla ice cream, while we brown Hispanos were the sauce. The nun, with her starched white headdress under her cowl, could have been the whipped cream except that I figured she was too sour for that.

I had never been among so many Anglo children before; they outnumbered us two to one. In the country church on Sundays it was rare to see an Anglo. The only time I saw many of these foreigners — except for a few friends of my father's — was when my parents took me into town shopping.

"One thing more," Sister Mary Margaret said. She stiffened, and her face turned to granite. It was the look that I later learned meant the ruler for some sinner's outstretched hands. Her hard eyes focused directly on me. "The language of this classroom is English. This is America. We will only speak English in class and on the school grounds." The warning hung ominously in the silent, crackling air. She didn't need to say what we brownfaces knew: If I hear Spanish, you're in trouble.

As we burst from the confines of the room for our first recess, I searched for that tough whose foot I had stomped on the way in. But surprise! He was not in our class. This puzzled me, because I had thought there was only one first grade.

I found him out on the school grounds, though. Or rather, he found me. When he saw me, he swaggered across the playground tailed by a ragtag bunch of boys like odds and ends of torn cloth tied to a kite. One of the boys from my class whispered to me in English with an accent that sounded normal — only Anglos really had accents. "Oh, oh! Chango, the third grader. Don't let his size fool you. He can beat up guys twice as big." With which my classmate suddenly remembered something he had to do across the way by the water fountain.

"¡Ojos largos!" Chango shouted at me. I looked up in surprise. Not so much for the meaning of the words, which was "big eyes," but for his audacity in not only speaking Spanish against the nun's orders, but shouting it in complete disregard of our jailers in black robes.

"Yes?" I said in English like an obedient student. I was afraid he would see my pounding heart bumping the cloth of my shirt.

Chango and his friends formed a semicircle in front of me. He placed his hands on his hips and thrust his challenging face at me, his words in the forbidden language. "Let's see you do that again."

"What?" I said in English, even though I knew what.

"And talk in Spanish," he hissed at me. "None of your highfalutin Anglo."

Warily I looked around to see if any of the nuns were nearby. "¿Qué?" I repeated when I saw that the coast was clear.

"You stepped on my foot, big eyes. And your big eyes are going to get it for that."

I shook my head urgently. "Not me," I said in all innocence. "It must have been somebody else."

But he knew better. In answer, he thrust a foot out and flicked his head at it in invitation. I stood my ground as if I didn't understand, and one of his orderlies laughed and hissed, "¡Gallina!"

The accusation angered me. I didn't like being called chicken, but a glance at the five of them waiting for me to do something did wonders for my self-restraint.

Then Chango swaggered forward, his arms out low like a wrestler's. He figured I was going to be easy, but I hadn't grown up with older cousins for nothing. When he feinted an arm at me, I stood my ground. At the next feint, I grabbed him with both hands, one on his wrist, the other at his elbow, and tripped him over my leg that snapped out like a jackknife. He landed flat on his behind, his face changing from surprise to anger and then to caution, all in an instant.

His cronies looked down at him for the order to jump me, but he ignored them. He bounced up immediately to show that it hadn't hurt or perhaps had been an accident and snarled, "Do that again."

I did. This time his look of surprise shaded into one of respect. His subordinates looked at each other in wonder and bewilderment. "He's only a first grader," one of them said. "Just think how tough he's going to be when he's older."

Meanwhile I was praying that Chango wouldn't ask me to do it a third time. I had a premonition that I had used up all of my luck. Somebody heard my prayer, because Chango looked up from the dirt and extended a hand. Was it an offer of friendship, or did he just want me to pull him to his feet?

To show that I was a good sport, I reached down. Instead of a shake or a tug up, he pulled me down so I sprawled alongside him. Everybody laughed.

"That's showing him, Chango," somebody said.

Then Chango grinned, and I could see why the nickname. With his brown face, small size, and simian smile there could be no other. "You wanna join our gang?" he asked. "I think you'll do." What if I say no? I thought. But the bell saved me, because they started to amble back to class. "Meet us on the steps after school," Chango shouted. I nodded, brushing the dust from my cords as I hurried off.

That was how I became one of Los Indios, which was what we called ourselves. It was all pretty innocent, not at all what people think of when they see brown faces, hear Spanish words, and are told about gangs. It was a club really, like any kid club. It made us more than nonentities. It was a recognition, like the medal for bravery given to the cowardly lion in *The Wizard of Oz*.

What we mostly did was walk home together through enemy territory. Since we were Los Indios, it was the cowboys and the settlers we had to watch out for. The Anglo ones. *Vaqueros y paisanos* were okay. Also, it was a relief to slip into Spanish again after guarding my tongue all day so it wouldn't incite Sister Mary Margaret. It got so I even began to dream in English, and that made me feel very uncomfortable, as if I were betraying something very deep and ancient and basic.

Some of the times, too, there were fights. As I said before, we were outnumbered two to one, and the sound of words in another language sometimes outraged other students, although they didn't seem to think about that when we all prayed in Latin. In our parish it was a twist on the old cliché: the students that pray together fight together — against each other.

But there was more to Los Indios than that. Most important were the movies. I forget the name of the theater. I think it was the Río. But no matter. We called it the Rat House. When it was very quiet during the scary part of the movie, just before the villain was going to pounce on the heroine, you could hear the scamper of little feet across the floor. We sat with our smelly tennis shoes up on the torn seats — we couldn't have done any more harm to those uncomfortable lumps. And one day someone swore he saw a large, gray furry something slither through the cold, stale popcorn in the machine in the lobby. None of us would ever have bought popcorn after that, even if we'd had the money.

For a dime, though, you still couldn't beat the Rat House. Saturday matinees were their specialty, although at night during the week they showed Spanish-language movies that parents and aunts and uncles went to see. Saturdays, though, were for American westerns, monster movies, and serials.

Since I was one of the few who ever had money, I was initiated into a special assignment that first Saturday. I was the front man, paying hard cash for a ticket that allowed me to hurry past the candy counter — no point in being tempted by what you couldn't get. I slipped down the left aisle near the screen, where behind a half-drawn curtain was a door on which was painted "Exit." No one could see the sign because the light bulb was burned out, and they never replaced it in all the years we went there. I guess they figured if the lights were too strong, the patrons would see what a terrible wreck the theater was and not come back.

The owner was a short, round, excitable man with the wrinkles and quavering voice of a person in his seventies but with black, black hair. We kept trying to figure out whether it was a toupee or not, and if it was, how we could snatch it off.

For all his wrinkles, though, he could rush up and down the aisles and grab an unruly kid by the collar and march him out like nothing you ever saw. So fast that we nicknamed him Flash Gordo. We would explode into fits of laughter when one of us saw him zoom down the aisle and whispered "Flash Gordo" to the rest of us. He gave us almost as many laughs as Chris-Pin Martín of the movies.

I counted out my money that first Saturday. I was nervous, knowing what I had to do, and the pennies kept sticking to my sweaty fingers. Finally, in exasperation, Flash Gordo's long-nosed wife counted them herself, watching me like a hawk so I wouldn't try to sneak in until she got to ten, and then she growled, "All right!"

Zoom! Past the candy counter and down the aisle like I said, looking for Flash. I didn't see him until I got right up front, my heart pounding, and started to move toward the door. That's when this circular shadow loomed in the semidark, and I looked up in fright to see him standing at the edge of the stage looking at the screen. Then he turned abruptly and scowled at me as if he could read my mind. I slipped into an aisle seat and pretended I was testing it by bouncing up and down a couple of times and then sliding over to try the next one.

I thought Flash was going to say something as he walked in my direction. But he suddenly bobbed down and picked something off the floor — a dead rat? — when a yell came from the back of the theater. "Lupe and Carlos are doing it again! Back in the last row!"

Flash bolted upright so quickly my mouth fell open. Before I could close it, he rushed up the aisle out of sight, toward those sex maniacs in the last row. Of all the things Flash Gordo could not tolerate, this was the worst. And every Saturday some clown would tattle on Lupe and Carlos, and Flash would rush across the theater. Only later did I learn that there never was any Lupe or Carlos. If there had been, I'm sure Los Indios would have kept very quiet and watched whatever it was they were doing back there.

"Oh, Carlos!" someone yelled in a falsetto. "Stop that this minute!"

I jumped out of my seat and rushed to the door to let Los Indios in. By the time Flash Gordo had shined his flashlight over and under the seats in the back, we were all across the theater at the edge of the crowd where we wouldn't be conspicuous. Later we moved to our favorite spot in the front row, where we craned our necks to look up at the giant figures acting out their adventures.

While the movies were fantastic — the highlight of our week — sometimes I think we had almost as much fun talking about them afterwards and acting them out. It was like much later when I went to high school; rehashing the Saturday night dance or party was sometimes better than the actual event.

We all had our favorites and our definite point of view about Hollywood movies. We barely tolerated those cowboy movies with actors like Johnny Mack Brown and Wild Bill Elliot and Gene Autry and even Hopalong Cassidy. Gringos! we'd sniff with disdain. But we'd watch them in preference to roaming the streets, and we'd cheer for the Indians and sometimes for the bad guys if they were swarthy and Mexican.

They showed the Zorro movies several times each, including the serials, with one chapter each Saturday. Zorro drew mixed reviews and was the subject of endless argument. "Spanish dandy!" one would scoff. "¿Dónde están los mejicanos?" Over in the background hanging on to their straw sombreros and smiling fearfully as they bowed to the tax collector, I remember.

"But at least Zorro speaks the right language."

Then somebody would hoot, "Yeah. Hollywood inglés. Look at the actors who play Zorro. Gringos every one. John Carroll. Reed Handley. Tyrone Power. ¡Mierda!"

That was what Zorro did to us. Better than Gene Autry but still a phony Spaniard, while all the *indios y mestizos* were bit players.

That was no doubt the reason why our favorite was the Cisco Kid. Even the one gringo who played the role, Warner Baxter, could have passed for a Mexican. More than one kid said he looked like my old man, so I was one of those who accepted Warner Baxter. Somebody even thought that he was Mexican but had changed his name so he could get parts in Hollywood — you know how Hollywood is. But we conveniently leaped from that to cheering for the "real" Cisco Kids without wondering how *they* ever got parts in that Hollywood: Gilbert Roland, César Romero, Duncan Renaldo. With the arch-sidekick of all time, Chris-Pin Martín, who was better any day than Fuzzy Knight, Smiley Burnette, or Gabby Hayes.

"Si, Ceesco," we'd lisp to each other and laugh, trying to sound like Chris-Pin.

We'd leave the theater laughing and chattering, bumping and elbowing each other past the lobby. There Flash Gordo would stare at us as if trying to remember whether or not we had bought tickets, thoughtfully clicking his false teeth like castanets. We'd quiet down as we filed past, looking at that toupee of his that was, on closer inspection, old hair blackened with shoe polish that looked like dyed rat fur. Hasta la vista, Flash, I'd think. See you again next week.

One Saturday afternoon when I returned home there was a beat-up old truck parked in front of the empty house next door and a slow parade in and out. In the distance I saw the curious stare of a towhead about my age.

When I rushed into the house, my three-year-old brother ran up to me and excitedly told me in baby talk, "La huera. La huera, huera."

"Hush," Mama said.

Uncle Tito, who was Mama's unmarried younger brother, winked at me. "Blondie's wearing a halter top and shorts," he said. "In the backyard next door."

"Hush," Mama said to him, scowling, and he winked at me again.

That night when I was supposed to be sleeping, I heard Mama and Papa arguing. "Well," Mama said, "what do you think about that? They swept up the gutters of Oklahoma City. What was too lightweight to settle got blown across the panhandle to New Mexico. Right next door."

"Now, Josefa," Papa said, "you have to give people a chance."

"Halter top and shorts," Mama snipped. "What will the children think?"

"The only child who's going to notice is Tito, and he's old enough, although sometimes he doesn't act it."

But then my eyelids started to get heavy, and the words turned into a fuzzy murmur.

One day after school that next week, Chango decided that we needed some new adventures. We took the long way home all the way past Fourth Street Elementary School, where all the pagan Protestants went. "Only Catholics go to heaven," Sister Mary Margaret warned us. "Good Catholics." While her cold eye sought out a few of us and chilled our hearts with her stare.

But after school the thaw set in. We wanted to see what those candidates for hell looked like — those condemned souls who attended public school. And I wondered: if God had only one spot left in heaven, and He had to choose between a bad Catholic who spoke Spanish and a good Protestant who spoke English, which one He would let in. A fearful possibility crossed my mind, but I quickly dismissed it.

We rambled along, picking up rocks and throwing them at tree trunks, looking for lizards or maybe even a lost coin dulled by weather and dirt but still very spendable. What we found was nothing. The schoolyard was empty, so we turned back toward home. It was then, in the large empty field across from the Río Valley Creamery, that we saw this laggard, my new neighbor, the undesirable Okie.

Chango gave a shout of joy. There he was. The enemy. Let's go get him! We saddled our imaginary horses and galloped into the sunset. Meanwhile, John Wayne, which was the name I called him then, turned his flour-white face and blinked his watery pale eyes at us in fear. Then he took off across the field in a dead run, which only increased our excitement, as if it were an admission that he truly was the enemy and deserved thrashing.

He escaped that day, but not before he got a good look at us. I forgot what we called him besides Okie *gabacho gringo cabrón*. In my memory he was John Wayne to our Cisco Kid, maybe because of the movie about the Alamo.

That then became our favorite after-school pastime. We'd make our way toward the Fourth Street Elementary School looking for our enemy, John Wayne. As cunning as enemies usually are, we figured that he'd be on the lookout, so we stalked him Indian-style. We missed him the next day, but the day after that when we were still a long block away, he suddenly stopped and lifted his head like a wild deer and seemed to feel or scent alien vibrations in the air, because he set off at a dogtrot toward home.

"Head him off at the pass!" Chango Cisco shouted, and we headed across toward Fifth Street. But John Wayne ran too fast, so we finally stopped and cut across to Lomas Park to work out a better plan.

We ambushed him the next day. Four of us came around the way he'd expect us to, while the other two of us sneaked the back way to intercept him between home and the elementary school. At the first sight of the stalkers he ran through the open field that was too big to be called a city lot. Chango and I waited for him behind the tamaracks. When he came near, breathing so heavily we could hear his wheeze, and casting quick glances over his shoulder, we stepped out from behind the trees.

He stopped dead. I couldn't believe anyone could stop that fast. No slow down, no gradual transition. One instant he was running full speed; the next instant he was absolutely immobile, staring at us with fright.

"You!" he said breathlessly, staring straight into my eyes.

"You!" I answered.

"¿Que hablas español?" Chango asked.

His look of fear deepened, swept now with perplexity like a ripple across the surface of water. When he didn't answer, Chango whooped out a laugh of joy and charged with clenched fists. It wasn't much of a fight. A couple of punches and a bloody nose and John Wayne was down. When we heard the shouts from the others, Chango turned and yelled to them. That was when John Wayne made his escape. We didn't follow this time. It wasn't worth it. There was no fight in him, and we didn't beat up on sissies or girls.

On the way home it suddenly struck me that since he lived next door, he would tell his mother, who might tell my mother, who would unquestionably tell my father. I entered the house with apprehension. Whether it was fear or conscience didn't matter.

But luck was with me. That night, although I watched my father's piercing looks across the dinner table with foreboding (or was it my conscience that saw his looks as piercing?), nothing came of it. Not a word. Only questions about school. What were they teaching us to read and write in English? Were we already preparing for our First Communion? Wouldn't Grandma be proud when we went to the country next Sunday. I could read for her from my schoolbook, *Bible Stories for Children*. Only my overambitious father forgot that *Bible Stories for Children* was a third-grade book that he had bought for me at a church rummage sale. I was barely at the reading level of "Run, Spot. Run." Hardly exciting fare even for my blind grandmother, who spoke no English and read nothing at all.

Before Sunday, though, there was Saturday. In order to do my share of the family chores and "earn" movie money instead of accepting charity, my father had me pick up in the backyard. I gathered toys that belonged to my little sister and brother, carried a bag of garbage to the heavy galvanized can out back by the shed, even helped pull a few weeds in the vegetable garden. This last was the "country" that my father carried with him to every house we lived in until I grew up and left home. You can take the boy out of the country, as the old saying goes. And in his case it was true.

I dragged my feet reluctantly out to the tiny patch of yard behind the doll's house in which we lived, ignoring my mother's scolding about not wearing out the toes of my shoes.

I must have been staring at the rubber tips of my tennis shoes to watch them wear down, so I didn't see my arch-enemy across the low fence. I heard him first. A kind of cowardly snivel that jolted me like an electric shock. Without looking I knew who it was.

"You!" he said as I looked across the fence.

"You!" I answered back with hostility.

Then his eyes watered up and his lips twitched in readiness for the blubbering that, in disgust, I anticipated.

"You hate me," he accused. I squatted down to pick up a rock, not taking my eyes off him. "Because I don't speak Spanish and I have yellow hair."

No, I thought, I don't like you because you're a sniveler. I wanted to leap the fence and punch him on those twitching lips, but I sensed my father behind me watching. Or was it my conscience again? I didn't dare turn and look.

"I hate Okies," I said. To my delight it was as if my itching fist had connected. He all but yelped in pain, though what I heard was a sharp expulsion of air.

"Denver?" The soft, feminine voice startled me, and I looked toward the back stoop of their house. I didn't see what Tito had made such a fuss about. She was blond and pale as her son and kind of lumpy, I thought, even in the everyday housedress she wore. She tried to smile — a weak, sniveling motion of her mouth that told me how Denver had come by that same expression. Then she stepped into the yard where we boys stared at each other like tomcats at bay.

"Howdy," she said in a soft funny accent that I figured must be Oklahoma. "I was telling your mother that you boys ought to get together, being neighbors and all. Denver's in the second grade at the public school."

Denver backed away from the fence and nestled against his mother's side. Before I could answer that Immaculate Heart boys didn't play with sniveling heathens, I heard our back door squeak open, then slam shut.

"I understand there's a nice movie in town where the boys go Saturday afternoons," she went on. But she was looking over my head toward whoever had come out of the house.

I looked back and saw Mama. Through the window over the kitchen sink I saw Papa. He's making sure she and I behave, I thought.

"It would be nice for the boys to go together," Mama said. She came down the steps and across the yard.

You didn't ask me! my silent angry self screamed. It's not fair! You didn't ask me! But Mama didn't even look at me; she addressed herself to Mrs. Oklahoma as if Snivel Nose and I weren't even there.

Then an unbelievable thought occurred to me. For some reason Denver had not told his mama about being chased home from school. Or if he did, he hadn't mentioned me. He was too afraid, I decided. He knew what would happen if he squealed. But even that left me with an uneasy feeling. I looked at him to see if the answer was on his face. All I got was a weak twitch of a smile and a blink of his pleading eyes.

I was struck dumb by the entire negotiation. It was settled without my comment or consent, like watching someone bargain away my life. When I went back into the house, all of my pent-up anger exploded. I screamed and kicked my heels and even cried — but to no avail.

"You have two choices, young man," my father warned. "Go to the matinee with Denver or stay in your room." But his ominous tone of voice told me that there was another choice: a good belting on the rear end.

Of course, this Saturday the Rat House was showing a movie about one of our favorite subjects where the mejicanos whipped the gringos: the Alamo. I had to go. Los Indios were counting on me to let them in.

I walked the few blocks to town, a boy torn apart. One of me hurried eagerly toward the Saturday afternoon adventure. The other dragged his feet, scuffing the toes of his shoes to spite his parents, all the while conscious of this hated stranger walking silently beside him.

When we came within sight of the theater, I felt Denver tense and slow his pace even more than mine. "Your gang is waiting," he said, and I swear he started to tremble.

What a chicken, I thought. "You're with me," I said. But then he had reminded me. What would I tell Chango and the rest of Los Indios?

They came at us with a rush. "What's he doing here?" Chango snarled.

I tried to explain. They deflected my words and listened instead to the silent fear they heard as they scrutinized Denver. My explanation did not wash, so I tried something in desperation.

"He's not what you think," I said. Skepticism and disbelief. "Just because he doesn't understand Spanish doesn't mean he can't be one of us." Show me! Chango's expression said. "He's — he's —" My voice was so loud that a passer-by turned and stared. "He's an Indian from Oklahoma," I lied.

"A blond Indian?" They all laughed.

My capacity for lying ballooned in proportion to their disbelief. I grew indignant, angry, self-righteous. "Yes!" I shouted. "An albino Indian!"

The laughs froze in their throats, and they looked at each other, seeing their own doubts mirrored in their friends' eyes. "Honest to God?" Chango asked.

"Honest to God!"

"Does he have money?"

Denver unfolded a sweaty fist to show the dime in his palm. Chango took it quickly, like a rooster pecking a kernel of corn. "Run to the dime store," he commanded the fastest of his lackeys. "Get that hard candy that lasts a long time. And hurry. We'll meet you in the back."

Denver's mouth fell open but not a sound emerged. "When we see him running back," Chango said to me, "you buy the ticket and let us in." Then he riveted his suspicious eyes on Denver and said, "Talk Indian."

I don't remember what kind of gibberish Denver faked. It didn't have to be much, because our runner had dashed across the street and down the block and was already sprinting back.

Our seven-for-the-price-of-one worked as always. When the theater was dark, we moved to our favorite seats. In the meantime, I had drawn Denver aside and maliciously told him he had better learn some Spanish. When we came to the crucial part of the movie, he had to shout what I told him.

It was a memorable Saturday. The hard sugar candy lasted

through two cartoons and half of the first feature. We relived the story of the Alamo again — we had seen this movie at least twice before, and we had seen other versions more times than I can remember. When the crucial, climactic attack began, we started our chant. I elbowed Denver to shout what I had taught him.

"Maten los gringos!" Kill the gringos! Then others in the audience took up the chant, while Flash Gordo ran around in circles trying to shush us up.

I sat in secret pleasure, a conqueror of two worlds. To my left was this blond Indian shouting heresies he little dreamed of, while I was already at least as proficient in English as he. On my right were my fellow tribesmen, who had accepted my audacious lie and welcomed this albino redskin into our group.

But memory plays its little tricks. Years later, when I couldn't think of Denver's name, I would always remember the Alamo — and John Wayne. There were probably three or four movies about that infamous mission, but John Wayne's was the one that stuck in my mind. Imagine my shock when I learned that his movie had not been made until 1960, by which time I was already through high school, had two years of college, and had gone to work. There was no way we could have seen the John Wayne version when I was in the first grade.

Looking back, I realized that Wayne, as America's gringo hero, was forever to me the bigoted Indian hater of *The Searchers* fused with the deserving victim of the attacking Mexican forces at the Alamo — the natural enemy of the Cisco Kid.

Another of my illusions shattered hard when I later learned that in real life Wayne had married a woman named Pilar or Chata or maybe both. That separated the man, the actor, from the characters he portrayed and left me in total confusion.

But then life was never guaranteed to be simple. For I saw the beak of the chick I was at six years old pecking through the hard shell of my own preconceptions. Moving into an alien land. First hating, then becoming friends with aliens like my blond Indian Okie friend, Denver, and finally becoming almost an alien myself.

NICHOLASA MOHR

Mr. Mendelsohn

"Psst . . . psst, Mr. Mendelsohn, wake up. Come on now!" Mrs. Suárez said in a low quiet voice. Mr. Mendelsohn had fallen asleep again, on the large armchair in the living room. He grasped the brown shiny wooden cane and leaned forward, his chin on his chest. The small black skullcap that was usually placed neatly on the back of his head had tilted to one side, covering his right ear. "Come on now. It's late, and time to go home." She tapped him on the shoulder and waited for him to wake up. Slowly, he lifted his head, opened his eyes, and blinked.

"What time is it?" he asked.

"It's almost midnight. Caramba! I didn't even know you was still here. When I came to shut off the lights, I saw you was sleeping."

"Oh . . . I'm sorry. Okay, I'm leaving." With short, slow steps he followed Mrs. Suárez over to the front door.

"Go on now," she said, opening the door. "We'll see you tomorrow."

He walked out into the hallway, stepped about three feet to the left, and stood before the door of his apartment. Mrs. Suárez waited, holding her door ajar while he carefully searched for the right key to each lock. He had to open seven locks in all.

A small fluffy dog standing next to Mrs. Suárez began to whine and bark.

"Shh-sh, Sporty! Stop it!" she said. "You had your walk. Shh."

"Okay," said Mr. Mendelsohn, finally opening his door. "Good night." Mrs. Suárez smiled and nodded.

"Good night," she whispered as they both shut their doors simultaneously.

Mr. Mendelsohn knocked on the door and waited; then tried the doorknob. Turning and pushing, he realized the door was locked, and knocked again, this time more forcefully. He heard Sporty barking and footsteps coming toward the door.

"Who's there?" a child's voice asked.

"It's me — Mr. Mendelsohn! Open up, Yvonne." The door opened, and a young girl, age nine, smiled at him.

"Mami! It's el Señor Mr. Mendelsohn again."

"Tell him to come on in, muchacha!" Mrs. Suárez answered.

"My mother says come on in."

He followed Yvonne and the dog, who leaped up, barking and wagging his tail. Mr. Mendelsohn stood at the kitchen entrance and greeted everyone.

"Good morning to you all!" He had just shaved and trimmed his large black mustache. As he smiled broadly, one could see that most of his teeth were missing. His large bald head was partially covered by his small black skullcap. Thick dark gray hair grew in abundance at the lower back of his head, coming around the front above his ears into short sideburns. He wore a clean white shirt, frayed at the cuffs. His worn-out pinstripe trousers were held up by a pair of dark suspenders. Mr. Mendelsohn leaned on his brown shiny cane and carried a small brown paper bag.

"Mr. Mendelsohn, come into the kitchen," said Mrs. Suárez, "and have some coffee with us." She stood by the stove. A boy of eleven, a young man of about seventeen, and a young pregnant woman were seated at the table.

"Sit here," said the boy, vacating a chair. "I'm finished eating." He stood by the entrance with his sister Yvonne, and they both looked at Mr. Mendelsohn and his paper bag with interest.

"Thank you, Georgie," Mr. Mendelsohn said. He sat down and placed the bag on his lap.

The smell of freshly perked coffee and boiled milk permeated the kitchen.

Winking at everyone, the young man asked, "Hey, what you got in that bag you holding on to, huh, Mr. Mendelsohn?" They all looked at each other and at the old man, amused. "Something special, I bet!"

"Well," the old man replied, "I thought your mama would be so kind as to permit me to make myself a little breakfast here today . . . so." He opened the bag and began to take out its contents. "I got two slices of rye bread, two tea bags. I brought one extra, just in case anybody would care to join me for tea. And a jar of herring in sour cream."

"Sounds delicious!" said the young man, sticking out his tongue and making a face. Yvonne and Georgie burst out laughing.

"Shh . . . sh." Mrs. Suárez shook her head and looked at her children disapprovingly. "Never mind, Julio!" she said to the young man. Turning to Mr. Mendelsohn, she said, "You got the same like you brought last Saturday, eh? You can eat with us anytime. How about some fresh coffee? I just made it. Yes?" Mr. Mendelsohn looked at her, shrugging his shoulders. "Come on, have some," she coaxed.

"Okay," he replied. "If it's not too much bother."

"No bother," she said, setting out a place for the old man. "You gonna have some nice fresh bread with a little butter — it will go good with your herring." Mrs. Suárez cut a generous slice of freshly baked bread with a golden crust and buttered it. "Go on, eat. There's a plate and everything for your food. Go on, eat . . ."

"Would anyone care for some?" Mr. Mendelsohn asked. "Perhaps a tea bag for a cup of tea?"

"No . . . no thank you, Mr. Mendelsohn," Mrs. Suárez answered. "Everybody here already ate. You go ahead and eat. You look too skinny; you better eat. Go on, eat your bread."

The old man began to eat vigorously.

"Can I ask you a question?" Julio asked the old man. "Man, I don't get you. You got a whole apartment next door all to yourself — six rooms! And you gotta come here to eat in this crowded kitchen. Why?"

"First of all, today is Saturday, and I thought I could bring in my food and your mama could turn on the stove for me. You know, in my religion you can't light a fire on Saturday."

"You come here anytime. I turn on the stove for you, don't worry," Mrs. Suárez said.

"Man, what about other days? We been living here for about six months, right?" Julio persisted. "And you do more cooking here than in your own place."

"It doesn't pay to turn on the gas for such a little bit of cooking. So I told the gas company to turn it off . . . for good! I got no more gas now, only an electric hot plate," the old man said.

Julio shook his head and sighed. "I don't know —"

"Julio, chico!" snapped Mrs. Suárez, interrupting him, "Basta — it doesn't bother nobody." She looked severely at her son and shook her head. "You gotta go with your sister to the clinic today, so you better get ready now. You too, Marta."

"Okay, Mama," she answered, "but I wanted to see if I got mail from Ralphy today."

"You don't got time. I'll save you the mail, you read it when you get back. You and Julio better get ready. Go on." Reluctantly, Marta stood up and yawned, stretching and arching her back.

"Marta," Mr. Mendelsohn said, "you taking care? . . . You know, this is a very delicate time for you."

"I am, Mr. Mendelsohn. Thank you."

"I raised six sisters," the old man said. "I ought to know. Six . . . and married them off to fine husbands. Believe me, I've done my share in life." Yvonne and Georgie giggled and poked each other.

"He's gonna make one of his speeches," they whispered.

". . . I never had children. No time to get married. My father died when I was eleven. I went to work supporting my mother and six younger sisters. I took care of them, and today they are all married, with families. They always call and want me to visit them. I'm too busy and I have no time . . ."

"Too busy eating in our kitchen," whispered Julio. Marta, Georgie, and Yvonne tried not to laugh out loud. Mrs. Suárez reached over and with a wooden ladle managed a light but firm blow on Julio's head.

". . . Only on the holidays, I make some time to see them. But otherwise, I cannot be bothered with all that visiting." Mr. Mendelsohn stopped speaking and began to eat again.

"Go on, Marta and Julio, you will be late for the clinic," Mrs. Suárez said. "And you two? What are you doing there smiling like two monkeys? Go find something to do!"

Quickly, Georgie and Yvonne ran down the hallway, and Julio and Marta left the kitchen.

Mrs. Suárez sat down beside the old man.

"Another piece of bread?" she asked.

"No, thank you very much . . . I'm full. But it was delicious."

"You too skinny — you don't eat right, I bet." Mrs. Suárez shook her head. "Come tomorrow and have Sunday supper with us."

"I really couldn't."

"Sure, you could. I always make a big supper and there is plenty. All right? Mr. Suárez and I will be happy to have you."

"Are you sure it will be no bother?"

"What are you talking for the bother all the time? One more person is no bother. You come tomorrow. Yes?"

The old man smiled broadly and nodded. This was the first time he had been invited to Sunday supper with the family.

Mrs. Suárez stood and began clearing away the dishes. "Okay, you go inside, listen to the radio or talk to the kids — or something. I got work to do."

Mr. Mendelsohn closed his jar of herring and put it back into the bag. "Can I leave this here till I go?"

"Leave it. I put it in the refrigerator for you."

Leaning on his cane, Mr. Mendelsohn stood up and walked out of the kitchen and down the long hallway into the living room. It was empty. He went over to a large armchair by the window. The sun shone through the window, covering the entire armchair and Mr. Mendelsohn. A canary cage was also by the window, and two tiny yellow birds chirped and hopped back and forth energetically. Mr. Mendelsohn felt drowsy; he shut his eyes. So many aches and pains, he thought. It was hard to sleep at night, but here, well . . . The birds began to chirp in unison and the old man opened one eye, glancing at them, and smiled. Then he shut his eyes once more and fell fast asleep.

When Mr. Mendelsohn opened his eyes, Georgie and Yvonne were in the living room. Yvonne held a deck of playing cards and Georgie read a comic book. She looked at the old man and, holding up the deck of cards, asked, "Do you wonna play a game of war? Huh, Mr. Mendelsohn?"

"I don't know how to play that," he answered.

"Its real easy. I'll show you. Come on . . . please!"

"Well," he shrugged, "sure, why not? Maybe I'll learn something."

Yvonne took a small maple end table and a wooden chair, and set them next to Mr. Mendelsohn. "Now," she began, "I'll shuffle the cards and you cut, and then I throw down a card and you throw down a card and the one with the highest card wins. Okay? And then, the one with the most cards of all wins the game. Okay?"

"That's all?" he asked.

"That's all. Ready?" she asked, and sat down. They began to play cards.

"You know, my sister Jennie used to be a great card player," said Mr. Mendelsohn.

"Does she still play?" asked Yvonne.

"Oh . . ." Mr. Mendelsohn laughed. "I don't know anymore. She's already married and has kids. She was the youngest in my family — like you."

"Did she go to P.S. Thirty-nine? On Longwood Avenue?"

"I'm sure she did. All my sisters went to school around here."

"Wow! You must be living here a long time, Mr. Mendelsohn."

"Forty-five years!" said the old man.

"Wowee!" Yvonne whistled. "Georgie, did you hear? Mr. Mendelsohn been living here for forty-five whole years!"

Georgie put down his comic book and looked up.

"Really?" he asked, impressed.

"Yes, forty-five years this summer we moved here. But in those days things were different, not like today. No sir! The Bronx has changed. Then, it was the country. That's right! Why, look out the window. You see the elevated trains on Westchester Avenue? Well, there were no trains then. That was once a dirt road. They used to bring cows through there."

"Oh, man!" Georgie and Yvonne both gasped.

"Sure. These buildings were among the first apartment houses to go up. Four stories high, and that used to be a big accomplishment in them days. All that was here was mostly little houses, like you still see here and there. Small farms, woodlands . . . like that."

"Did you see any Indians?" asked Georgie.

"What do you mean, Indians?" laughed the old man. "I'm not that old, and this here was not the Wild West." Mr. Mendelsohn saw that the children were disappointed. He added quickly, "But we did have carriages with horses. No cars and lots of horses."

"That's what Mami says they have in Puerto Rico — not like here in El Bronx," said Yvonne.

"Yeah," Georgie agreed. "Papi says he rode a horse when he was a little kid in Puerto Rico. They had goats and pigs and all them things. Man, was he lucky."

"Lucky?" Mr. Mendelsohn shook his head. "You — you are the lucky one today! You got school and a good home and clothes. You don't have to go out to work and support a family like your papa and I had to do, and miss an education. You can learn and be somebody someday."

"Someday," said Yvonne, "we are gonna get a house with a yard and all. Mami says that when Ralphy gets discharged from the army, he'll get a loan from the government and we can pay to buy a house. You know, instead of rent."

Mrs. Suárez walked into the living room with her coat on, carrying a shopping bag.

"Yvonne, take the dog out for a walk, and Georgie, come on! We have to go shopping. Get your jacket."

Mr. Mendelsohn started to rise. "No," she said, "stay . . . sit down. It's okay. You can stay and rest if you want."

"All right, Mrs. Suárez," Mr. Mendelsohn said.

"Now don't forget tomorrow for Sunday supper, and take a nap if you like."

Mr. Mendelsohn heard the front door slam shut, and the apartment was silent. The warmth of the bright sun made him drowsy once more. It was so nice here, he thought, a house full of people and kids — like it used to be. He recalled his sisters and his parents

... the holidays ... the arguments ... the laughing. It was so empty next door. He would have to look for a smaller apartment, near Jennie, someday. But not now. Now, it was just nice to sleep and rest right here. He heard the tiny birds chirping and quietly drifted into a deep sleep.

Mr. Mendelsohn rang the bell, then opened the door. He could smell the familiar cooking odors of Sunday supper. For two years he had spent every Sunday at his neighbors'. Sporty greeted him, jumping affectionately and barking.

"Sh — sh ... down. Good boy," he said, and walked along the hallway toward the kitchen. The room was crowded with people and the stove was loaded with large pots of food, steaming and puffing. Mrs. Suárez was busy basting a large roast. Looking up, she saw Mr. Mendelsohn.

"Come in," she said, "and sit down." Motioning to Julio, who was seated, she continued, "Julio, you are finished, get up and give Mr. Mendelsohn a seat." Julio stood up.

"Here's the sponge cake," Mr. Mendelsohn said, and handed the cake box he carried to Julio, who put it in the refrigerator.

"That's nice, thank you," said Mrs. Suárez, and placed a cup of freshly made coffee before the old man.

"Would anyone like some coffee?" Mr. Mendelsohn asked. Yvonne and Georgie giggled, looked at one another, and shook their heads.

"You always say that!" said Yvonne.

"One of these days," said Ralphy, "I'm gonna say, 'Yes, give me your coffee,' and you won't have none to drink." The children laughed loudly.

"Don't tease him," Mrs. Suárez said, half smiling. "Let him have his coffee."

"He is just being polite, children," Mr. Suárez said, and shifting his chair closer to Mr. Mendelsohn, he asked, "So ... Mr. Mendelsohn, how you been? What's new? You okay?"

"So-so, Mr. Suárez. You know, aches and pains when you get old. But there's nothing you can do, so you gotta make the best of it."

Mr. Suárez nodded sympathetically, and they continued to talk.

Mr. Mendelsohn saw the family every day, except for Mr. Suárez and Ralphy, who both worked a night shift.

Marta appeared in the entrance, holding a small child by the hand.

"There he is, Tato," she said to the child, and pointed to Mr. Mendelsohn.

"Oh, my big boy! He knows, he knows he's my best friend," Mr. Mendelsohn said, and held the brown shiny cane out toward Tato. The small boy grabbed the cane and, shrieking with delight, walked toward Mr. Mendelsohn.

"Look at that, will you?" said Ralphy. "He knows Mr. Mendelsohn better than me, his own father."

"That's because they are always together." Marta smiled. "Tato is learning to walk with his cane!"

Everyone laughed as they watched Tato climbing the old man's knee. Bending over, Mr. Mendelsohn pulled Tato onto his lap.

"Oh . . . he's getting heavy," said Mrs. Suárez. "Be careful."

"Never mind," Mr. Mendelsohn responded, hugging Tato. "That's my best boy. And look how swell he walks, and he's not even nineteen months."

"What a team," Julio said. "Tato already walks like Mr. Mendelsohn, and pretty soon he's gonna complain like him, too." Julio continued to tease the old man, who responded good-naturedly as everyone laughed.

After coffee, Mr. Mendelsohn sat on the large armchair in the living room, waiting for supper to be ready. He watched with delight as Tato walked back and forth with the cane. Mr. Mendelsohn held Tato's blanket, stuffed bear, and picture book.

"Tato," he called out, "come here. Let me read you a book — come on. I'm going to read you a nice story."

Tato climbed onto the chair and into Mr. Mendelsohn's lap. He sucked his thumb and waited. Mr. Mendelsohn opened the picture book.

"Okay. Now . . ." He pointed to the picture. "A is for Alligators. See that? Look at that big mouth and all them teeth." Tato yawned, nestled back, and closed his eyes. The old man read a few more pages and shut the book.

The soft breathing and sucking sound that Tato made assured

Mr. Mendelsohn that the child was asleep. Such a smart kid. What a great boy, he said to himself. Mr. Mendelsohn was vaguely aware of a radio program, voices, and the small dog barking now and then, just before he too fell into a deep sleep.

This Sunday was very much like all the others: coffee first, then he and Tato would play a bit before napping in the large armchair. It had become a way of life for the old man. Only the High Holy Days and an occasional invitation to a family event, such as a marriage or funeral and so on, would prevent the old man from spending Sunday next door.

It had all been so effortless. No one ever asked him to leave, except late at night when he napped too long. On Saturdays, he tried to observe the Sabbath and brought in his meal. They lit the stove for him.

Mrs. Suárez was always feeding him, just like Mama. She also worried about me not eating, the old man had said to himself, pleased. At first, he had been cautious and had wondered about the food and the people that he was becoming so involved with. That first Sunday, the old man had looked suspiciously at the food they served him.

"What is it?" he had asked. Yvonne and Georgie had started giggling and looked at one another. Mrs. Suárez had responded quickly and with anger, cautioning her children, speaking to them in Spanish.

"Eat your food, Mr. Mendelsohn. You too skinny," she had told him.

"What kind of meat is it?" Mr. Mendelsohn insisted.

"It's good for you, that's what it is," Mrs. Suárez answered.

"But I —" Mr. Mendelsohn started.

"Never mind — it's good for you. I prepare everything fresh. Go ahead and eat it," Mrs. Suárez had interrupted. There was a silence as Mr. Mendelsohn sat still, not eating.

"You know, I'm not allowed to eat certain things. In my religion we have dietary laws. This is not pork or something like it, is it?"

"It's just . . . chicken. Chicken! That's what it is. It's delicious . . . and good for you," she had said with conviction.

"It doesn't look like chicken to me."

"That's because you never ate no chicken like this before. This here is — is called Puerto Rican chicken. I prepare it special. So you gonna eat it. You too skinny."

Mr. Mendelsohn had tried to protest, but Mrs. Suárez insisted. "Never mind. Now, I prepare everything clean and nice. You eat the chicken. You gonna like it. Go on!"

And that was all.

Mr. Mendelsohn ate his Sunday supper from then on without doubt or hesitation, accepting the affection and concern that Mrs. Suárez provided with each plateful.

That night in his own apartment, Mr. Mendelsohn felt uneasy. He remembered that during supper, Ralphy had mentioned that his GI loan had come through. They would be looking for a house soon, everyone agreed. Not in the Bronx; farther out, near Yonkers. It was more like the country there.

The old man tossed and turned in his bed. That's still a long way off. First, they have to find the house and everything. You don't move just like that! he said to himself. It's gonna take a while, he reasoned, putting such thoughts out of his mind.

Mr. Mendelsohn looked at his new quarters.

"I told you, didn't I? See how nice this is?" his sister Jennie said. She put down the large sack of groceries on the small table.

It was a fair-sized room with a single bed, a bureau, a wooden wardrobe closet, a table, and two chairs. A hot plate was set on a small white refrigerator and a white metal kitchen cabinet was placed alongside.

"We'll bring you whatever else you need, Louis," Jennie went on. "You'll love it here, I'm sure. There are people your own age, interested in the same things. Here — let's get started. We'll put your things away and you can get nicely settled."

Mr. Mendelsohn walked over to the window and looked out. He saw a wide avenue with cars, taxis, and buses speeding by. "Its gonna take me two buses, at least, to get back to the old neighborhood," he said.

"Why do you have to go back there?" Jennie asked quickly.

"There is nobody there anymore, Louis. Everybody moved!"

"There's shul . . ."

"There's shul right here. Next door you have a large temple. Twice you were robbed over there. It's a miracle you weren't hurt! Louis, there is no reason for you to go back. There is nothing over there, nothing," Jennie said.

"The trouble all started with that rooming house next door. Those people took in all kinds . . ." He shook his head. "When the Suárez family lived there we had no problems. But nobody would talk to the landlord about those new people — only me. Nobody cared."

"That's all finished," Jennie said, looking at her watch. "Now look how nice it is here. Come on, let's get started." She began to put the groceries away in the refrigerator and cabinet.

"Leave it, Jennie," he interrupted. "Go on . . . I'll take care of it. You go on home. You are in a hurry."

"I'm only trying to help," Jennie responded.

"I know, I know. But I lived in one place for almost fifty years. So don't hurry me." He looked around the room. "And I ain't going nowhere now."

Shaking her head, Jennie said, "Look, this weekend we have a wedding, but next weekend Sara and I will come to see you. I'll call the hotel on the phone first, and they'll let you know. All right?"

"Sure." He nodded.

"That'll be good, Louis. This way you will get a chance to get settled and get acquainted with some of the other residents." Jennie kissed Mr. Mendelsohn affectionately. The old man nodded and turned away. In a moment, he heard the door open and shut.

Slowly, he walked to the sack of groceries and finished putting them away. Then, with much effort, he lifted a large suitcase onto the bed. He took out several photographs. Then he set the photographs upright, arranging them carefully on the bureau. He had pictures of his parents' wedding and of his sisters and their families. There was a photograph of his mother taken just before she died, and another one of Tato.

That picture was taken when he was about two years old, the old man said to himself. Yes, that's right, on his birthday . . . There was a party. And Tato was already talking. Such a smart kid, he thought, smiling. Last? Last when? he wondered. Time was going fast for him. He shrugged. He could hardly remember what year it was lately. Just before they moved! he remembered. That's right, they gave him the photograph of Tato. They had a nice house around Gun Hill Road someplace, and they had taken him there once. He recalled how exhausted he had been after the long trip. No one had a car, and they had had to take a train and buses. Anyway, he was glad he remembered. Now he could let them know he had moved, and tell them all about what happened to the old neighborhood. That's right, they had a telephone now. Yes, he said to himself, let me finish here, then I'll go call them. He continued to put the rest of his belongings away.

Mr. Mendelsohn sat in the lobby, holding on to his cane and a cake box. He had told the nurse at the desk that his friends were coming to pick him up this Sunday. He looked eagerly toward the revolving doors. After a short while, he saw Ralphy, Julio, and Georgie walk through into the lobby.

"Deliveries are made in the rear of the building," he heard the nurse at the desk say as they walked toward him.

"These are my friends, Mrs. Read," Mr. Mendelsohn said, standing. "They are here to take me out."

"Oh, well," said the nurse. "All right, I didn't realize. Here he is, then. He's been talking about nothing else but this visit." Mrs. Read smiled.

Ralphy nodded, then spoke to Georgie. "Get Mr. Mendelsohn's overcoat."

Quickly, Mr. Mendelsohn put on his coat, and all four left the lobby.

"Take good care of him now," they heard Mrs. Read calling. "You be a good boy now, Mr. Mendelsohn."

Outside, Mr. Mendelsohn looked at the young men and smiled. "How's everyone?" he asked.

"Good," Julio said. "Look, that's my pickup truck from work. They let me use it sometimes when I'm off."

"That's a beautiful truck. How's everyone? Tato? How is my

best friend? And Yvonne? Does she like school? And your mama and papa? . . . Marta?"

"Fine, fine. Everybody is doing great. Wait till you see them. We'll be there in a little while," said Julio. "With this truck, we'll get there in no time."

Mr. Mendelsohn sat in the kitchen and watched as Mrs. Suárez packed food into a shopping bag. Today had been a good day for the old man: he had napped in the old armchair and spent time with the children. Yvonne was so grown up, he almost had not recognized her. When Tato remembered him, Mr. Mendelsohn had been especially pleased. Shyly, he had shaken hands with the old man. Then he had taken him into his room to show Mr. Mendelsohn all his toys.

"Now, I packed a whole lotta stuff in this shopping bag for you. You gotta eat it. Eat some of my Puerto Rican chicken — it's good for you. You too skinny. You got enough for tomorrow and for another day. You put it in the refrigerator. Also I put some rice and other things."

He smiled as she spoke, enjoying the attention he received.

"Julio is gonna drive you back before it gets too late," she said. "And we gonna pick you up again and bring you back to eat with us. I bet you don't eat right." She shook her head. "Okay?"

"You shouldn't go through so much bother," he protested mildly.

"Again with the bother? You stop that! We gonna see you soon. You take care of yourself and eat. Eat! You must nourish yourself, especially in such cold weather."

Mr. Mendelsohn and Mrs. Suárez walked out into the living room. The family exchanged goodbyes with the old man. Tato, feeling less shy, kissed Mr. Mendelsohn on the cheek.

Just before leaving, Mr. Mendelsohn embraced Mrs. Suárez for a long time, as everybody watched silently.

"Thank you," he whispered.

"Thank you? For what?" Mrs. Suárez said. "You come back soon and have Sunday supper with us. Yes?" Mr. Mendelsohn nodded and smiled.

It was dark and cold out. He walked with effort. Julio carried the shopping bag. Slowly, he got into the pickup truck. The ride back was bumpy and uncomfortable for Mr. Mendelsohn. The cold wind cut right through into the truck, and the old man was aware of the long winter ahead.

His eyelids were so heavy he could hardly open them. Nurses scurried about busily. Mr. Mendelsohn heard voices.

"Let's give him another injection. It will help his breathing. Nurse! Nurse! The patient needs . . ."

The voices faded. He remembered he had gone to sleep after supper last — last when? How many days have I been here . . . here in the hospital? Yes, he thought, now I know where I am. A heart attack, the doctor had said, and then he had felt even worse. Didn't matter; I'm too tired. He heard voices once more, and again he barely opened his eyes. A tall thin man dressed in white spoke to him.

"Mr. Mendelsohn, can you hear me? How do you feel now? More comfortable? We called your family. I spoke to your sister, Mrs. Wiletsky. They should be here very soon. You feeling sleepy? Good. Take a little nap — go on. We'll wake you when they get here, don't worry. Go on now."

He closed his eyes, thinking of Jennie. She'll be here soon with Esther and Rosalie and Sara. All of them. He smiled. He was so tired. His bed was by the window and a bright warm sash of sunshine covered him almost completely. Nice and warm, he thought, and felt comfortable. The pain had lessened, practically disappeared. Mr. Mendelsohn heard the birds chirping and Sporty barking. That's all right, Mrs. Suárez would let him sleep. She wouldn't wake him up, he knew that. It looked like a good warm day; he planned to take Tato out for a walk later. That's some smart kid, he thought. Right now he was going to rest.

"This will be the last of it, Sara."

"Just a few more things, Jennie, and we'll be out of here." The two women spoke as they packed away all the items in the room. They opened drawers and cabinets, putting things away in boxes and suitcases.

"What about these pictures on the bureau?" asked Sara.

Jennie walked over and they both looked at the photographs.

"There's Mama and Papa's wedding picture. Look, there's you, Sara, when Jonathan was born. And Esther and . . . look, he's got all the pictures of the entire family." Jennie burst into tears.

"Come on, Jennie. It's all over, honey. He was sick and very old." The older woman comforted the younger one.

Wiping her eyes, Jennie said, "Well, we did the best we could for him, anyway."

"Who is this?" asked Sara, holding up Tato's photo.

"Let me see," said Jennie. "Hummm . . . that must be one of the people in that family that lived next door in the old apartment on Prospect Avenue. You know — remember that Spanish family? He used to visit with them. Their name was . . . Díaz or something like that, I think. I can't remember."

"Oh yes," said Sara. "Louis mentioned them once in a while, yes. They were nice to him. What shall we do with it? Return it?"

"Oh," said Jennie, "that might be rude. What do you think?"

"Well, I don't want it, do you?"

"No." Jennie hesitated. "But let's just put it away. Maybe we ought to tell them what happened. About Louis." Sara shrugged her shoulders. "Maybe I'll write to them," Jennie went on, "if I can find out where they live. They moved. What do you say?"

TOMÁS RIVERA

On the Road to Texas:
Pete Fonseca

H E'D ONLY JUST gotten there and he already wanted to leave.
He arrived one Sunday afternoon walking from the little
town where we bought our food Saturdays and where they didn't
mind that we came in the afternoon all dirty from work. It was
almost dark when we saw this shape crossing the field. We'd been
fooling around in the trees and when we saw him we were almost
scared, but then we remembered there was more of *us* so we
weren't so scared. He spoke to us when he got near. He wanted to
know if there was any work. We told him that there was and there
wasn't. There was, but there wasn't till the weeds grew. It'd been
pretty dry and the weeds didn't grow. It'd been pretty dry and the
weeds didn't grow and all the fields were real clean. The boss was
pretty happy about it since he didn't have to pay for weeding the
onion fields. Our parents cursed the weather and prayed for rain so
the weeds'd grow and we had to make like we cared too, but really
we liked getting up late, wandering around in the trees and along
the stream killing crows with our slingshots. That's why we said
there was but there wasn't. There was work but not tomorrow.

"Aw, fuck it all."

We didn't mind him talking like that. I think we realized how
good his words went with his body and clothes.

"There's no goddamned work no fuckin' place. Hey, can you give me something to eat? I'm fuckin' hungry. Tomorrow I'm going to Illinois. There's work there for sure . . ."

He took off his baseball cap and we saw that his hair was combed good with a pretty neat wave. He wore those pointed shoes, a little dirty, but you could tell they were expensive ones. And his pants were almost pachuco pants. He kept saying *chale* and also *nel* and *simón* and we finally decided that he was at least half pachuco. We went with him to our chicken coop. That's what we called it because it really was a turkey coop. The boss had bought ten little turkey coops from a guy who sold turkeys and brought them to his farm. We lived in them, though they were pretty small for two families, but pretty sturdy. They didn't leak when it rained, but even though we cleaned them out pretty good inside they never really lost that stink of chicken shit.

His name was Pete Fonseca and Dad knew a friend of his pretty good. Dad said he was a bigmouth since he was always talking about how he had fourteen gabardine shirts and that's why they called him El Catorce Camisas. They talked about fourteen shirts a while and when we went to eat beans with slices of Spam and hot flour tortillas, Dad invited him to eat with us. He washed his face good and his hands too, and then he combed his hair real careful, asked us for brilliantine and combed his hair again. He liked the supper a lot and we noticed that when Mom was there he didn't use pachuco words. After supper he talked a little more and then lay down on the grass, in the shadow where the light from the house wouldn't hit him. A little while later he got up and went to the outhouse and then he lay down again and fell asleep. Before we went to sleep I heard Mom say to Dad that she didn't trust that guy.

"Me neither. He's a real con man. Gotta be careful with him. I've heard about him. Catorce Camisas is a bigmouth, but I think it's him who stabbed that wetback in Colorado and they kicked him out of there or he got away from the cops. I think it's him. He also likes to smoke marijuana. I think it's him. I'm not too sure . . ."

Next morning it was raining and when we looked out the

window we saw that Pete had gotten in our car. He was sitting up but it looked like he was sleeping because he wasn't moving at all. I guess the rain waked him up and that's how come he got in the car. Around nine it stopped raining so we went out and told him to come have breakfast. Mom made him some eggs and then he asked if there was any empty house or some place he could live. And when was work going to start? And how much did they pay? And how much could you get a day? And how many of us worked? Dad told him that we all worked, all five of us, and that sometimes we got almost seventy bucks a day if we could work about fourteen hours. After breakfast Dad and Pete went out and we heard him ask Dad if there was any broads on the farm. Dad answered laughing that there was only one and she was sort of a loser. La Chata, snub-nose. And they went on talking along the path that went round the huts and to the water pump.

They called her La Chata because when she was little she got sick with something like mange on her face and the nose bone had got infected. Then she got better but her nose stayed small. She was real pretty except for her nose and everyone spoke bad about her. They said that even when she was little she liked men a lot and everything about them. When she was fifteen she had her first kid. Everyone blamed one of her uncles but she never told who it was. Her mom and dad didn't even get angry. They were pretty nice. Still are. After that, she'd shack up with one guy and then another and each one left her at least one kid. She gave some away, her parents took care of others, but the two oldest stayed with her. They were big enough to work now. When Pete arrived, it was just two weeks after she'd lost again: her last husband had left, he didn't even get mad at her or anything. Just left. La Chata lived in one of the biggest chicken coops with her two sons. That's why Dad told Pete there was only one and she was sort of a loser. We figured Pete was pretty interested in what Dad said, and it seemed pretty funny since La Chata must've been about thirty-five and Pete, well he couldn't be more than twenty-five.

Anyhow, it turned out he *was* interested in what Dad said because later, when we were fooling around near the pump, he asked us about La Chata. Where did she live, how old was she, was she any good? We were just talking about that when La Chata came down to get water and we told him that was her. We said hello to her and she said hello to us, but we noticed that she kept on looking at Pete. Like the people say, she gave him the eye. And even more when he asked her her name.

"Chavela."

"Hey, that's my mother's name."

"No kidding."

"Honest, and my grandmother's, too."

"You son of a bitch."

"You don't know me yet."

La Chata left the pump and when she was pretty far away, Pete sighed and said real loud:

"Hey, mamasita, mamasota linda!"

So she could hear, he told us after. Because according to him broads like to be called that. From then on we noticed that every time La Chata was near Pete he would always call her *mi chavelona* real loud. He said it loud so she'd hear and I think La Chata liked it because when work started she always chose the rows nearest Pete and if he got ahead of her she'd try and catch up. And then when the boss brought us water Pete always let her drink first. Or he helped her get on and off the truck. The first Saturday they paid us after Pete got there, he bought some fritos for La Chata's kids. That's how it began.

I liked it best when he sang her songs. Pete was going to stay and work, he'd say, until everything was over. He went to live with two other guys in an old trailer they had there. We used to go after supper to talk to them, and sometimes we'd sing. He'd go outside, turn toward La Chata's house, and sing with all his might. In the fields too we'd just get close to her or she'd come along and Pete would let go with one of his songs. Sometimes he even sang in English: *Sha bum sha bum* or *Lemi go, lemi go lober*, and then in Spanish: *Ella quiso quedarse, cuando vió mi tristeza . . . Cuando te hablen de amor y de ilusiones*. Sometimes he'd even stop working and stand up in the row, if the boss wasn't there, and he'd sort of move his hands and his body. La Chata'd look out of the corner of her eye, like it bothered her, but she always went on taking the rows next to Pete, or meeting him, or catching up to him. About two weeks later they both started going to get water at the truck together, when the boss didn't bring it, and then they'd go behind the truck a while and then La Chata would come out fixing her blouse.

Pete would tell us everything afterwards. One day he told us that if we wanted to see something we should hide behind the trailer that night and he'd try and get her to go in the trailer.

"You know what for . . . to give her some candy . . ."

Us and the guys who lived with him hid behind the trailer that night and then after a long time we saw La Chata coming toward the trailer. Pete was waiting for her and she'd just got there and he took her hand and pulled her toward him. He put his hand up under her skirt and started kissing her. La Chata didn't say nothing. Then he leaned her up against the trailer, but she got away and told him you son of a bitch, not so fast. Pete was inviting her to come into the trailer but she didn't want to and so they stayed outside. Do you love me, will you marry me, yes I will, when, right now, what about that other cat. Finally she left. We came out of the dark and he told us all about it. Then he started telling us all about other broads he'd made. Even white ones. He'd brought one from Chicago and set up his business in Austin. There, according to him, the bastards would line up at five bucks a throw. But he said that the broad he'd really loved was the first one he married the right way, in the Church. But she'd died with the first kid.

"I sure cried for that woman, and since then nothing. This fuckin' life . . . Now with this chavelona, I'm beginning to feel something for her . . . She's a good person, if you know what I mean."

And sometimes he'd start thinking. Then he'd say real sincere like:

"Ay, mi chavelona . . . man, she's a hot one . . . but she won't let me . . . until I marry her, she says."

Three days after we'd hid, Pete decided to get married. That's why all that week that's all he talked about. He had nothing to lose. Why, him and La Chata and the two boys could save a lot. He'd also have someone to cook his *gorditas* for him and his nice hot coffee, and someone to wash his clothes and, according to Pete, she could handle at least one John a night. He'd start calculating: at four dollars a throw at least, times seven nights, that was twenty-eight dollars a week. Even if *he* couldn't work things'd be pretty good. He also said he liked La Chata's boys. They could buy a jalopy and then Sundays they could take rides, go to a show, go fishing or to the dump and collect copper wire to sell. In fact, he said, him marrying La Chavelona was good for all of them. And the sooner the better.

A little while later he came to talk to Dad one night. They went out on the road where no one could hear them and they talked a pretty long time. That night we heard what Dad and Mom were saying in the dark:

"Get this: he wants to marry La Chata! He wanted to elope with her, but what in? So it's better to get married for real. But — get this — he's got some sickness in his blood so he doesn't want to go into town and get the papers. So what he wants is for me to go and ask La Chata's father, Don Chon, for her hand. He wants me to go right away, tomorrow . . . Don Chon, I've come today commissioned to ask you for the hand of your daughter, Isabel, in matrimony with young Pedro Fonseca . . . How's that, eh? . . . How's it sound, old lady? . . . Tomorrow after work, right before supper."

Next day all you heard about was how they were going to ask for La Chata's hand. That day Pete and Chavela didn't even talk to each other. Pete went around all day real quiet and sort of glum, like he wanted to show us how serious he was. He didn't even tell us any jokes like he always did. And La Chata also looked real serious. She didn't laugh any all day and every now and then she'd yell at her kids to work faster. Finally the workday finished and before supper Dad washed up, parted his hair four or five times, and went straight to Don Chon's house. Pete met him in the front yard and they both knocked at the door. They went in. *It was okay— they'd asked them to come in.* About half an hour later they all came out of the house laughing. *They'd agreed.* Pete was hugging La Chata real tight. Pretty soon they went into Chavela's house and when it got dark they closed the doors and pulled down the rags on the windows too. That night Dad told us about ten times what happened when he went to ask for her hand.

"Man, I just spoke real diplomatic and he couldn't say no . . ."

Next day it rained. It was Saturday and that was when we really celebrated the wedding. Almost everyone got drunk. There was a little dancing. Some guys got into fights but pretty soon everything calmed down.

They were real happy. There started to be more and more work. Pete, La Chata and the boys always had work. They bought a car. Sundays they'd go driving a lot. They went to Mason City to visit some of La Chata's relatives. She was sort of strutting around real proud. The boys were cleaner now than ever. Pete bought a lot of clothes and was also pretty clean. They worked together, they helped each other, they took real good care of each other, they even sang together in the fields. We all really liked to see them because sometimes they'd even kiss in the fields. They'd go up and down the rows holding hands . . . *Here come the young lovers.* Saturdays they'd go shopping, and go into some little bar and have a couple after buying the groceries. They'd come back to the farm and sometimes even go to a show at night. They really had it good.

"Who would of said that that son of a gun would marry La Chata and do her so right? It looks like he really loves her a lot. Always calling her *mi chavelona.* And can you beat how much he loves those kids? I tell you he's got a good heart. But who was to say that he did. Boy, he looks like a real pachuco. He really loves her, and he doesn't act at all high and mighty. And she sure takes better care of him than that other guy she had before, don't you think? And the kids, all he does is play with them. They like him a lot too. And you gotta say this about him, he's a real hard worker. And La Chata too, she works just as hard. Boy, they're gonna pick up a pretty penny, no? . . . La Chata finally has it pretty good . . . Man, I don't know why you're so mistrusting, old lady . . ."

Six weeks after the wedding the potato picking ended. There was only a couple of days more work. We figured Tuesday everything would be over and so we fixed up the car that weekend since our heads were already in Texas. Monday I remember we got up early and Dad like always beat us to the outhouse. But I don't even think he got there because he came right back with the news that Pete had left the farm.

"But what do you mean, old man?"

"Yeah, he left. He took the car and all the money they'd saved between him and La Chata and the boys. He left her without a cent. He took everything they'd made . . . What did I tell you? . . . He left . . . What did I tell you?"

La Chata didn't go to work that day. In the fields that's all people talked about. They told the boss about it but he just shook his head, they said. La Chata's folks were good and mad, but I guess we weren't too much. I guess because nothing had happened to us.

Next day work ended. We didn't see La Chata again that year. We came to Texas and a couple of months later, during Christmas, Dad talked to Don Chon who'd just come from Iowa. Dad asked about Pete and he said he didn't know, that he heard he'd been cut up in a bar in Minnesota and was going around saying the cops had taken all his money and the car, and that the boss had told the cops and they'd caught him in Albert Lea. Anyhow, no one had given any money to Don Chon or La Chata. All we remembered was how he'd only just gotten there and he already wanted to leave. Anyhow, Pete sure made his pile. But, like they say, no one knows who his boss is. That all happened around '48. I think La Chata must be dead by now, but her kids must be grown men.

JESÚS COLÓN

Kipling and I

SOMETIMES I pass Debevoise Place at the corner of Willoughby Street . . . I look at the old wooden house, gray and ancient, the house where I used to live some forty years ago . . .

My room was on the second floor at the corner. On hot summer nights I would sit at the window reading by the electric light from the street lamp which was almost at a level with the windowsill.

It was nice to come home late during the winter, look for some scrap of old newspaper, some bits of wood and a few chunks of coal, and start a sparkling fire in the chunky fourlegged coal stove. I would be rewarded with an intimate warmth as little by little the pigmy stove became alive puffing out its sides, hot and red, like the crimson cheeks of a Santa Claus.

My few books were in a soap box nailed to the wall. But my most prized possession in those days was a poem I had bought in a five-and-ten-cent store on Fulton Street. (I wonder what has become of these poems, maxims and sayings of wise men that they used to sell at the five-and-ten-cent stores?) The poem was printed on gold paper and mounted in a gilded frame ready to be hung in a conspicuous place in the house. I bought one of those fancy silken picture cords finishing in a rosette to match the color of the frame.

I was seventeen. This poem to me then seemed to summarize,

in one poetical nutshell, the wisdom of all the sages that ever lived. It was what I was looking for, something to guide myself by, a way of life, a compendium of the wise, the true and the beautiful. All I had to do was to live according to the counsel of the poem and follow its instructions and I would be a perfect man — the useful, the good, the true human being. I was very happy that day, forty years ago.

The poem had to have the most prominent place in the room. Where could I hang it? I decided that the best place for the poem was on the wall right by the entrance to the room. No one coming in and out would miss it. Perhaps someone would be interested enough to read it and drink the profound waters of its message . . .

Every morning as I prepared to leave, I stood in front of the poem and read it over and over again, sometimes half a dozen times. I let the sonorous music of the verse carry me away. I brought with me a handwritten copy as I stepped out every morning looking for work, repeating verses and stanzas from memory until the whole poem came to be part of me. Other days my lips kept repeating a single verse of the poem at intervals throughout the day.

In the subways I loved to compete with the shrill noises of the many wheels below by chanting the lines of the poem. People stared at me moving my lips as though I were in a trance. I looked back with pity. They were not so fortunate as I who had as a guide to direct my life a great poem to make me wise, useful and happy.

And I chanted:

If you can keep your head when all about you
Are losing theirs and blaming it on you . . .

If you can wait and not be tired by waiting,
  Or being lied about, don't deal in lies,
Or being hated don't give way to hating . . .

If you can make one heap of all your winnings;
  And risk it on one turn of pitch-and-toss,
And lose, and start again at your beginnings . . .

"If —," by Kipling, was the poem. At seventeen, my evening prayer and my first morning thought. I repeated it every day with the resolution to live up to the very last line of that poem.

I would visit the government employment office on Jay Street. The conversations among the Puerto Ricans on the large wooden benches in the employment office were always on the same subject. How to find a decent place to live. How they would not rent to Negroes or Puerto Ricans. How Negroes and Puerto Ricans were given the pink slips first at work.

From the employment office I would call door to door at the piers, factories and storage houses in the streets under the Brooklyn and Manhattan bridges. "Sorry, nothing today." It seemed to me that that "today" was a continuation and combination of all the yesterdays, todays and tomorrows.

From the factories I would go to the restaurants, looking for a job as a porter or dishwasher. At least I would eat and be warm in a kitchen.

"Sorry" . . . "Sorry" . . .

Sometimes I was hired at ten dollars a week, ten hours a day including Sundays and holidays. One day off during the week. My work was that of three men: dishwasher, porter, busboy. And to clear the sidewalk of snow and slush "when you have nothing else to do." I was to be appropriately humble and grateful not only to the owner but to everybody else in the place.

If I rebelled at insults or at a pointed innuendo or just the inhuman amount of work, I was unceremoniously thrown out and told to come "next week for your pay." "Next week" meant weeks of calling for the paltry dollars owed me. The owners relished this "next week."

I clung to my poem as to a faith. Like a potent amulet, my precious poem was clenched in the fist of my right hand inside my secondhand overcoat. Again and again I declaimed aloud a few precious lines when discouragement and disillusionment threatened to overwhelm me.

If you can force your heart and nerve and sinew
To serve your turn long after they are gone . . .

The weeks of unemployment and hard knocks turned into months. I continued to find two or three days of work here and there. And I continued to be thrown out when I rebelled at the ill treatment, overwork and insults. I kept pounding the streets looking for a place where they would treat me half decently, where my devotion to work and faith in Kipling's poem would be appreciated. I remember the worn-out shoes I bought in a second-hand store on Myrtle Avenue at the corner of Adams Street. The round holes in the soles that I tried to cover with pieces of carton were no match for the frigid knives of the unrelenting snow.

One night I returned late after a long day of looking for work. I was hungry. My room was dark and cold. I wanted to warm my numb body. I lit a match and began looking for some scraps of wood and a piece of paper to start a fire. I searched all over the floor. No wood, no paper. As I stood up, the glimmering flicker of the dying match was reflected in the glass surface of the framed poem. I unhooked the poem from the wall. I reflected for a minute, a minute that felt like an eternity. I took the frame apart, placing the square glass upon the small table. I tore the gold paper on which the poem was printed, threw its pieces inside the stove and, placing the small bits of wood from the frame on top of the paper, I lit it, adding soft and hard coal as the fire began to gain strength and brightness.

I watched how the lines of the poem withered into ashes inside the small stove.

AMÉRICO PAREDES

The Hammon and the Beans

ONCE WE LIVED in one of my grandfather's houses near Fort
Jones. It was just a block from the parade grounds, a big
frame house painted a dirty yellow. My mother hated it, especially
because of the pigeons that cooed all day about the eaves. They had
fleas, she said. But it was a quiet neighborhood at least, too far from
the center of town for automobiles and too near for musical,
night-roaming drunks.

At that time Jonesville-on-the-Grande was not the thriving
little city that it is today. We told off our days by the routine on
the post. At six sharp the flag was raised on the parade grounds to
the cackling of the bugles, and a field piece thundered out a salute.
The sound of the shot bounced away through the morning mist
until its echoes worked their way into every corner of town.
Jonesville-on-the-Grande woke to the cannon's roar, as if to battle,
and the day began.

At eight the whistle from the post laundry sent us children off
to school. The whole town stopped for lunch with the noon
whistle, and after lunch everybody went back to work when the
post laundry said that it was one o'clock, except for those who
could afford to be old-fashioned and took the siesta. The post was
the town's clock, you might have said, or like some insistent elder
person who was always there to tell you it was time.

At six the flag came down, and we went to watch through the high wire fence that divided the post from the town. Sometimes we joined in the ceremony, standing at salute until the sound of the cannon made us jump. That must have been when we had just studied about George Washington in school, or recited "The Song of Marion's Men," about Marion the Fox and the British cavalry that chased him up and down the broad Santee. But at other times we stuck out our tongues and jeered at the soldiers. Perhaps the night before we had hung at the edges of a group of old men and listened to tales about Aniceto Pizaña and the "border troubles," as the local paper still called them when it referred to them gingerly in passing.

It was because of the border troubles, ten years or so before, that the soldiers had come back to old Fort Jones. But we did not hate them for that; we admired them even, at least sometimes. But when we were thinking about the border troubles instead of Marion the Fox, we hooted them and the flag they were lowering, which for the moment was theirs alone, just as we would have jeered an opposing ball team, in a friendly sort of way. On these occasions even Chonita would join in the mockery, though she usually ran home at the stroke of six. But whether we taunted or saluted, the distant men in khaki uniforms went about their motions without noticing us at all.

The last word from the post came in the night when a distant bugle blew. At nine it was all right because all the lights were on. But sometimes I heard it at eleven, when everything was dark and still, and it made me feel that I was all alone in the world. I would even doubt that I was me, and that put me in such a fright that I felt like yelling out just to make sure I was really there. But next morning the sun shone and life began all over again, with its whistles and cannon shots and bugles blowing. And so we lived, we and the post, side by side with the wire fence in between.

The wandering soldiers whom the bugle called home at night did not wander in our neighborhood, and none of us ever went into Fort Jones. None except Chonita. Every evening when the flag came down she would leave off playing and go down toward what was known as the lower gate of the post, the one that opened not on Main Street but against the poorest part of town. She went into the grounds and to the mess halls and pressed her nose against the screens and watched the soldiers eat. They sat at long tables calling to each other through food-stuffed mouths.

"Hey bud, pass the coffee!"

"Give me the ham!"

"Yeah, give me the beans!"

After the soldiers were through, the cooks came out and scolded Chonita, and then they gave her packages with things to eat.

Chonita's mother did our washing, in gratefulness — as my mother put it — for the use of a vacant lot of my grandfather's which was a couple of blocks down the street. On the lot was an old one-room shack which had been a shed long ago, and this Chonita's father had patched up with flattened-out pieces of tin. He was a laborer. Ever since the end of the border troubles there had been a development boom in the Valley, and Chonita's father was getting his share of the good times. Clearing brush and building irrigation ditches, he sometimes pulled down as much as six dollars a week. He drank a good deal of it up, it was true. But corn was just a few cents a bushel in those days. He was the breadwinner, you might say, while Chonita furnished the luxuries.

Chonita was a poet, too. I had just moved into the neighborhood when a boy came up to me and said, "Come on! Let's go hear Chonita make a speech."

She was already on top of the alley fence when we got there, a scrawny little girl of about nine, her bare dirty feet clinging to the fence almost like hands. A dozen other kids were there below her, waiting. Some were boys I knew at school; five or six were her younger brothers and sisters.

"Speech! Speech!" they all cried. "Let Chonita make a speech! Talk in English, Chonita!"

They were grinning and nudging each other, except for her brothers and sisters, who looked up at her with proud, serious faces. She gazed out beyond us all with a grand, distant air and then she spoke.

"Give me the hammon and the beans!" she yelled. "Give me the hammon and the beans!"

She leaped off the fence and everybody cheered and told her how good it was and how she could talk English better than the teachers at the grammar school.

I thought it was a pretty poor joke. Every evening almost, they would make her get up on the fence and yell, "Give me the hammon and the beans!" And everybody would cheer and make her think she was talking English. As for me, I would wait there until she got it over with so we could play at something else. I wondered how long it would be before they got tired of it all. I never did find out, because just about that time I got the chills and fever, and when I got up and around, Chonita wasn't there anymore.

In later years I thought of her a lot, especially during the thirties when I was growing up. Those years would have been just made for her. Many's the time I have seen her in my mind's eye, on the picket lines demanding not bread, not cake, but the hammon and the beans. But it didn't work out that way.

One night Doctor Zapata came into our kitchen through the back door. He set his bag on the table and said to my father, who had opened the door for him, "Well, she is dead."

My father flinched. "What was it?" he asked.

The doctor had gone to the window and he stood with his back to us, looking out toward the light of Fort Jones. "Pneumonia, flu, malnutrition, worms, the evil eye," he said without turning around. "What the hell difference does it make?"

"I wish I had known how sick she was," my father said in a very mild tone. "Not that it's really my affair, but I wish I had."

The doctor snorted and shook his head.

My mother came in and I asked her who was dead. She told me. It made me feel strange but I did not cry. My mother put her arm around my shoulders. "She is in heaven now," she said. "She is happy."

I shrugged her arm away and sat down in one of the kitchen chairs.

"They're like animals," the doctor was saying. He turned around suddenly and his eyes glistened in the light. "Do you know what that brute of a father was doing when I left? He was laughing! Drinking and laughing with his friends."

"There's no telling what the poor man feels," my mother said.

My father made a deprecatory gesture. "It wasn't his daughter anyway."

"No?" the doctor said. He sounded interested.

"This is the woman's second husband," my father explained. "First one died before the girl was born, shot and hanged from a mesquite limb. He was working too close to the tracks the day the Olmito train was derailed."

"You know what?" the doctor said. "In classical times they did things better. Take Troy, for instance. After they stormed the city they grabbed the babies by the heels and dashed them against the wall. That was more humane."

My father smiled. "You sound very radical. You sound just like your relative down there in Morelos."

"No relative of mine," the doctor said. "I'm a conservative, the son of a conservative, and you know that I wouldn't be here except for that little detail."

"Habit," my father said. "Pure habit, pure tradition. You're a radical at heart."

"It depends on how you define radicalism," the doctor answered. "People tend to use words too loosely. A dentist could be called a radical, I suppose. He pulls up things by the roots."

My father chuckled.

"Any bandit in Mexico nowadays can give himself a political label," the doctor went on, "and that makes him respectable. He's a leader of the people."

"Take Villa, now —" my father began.

"Villa was a different type of man," the doctor broke in.

"I don't see any difference."

The doctor came over to the table and sat down. "Now look at it this way," he began, his finger in front of my father's face. My father threw back his head and laughed.

"You'd better go to bed and rest," my mother told me. "You're not completely well, you know."

So I went to bed, but I didn't go to sleep, not right away. I lay there for a long time while behind my darkened eyelids Emiliano Zapata's cavalry charged down to the broad Santee, where there were grave men with hoary hairs. I was still awake at eleven when the cold voice of the bugle went gliding in and out of the dark like something that couldn't find its way back to wherever it had been. I thought of Chonita in heaven, and I saw her in her torn and dirty dress, with a pair of bright wings attached, flying round and round like a butterfly shouting, "Give me the hammon and the beans!"

Then I cried. And whether it was the bugle, or whether it was Chonita or what, to this day I do not know. But cry I did, and I felt much better after that.

JOSÉ ANTONIO VILLAREAL

Pocho

I

I T WAS SPRING in Santa Clara. The empty lots were green with new grass, and at the edge of town, where the orchards began their indiscernible rise to the end of the valley floor and halfway up the foothills of the Diablo Range, the ground was blanketed with cherry blossoms, which, nudged from their perch by a clean, soft breeze, floated down like gentle snow. A child walked through an empty lot, not looking back, for the wake of trampled grass he created made him sad. A mild, almost tangible wind caressed his face and hair like a mother's hands, washing him clean as it fondled him and passed to who knows where. Suddenly a jackrabbit, startled by his unseen presence, leaped past his feet and bounded across the city street, and meanwhile the multicolored birds blended, lending their opulence to the scene. His every sense responded to life around him. He thought the robin and the rabbit were God's favorites, because they were endowed with the ability to make play out of life. And, as young as he was, things were too complex for him.

The small boy was on his way home from his first confession. In one hand he carried a brand-new cap; in the other a small picture of the Virgin Mary in a gilt-edged frame. The object, of itself, had little value for him, but he had wrapped it in his handkerchief to protect it, because he had won it by being the first in his age group to learn the catechism and, as his first symbol of recognition, it gave him a pleasant feeling. He walked diagonally across an empty block, stopping now and again to listen to some sound or to inspect a green insect. Every bug he saw was green, and he idly wondered why.

Such things worried him, always. The sky was his biggest problem these days. In the beginning, there was darkness — nothing, he was told, and accepted, before God made the world.

Who made the world?

God made the world.

Who is God?

God is the Creator of Heaven and Earth and of all things.

He knew this. He did not have to think to know — like the way he knew his prayers, like the way he turned when someone called his name or the way his eye closed when a fly came near it. It had occurred to him once that the answer to the second question was nothing more than the answer to the first. That he still did not know who God was. But upon reflection he remembered that one does not question God, and was satisfied.

But if there was nothing at the beginning, what was there? Just a big bunch of empty sky? But if it was even just empty sky, it was *something!* And the darkness! Was not the darkness *something?*

Someday he would ask, when he could ask it without getting all mixed up; he was certain someone would tell him.

He stopped in the shade of a giant oak that grew in the center of the field, and thought how wonderful it was that birds were able to fly, and lived in trees, thus exposing their red breasts. If they had been made like a bug, only their ugly grayish-brown backs would be seen. When he reached the other side of the square and turned down his street, he hastily put his cap on. It would not do to have his father catch him bareheaded. Only two weeks ago his father had made him walk three miles because he had forgotten his cap. They had been out in the country gathering wood, and when the man suddenly realized the boy was bareheaded, he scolded him and sent him home. To his father, a hat was an essential part of a man, and the boy had not imagined that it meant such a thing to him.

The red ugly building that was his home was before him now. It had been a store at one time, and faded lettering was still legible on its high front. "CROCKERIES" and "SUNDRIES," it read. Below that, in smaller lettering, "Livery Stable." The "sundries" had bothered him for a long time, until finally, one day, he asked his teacher what "soondries" meant and she did not understand him. When he spelled the word out for her, she laughed and told him it meant "a great many things." She then taught him to pronounce the word. Although he liked his teacher, he never forgave her for laughing at him, and from that day he was embarrassed whenever he was corrected by anyone. And when he daydreamed in class and she asked, in exasperation, "Richard, of what are you thinking?" he answered, "Sundries." He waited patiently for the day he would run across the word when reading aloud in class, and when that day came, it was before a different teacher, and instead of the elation he had anticipated, he was left with a curious dissatisfaction. Now, as he stood before his house, he pronounced the word almost soundlessly. He was afraid of being caught talking to himself.

He walked into the house and heard his mother singing in the kitchen. In a clear, fine voice, she sang ballads of the old days in her country, and the child was always caught in their magic. He was totally unaware that his imaginary remembrances, being free of pathos, were far more beautiful than her real ones.

"You are home, my son?" she asked.

"Sí, Mamá." He kissed her and then handed her the small picture. "Here. It is my prize."

"Ah! What a good son you are. Your father will be proud." She kissed him again. "Now, change your clothes. You must save these for school."

"Yes, but first I must ask you something."

She stopped suddenly as she was turning from him. She had an instinctive fear of her son's questions, for she sensed that although he was but nine years old, he would soon ask her things she did not discuss even with her husband. She looked at him. His dark face was cupped in his frail hands, and his thin elbows rested on the table. His face was a miniature replica of hers. High cheekbones, small chin, black eyes; the nose was long, and it hooked down at the tip, exactly as hers did. Only his earlobes were different. They were extraordinarily large, like her husband's. His fingers were long and nervous.

All *indio*, this boy of mine, she thought, except inside. The Spanish blood is deep within him.

She was concerned for this child of her heart. Eight girls she had borne in her thirty-four years, and this was her only son. He had brought her and her man back together, and for that she could never love him enough. But he was such a rare one! Her face softened and she said:

"Very well, son. What is it that you want to know?"

He turned a perplexed face to her. "The good Father asked me some strange things today, Mamá," he said.

"Is that what you want to talk about?" she asked, and her voice showed gentle reproof. "You know it is a sin to discuss a holy confession with anyone." She prepared to dismiss him, thankful for the opportunity.

He spoke again, before she could say another word. "He asked me if I liked to play with myself, and I said yes, and he was angry." With his limited knowledge of English, the translation into Spanish was a literal one, and she did not fully understand his meaning. "I could not say no, because it is true that I would rather be alone than with the Portuguese and the Spaniards. They always hit me, anyway, and make fun of me. Tell me, why should I play with the others if they do not like me?"

She would not try to explain to him the importance of companionship and the security of belonging to a group. It would only make her think of how she herself was sometimes lonely here without any of her people. "Talk to your father later. He will tell you," she said. "Now, go do what I told you."

"There is more, Mamá. He asked me also if I sometimes play with Luz. You yourself make me play with her, so I answered yes. Then he wanted to know if I ever touch her, and I said I do, and he was angrier. After a while, his voice was kind and he told me it is a mortal sin to touch a girl, and even worse to touch your own sister. I never knew that one mortal sin could be worse than another mortal sin. Fifty Our Fathers and fifty Hail Marys he gave me to say for penance."

The full meaning of what he was saying struck her, so she perceptibly shrank from him. What can I say? she thought. How can I tell him? Near panic, she started to refer him to his father again, but he said:

"I know what he meant about touching Luz. I did not remember before, but right now I know."

She grasped the table for support. ¡Por Dios! she thought. He knows all about being with a woman! Her face was white, and she hoarsely whispered through her teeth, "Tell me how you know what he meant! Tell me now!"

"It is nothing," he said quietly, but her vehemence frightened him. "It happened so long ago I had forgotten — and I do not see why it is a mortal sin."

"A long time ago!" The initial shock was past, and she was at the point of violent anger. "What happened a long time ago? What did you do? Tell me!"

He could not understand the reason for her wrath. "You remember the Mangini girls when I was little and we lived in the other house? You liked them because they were good to me and always took me with them when they went out into the empty lots to get milkweed for their rabbits. When we were out in the fields, they took my trousers off and played with my palomas and laughed and laughed. Then they took their clothes off, and hugged me and rolled around in the grass. And they would say they wished I was older but if I was older they could not play with me like that. And you know? The big ones had hair on their body, except that one of them had only a little bit."

"Pig! Pig! Ah, what has God given me? A shameless!"

He continued in a calm voice, now seemingly apathetic to her fury, "And then, one day, the girls were starting to get dressed when the biggest one grabbed me, and she started to moan like she was crying, and she bit me on the shoulder and made me cry. I never went out with them again."

"Why did you not tell me of this before?" she shouted.

"They told me it was our secret, and they bought me ice cream cones if I promised not to tell anyone." He paused a moment. "I guess that is what the priest meant. Now I will have to make another confession, because I have never played like that with Luz and I told him I did. And I think I did not say all my penance — I lost count."

"You are bad! Filthy!" She pushed him roughly into the large room that was the bedroom for the whole family. "Tomorrow, early, you go to confession and tell all that to the Father. Now you better pray that you do not die tonight!" She sat at the table and, with her head on her arms, began to cry.

The frightened and bewildered boy sat on the bed where four of his sisters slept. He took off his clothes, crying silently. As his sobs subsided, he wondered why his parents, who were so good to him, could change so suddenly to become almost vicious. The very bed he sat on was an example of their goodness, for they preferred to sleep on the floor so that their children could have it. There was something here that he did not know. A mystery so great that it could not be spoken about, so great that it could only be mentioned indirectly. Why did they not want to tell him? *God made the world. Who is God?* But if He was good and kind, why did He make darkness? Night was the scariest time of the day, because a day is twenty-four hours and night is a day. But not daytime. He was scared at night because he could not see, and he was frightened now because he could not know, and somehow God was in the middle of the whole thing. To do "bad" things had something to do with being alive, but really what were "bad" things? As he thought, he almost marveled, because experiences that had left him shaken and afraid were nearly always somehow connected with the mystery. It seemed years ago that he had sat on a box at an old squeaky table under the prune trees. Across from him, his father sat eating his food. His sisters sat around the table on both sides of them. They were eating, too, but he could not eat. He just sat there staring at his frijoles, and all the time his stomach kept bothering him, just as it did when he took castor oil. He felt the corner of his mouth jerk down, but he could not cry. Not yet. He could hear the little animals chirping and making noises in the darkness around him. The little boys from the other families were playing hangol-seek in the orchard, stepping all over the fruit, probably. Once in a while, a prune would fall from the limb on top of him and make a funny little noise when it hit the table. He used to like that before, because once one fell on his father's plate and he got mad, but now he did not feel good. He looked up when his father spoke in a strong voice:

"Eat! Are we so rich that our food can be thrown away?"

"No, Papá. It is only that I don't feel good. I am worried about my mother."

"Do not worry, son." He did not sound mean this time. "Your mother is all right. Go in and see her if you wish. Give me your plate. I will finish it myself."

"Sí, señor," he said, and jumped off the box. He opened the flap of the tent, and now he wanted to turn back. His mother was making terrible noises. Funny, he had not heard her moaning when he was outside. He could not turn back, and he really wanted to, because he was scared. There was a dirty old blanket that his father had put across the middle of the tent so they would not bother Mamá. They all slept in the tent — his six sisters, too — and Papá wanted to be sure they would not bother Mamá. He got down like a little cat and crept under the blanket, and then he kneeled down next to his mother. She stopped moaning for a little while and she was sweating. In her hands she had her rosary beads, the good ones. His uncle Juan had given them to her when she married his father. His uncle had just come back from walking like a little cat all the way to the shrine of the Dark Virgin, almost eight leagues away, and he felt very good inside. So he gave her his rosary. Everyone said that that was a bad sign, to give your own rosary beads away, but his uncle Juan just laughed and drank more tequila. He died the next day. He just got a pain and died. Richard knew the story; his father had told him about it over and over.

His mother's lips were very wet when he kissed her, and they did not smell too good.

"¿Cómo está, Mamá?" he started to ask. She turned her face, and her eyes were not there for him. It looked like she was looking right through him, but when she talked, she talked to him and nobody else.

"I am all right, little one." She talked like she was very tired. "The Virgin is looking out for me."

He wanted to holler out against the Lord and the Virgin for making her suffer, but he got scared and crossed himself because he had a bad thought. He lied to his mother. "I ate all my food, Mamacita, but the tortillas were not like you make them. You make them much better."

She said, "That is good, son. Now, go outside for a while." But when she said that, she gave a big yell and pulled her hands apart. The rosary beads broke, and part of them fell to the dirt floor. He looked at her face and his body was very cold, and he could not move, but then he jumped up and ran out, shouting, "My mother is dying! My mother is dying, and it's my fault. I thought against God, and the rosary broke! It's the sign! She is going to die, and it's my fault — my fault — my grievous fault!"

Everybody ran around and left him by himself, so he fell on his stomach and cried very hard and his face got dirty. After a while, he stopped crying. His mother was shouting so much that he could even hear her outside. He walked away into the orchard. He began to think.

Maybe it isn't my fault, he thought. Maybe Mamá got bit by a little animal. But when he thought of that, he got scared all over again, because only last week Papá had caught him playing with a little animal that had a red stomach. He had been poking it with a stick and Papá stepped on it and took his stick away from him and hit him with it, because he said that the animal would kill him. After a while, he had asked his father how a funny little animal with a red stomach could kill him, and he answered that it would bite him and he would just swell up and die. He remembered that when he went in to see his mother, she was all swelled up. He ran back to the tent, and went inside to the corner where his mattress of potato sacks was, and stood there on his knees praying. He said more than ten Hail Marys and Our Fathers, and then began to make up his own prayers. He promised Him so many things that he could not remember, and all the time his mother kept screaming, and his father came to him and fell asleep on his mattress of potato sacks like nothing was happening. He wanted to sleep, too, as his father was doing, but he could not. Instead of trying to sleep some more, he finally got a coal-oil lamp and lit it. He tried to read from his book, *Toby Tyler, or Ten Weeks with the Circus*. He would never forget the name of it, because he liked it so much and had read it five times before. His teacher in Brawley had given it to him, once when he went to school for about a month, and told him he should keep it until he learned to read. He read the same page over two times, and put the book away in his hiding place, because once he put it under his mattress and his baby sister wet all over it; that was why the pages were bumpy and hard. All this time, his mother kept hollering, until he thought he would bust before she did. Pretty soon, his oldest sister came and waked his father, and he went behind the blanket with her. And pretty soon his mother was quiet, and he stood there waiting, but he did not know what he was waiting for. There was one more cry, and that one was different; that was not his mother. All at once, he felt good again and knew that he could go to sleep. He forgot about God and lay down. His mother was all right. He was sure of it. Maybe he was as sure of that as he was that in a couple of days his mother would be out in the orchard picking prunes with the rest of them.

Very clearly he now knew this was a part of the mystery. He could look back to that time with the sophistication of his nine years. Since that first time, he had seen his mother big with child twice, and each time remembered the horrible fantasy of the black widow spider. So she *must* know, she had to know, and of course as long as *she* knew, it could not be too evil — and yet how did she find out? He was certain his father did not know, else he would tell him. Somehow his mother and the priest were a part of this thing that was such evil . . . But if he had done such a great wrong, why was it that nothing had happened to him because of it? He began to cry again, because it was afternoon and it would be night soon and his punishment would come at night. He knew that bad things happen in the dark. He had not made a good confession, and he might indeed die in the night and go to hell. *The third day He rose again from the dead.* Do many people go to hell? He knew a boy

who went to hell, although he had never thought of this before.
And he also knew that the boy was in hell because of something
having to do with the Sin. Suddenly he very nearly had the answer
to the whole thing, and he was calm. Now he could remember
other times the Sin had come up . . . They told them that it was
just a feeling and that they were too little to get it yet. It was
nighttime almost, and the big guys were standing by the gas station
talking. They were going to a hookshop, they said, and he and
Ricky wanted to know what it was. The big guys laughed at them,
because they were little kids and did not know nothing, and they
were smarter. One of the big guys was always mean to him,
because he was Spanish and Richard was Mexican . . . He had asked
him one day why he was always picking on him, and he told him
because he was Mexican and everybody knew that a Spaniard was
better than a Mexican any old day, and Richard told him that his
father said that in Spain if a guy had a burro, he was a king; but he
did not know what Richard was talking about. Richard did not
stand too close to him, because he was always trying to pants him,
and he would have died of shame if he did it tonight, because he
knew his BVDs were dirty at the trap door. The boy talked louder
than any of the others, and kept saying, "Let's go — I got ants in my
pants," and all that, and he kept walking back and forth and holding
the front of his pants with both hands. He was pretty dumb, and
he was the one that got drowned in the river one time his folks
went up to Sacramento to work in the asparagus. He kept hollering, "Let's go," but they had to wait for the guy with the car, and
then he told Richard to get the hell away from there, cholo,
because they did not want any chilebeans hanging around. Richard
did not go, but he watched and was ready to start running, but the
other did not chase him. Instead, he started saying things to him to
make everybody laugh, like "Why don't you go home and eat some
tortillas," and Richard told him he had just finished eating, and
anyway he did not see anything funny about it, because he liked
tortillas better than bread any old day. But it was funny to the rest
of them, except Ricky, because he used to eat over Richard's house
all the time. And then the guy asked him to go home and listen to
the radio, although he knew Richard's family did not even have

electric lights. And that was not funny either, but they kept laughing and saying all kinds of dingy things, and then the same guy told Richard to go tell his sister Concha he wanted to fuck with her. And everybody laughed louder and almost died laughing, and Richard did not know what to say, because he did not really know what the guy meant, but he did know it was bad, and he got mad and started to cry and told the guy that someday he was going to grow up bigger and beat him up. But the guy said again to call her and tell her what he said, and Richard told him that he was going to tell his father on him, and the guy said to go ahead and call him and he'd give the old bastard a highster in the ass, and everybody laughed some more and he chased him, but only a little way. They laughed at Richard's father, but they did not know about him.

II

At this time, Richard's most enjoyable moments were those spent in the company of his father. He loved his mother. She was always there when he needed her, and her arms and her songs were warmth and comfort and security, but with his father it was a different thing, because pleasure is far different from security. And suddenly he began to look forward to the time his father would return from work. Whenever possible, Juan Rubio took him with him in his travels around the valley. There were not many Mexican people in Santa Clara in those days, and the few families scattered throughout the far reaches of the valley became close friends. It was another thing in the summer, when people arrived by the hundreds from southern California, first for the apricot and then the prune harvest; but in the remaining months it was not an easy thing for the people to have intercourse with someone from their own country.

With his father, Richard sat around campfires or in strange kitchens, with wood stoves burning strongly and the ever-present odor of a pot of pink beans boiling, freshly cooked tortillas filling the close, warm room, and listened to the tales of that strange country which seemed to him a land so distant, and the stories also seemed of long, long ago. It was then, listening and weaving a parallel fantasy in his mind, that he felt an enjoyment so great that he knew he could not possibly savor it all. He listened to the men speak until he grew drowsy, and he climbed onto his father's lap, and Juan Rubio held him easily against his body, close to his chest, and the boy associated the smell of the man with his happiness.

In the summer also now, it became the custom for his father to allow two or three families to pitch their tents in the large backyard, or to use a portion of the barn to live in until the prune season was over and they would return to their own part of the state. And so Richard had Mexican friends and learned more about them from living with them. They held small Mexican fiestas and sang Mexican songs, and danced typical dances, so that there, in the center of Santa Clara, a small piece of Mexico was contained within the fences of the lot on which Juan Rubio kept his family.

Thus the summers were glorious for Richard — marred only by an occasional happening of life that is intrinsically sad, for in the Rubio yard children were born, people were married, and sometimes someone, usually a newborn baby, died. Richard could not accept the idea of death, even with the knowledge that he would go to heaven. To die was easy, but to give up life was not an easy thing even to think about, and yet it was obvious to him that it could not be too difficult a thing, for even cowards somehow managed to die. He had seen a man die this summer, and the ease with which he had expired was frightening, and in the moment before he died there was no difference in him from the moment after he was dead — yet suddenly he was dead, irrevocably dead.

Richard was with his father talking to Don Tomás that night when it happened, and Don Tomás said good night to Juan Rubio and walked to his house in the backyard. A short time later, his stepson came over to ask for some yerba buena, because his father — he always called him his father — had a bad stomachache. Soon he returned and asked for some alcohol to rub him down, because he was in great pain. By then, Don Tomás could be heard moaning and calling to God to ease his suffering. Richard went out to the backyard to a point where he could see into the room. The bed was by the door, and it was not really dark yet, so he could see him very plainly on the bed. Don Tomás moved his head from one side to the other, and he doubled up his body with big jerks. Once, he let out a big, long fart. In the rear of the room, a candle was lighted to the Virgin and the women of the house were praying. Richard could hear the murmur all the way outside. He wanted to go into the room and look at Don Tomás up close, but he was afraid he was going to die, and he did not want to watch him when he died. Juan Rubio sent him away to get the enema bag, because Don Tomás kept saying he had a great constipation, but by the time he returned with the bag, his father was talking to the stepson, and the stepson got on his bicycle and went away very fast. Don Tomás was not conscious anymore, and he was very sick, and the boy was sent to bring an ambulance. Don Tomás was quiet, lying on his back, staring at the rafters. Every once in a while he took a deep, loud breath, and then one time he did not breathe again but kept on staring at the rafters. Juan Rubio came then and put two rocks on his eyes, and took Richard away from there. The stepson came back and said the ambulance would not come because there was no one to pay for it, and Juan Rubio sent him back to call the cops. After a while the chief of police came, and then the county hearse, gray with black curtains, came, and then an ambulance came.

The next day they buried Don Tomás, and the coroner told Juan Rubio that he had died of peritonitis, caused by a ruptured appendix, and the county buried Don Tomás in the Catholic cemetery at one end near the cherry trees, because that is where the county buried people who did not have money. Juan Rubio and Richard stayed behind under the cherry trees after everybody left, and they talked because Richard was still afraid, and the boy told his father that he was afraid to die because it seemed like a big darkness and that he did not want to die ever, and his father put his arms around him, and he said that if he did not want to die ever and he wanted that very much, then he would never die. He made Richard very happy when he said that, and he believed him because his armpits smelled so nice. And then they saw that the hearse had come back to the grave. They watched them lift the coffin back out, and waited to see them throw Don Tomás back in the hole and keep the coffin, but they just filled up the hole and took Don Tomás away with them, coffin and all. Richard asked his father why he was crying, and Juan Rubio said that it was the only thing he could do.

That night, Don Tomás returned to the backyard. An idiot girl named Dora, who had runny sores, saw him first and came running to tell everybody, and they were all frightened and closed their doors. Richard was outside under a tree when it happened, and was so frightened that he could not move and Don Tomás found him there. Don Tomás looked at him sadly, and his face was very white, because he did not have any blood. He did not talk and Richard did not talk, but he knew Don Tomás wanted him to put him back in his grave.

III

Near the primary school that Richard attended, there still stands a large red barn, old and abandoned, its windows boarded and its roof unshingled. Like all inutile inanimates, it gives no hint that it, too, has a past. In the early days of the motorcar, it housed the wagons and horses of one of the most successful draymen in Santa Clara. Mat Madeiros was one of those men who, being poor all their lives, become authorities on commerce and economic trends when they find themselves in the secure position of moderate wealth. Mat knew business was booming and would get even better. Soon he would not be able to handle all his orders with his modest equipment. He talked loud and long on the importance of the machine in business, and sold his horses to a farmer in Cupertino. His wagons were too heavy to be used in orchards, so he dismantled them and put them in a far corner of the barn.

Mat learned to drive his Reo truck and prospered, so that before the end of one year the vehicle was paid for, and in the second year he had visions of a fleet of trucks and an important position in the community. Every evening, he stood in front of the pool hall, sucking on a black cigar, renewing friendships with old acquaintances, thinking forward to the day he would run for the town council — he might even receive enough votes to become mayor. Gradually he became so engrossed in reveries of social accomplishment that he scarcely noticed that his hauls were becoming fewer in number. Soon his clients stopped coming altogether, and he had to drive to the neighboring towns of Berryessa, Sunnyvale and Saratoga in search of jobs. Once, he even went all the way to Old Almaden, but to no avail. Now the household was run on the money he had saved to put into his business, and he was finally forced to work in a cannery and to put his rig up on blocks. Every evening, he went into the barn and sat at the wheel of the truck, as a child will sometimes do. With a yardstick, he measured the contents of the gas tank and then checked the tires with a hand gauge, thumping each of them with the heel of his hand. Thus reassured that his truck was ready for the time hauls would begin to come up, he stood back and gave it a look of approval, then went in to his supper.

These days, Mat bolstered his spirits by declaring to his wife and children, and even to himself, that of a certainty things would soon be better. Business was bound to improve, and his rig would once again be in demand. He explained in detail how he would add more rigs and how he would have to hire a man to help out as the business grew. At the plant, he told his fellow workers that he was there only temporarily, and because he had acquired an independence when he was his own boss, he was not a good worker, and one day found himself out of a job. His small reserve had dwindled steadily and he had no money. He would not think of selling his truck, until finally, in desperation, he was forced to try, but by now he could not find a buyer. All this led to a period of notoriety for Mat's big barn.

The year was 1931, and the people of Santa Clara were hungry. The little food they could buy with their meager income was augmented only because the valley was so fertile, and now it was common practice to go into the fields and take fruits and vegetables. The smaller farmers, who could not afford to harvest their crops, willingly let the people have them. Richard's family did not suffer as much as the others, because the Depression had not changed their diet. They had never had much more than they were now getting. His father had always managed to bring vegetables home to add to their basic staples. The boy was no longer greeted at noon recess with jeers and hoots. The hated, oft-repeated cries of his schoolmates — "Frijoley bomber!" "Tortilla strangler!" — now disappeared, as did the accompanying laughter, and he sometimes shared his lunch with them. He did this with a sense of triumph, because he felt he had defeated them by enduring their contempt and derision openly. For almost a year, he had purposely eaten where he could be easily observed, refusing to be driven into hiding because they laughed about the food he ate. He did not suspect the real reason for his victory.

The state of the community was reflected in the school in other ways. A new ruling made it permissible to attend classes in bare feet, and another suspended school during bad weather. The rainy-day session was a godsend to the children and, of course, defeated its purpose, for they had more time to spend on the wet streets.

The townspeople demanded help from the county, and learned that their success in this would be greater if it was done collectively rather than individually, so the Unemployed Council was born. Mat's barn was cleaned and used as a meeting place and headquarters for the organization. Committees were formed to go before the Board of Supervisors, the County Welfare Department, and the mayor of Santa Clara to petition aid for the needy. And the government agencies responded as well as they possibly could. They gave commodities labeled as surplus, and distributed clothing to the worst cases. At first, the meetings were conducted in four languages — English, Spanish, Portuguese, and Italian — but as the group grew, it became increasingly difficult to maintain order. The original organizers felt that tenure should give them leadership, and refused to give the newcomers a voice. Petty jealousies were born and nurtured, until the meetings were often disrupted by violent arguments. There was soon complete demoralization, and collapse was impending, for the people had little knowledge of administrative procedure and were not overly literate. Into this chaos came the man from the city, the professional organizer.

Unemployed councils had developed in other cities throughout the state, and Communist affiliations made a concentrated effort to unite these groups into one strong structure. When the absorption of the councils was accomplished, the heretofore amicable relationship between the local groups and the authorities ended, and Mat's truck was once more on the road. Working parties forayed the bakeries for stale bread, the dairies for skim milk, and anyplace else where they might find something to help feed the people.

Richard and his father walked into the red barn. It was different inside from the first time he had seen it. The walls were newly whitewashed and a wooden floor had been installed. At one end of the building was a raised platform on which stood a long table and several chairs. The wall behind the table was bedecked with bunting, of which a red flag with hammer and sickle was the centerpiece. This object always reminded the child of the picture on the box that held his father's indigestion medicine. The boy and his father always sat with a group of Spanish men, because, as his father said, while they were not the best people with whom to associate, they at least spoke the language of Christians. They took seats, and Richard waited for things to begin. First they would play that march on the old gramophone while everyone stood, and then they would all sing their own songs. Words had been written to the tunes of popular songs of the day and to old favorites. "Auld Lang Syne," "Home, Sweet Home," and the "Stanford Fight Song" were the most popular with the crowd. Many of these songs were simple, straightforward pleas for food and clothing, while others called on the people to rise and throw off the shackles of serfdom.

Richard had anticipated tonight with pleasure, for on this night the delegate from San Francisco came, and he always put on a performance that was better than the one-ring Mexican circus Richard once saw in Milpitas. The man would pace back and forth, at times almost falling off the platform in his enthusiasm; he would wildly wave his arms and scream in a high-pitched voice. Because he was a small man, his antics were all the more ludicrous to the boy.

The songs were now over, and the man walked toward the platform. He shook hands with everyone in his path as he made his way to the front. The local chairman said a few words of needless introduction, and the delegate began to speak. He spoke in a different voice from the one Richard knew, slowly and carefully enunciating, almost stentoriously, as if he suddenly realized that most of the assemblage had never understood a word he said.

"Comrades," he said, "the time has come for us to show the instruments of our capitalistic government that we are tired of being stepped upon. The supervisors have refused to see our committees, so from now on we will be one big committee. We are going to raise such a racket that they will not dare refuse to see us. We are hungry and will be heard. This is just the beginning of a program that will tell the world how we have been let down. If they refuse to help us, then we must redouble our efforts to help ourselves.

"And I have good news for you, Comrades — yes, good news! One day soon, people like you and I will march to Sacramento and demand an audience with the governor . . . You realize what that will mean, a thing like that? People from every town and city in California, converging on the state capital? Washington will hear of it, and they will not be able to ignore us then. Plans are already in progress for the hunger march, and I personally promise you that we will make it soon. I have been assigned to remain here with you, and a Comrade will be sent to help me instruct. One day we will have our own schools, and your children will receive the education they deserve. Now we can continue with the meeting."

He sat down amid thunderous applause, and very interestedly listened to the remainder of the meeting. Plans were made for the execution of the hunger march, and when the business at hand was out of the way, portable tables were set up and the people were served hot cocoa and bread. Many who were not local people came in to get food, and Richard watched in fascination. The men from hobo jungles interested him, because they, in spite of their obvious hunger, courteously took only one helping and withdrew, while others, whom he knew to have some food at home, returned again and again to be fed. The diverse types among these men of the road also made him curious. Some were in tatters, their dirty ankles showing between their shrunken trousers and battered shoes. There were those who wore the sturdy clothing of the farmhand and looked no different from the people of the town. There were others who, in spite of their present circumstances, still attempted to affect a manner of respectability. They wore badly wrinkled unmatched suits with chambray shirts and soiled but neatly tied neckties. Regardless of their appearance, these men all had a common, haunted look of despair. Young and old walked with the same dazed air of incomprehensibility, except the Negroes. Richard, who had never seen Negroes in his life, mistook their attitude for morbid stoicism and was frightened by the black faces. Soon, however, he easily lost himself in their laughter and horseplay, and their color lost its strange ominousness. He learned to love the amazing beauty of their wide, toothy grins. When he talked to them, they told him about Alabam', the C'linas, and other such alien and mysterious places.

The next morning began a series of events that for a while kept Richard in a state of constant excitement. Always, however, there was a part of his mind that carefully observed from a detached point of view, and he was aware that he was learning something. There was a demonstration at the county courthouse in San Jose, which was in itself orderly, but the aftermath was one of spontaneous violence. What happened occurred without any apparent leadership, because the instigators kept well in the background. Food and produce trucks were marauded as they passed through town, for the old 101 highway did not bypass Santa Clara then. It was not an uncommon sight to see a truck lying on its side, with men scurrying antlike, back and forth, carrying pilfered food to their homes. Richard was often nearby, not showing his impatience, quietly calculating until he saw what he wanted. But, in spite of his careful planning, his choice of foods was bad, because he was driven by the mania of a child who had not had certain things, and by the end of the third day he had fifty loaves of bread and a hundred tins of deviled meat. He was unaware that he would have benefited had he gone about his plundering in a haphazard manner.

One Saturday morning, Richard accompanied his father to the pear groves at the north end of the valley. Although it was late in October and the Bartletts had long been harvested, the Winter Nellies were ready to be picked for shipment east. The ranchers had put out a call for workers. When Richard and his father arrived at the ranch where his father worked every season, cars were lined on both sides of the dirt driveway that led from the road to the house and the main buildings. About two hundred men were gathered in the loading area, talking quietly in small groups. Their lack of cheerfulness seemed strange to Richard, who had seen many such congregations joking and skylarking, waiting for the boss to come out. Then they would stand quietly while the straw bosses picked out the old hands, then selected the healthier-appearing and more serious of the remaining. No one would pay an hourly wage to a clown.

The steady help arrived and got to their jobs. Two men took ladders and buckets out of the big barn, while others, wearing hipboots and foul-weather clothing, coupled hoses and hitched horses to tank wagons, preparatory to spraying the Bartlett trees. Some walked into the orchard with pruning shears and saws, and others went off with axes, mattocks, and shovels to dig out dead trees.

The owner walked out then, wiping his mouth with a huge red handkerchief. Beside him was his eighteen-year-old daughter, who, since he had never had a son, kept his accounts and helped him in his business. She knew every phase of it, and would someday own one of the richest and largest orchards in the valley. She was a special friend of Richard's, for whenever his father worked there, the boy spent hours with her, and she sometimes took him into her library, where he lost himself in the books her father had bought for the son he never had.

The man and the young woman walked out to the center of the large yard. He was a good man, Mr. Jamison, and no one who had ever worked for him could say otherwise. He was not averse to taking his workers into his immaculate living room on cold mornings, where his wife would serve them hot coffee and a jigger of his good brandy. At the end of the working season, he always gave them enough wine for a party, and even got drunk in their company.

He smiled at them. "I'm sorry so many of you made an unnecessary trip out this morning," he said. "You see, I have my own packing plant and can handle only so much fruit a day, so I'm hiring only thirty men. Of course, my old help will be hired first, so those of you who've never worked for me better try somewhere else before it gets too late. If you're new in the valley, my daughter will tell you what ranches to try." No one made a move to leave, and the rancher sensed something was wrong. "What's the matter?" he asked.

None of the men who knew him would look up. An unidentified voice called out, "What are you paying, Mr. Jamison?"

"Fifteen cents. You all know that."

"We want twenty-five, Mr. Jamison!"

The rancher shook his head in a negative gesture. "I can't do that. I'm already in trouble for paying fifteen cents, but the truth is that I just can't afford to pay more than that."

"Then your fruit'll rot, 'cause none of us will work for less'n twenty!"

The girl had been sitting on the bumper of a car talking to Richard. She got up and returned to her father's side. "Listen," she said. "Dad's telling you the truth. The Association held a special meeting last night, and we argued all night for fifteen cents. They wouldn't agree to it . . . Twelve cents an hour is all they're paying. If you don't believe it, go see Robertson, or Black, or Genovese. Right now they're paying twelve, and the men are probably working already. Dad's offering you fifteen, the same as last year. And he'll probably get thrown out of the Growers for it."

The unidentified man spoke again. "We want twenty — or we won't work. You better make up your mind, 'cause it'll start raining soon, and then where will you be? Look at the sky. It looks like it will rain today." Someone snickered in the background. It was obvious that the man doing the talking was an outsider, for a light wind was coming in from San Francisco Bay, two miles to the north, a good indication in Santa Clara that there would be no rain.

The girl became angry then, and took a defiant step toward the approximate location of the voice.

In her blue denims and plaid shirt, her hair splashing yellow on her shoulders, her arms akimbo, she faced them, and to Richard she was the most beautiful thing he had ever seen. He did not really understand what was happening, but was in immediate sympathy with her. He moved to her side and aped her stance, and oddly his small figure was not farcical to the men.

"Just who are you?" she asked the man who had spoken. "Step out so I can see you!" When the man did not come forward, she said, "All right! So this is a strike! We were warned that this might happen this year, but Dad wouldn't believe his friends would let him down. He's always been so good to you, and even now is doing the best he can. Do you think you're the only ones having a hard time?" She paused, then tried to reason with them; she appealed to their sense of fairness. "If that crop isn't picked, we'll be running the ranch for Giannini next year. If we pay you what you ask, we lose not only money but the ranch as well — but you don't care anything about that, do you? You forgot the things he's done for you." She was angry once more at their silence. "Cowards — you should be ashamed! Standing there without even the guts to talk, without even the guts to look squarely at us . . . Hiding a stranger in the background to shoot off his big mouth!" She called out to them individually, talking to boys her own age, boys who had gone to school with her. "You, Mike, and Pete, and Charlie — aren't *you* ashamed of what you're doing? And you, Jack, especially you . . . Have you forgotten too, so soon?" And because Jack meant more to her than the others, she could be cruel to him. She spoke the bitter words brutally. "It means a lot to my old man to have his pears picked right away. Didn't it mean a lot to your folks when they got that box of groceries last week and that store order for clothing for the kids?"

"Please don't, daughter," said her father embarrassedly.

"I don't care, Pop!" She shook his hand from her arm. "Maybe I'll shame them into behaving like men." She spoke to Jack again. "You didn't know he'd done that, did you, Jack? Because he's so kind, he tried to help. Because of his goodness, he can't even be angry toward you men — if you can call yourselves men! But I'm not kind, and I'm mad! What do you think of your strike now, Jack?"

The young man was forced to speak, not only because of what she had just told him but because they had once been something special in each other's young lives, and because her father had raised her to be the kind of girl who would go with him, Jack

Perreira, to the high school senior prom. He spoke softly, almost intimately, as if the two were alone, and yet there was a hint of humility in his voice. "I knew who sent the food, Marla. I knew it right away, but now the men are striking, and no matter what I think about it and how I feel about you, I have to follow along. When you have a chance to think, you'll understand."

She did not think she could ever understand, but she somehow respected him for his words. "The offer still stands," she spoke out to the crowd. "The ladders and buckets are there for those who want to work." There was still no movement from the men. She had worked among men all her life, and knew their vernacular well. "Okay, then, you goddamn bastards!" she shouted. "Get the hell off our property, and don't come back until you're ready to go to work . . . And the wage has just gone down! When you come back, it'll be at twelve cents an hour. Twelve goddamn cents is all you'll get! Right now I'm going to call the sheriff, and then I'm going to get a shotgun and shoot any son of a bitch who's still on our land and doesn't want to work." She walked to the house so rapidly that Richard was forced to run to keep up with her. Her father went off into the orchard, and the men moved their cars out to the highway. They did not trust her not to carry out her threat.

She sat under a tree, with the boy beside her and a twelve-gauge shotgun across her lap, waiting for the sheriff to arrive. After a while, she sent Richard to tell the men that they were welcome to water if they were thirsty. When the sheriff and his deputies arrived, Richard stayed beside his father. Policemen frightened him, and he thought his father would be arrested. The sheriff told the men to go to work, but they ignored him. The road was public domain, and he lacked the authority to make them leave. He left his men there and moved on, for there were strikes all over the countryside.

The road where the men were keeping their vigil, although paved, was not really a highway but a county road. Therefore they were surprised to see a truck, loaded with watermelons, approach and come to a stop in their midst. A lean, fair-skinned young man jumped from the cab and looked around.

"Help yourself," he said casually, and walked toward an old man who was talking to Richard's father. "They told me I'd find you here," he said, and embraced the old man warmly.

"How are you, my son? How good it is to see you!" said the old man. He turned to Richard's father. "This is my son Victor, Don Juan. A grown man, no?"

"Much pleasure, sir," said the young man, taking Juan Rubio's hand.

"Equally. You have come a long way, eh?"

"Imperial Valley," answered Victor. "I left two days ago and was making good time but, coño, that Pacheco Pass is more difficult than the portals of heaven!"

"I know. I have suffered it."

The old man grabbed his son's arm. "But, man, me cago en Dios! Do you not see that those men are stealing your watermelons?" He shouted excitedly to the men, "¡Hola! ¡Maldita sea! Take yourselves from that truck, jackoffers of the devil! Respect another's goods!" He shook his head with indignant disgust and said, "I excrete on the milk of such abusers!"

Victor laughed. "Calm yourself, old one," he said. "I told them to have some so they would not wreck my truck. Watch how careful they are and how they do not make pigs of themselves. An old one like you should know that people behave better if they are made responsible for something." He put his hand on Richard's head and said, "Go, little one, and bring us back a good one."

They sat on a runningboard and ate the melon. A man wandered over to them and said that some of the new men had left, on the pretense of looking elsewhere for work, but had secreted themselves into the ranch by walking on a creekbed, and had been picking all along. Some of the strikers wanted to go in and drag them out, but the idea was rejected when they realized that the fruit would have to be taken out through the driveway. They would stay there and not let the truck pass through.

"I will move my rig out of the way," said Victor. Richard had immediately liked him, and asked if he could go with him. "Come on," Victor said. They had to go a quarter of a mile before they found a suitable place to park the truck. When they returned, the first load of pears was ready to leave for the packing house. The men were milling around the driveway.

"Out of my way!" yelled the truck driver. "I'm coming through!" He picked up speed, ready to take a fast, wide turn onto the pavement. The men scattered in all directions, and for a moment it seemed that he would make his escape, but a young boy drove an old Essex up to the driveway, directly in the path of the oncoming truck. The driver did not have time to stop, and the truck ran into the car, turning it on its side. Immediately the men jumped on the truck and scattered fruit in all directions. Within minutes, the three hundred boxes were demolished, pears were strewn all over the ground, and the truck itself was practically useless. From the beginning, the deputies tried to stop the men, threatening them with their guns, but when the men did not obey, the deputies did not fire, and instead attacked the rioters with nightsticks.

Richard stood to one side, holding fast to his new friend's hand. He saw Victor's father get hit on the head with a club and slump to the pavement. He put both arms around Victor's legs and tried to hold him back, but Victor shook him off and the boy fell into an irrigation ditch. When he got up, he saw Victor, a rock in his hand, looking for the man who had hit his father. And, not ten feet away, he saw him find him, and then saw him smash the man's forehead in, away from his face, with the rock.

Victor picked his father up and carried him to the side of the road, away from the melee. The old man sat up and held his head.

"Ay, what an ache of the head! What an ache of the head!" he repeated.

The fighting ended, and the two factions withdrew. Juan Rubio found his son crying under a tree and carried him to where Victor and his father sat. The young man looked at his clothes; by an unexplained miracle, he had no blood on him. A number of men had minor injuries, but the man Victor hit was still lying in the road, on the smashed pears and watermelon rinds. One of the deputies ran to the house to call an ambulance, while the others gathered around the fallen man. Almost immediately another ran after the first. "Never mind the ambulance!" he shouted. "Try to reach the sheriff instead! Joe's dead!"

"Here's the rock he was hit with," someone said. By the time the sheriff arrived, the weapon had been handled by most of the deputies.

"We questioned everybody already, Sheriff," said the deputy who had been left in charge. "No one knows who hit him, or they ain't telling."

"Let me get the son of a bitch and he'll never go to trial, I guarantee that!" said the sheriff.

"This guy is the only one who could've seen it. Says he wasn't in the fight at all. Says he was standing with the kid there, just watching."

"Come 'ere, you!" snapped the sheriff. "What's your name?"

"Victor Morales."

"What the hell you doing here if you don't belong to this here mob?"

"I stopped to see my old man. Got a load of melons I'm taking up to the city," answered Victor.

"That's right, Sheriff," said the deputy. "He give us some of them melons before the fight started. Truck's right over there."

"Okay, so you got a load of melons," said the sheriff. "Now, tell us what you know. Did you see the guy that did this to Joe?"

"No," said Victor. "I didn't see it happen. Guys were fighting all over the place, and boxes were flying off the truck . . . Then I saw my old man get hurt, and I helped him across the road. Next thing I know, the fight's over and the guy's laying there."

The sheriff was pacing back and forth. "Goddamn it!" he shouted. "This is some mess! Joe's dead and all we've got is a bloody rock and a couple of hundred sonsabitches who could've killed 'im!" He inspected the rock again, then said excitedly, "Somebody's got some blood on him. Look them all over!"

"We thought of that already. Nobody's went, and we give them all a good check," said the deputy. "No blood! Somebody musta just throwed that rock."

"How about the kid?" asked the sheriff. "You bother to question the kid?"

"I guess I forgot in all the excitement."

Richard was brought forward. "Look, sonny," said the sheriff, "did you see who hit that man? Come on, speak up!" The boy was frightened, and had difficulty phrasing his answer in English. He could not speak. "You musta seen it," continued the sheriff, "or else you wouldn't be so scared!"

The boy was finally able to talk. The sound of his voice gave him courage, and he became almost voluble. "I didn't see it. It was just like he said, everybody was running around and everything. I don't know who hit him." He looked directly into the officer's eyes to keep from turning his head to where Victor stood.

"Then why were you so afraid to talk? How come you were crying?"

"I don't talk English too good," answered Richard. "I almost answered you in Spanish."

The sheriff looked at him for a long moment, and then said, in a stern voice, "Stop lying! You know who it was! You're so scared you're shaking!"

Richard gave him a look of hurt dignity. He was not crying, now that he knew he was past the most dangerous part of this thing in which he had somehow become involved, but his voice quavered. "If you were little like me and watched a big fight and knew a man was killed, you'd be scared, too," he said as seriously as he could. He walked back to his father, and the officer did not bother him again.

"I guess the only witness was Joe," said the sheriff. "And Joe's dead." He waved his arms in a helpless gesture and, in his frustration, ordered the road cleared. He was in an uncomfortable position, he knew, for the people were not itinerant laborers, but lived in town and were taxpayers. A few of them were even voters, and his treatment of them at this time could affect his reelection, but he *must* do something.

The boy who drove the car into the path of the truck was charged with reckless driving and operating a vehicle without a license, and the men were then ordered home. Only two people ever knew what really happened that morning.

The next day, the old hands went to work for Mr. Jamison and he paid them fifteen cents.

*   *   *

After the excitement and violence of that day, the hunger march to Sacramento was anticlimactic to Richard. He took a lunch, and there was much singing, and new country to see, but it was not more than a holiday outing to him — a happy but uneventful one. And one day Franklin D. Roosevelt was President of the United States, and another phase of Richard's life was over. The Unemployed Council was a thing of the past, and the big red barn was once more thrust into oblivion.

OSCAR "ZETA" ACOSTA

The Autobiography of
a Brown Buffalo

W ITH THUNDERING hoofbeats hammering and kicking whirlwinds of dust to my rear, I eat up the burning sands and concentrate on the white line, my only guide. Sacramento, Lake Tahoe and Shell stations. I pass up long-haired hitchhikers. I discard empty Budweisers along the trail just in case I lose my direction now that I am without my shrink, my guru and their magic. Tall buildings and rectangular slabs of pavement sink behind me as I dig my claws into the gas pedal of my green '65 Plymouth. With a head full of speed, a wilted penis and a can in my hand, my knuckles redden as I hold tightly to the wheel and plunge headlong over the mountains and into the desert in search of my past . . .

Although I was born in El Paso, Texas, I am actually a small-town kid. A hick from the sticks, a Mexican boy from the other side of the tracks. I grew up in Riverbank, California; post office box 303; population 3,969. It's the only town in the entire state whose essential numbers have remained unchanged. The sign that welcomes you as you round the curve coming in from Modesto says, "The City Of Action."

Manuel Mercado Acosta is an *indio* from the mountains of Durango. His father operated a mescal distillery before the revolutionaries drove him out. He met my mother while riding a motorcycle in El Paso.

Juana Fierro Acosta is my mother. She could have been a singer in a Juárez cantina but instead decided to be Manuel's wife because he had a slick mustache, a fast bike, and promised to take her out of the slums across from the Rio Grande. She had only one demand in return for the two sons and three daughters she would bear him: "No handouts. No relief. I never want to be on welfare."

I doubt he really promised her anything in a very loud, clear voice. My father was a horsetrader, even though he got rid of both the mustache and the bike when FDR drafted him, a wetback, into the U.S. Navy on June 22, 1943. He tried to get into the Marines, but when they found out he was a good swimmer and a noncitizen, they put him in a sailor suit and made him drive a barge in Okinawa.

We lived in a two-room shack without a floor. We had to pump our water and use kerosene if we wanted to read at night. But we never went hungry. My old man always bought the pinto beans and the white flour for the tortillas in one-hundred-pound sacks which my mother used to make dresses, sheets and curtains. We had two acres of land which we planted every year with corn, tomatoes and yellow chiles for the hot sauce. Even before my father woke us, my old ma was busy at work making the tortillas at 5 A.M. while he chopped the logs we'd hauled up from the river on the weekends.

Reveille was at 6 A.M. sharp for me and my older brother, Bob. Radio station KTRB came on the air each morning with "The Star-Spangled Banner." A shrill, foggy whistle woke us to the odors of crackling wood in the cast-iron stove cooking the perfectly rounded, soft, warm tortillas.

"All right, boys. Up and at 'em," the wiry *indio* calls out to me and Bob. Sleep is for the lazy, those whom my parents detest, the slow-minded types afraid of the sunlight. And so to prove my worth I'm always the first one to jump up, stand on the bed and place my hand respectfully over my heart — I'm only a civilian — to show my allegiance to my father's madness for a country that has given him a barge and a badge at Okinawa in exchange for an honorable discharge. And made him a citizen of the United States of America to boot.

After the salute we scramble to dress while on KTRB one of the Maddox brothers says to Rose, "Give us a great big smile, Rose." She giggles and they stomp away to an Okie beat. Roll call comes on the Acosta ship at exactly 6:10 on the button. My father waits for his crew outside. We stand in line, my brother, myself and my mother, who is trying to lose weight.

She has been on a diet all my life. She has a definite concern about people being overweight. She has nagged me and my sisters — my brother Bob was always skinny — until we all ended up with some doctor or another; but I stayed fat and she has always had a fine body, even sexy you might say.

After we eat our scrambled eggs and chorizo guzzled down with Mexican chocolate, we trudged through the well-worn paths across empty lots with wild wheat to Riverbank Grammar School, where I learned my p's and q's from Miss Anderson. At noon we ran down Patterson Road for lunch. Two miles in fifteen minutes flat. My mother was of the strict opinion that you cannot learn without a hot lunch in your stomach. So we were permitted exactly thirty minutes to finish up our daily fights at the old black oak tree. A tree with gnarled branches with small, corklike, burnt balls we used for floaters when we waited for catfish down at the river near the Catholic church, where the sisters taught us about sin and social politics.

Bob and I had to chop wood for the evening meal. We had to pump the water into tin tubs for our nightly bath. And unless we bathed and washed the dishes, we couldn't turn on the little brown radio to listen to *The Whistler*, *The Shadow*, or *The Saturday Night Hit Parade* with Andy Russell, the only Mexican I ever heard on the radio as a kid. We would sit and listen while we shined our shoes. During the commercials my mother would sing beautiful Mexican songs, which I then thought were corny, while she dried the dishes. "When you grow up, you'll like this music too," my ma always prophesied. In the summer of '67, as a buffalo on the run, I still thought Mexican music was corny.

Usually, my old man would wait until we got in bed before he gave us our nightly lectures. Then he'd pull out a blue-covered book they'd given him in the navy called *The Seabee's Manual*. It was the only book I ever saw him read. He used to say, "If you boys memorize this book, you'll be able to do anything you want." It showed you how to do things like tie fantastic knots, fix boilers on steamships and survive without food and water when lost at sea. Admittedly, it helped when I took my entrance exams into Boy Scout Troop 42, but it didn't offer any advice on how to get rid of ulcers or the ants in my stomach. Its primary wisdom was its advice against waste. The horsetrader was so hung up on this principal sin that once he made me go to bed without supper because I'd filled a glass with water when I required only half the precious liquid.

"Why can't you fill it halfway? Then if you want more, fill it about one fourth . . . et cetera," he'd tell us in total seriousness. To this day I get a twinge of guilt when I throw away water, leftovers and old clothes that I can't possibly use.

We used to go to the garbage dump down by the old aluminum plant, which to my knowledge never produced aluminum. Immediately after its construction Tojo and FDR got into it and the place was converted into a shell-casing plant. That event, along with the Riverbank Canning Company, placed Riverbank on the map. We had one of the three shell-casing plants in the country during the Second World War and the largest tomato paste cannery in the world.

We'd take a truckful of junk to the dump and spend the entire morning searching through the rotting, burning piles of trash, broken furniture, old clothes, busted tools and old family items, all of us in search of things that the horsetrader thought could still be saved under the rules of *The Seabee's Manual*. By the time we got done, the truck was as full as when we left. Then the singer and the *indio* would get into it. And when he'd turn his back to her, shake his head and say "You just don't understand," she'd start in on me and Bob. But she never contradicted him in our presence.

"You'd better do what your dad tells you, hijo," she'd warn us. Even when she knew it was madness, when she suspected he was suffering from shell shock, still she never disagreed with his instructions to his sons. She'd simply take another aspirin and sing

Mexican songs, dreaming maybe of what might have been had she not become a captain's wife.

Even the time he gave us the ultimate lesson on becoming "a man," she didn't say a word. We were all at the supper table. I was wolfing down hot, fresh corn with huge glasses of milk. I'd eat so fast that even when I dropped a piece of meat on the adobe floor or spilled the Kool-Aid, I wouldn't miss a stroke. He warned me of the effect it would have on both my character and my stomach. Every single night of my childhood, my folks bugged me about my speed. It got to where I even tried eating with my left hand to slow me down, but after three weeks I became ambidextrous and it wouldn't work anymore. I consoled myself with the idea that even though it didn't help my diet any, it would still be of use in case I ever got my right hand chopped off by the Japs.

That night my old man said, "If you can eat a spoonful of your mother's chile, I'll give you a penny."

I looked at my brother. He wasn't about to take up the challenge. He didn't pay as much attention to my dad as I did. For some reason, he wasn't that interested in becoming a man.

"Right away? A penny for every spoonful?" The six-year-old kid said.

"Don't you trust me?"

My brother merely laughed when he saw the tears running down my fat, brown cheeks after the third spoonful. But I proved my point. I never backed off from any challenge.

My mother just shook her head. She disapproved of his madness. She even tried to imagine there might be some mystery that she, as a mere woman, couldn't understand.

Frugality and competition were their lot. The truth of it was they both conspired to make men out of two innocent Mexican boys. It seemed that the sole purpose of childhood was to train boys how to be men. Not men of the future, but *now*. We had to get up early, run home from school, work on weekends, holidays and during vacations, all for the purpose of being men. We were supposed to talk like *un hombre*, walk like a man, act like a man and think like a man. When they called us from the corner lot to play keep-away, we couldn't go until we finished pulling weeds from the garden. And while the gang gathered behind the grocery store to smoke cigarette butts, we had to shine our shoes and read *The Seabee's Manual*. In fact, the only times we could read funny books was when my father was in the navy. Nothing would infuriate him more than to catch us browsing through *Captain Marvel* or *Plastic Man*. Men, after all, didn't waste their time reading funny books. Men, he'd tell us, took life seriously. Nothing could be learned from books that were funny.

I used to think that only my father was mad. I doubted that the fathers of my friends in the barrio taught them the same things. But one day I learned differently. Walking home from school on a Tuesday afternoon, I spit on the picture of an American flag. It was Victory Stamp Day. We used to save them the way some people collect green stamps.

We had been lectured by Miss Anderson on the art of self-preservation in case of an enemy attack. Although she spoke strictly about the Japanese, I always pictured the real enemy as not only a kamikaze with the red rising sun on his wings, but also some old man with an enormous fountain pen who sent printed letters to the poor families living in small towns. FDR was as much my enemy as were the Japs. After all, it was he, not Tojo, who drafted my old man. He's the one who made my mother and my brother cry for a whole month after we drove my dad down to the post office. He's the one who took a razor blade and cut out entire sentences from the little letters that looked like telegrams that my father wrote us from Okinawa, Iwo Jima and Tarawa. And when my father said *they* hadn't told him how much longer he'd have to drive the barge, we knew he referred to FDR, not Tojo.

So you have eight ragtag ten-year-old brown-baked Mexican boys marching single file along the curb in front of the old PT&T. Oscar sees a leaflet with the picture of the American flag. He spits!

"Hey, look what Oscar did," Johnny Gomez tells the others. He stands back, points to the leaflet as if it were some snake. The others circle around and shake their heads.

"What'd you do that for?" his brother David demands of me.

"Why not? It's just a picture," I explain.

"That's the American flag, stupid!"

"So what?"

"So don't do it no more."

"Why? You gonna make me?"

David beat the shit out of me. While I dusted my pants off and wiped the blood from my elbows, they all laughed at me.

"You ain't so tough," the short little Indian said to me.

"Oh, yeh?" He got on top of me and pinned my arms to the ground with his knees. I had to give up . . . but only to start again with Alfonso when he said I was a chicken. As things turned out, I had to fight each of them that afternoon. I lost every single fight.

The seven whipped my ass on that day that I spit on the picture of my father's flag. I have never, to this day, had any respect for that flag or that country. You can blame it on my childhood experiences. Politics has nothing to do with it. I have no ideology. I've been an outlaw out of practical necessity ever since. And I have never backed off from a fight.

My old man taught me to fight dirty. He said, "Don't start anything. But if you have to fight, don't fool around. Pick up a stick, a rock or anything that's hard. You hit them on the head a few times and they'll never pick on you again."

He bought us boxing gloves and a punching bag for Christmas. After a while, none of the guys in the neighborhood my age wanted to come over and work out. Years later, as a senior in high school, I won the heavyweight boxing championship by hitting Harry Greene below the belt until he couldn't stand up. When his manager ran into the ring to protest, I punched him too. Some of his followers chased me into the locker room after they gave me the medal. I picked up a track shoe with spikes and held them at bay until my football coach, Joe Sigfried, ordered them out.

Living in Riverbank was no different from living in a strange, foreign town. I was an outsider then as much as I am now. Particularly during the first three years, Bob and I had to defend ourselves against the meanest and toughest boys on the list because we were considered "easterners." They said we weren't *real* Mexicans because we wore long, black patent leather boots and short pants, which my mother bought for us in Juárez just before we boarded the Greyhound bus to join up with my father, who'd left the year before to seek the riches of California's golden peach orchards.

California, then, was a land of *pochos*. These California Mexicans were not much higher than the Okies with whom they lived. They spoke English most of the time, while we looked upon life "out west" simply as a temporary respite from the Depression. The five bucks a week my old man earned as a mechanic in El Paso hadn't been quite enough to satisfy my mother's dreams. She wanted a sewing machine, a house with electricity and running water. She never dreamed of actually owning a house; she just wanted to live in one with all the modern conveniences she read about in the Sears, Roebuck catalogue. So, when we left El Segundo Barrio across the street from the international border, we didn't expect the Mexicans in California to act like *gringos*.

But they did. We were outsiders because of geography, and outcasts because we didn't speak English and wore short pants. And so we had to fight every single day. Until the day Bob beat up Jimmy Pacheco, the youngest of a bunch of Apaches who lived on the edge of the barrio with ten brothers and about seven dogs. They were the only ones in the entire neighborhood that had a wire fence around their property. They were always slaughtering pigs and goats and young bulls, getting drunk on tequila and drinking raw blood with fresh onions. But one day Bob grabbed Jimmy by the wrist and flung him against the trunk of an old black oak tree, and that was that. Jimmy didn't fool anyone with the long-sleeved shirts he wore for weeks after the incident. We all knew he had a cast underneath. Generally, the *pochos* quit picking on us after that. Not that they accepted us as part of their tribe, but they simply quit fucking with us. I never had to fight a Mexican again until I joined the revolution some thirty years later.

The fight with Pacheco didn't end the war, however. Our biggest battlefront opened at seven-thirty in the morning at the railroad tracks which marked the edge of Okie Town. At night and on weekends we fought the Mexicans in the neighborhood, but during the day and at school we had to fight off the Okies. We had an unspoken rule that you never fought one of your own kind in front of others. In the battle for group survival you simply don't weaken your defenses by getting involved in family squabbles in front of the real enemy.

We had to fight the Okies because we were Mexicans! It didn't matter to them that my brother and I were outcasts on our own turf. They'd have laughed if we'd told them that we were easterners. To them we were greasers, spics and niggers. If you lived on the West Side, across from the tracks, and had brown skin, you were a Mexican.

Riverbank is divided into three parts, and in my corner of the world there were only three kinds of people: Mexicans, Okies and Americans. Catholics, Holy Rollers and Protestants. Peach pickers, cannery workers and clerks.

We lived on the West Side, within smelling distance of the world's largest tomato paste cannery. With its hordes of flies and the ugly stench of rotting waste on hot summer days, the West Side was tucked a safe distance from the center of town, where the Americans lived. Every home had a garden, at least a rosebush or two, and if nothing else a couple of chickens. We grew vegetables not for victory but for survival during the frosted, tully-fogged winter months after the peaches, walnuts, tomatoes, grapes and olives had been picked. And long before it became fashionable for the American women to plant flowers and lemon trees in cute little bonnets and white gloves, the Mexican women were watering their roses and chile plants on Saturday mornings while we went to our catechism classes at the Lady of Guadalupe.

The West Side is still enclosed by the Santa Fe Railroad tracks to the east, the Modesto–Oakdale highway to the north and the irrigation canal to the south. Within that concentration only Mexicans were safe from the neighborhood dogs, who responded only to Spanish commands. Except for Bob Whitt and Emitt Brown, both friends of mine who could cuss in better Spanish than I, I never saw a white person walking the dirt roads of our neighborhood.

If you climb the water tower next to the railroad depot, you can see Okie Town to the east. Riverbank is flat, farming country. Except for the bank and the Masonic lodge, there are no three-story dwellings or structures for miles around. I always wanted to climb that aluminum-colored, ten-thousand-gallon water storage tank, but Harry March, who owned the five-and-dime, always warned against it. He looked like John L. Lewis and sold us cigarettes if we scribbled a note and pretended it was from our parents. I used to ask for Wings and sign my father's name, even though we both knew he was away in the navy. "If they catch you, they'll put you in the hoosegow," he'd tell us when we stopped by on the way home from school for our afternoon ice cream cone.

One day I couldn't wait anymore to do my part for the war effort Miss Anderson kept talking about. I wanted my father home because my mother was going crazy. She ate nothing but aspirins and oranges, drank black coffee and beat us with belts, rubber hoses, ice hooks. Even though I'd sort of taken over the family at the age of ten, got to zip up my mother's dresses when she dressed for the cannery and had the final word on whether my sisters could go to the movies, still I wanted the sailor back home.

The headlines of the *Modesto Bee* made us cry every day, even when Mr. McClatchy said we'd pounded the daylights out of the Japs. The constant flow of mile-long troop trains with soldiers herded in like cattle was a daily reminder of my uselessness as a civilian. We'd go down to the railroad and wave at the brave men headed for San Francisco on their way to fight the Japs. They'd give us pennies and nickels and once in a while ask us to bring our sisters to say hello. Mine was practically still in diapers, so I couldn't offer much of that.

I had even taken to looking for the red cellophane strips from Lucky Strike packs, which Harry March had told us could be exchanged for German shepherd Seeing Eye dogs for the crippled veterans. After a year I had only two hundred of them. I'd had enough arithmetic to know that at that rate I'd be picking up dirty, empty cigarette packs for five more years. We tried to save newspapers, but it didn't amount to much. And I knew it would take the rest of my life to save ten pounds of tinfoil from Juicy Fruit and the insides of the cigarette packs.

So one day I finally made my decision to join the resistance. I climbed to the top of the lily tree in our backyard. This tree with the purple blossoms and little green balls the size of steelies — the best marble you can pick for playing fish — this was my own personal, private place. Bob was the owner of the eucalyptus tree, and we all shared the fruits of the plum, the fig and the almond trees; but no one could climb my lily tree without my permission.

I carry my pump-action .22 strapped to my shoulder as I carefully and quietly climb the thirty-foot-tall sniper post. The enemy planes fly day and night over this land. I just have to wait. Gary Cooper didn't complain when he had to sit in that tree with the Japs marching underneath, the flies and gnats driving him crazy in that hot, steaming jungle, did he? . . . I hear the drone in the distance. I close my eyes. You can tell by the hum of the motor whose side he's on. And when it is overhead I take careful aim. I know it *looks* like a P-38, but that's a disguise . . . I shoot.

I wait for it to fall, but somehow it keeps flying toward the aluminum plant . . . I wipe the sweat from my brow and think it through again. What would Coop do in this situation? I have only one bullet left. One shot. Do I wait for another plane? Of course they heard the blast from my rifle. Soon they'll be here. I'm not afraid of the torture. I can take anything, remember? But a man has to destroy any target, any supply of war material, do anything that will hurt the Nips. It doesn't have to be a moving target. It doesn't have to be a human . . .

And there it sits, big as day. No more than one block from my scope is the infamous water tower. The whole town depends upon it. Cut off their water supply and you'll have them in the palm of your hand in a week. Does the Geneva Convention actually prohibit sniper action against the civilian population? What would Miss Anderson say about this? Fuck it! I've got to help my father get home any way that I can. After all, *this is war!* Surely God will understand even if the sisters don't. Look at Humphrey Bogart. He's still alive, isn't he? And how many has he snuffed out? I squeeze the trigger and close my eyes.

Two days later I take a casual stroll to the railroad depot. Just going down to say hello to the troops, I tell my ma. For two whole days and nights I've not even dared to look toward the east. It's bad luck to look for death and destruction. No one's mentioned it, but I've been certain all weekend that the entire population will soon be dying of thirst. The fact that our faucet keeps pumping clear water doesn't throw me; I know they're on the spare tank now. By tomorrow it'll be all over with.

Without looking up, I stand under the palm trees in the little park behind the Santa Fe depot. When I'm certain no one is watching, I look up toward the water tank. I squint my eyes to see the damage. I look for evidence of a flood. Something. It's possible, of course, that they already dried it out, sucked the water up with some huge pump. Good soldiers always hide their true battle conditions. Besides, how can I really be sure? I haven't binoculars to be positive. I'll merely report it as an "attempt." I didn't do it for any goddamn Purple Heart anyway! The old man will simply have to take my word for it. He knows I never lie to him. He knows perfectly well I've never lied to him since that day he hung me from a rafter in the chicken coop.

We had been pulling weeds from the tomatoes. My young uncle Hector started it all. He threw the first rock at Bob. My brother thought it was me and threw a clod the size of a pumpkin. The captain warned us twice. The third time he ordered us inside. Before he found a belt, some Americans stopped by to purchase some corn. We sold it for fifty cents a dozen, and put in an extra one in case you found one with worms. While the horsetrader picked the corn from the stalks, Hector talked us into stuffing newspapers under our V-8's. "Don't forget to pretend when he hits us," my uncle said . . . Well, I blew it. I forgot. I should have rubbed onions in my eyes.

When the captain discovered the sports pages of the *Modesto Bee* under my shorts, he asked, "Okay, you cheaters, whose idea was it?"

Shit, not even my old man can make me talk once I've made up my mind. I am loyal to the core. Even when he marched us to the chicken coop under the plum tree, did you see me cry? When he made the three of us stand on that four-by-four, tied the rope around our necks, did you hear me beg for mercy?

"When you're ready to talk, I'll cut you down," he said.

Even when he walked out, leaving us there to die, I said nothing. Despite the fact I was the youngest of the three, you didn't see me holding up any white flag of surrender. Though as the blood curdled in my legs, even cramps of electrical shocks up my spine didn't do a thing. I knew my mother would find us with our tongues hanging out when she came for the eggs in the morning. And when that mean bantam rooster pecked at my feet, when we could no longer hear my father's voice outside, you still didn't hear me cry, did you?

It was Hector who chickened out and called for help. "Manuel, you better cut me down or I'll tell 'Ama." Who knows how long the captain would have let us hang if Hector hadn't been his kid brother? Whatever influence or authority Hector had over me because he was my uncle and five years older, he lost it that afternoon in the chicken coop. And but for his lack of character, I'd probably have never started on those nasty habits in the shower.

During the summers we used to pick peaches. My father would challenge the three of us to a race. If Bob, Hector and me could pick more lugs of peaches than the captain, he'd buy us a water-melon and take us to the canal after work. We always lost because we took an hour for lunch while the old man kept picking away, but he took us to swim anyway. The sweltering heat and the itching peach fuzz didn't bother Indians like him. But laggards and sissies such as we were had to plunge and dip and show off in front of girls at the canal during the lunch hour to feel better.

If it hadn't been for my fatness, I'd probably have been able to do those fancy-assed jackknifes and swan dives as well as the rest of you. But my mother had me convinced I was obese, ugly as a pig and without any redeeming qualities whatsoever. How then could I run around with just my Jockey shorts? V-8's don't hide fat, you know. That's why I finally started wearing boxers. But by then it was too late. Everyone knew I had the smallest prick in the world. With the girls watching and giggling, the guys used to sing my private song to the tune of "Little Bo Peep": "Oh, where, oh where can my little boy be? Oh, where, oh where can he be? He's so chubby, panson, that he can't move along. Oh, where, oh where can he be?"

I tried like hell to stop eating ice cream and tortillas with mayonnaise, but I still always stayed five or ten pounds overweight. And no matter what I did or what I thought, even when I asked the Virgin Mary to make me a man and give me at least a bit of pubic hair, still my prick was an inch or two smaller than all the rest.

In fact, if it hadn't been for Vernon Knecht, I might have remained the deformed freak that I was to this day. He was a big, red-headed German kid who taught me how to leave markings on trees and traffic arrows made of rocks when I studied for my merit badges with Troop 42. When I was twelve, we went on a hiking and camping weekend with our fag Boy Scout leader out at the Oakdale Reservoir, and I was instructed to be Vernon's *buddy.* In case you drowned, got lost or were attacked by Indians, you were supposed to have a buddy. Since Vernon was a First Class Scout and about three years older, the Tenderfoot that I was leaned on his every word. So that night, under the pup tent while the summer rain kept us all inside, I asked him how to make the bugger grow.

"Shit, you mean you don't know how to jack off?"

"You mean pull it?" I asked my guide.

He whipped out his long, white dick and said, "Yeh, man. Push and pull . . . just like this."

When Hector, brother Bob and cousin Manuel used to make fun of my obesity and little penis, I would yell through my teeth, "At least I don't pull it." They always got a kick out of that and called me a liar. I had to show them the palms of both my hands to prove that I didn't masturbate.

"You see any warts?" I'd ask.

So that weekend at the Oakdale Reservoir, I told Vernon Knecht, "I don't want to do anything dirty. I haven't made my confirmation yet."

"What do you mean?" the German infidel asked.

"Shit, man, how would you confess that to a priest? You think he'd believe me if I told him I did it to make it grow?"

"Well, fuck, man. Just don't tell him."

I lost most of my religion the same night I learned about sex from old Vernon. When I saw the white, foamy suds come from under his foreskin, I thought he had wounded himself from yanking on it too hard with those huge farmer hands of his. And when I saw his green eyes fall back into his head, I thought he was having some sort of a seizure like I'd seen Toto, the village idiot, have out in his father's fig orchard after he fucked a chicken.

I didn't much like the sounds of romance the first time I saw jizz.

I knew that Vernon was as tough as they came. Nothing frightened or threatened him. He'd cuss right in front of John Hazard, our fag Boy Scout leader, as well as Miss Anderson. But when I heard him oooh and aaah as the soapsuds spit at his chest while we lay on our backs inside the pup tent, I wondered for a minute if sex wasn't actually for sissies. I tried to follow his example, but nothing would come out. With him cheering me on, saying, "Harder, man. Pull on that son of a bitch. Faster, faster!" it just made matters worse. The thing went limp before the soapsuds came out.

He advised me to try it more often. "Don't worry, man. It'll grow if you work on it."

When I got home the next day, my mother wouldn't let me in the kitchen until I cleaned up. I was starving from being on pork and beans all weekend, so I hurried into the shower.

Maybe if I put soap on it, just to warm up, I said to myself.

Sure enough, the bugger's big spit jumped in my eyes for the first time in my life. Every time I've heard the saying about cleanliness being next to godliness, I really get a bang.

Songs of Self-Discovery

EDWARD RIVERA

First Communion

I SPENT the first grade of school under Luisa Lugones ("Mees Lugones"), the first-grade teacher of Bautabarro, who never laid a hand on anybody. She might hug one of her thirty-something students for standing out in class, but hit one of her neighbors' children for whatever infraction, never. "That's not what I get paid to do," she used to say. (She earned a couple of dollars a week, maybe less.) She took any complaints against you to your father and mother, or your guardians if you were an orphan, and let them handle the situation, which she explained, in front of you, briefly and honestly. If your parents wanted details, she gave them the details, in a serious but not morbid way and without dramatics or sermons. If they wanted to make a big deal out of it, that was their business, and your misfortune, part of the price you had to pay for disturbing her class. It was a well-run class.

I was doubly lucky, because Papi had taken off for New York years before I started school, so I escaped getting it from him during that year I spent in the first grade. Not that I gave Mees Lugones much reason to complain about me. She chose to do it only once, the time I got into a fight with Antonio Carretas. My adopted brother, Chuito, had instigated it when I told him Antonio had stolen a piece of buttered bread Chuito had bought me that morning for lunch. As usual, whenever he could get away from his peon's job, Chuito had waited for me outside the schoolhouse — the same site my father and uncle Mito had tried turning into a general store — and walked home with me.

"You look a little hungry today, Santos," he told me. "Anemic. Tomorrow I'll buy you a two-cents piece of bread. I'll tell Arsenio to smear extra butter on it." He was on good terms with Arsenio Pagán, the eight-fingered grocer.

"I didn't eat that bread you gave me, Chuito," I confessed. "That's why I'm anemic today."

"You lost it? A serpent got to it before you did?"

"Antonio Carretas took it. He stole it."

He threw up his hands. "Jesus Christ! It runs in his family, that little punk. They're all crooks. *Ladrones maricones.* Even the grandfather. He's still stealing chickens when you turn your back on them." And one of the Carretas brothers had stolen a good-looking girl from under Chuito's nose. He couldn't come right out and hit the thief for that kind of theft, but he had it in for him; he was waiting for any excuse to get him. "And you didn't grab that piece of bread back from that little cowshit?" he asked me.

"I couldn't. He ate it all up right away. In one swallow. You should have seen his mouth."

"I'll tell you how I want to see his mouth tomorrow, Santos. Without teeth. All gums. And you're going to be his dentist. Let me see your right fist." I made a tight fist and showed it to him. "Fine," he said. "Maybe it's not as big as Antonio's mouth, but it's big enough to destroy it. No?"

Under the circumstances, yes. I should have kept my mouth shut about that piece of bread. Too late. I'd have to fight Antonio for it, and for Chuito's grievance over that stolen anonymous girl.

He took the rest of that afternoon off to give me "special lessons" on how to destroy Antonio Carretas next morning. We had to do it a good distance from the house, because Mami wanted nothing to do with violence and would have given us no end of hell, and no dinner that night, if she had caught us working out (situps, pushups, side-to-side twists, squats, chinning from branches, jogging up and down hills, swinging the arms windmill fashion to, as he put it, "loosen up your muscles, Santos") and sparring. He cautioned me against leading with my right — or maybe my left; I couldn't remember which next morning, after a night of uneasy dreams, and too much breakfast "for stamina" — and when I walked up to Antonio Carretas outside the school-shack, tapped him on the shoulder, and took a good swing at his mouth when he turned around, I missed. Not by much, but with someone like Antonio you didn't have to miss by much to lose the fight. He caught me on the nose right away — if his big mouth was an "easy" target, so was my oversized nose — and drew blood. He hadn't needed a workout or an extra serving of breakfast to put me out of contention. And he took the two-cents piece of extra-buttered bread Chuito had bought me that morning. He ran off with it before Mees Lugones arrived on the scene of my defeat, my second in two days.

She told one of the other students to go pick a handful of medicinal grass for my nose and took me inside the shack, where I had to lie on her two-plank desk, flat on my back and feeling pretty demolished, circled by about twenty-eight fellow students of both sexes, for about thirty minutes. It took the medicinal grass that long to stop the flow of blood from my swollen nose. She and a couple of students had taken turns chewing the grass into compresses, one to a nostril, with frequent changes of compress, before the flow let up and finally stopped.

"I wouldn't go into boxing if I were you, Santos," Chuito was to tell me that night (our beds adjoined). "I think you're the kind that's going to need a friend or a weapon when you get into trouble with the Antonio Carretases of this shitty world." The day before my defeat, he had called it "the greatest world ever invented" and even gave God some credit for it. Now it was a shitty world all of a sudden. He had some confusions to straighten out.

And Mees Lugones, without giving me a sermon on decent behavior and other moralities, took me home after class let out for that day. "By swinging at Antonio first, you put yourself in the wrong, Santos" was all she told me on the walk home, trailed by all my fellow students except Antonio Carretas, who had made himself scarce.

Chuito had been spying on us from behind the bushes all along. He had seen me get it in the nose and failed to show himself all morning; and unknown to any of us, he followed us all the way home and stayed within easy reach, hiding until it was time for him to come back from "work" in my grandfather's fields. Papagante reported his absence to Mami next day, and he had to make up a quick lie to get out of it. I don't think they were taken in by it — he wasn't a good liar; his lips always shook when he wasn't being honest — but there was nothing they could do about it. He was on his own.

So I was the one who ended up paying the price for his unsuccessful revenge on the Carretas brother who had swiped his sweetheart. "I don't think it was all Santos's fault, Doña Lilia," Mees Lugones told Mami (she was older than Mami). "But — well, I don't want to preach, but just take a look at him. His poor nose."

"Poor nose, nothing," Mami said. She must have been trying to sound as Papi would have if he had been there to take charge. "If it stays swollen like that, he may keep out of trouble the rest of his life and live longer." Then she thanked Mees Lugones and walked out with her as far as our chicken coop, where four hens were keeping our breakfast eggs warm.

She was applying a damp rag to my nose when Chuito got back from his labors, put on a startled look to disguise his guilt — taking it for granted I wasn't going to rat on him — and said, after shaking his head, "It'll come off by itself, Mami." He was talking about the blood that had caked in my nostrils. "It's *dry* blood. Let him suffer a little." He couldn't hold back a big grin.

"Get out!" she told him. "I'll call you when it's time to eat." But when she stepped out and called him, about an hour later, he was gone off somewhere.

Less than a year after I graduated from Mees Lugones's class, I was enrolled in St. Misericordia's Academy for Boys and Girls, a parochial school in East Harlem, on the advice of our next-door neighbors, whose daughter and son were in the sixth and seventh grades at "St. Miseria's," as they called the school. So did I, after a while.

It turned out to be a very strict institution. Penalties galore. Maybe that was why our neighbors in apartment 19 had enrolled their kids there: for discipline — *fuetazos*, whiplashings, as the husband called it — and not for a good education and an old-fashioned religious "indoctrination," as our priests and teachers called it. Whatever it was, it was way beyond what my future public-school friends got: next to nothing, except for sports and a way with girls that left us "parochials" in the dust.

Another advantage the "publics" had over us was that their teachers couldn't lay a hand on them. By law. The opposite was true in St. Miseria's. The law there seemed to be that if your teacher didn't let you have it good from time to time, there was something morally wrong with him or her. It was as if our hands had been made for the Cat's Paw rubber strap that could leave the imprint of a winking, smiling cat on your palm, or the twelve-inch metal-edged ruler (centimeters on one side, inches on the other) that could draw blood from your knuckles if you acted up once your mother delivered you into "their" hands at 8:30 A.M. in front of the church, where you began the day with mass.

Just as bad as corporal punishment — or worse, because it made you feel like a rat on the run from hell for a long time afterward — was the message they gave you about losing your soul if you persisted in sinning. Meaning you hadn't done your homework by Catholic standards, or had talked out of turn in class; in fact, almost anything they decided wasn't "right" or — as Sister Mary McCullough, our principal, used to put it, with her eyebrows bunched up and her lips pursed — anything that did not "redound to the greater honor and glory of Holy Mother." "Holy Mother" was always Church. The other mother, the Mother of our Lord, was usually referred to as Our Blessed Mother or Blessed Mary or Holy Virgin. She had lots of nicknames. She was seldom called simply Mary. That might encourage vulgar liberties, abusive adjectives.

There was something both cold-hearted and generous about our nuns that gave at least some of us reason to be grateful our parents had signed us up at St. Miseria's. Sister Mary Felicia, for example. Third grade. The nicest thing Sister Felicia did for me was buy me an unused First Communion outfit in the Marqueta on Park Avenue when she found out I was a welfare case. She didn't have to do that, because Papi somehow always found a way to scrounge up the funds for whatever we needed. I think he had credit everywhere, though he wasn't one to abuse it. But Sister didn't bother consulting him or Mami about their resources. Maybe my plain Third Avenue clothes and my apologetic look gave her the impression we were in such bad shape at home that Papi couldn't put out the money for a cheap Communion outfit: a white shirt without a label inside the collar, a pair of Thom McAn shoes (blisters guaranteed) that expanded like John's Bargain Store sponges as soon as it rained, and an even cheaper Howard Clothes suit with a vest and a big label over the jacket's wallet pocket, so that whenever a man opened up that jacket and reached inside for his wallet, others could see he was moving up in this world. No more Third Avenue cheap stuff for this *elemento*. Unless he had somehow stolen that label and had his wife the seamstress sew it onto the wallet pocket just to impress the kind of people who kept an eye on labels. If Sister Felicia was one of those types, she kept it to herself. All she wanted was for every boy and girl in her class to show up at First Communion ceremonies in a prescribed, presentable outfit: the girls in white, the boys in black, with an oversized red ribbon around the elbow.

"Making your First Communion," Mami told me in private one day when she was in a joking mood, "is almost as important as making your first caca all by yourself."

"So why do I have to wear this uniform, then?" I said, confused.

"Because it's a ceremony. The most important of your life so far. Except for baptism. It's like when you get married for the first time." Meaning what, I didn't know or ask. And what was this about people getting married more than once? Another joke? Sometimes she went over my head and didn't explain the point. Some things I should find out for myself, I guessed. You can't always be depending on your mother to fill you in. She wouldn't even tell me how she felt about Sister Felicia's generosity.

At the time it may have been a nice favor on Sister's part — and on Sister Principal's, because she was the one who dispensed their funds — putting out all that money for a kid on ADC. For one thing, they were Irish, all of them, so why should they give a damn for people like me? But they did sometimes. More confusion on my side. And a long time later, when I thought back on it, I was still confused.

One afternoon, after the last class bell, Sister told me and a couple of other classmates not to leave the room because she wanted to talk to us about something important. Right away I figured she was going to bleed our knuckles with her twelve-incher for something, some sin we had committed unawares. Unawares was no excuse. Happened all the time in St. Miseria's. I started going over all the things I'd said and done that day in public, and then in private, and I couldn't come up with a single sin. Which didn't mean a thing. The nuns knew a lot better than you did what a sin was and wasn't; they'd had technical training in those things, and they didn't miss a thing. Almost every day somebody got extra homework for daydreaming in class, or the knuckles job for laughing at something serious somebody had said, or for picking his or her nose in public. That's what Marta Cuevas had done the week before I got my outfit. She was good-looking, too. She was short and hefty, she had a good profile, and she sat in the first row, right up there where every move you made was seen by everyone else, especially by Sister, who used to pace back and forth, with an open book in one hand and the twelve-inch ruler in the other, from the exit (closed) to the window (open just a crack for fresh oxygen). And she, Marta, nervous because Sister was going to call on her next, forgot the rule about picking your nose and committed that infraction right under Sister's own nose. She must have thought she was back home or something; in a dark movie, where nobody noticed what you were doing with your hands.

Sister shut her mouth in the middle of a question, placed her book face down on her desk — her hands were shaking — and put a difficult question to Marta: where had she learned such repulsive manners? Certainly not in school — hinting that in Marta's home personal habits were still primitive. One could just imagine, if one had that kind of stomach, what their table manners must be like, and what kind of "meals" they sat down to, if they bothered to sit at all. They probably all ate standing, or squatting right there on the kitchen floor, like their ancestors the Caribs, cannibalistic Indians from the jungles of South America (we had read about them already during the history hour; they ate their enemies raw). The only fire they knew anything about came from Huracán, their thunder god. She went on to tell us that the Caribs hadn't even discovered friction, that's how primitive they were. It was the Europeans, the Spaniards, who had brought them friction, the True Faith, and other forms of Christian civilization.

"The word *friction* comes from the Latin *fricare*, children," she said. "And when you rub two dry sticks or stones or bodies of certain things together, if you do it long enough and briskly enough, you produce fire. And fire is necessary for cooking and warmth."

She went on to demonstrate friction by rubbing her index fingers together. Briskly. I had seen a magician do the same thing in a movie, and it had worked. His fingers — all ten of them — went up in flames. I had tried it myself, and it hadn't worked. I knew I was no magician. I'd have to stick to matches. And now Sister Felicia was trying it herself, and it wasn't working, either. No flames. Not even sparks. So she stopped rubbing, looked around at no one, embarrassed for a few seconds, and said, "It doesn't always work, boys and girls. My hands are cold this morning." She began slapping her cold hands, as if to wipe off the failure of her friction magic. "No fire this time," she said, smiling. Then she became serious again. "Now open up your catechisms" — the Baltimore edition — "to page forty-three. Briskly, briskly." I felt let down and confused. And she never mentioned friction again in class.

But there was another kind of friction going on in our class all the time, and Marta Cuevas, who had no answer to Sister's tough question on her repulsive nose-picking, was demonstrating it. All she could do just then was stare up at Sister — I had a good view of her attractive cannibal profile — with a paralyzed, agonized look.

"Stand up, Marta Cuevas!" Sister commanded — boomed. She could have scared the loincloth off Huracán himself.

Marta stood up as if stone-faced José Bosquez, sitting right behind her, had given her the biggest goose of her life so far — and it wasn't likely she'd be getting another one like it soon — and before Sister asked her to, she put out her hand, the right one (she knew which one was going to get it), and made a tight fist, with her thumb curled outward and wagging away like the classy-looking stump of a fancy dog's former tail. Her fingernails needed trimming, too. This kid descended from pagans had a lot to learn. With her free hand she had to hold the other hand by the wrist, because it kept shaking so much, this hand that got it, that Sister swung and missed the first and third times she took a cut at it with her ruler. Marta didn't scream, thank God. And when it was all over she just sat back down, her jaw clenched as tight as she could make it, and dropped a few tears on her open book, a reader about a group of boys and girls, Jean and Paul, Monique and Simone, who lived in a place called Timber Town up in French Canada. From time to time Marta sneaked her right hand up to her mouth, unclenched her jaw, and blew on her knuckles. Sister pretended not to notice. She didn't even call on her the rest of the day. So in a way Marta got herself off the hook, because I don't think she had studied too much the night before. Probably spent her homework hours reading comic books. *The Living Hulk, Wonder Woman, Heart Throb* — enough to corrupt "an idle brain," as Sister said.

So as far as I could tell, when Sister asked a handful of us to stay behind after class let out that day, we had violated some rule and were going to get it, a mass purge, or "purgation," a word the sisters liked to throw around, the way Father Rooney back in church liked to throw around Latin things like *Dominus vobiscum* and *Hoc est* my body and blood, before the pope said you had to use English in church and spoiled the whole mystery. "Gave the whole game away, Gino," I heard one of the ushers say to another usher in church one Sunday.

But I was wrong about Sister's intentions. "We're going to purchase your First Communion outfits, boys and girls," Sister Felicia told us. Now she was smiling. A fine smile, too. They took good care of their teeth in that order. And all we could do was look at each other in wonder. First they hit you and make certain embarrassing hints about your family habits and your man-eating ancestors, and then they treat you to a free purchase of clothes. The whole bunch of us had a lot to learn about these women, and a lot to be grateful for as well. Not that we had much choice, but still . . .

Six boys and girls and two nuns. One of the girls was Marta Cuevas, who wasn't crying anymore or bringing her fingers anywhere near her nose, no sign on her face that she'd been "purgated" that very morning in front of the public. We split up as soon as we hit the first Marqueta stall on 110th and Park, where a pandemonium of merchants sold a mixed bag of merchandise: tropical products (mostly starchy tubers), religious articles (plastic and plaster statuettes and badly reproduced prints of wonder-working saints), "botanical" herbs with healing properties (Mami had a few back home, but they never healed anything from what I could tell; they just smelled up the house), voodoo pamphlets and recipes, evil-looking effigies with stringy hair, and charms for secret rituals of one kind or another. But that was only a fraction of the merchandise you could buy in those stalls. There was an immense assortment of private wear, too, most of it for women and girls: girdles, brassieres, skirts, blouses, panties; nylon stockings in every possible shade; slippers, plain or with bright-colored pompons over the toes; bathing suits, one-piece outfits for girls of all ages, or for women who could still fit into a girl's size and didn't mind looking like a case of arrested development; teenage girls' jumpers; widows' black shawls, chintzy mantillas for that special Spanish look, happily married women's polka-dot neckerchiefs, head kerchiefs of all kinds and colors; and a lot of other stuff, including smoked, boiled, and uncooked pork.

One of the stands we passed was displaying the close-shaved head of a pig with bent ears that had lost their pink — maybe it was embalmed to retard spoilage. It was wearing a sailor's cap on a slant, a pair of smoked glasses, and a red bow tie, and in its mouth the owner had stuck a half-smoked cigar, the long, thin panatela type. On the cap the embalmer had pinned a message in red: "Eat Me, Im' Delishious." Moses would have passed out.

"That man can't spell," said Sister Felicia, and turned her head away. The rest of her train, three boys, followed her timidly, no smiles. I was feeling a little snobbish about that man's lousy spelling. Here was a grown man, probably the father of half a dozen or more, and he didn't know where to put his apostrophe. This was the kind of father who handed down his ignorance to his children, and then they would pass it on to theirs and drive women like Sister Felicia out of their minds. She was looking mad, too, but under control, tolerant, long-suffering. And she was leading us through the mobs of shoppers at a fast clip. A lot of them, mostly mothers and their kids, made way for us when they saw her coming toward them with that long-suffering, angry look on her face. Their own surprised faces would turn serious all of a sudden, and they'd step out of our way and follow us with frightened eyes. Nobody was going to mess with us as long as we stuck close to her, this woman who was going to spend money on us even though the Sisters of Misericordia were always on a tight budget.

They carried all their funds for the day in a little black purse made of leather, or something that looked just like leather, with a silver-looking snap at the top; they kept it inside their plackets, the mysterious innards of their long plain gowns, and they always cast a cautious scan around them whenever they reached inside the placket for the purse. You could never tell who was a thief. One of the boys in my class had sneaked back inside the classroom once during lunch hour and stolen a red and white magnet she had confiscated from another student, who had been applying it to the head of the girl sitting in front of him. His excuse, when Sister caught him, was that he had been looking for lice in that girl's hair. He found a few, too, he said, but that didn't get him off the hook. And the other one, the one who sneaked upstairs and stole the magnet, was caught by Sister Mary Monitor, as we called whichever nun was guarding the stairs that day. They made him bring in his parents next day for a good dressing-down — all three of them were dressed down — and if the parents hadn't apologized with all their might, their son would have been expelled, exiled to public school, which as we saw it was as close as you could come to perdition before actually dying with all your sins confessed. "Let that be a lesson," Sister Felicia had told the rest of us, just in case we had missed the point. We hadn't.

Now she was smiling away as everyone in the Marqueta made

way for us. She was a fast walker, almost as if she were running to catch the New York Central, which was rumbling right over our heads: the market stalls were inside the arcade beneath the elevated railroad tracks, and I was always afraid one of those trains, crammed with well-dressed passengers headed for their homes in the country, would come crashing down through the ceiling of those stalls and destroy everyone in the place. A good headline for El Diario, worse than the Lisbon earthquake we had read about already.

With that peril rumbling overhead, I couldn't understand why Sister was all smiles all of a sudden, as if she were actually enjoying the sight of all that Marqueta merchandise. "It's all chit, man," one of the two boys I was with said. "Right?"

"That's your opinion, Almendras," I said. (During school hours we were all on a last-name basis, and as far as I was concerned, we were still in school just then.)

"So what's wrong with your opinion?" Almendras said.

"My mother shops here," I said. "Every Saturday."

"And you come with her, right?"

"Yeah, so what?"

"Nothing."

I knew what he was getting at, but with Sister right there I couldn't start anything. She wasn't speaking to anyone until we got to the stall she wanted.

"I want," she told Don Jorge Mercado, who specialized in ceremonial outfits, "three white shirts for these three boys, three red ties, three red armbands, the First Communion kind, three pairs of white socks, and three tie clasps with a cross, if you have them. If you don't have them with a cross, please tell me who does. We're in a hurry." Just like that. Brisk, no nonsense, always in character.

"Absolutelymente, Sister," said Don Jorge. What kind of answer was that? I thought he was avoiding her question about the three crucifixion clasps. I knew that at least one other merchant had them: Doña Dolores Flores of the Flores Botánica establishment on Park Avenue, a short walk away. Doña Flores, a widow without dependents, sold odds and ends on the side, almost like contraband; but Don Jorge wasn't about to put in a good word for one of his competitors, not even for the benefit of a nun. He had an extended family to feed.

He squatted behind his high counter for a few seconds, disappeared completely, and then reappeared with a big grin and a nine-by-twelve box full of those First Communion tie clasps. It was like looking at a large collection of dead grasshoppers. He sifted through the collection and picked three out in a showy, meticulous way, as if only the very best dried grasshoppers would do for Sister Felicia and her three timid charges. Then, like a master magician, still grinning away, he held them up for her inspection and approval.

She nodded, unsmiling, as if she could expect no better from a swindler of his sort. "We'll take them."

"They all come out of the same mother hopper, Malánguez," Almendras whispered in my ear. "Spooky." I gave him a little kick on the ankle to shut him up. His sarcasm might end up getting us in trouble with Sister.

". . . shirts," she was telling Don Jorge.

"What's your neck size, boys?" Don Jorge asked us.

Almendras and our other companion had no trouble telling him, and he pulled the same vanishing act behind the counter and came up with two identical-looking First Communion shirts and three red ties with a clasp at the back and a ready-made knot.

"Those came out of the same mother too," Almendras whispered to me. This time I ignored him. His type eventually got into trouble with the law and all kinds of authorities, because he couldn't take anything serious seriously.

"And what's your neck size, young man?" Sister asked me. I knew she would. I didn't know my neck size. Mami always took care of that. She had it written down somewhere in the house, along with my shoe size, my waist, the number and kind of vaccinations I'd already had and when, what other vaccinations I still had coming to me, and other vital statistics and records. And now, because I hadn't bothered to check any of that out, I was about to get into trouble with Sister, and to suffer a humiliation in front of my two classmates and Don Jorge the First Communion magician. And if all those shoppers around us got wind of my ignorance, I'd just have to live with the humiliation. I turned red while she and Don Jorge and the other two charges waited for my answer. This was turning into a test of my intelligence.

"Well, Mr. Malánguezzz?" she hissed, losing patience. She had things to do back at the nunnery.

"I am not sure, Seester," I said finally.

She couldn't believe it. "Do you mean to tell me, Ssantosss Malánguezzz, that you still don't know your own neck size?" Don Jorge and the other two charges chuckled. The merchant in the next stall was grinning.

"I think it is a fifteen and a half, Seester," I said. That was Papi's neck size. He kept it and other sizes written down in a little memo notebook inside our dining room closet. I'd peeked into it. I knew his sizes better than mine.

"Fifteen and a half?" Sister said. "That's impossible. I'm almost tempted to suspect you of lying, young man. Just look at your neck." I tried but I couldn't. "You're not a fifteen and a half. You're more like a *five* and a half. Isn't that what you meant?" She was trying to save face for me in front of Don Jorge and the others, so I nodded. Don Jorge was still smiling; so was the other merchant, and Almendras, and the other charge, someone named Macario something. I couldn't remember his last name just then. I didn't want to.

"That is okay, Sister," Don Jorge cut in. "I take care of it no trouble. I know from the experience long the sizes right." He disappeared behind the counter again and came up with a tape measure. It was long and yellow, a huge tapeworm that looked to be coming apart from years of use. So maybe I wasn't the only ignorant customer Don Jorge had ever had. "Here, Sister," he said, "you take the size from the neck of my friend Malánguez over here, and I will pull out for him the shirt. I will bet to you that it is a six, no?"

"I don't gamble, Mr. Mercado," she said, frowning at his familiarity, and took the tape measure from him with a look of disgust.

"Anyway, Sister," he went on, "if Jorge Mercado is wrong, he will give to you a free crucifixion claps. And if you are the one who is all wrong, I don't charge extra."

"It's *cruci-fix*, Mr. Mercado," she corrected. "And *clasp. Claps* is a verb, sir. Third person singular."

"That is what I say, Sister," he said, winking at the rest of us. I didn't like people pulling our nuns' legs, and pretended not to understand his prank.

She ringed the tapeworm around my neck and stooped to squint at the answer. For a second there I thought she might decide to choke me with that thing, and just then I couldn't blame her. "It's more than five and a half and less than six," she told Don Jorge, changing her mind about choking me.

"What kind of size that is?" Almendras asked Macario Something. His own neck was fat, too much starch in his diet. Rice and beans for breakfast, lunch, and dinner. He was one of those who went home for lunch and missed out on the peanut butter sandwiches, cold macaroni and cheese, and green apples the rest of us were treated to most of the time.

"I don't split the hairs," Don Jorge was telling Sister. "I will give to you one free cruficixion for the tie."

"As you wish," she told him, unsmiling. But I think she was pleased by his generosity; and he for his part was ensuring himself of more First Communion business from her and the other nuns. A shrewd merchant.

The other items Sister bought us — the red ribbon armband, the white socks, the belts with the cardboard lining — were no problem. The socks were the nylon stretch-hose type; the armbands, like the knotted ties, were all the same size; and the tape measure took care of our waists. We measured those ourselves.

The complete purchase must have come to over fifteen dollars, a lot of money to be spending on us. She pulled her purse out of her placket and pulled two fives and a ten out of the purse and handed them to Don Jorge, who gave her her change back, while Almendras, Macario, and I looked at each other in amazement: all that money changing hands for our benefit.

"Come back again fast, Seester," Don Jorge said, handing her three boxes, each box neatly tied with blue string.

She thanked him, he thanked her back and said any time, and then she told him she'd see him next day at the same time. "I have six other boys just like these three," she said, making us sound like her sons, and probably thinking of us as sons of a sort.

She handed each of us his gift box. My hands were shaking and I dropped mine, right there on the dirty Marqueta floor, among crushed vegetables and all kinds of garbage. She didn't say anything; nobody did. She just stood over me, looking down at me, while I stooped and quickly picked up the box. I was afraid to look her in the eye, and didn't. The ground was the only place fit for my stare just then. And she didn't say a thing to me, to any of us, on our way to the exit, or out on the street; nor did we say anything to her or to each other — a very solemn exit — until we got to the corner of 107th and Park, where I was going to make a right turn toward my block.

"Get your correct suit size and shoe size from your mother, Santos Malánguez," she told me.

"Yes, Seester," I said. Another surprise coming. I was afraid to ask her why, but I could guess.

"You too, Almendras," she said. "And you, Macario Iglesias." So that was his last name. Macario Churches, in translation. A future priest, it turned out.

Almendras couldn't control himself. "For why, Sister?"

"You mean *what for*, young man." A stickler for correctness. "Because we're not finished shopping for your outfits. This was only the first stage of our purchase. Next week we shop for suits and shoes." No comment, only looks of additional amazement exchanged by Almendras, Iglesias, and Malánguez.

"Well, Malánguez," she said, "take good care of that outfit. You'll look fine in it, I'm sure. Don't dawdle on the way home." They actually used words like that. Sometimes they even said "tarry." And don't be tardy for mass tomorrow morning."

Of course not. When had I ever been? She knew I knew what was good for me. I told her I wouldn't be, and thanked her for Part One of the outfit.

"You're welcome. And don't forget to ask your mother for those *sizes.*" Now she was rubbing it in about my neck again. I said I wouldn't, and made a quick turn toward my block, forgetting to say goodbye to Almendras and Iglesias, who would be walking with her for a couple more blocks. Her bodyguards, though she didn't need any protection. Nobody started trouble with our nuns, at least not before the drug pushers and their customers entered our neighborhood like that great medieval plague she had told us about during our history period.

I didn't dawdle on the way home, either. I double-timed it there, just in case some thief spotted me; and I ran up the stairs to our fifth-story apartment feeling like a thief myself. Taking gifts from anyone outside our family made me feel dishonest.

"Pues," Mami told me, suspicious, "if she gave you all this, I guess you'll have to keep it." I never doubted that. "Put it away in your bureau." I did, right away. I would have locked it up in there, just in case, if I'd had a lock.

And it was only much later, long after dinner and most of my homework for that night, that I told her and Papi about Stage Two of that First Communion outfit. I broke it to them timidly, almost as if it had been my fault. Maybe it was. I had no idea why, except that I was timid in school (I was timid everywhere, in fact) and that my English, broken and mispronounced, was a disgraceful version of the real thing, the one Sister Felicia and her fellow nuns threw around the way they were throwing their money away on some of us. Shyness and poor English were unmistakable signs of someone who needed to have his outfit bought for him. That was my explanation of Sister's charity. But I kept it to myself.

Papi and Mami kept it to themselves too, for a couple of minutes after I asked Mami for those sizes Sister wanted. "I'm not telling anybody," she said, looking depressed. In a minute she'd be calling down her favorite saints and asking them to explain just what it was she had done to deserve this.

"You have to tell him, Lilia," Papi said, trying to keep his cool.

"*You* tell him, then," she said.

"If I knew his sizes, I would."

"What kind of father are you that you don't know what size shoes your own son wears?"

"I guess I'm irresponsible," he said. I think he was being sarcastic. It was hard to tell; there was no emotion in his voice.

"I guess you are, Gerán." She wasn't going to let up on him too quickly.

"But I'm going to reform my ways. Right now. Santos, take off your right shoe." He gave me a big serious nod. No nonsense.

"Why that one?" I said. I had a hole in my right sock. The big toe of that foot was always twitching and boring holes into whatever socks it got hold of. Mami, who was getting a little tired of patching up those abused socks, had threatened to tie the guilty toe to its neighbor, the "index" toe, as a way of holding it down.

"That's right, why that one?" Mami said, keeping up her aggression.

"All right, take off the left one, then," he said. "One foot is as good as the other in this house."

Mami got up and left to go do something in the bedroom. Whenever she did that abruptly, it was either a sign of defeat or else a temporary withdrawal so she could come up with a new strategy in peace. And I had lost my ally.

I took off my left shoe and handed it to Papi, who had put on his telescopic eyeglasses for a good squint.

"I can't find the size, Santos. Where is it?" I could have saved him the trouble.

"I don't know, Papi. It was there when I looked for it. Yesterday."

"It wasn't there this morning?"

"I didn't look this morning."

"Why not?" I didn't have an answer to that one. Then he sat back, held the suspicious shoe at arm's length, and inflicted a careful inspection on it. "It's not only the odor," he said in Spanish. "Foh. It's also the condition it's in." And then, training his look on me through those gruesome spectacles he couldn't do without, he said, "Is that why you didn't want to show to me the right one?"

"I don't know what you are talking, Papi." I didn't.

"Because the other one is in a more bad condition. That is what I am talking, my son." English again. We could get confused sometimes.

And I didn't want to tell him about the hole in my sock, about my twitching big toe, and about what Mami had threatened if I didn't cut it out; so I nodded, and he said it figured (in Spanish). "So there's no sense inspecting that one for the size of your foot, is there?" I said no, there wasn't. "Maybe a mouse stole it last night," he said in Spanish. "When you was sleeping." That came out in English. He handed the shoe back to me and began laughing to himself. There was no malice in it that I could see, but I couldn't help feeling hurt, and instead of laughing with him — if I could have joined in, I would have — I shoved my left foot back inside its abused shoe and, without bothering to lace it, got up and went back to my own room, where I forced myself, a little less than happy, to finish Sister Felicia's homework for that day. While I was memorizing a couple of things that Saint Augustine supposedly had said (this was for catechism), I could hear him and Mami having a serious exchange in their bedroom. Since my bedroom door was shut (homework was a very private task, secret as well as sacred), I couldn't make out what they were telling each other, but I picked up enough snatches to conclude, undoubtfully, that what they were discussing, in their own privacy, and in such a serious tone of voice, was me and my First Communion outfit. And Sister, too. Her name kept coming up in their dialogue. From their tone, I could tell for certain that they weren't too happy with the charity she had imposed on me — on the three of us — and the unintended insult that came with the package.

"This time *you* tell him," Mami was telling him, her voice a little higher than her normal.

"Muy bien," he said. They never spoke English to each other. It would have been insulting, almost unforgivable, pretentious, in bad taste.

He came into my room, after knocking twice, to tell me that he and Mami, upon careful consideration, had decided against accepting more gifts from Sister Felicia, "or any Sister in that school, Santos, because we have the money, and if we didn't have it, we would find it. I think there was a misunderstanding."

"So why you don't write her a note?" I said. I was ready to rip out a clean sheet from my notebook and hand it to him, along with my combination fountain pen/retractable pencil (a recent present from him, bought at Kresge's, first day of classes; he had taken off from work that morning to accompany me because I'd been too nervous to stand up straight, and Mami had come down with a September virus, not for the first time).

"Because she doesn't understand Spanish, and my English is — imperfect."

"So I help you with the spelling."

"Is more than the spelling, Santos," he said, smiling. "Is also the gramática and the commas." Something I had trouble with myself. "I will take off from the job tomorrow morning and tell to her."

We went to church together next morning. He was dressed up in his best, which wasn't all that hot: a gray suit that made him look too solemn for my taste, and Mami's, but he insisted it was the right color for formal occasions and confrontations; and what was this private interview with Sister Felicia if not a formal occasion, as well as a confrontation of some kind? So gray suit it was. Gray suit, and tie (gray too, with blue stripes), a freshly laundered white shirt (courtesy of Mami, who mixed her own starch) with button-down collar, so the points wouldn't pop up perversely and embarrass him, as had happened, highly polished black shoes with formal-looking round tips, and matching cotton socks. (He had contempt for flammable nylon: "I don't want my feet catching on fire," he used to say.)

He talked to Sister, in his own timid, formal way, just before mass got going, and afterward I went to sit with my class in our designated section (between the eighth and eleventh Stations of the Cross), so I had no way of overhearing their confidential exchange. I hoped he wouldn't say anything that would get me into trouble with Sister, and I hoped his English held up so she wouldn't feel scornful of him, and of me in connection, and get the impression that he himself could use a change of outfit. He did, too, as I saw it; that gray suit was embarrassing me. If Almendras said anything even slightly sarcastic about it, the two of us were going to get it good for fighting like public school savages. But he didn't. He knew his limits, up to a point.

"I'll see you at six," Papi told me right after mass let out. He had sat through it, in the back, with other adults, on the side that adjoined the nunnery. We were already forming a double line, which meant no talking, so I couldn't ask him whether she had accepted his refusal. But he was smiling, so it must have gone well.

"Your father," Sister told me in class before we sat down to work, "has decided to buy you the rest of the First Communion outfit himself, Malánguez. I guess you knew that." I nodded. If she thought I was responsible for this setback, she didn't say, and I wasn't about to ask her.

"Why your father turn down Sister's outfit, Malánguez?" Almendras asked me after lunch.

"He got a big pay raise," I said. I didn't have to tell him the truth. "Mind your own business."

"So what?"

"So nothing."

"So suit yourself, if you want to talk like that."

"Okay. I suit myself."

Euclides Cruz got the shoes and suit I'd had coming to me.

You couldn't tell the charity cases from those boys and girls whose parents had paid for their outfits, or signed the credit agreement. Some sixty of us boys sat on the right-hand side of the center pews (best seats in the House); girls, more of them than of us, on the left. A traditional arrangement. Everything was prescribed, nothing left to impulse or accident. We boys were in black, with the red arm ribbon and the red tie. Each one of us had a new black missal and a matching rosary; the Sisters had passed them out to us outside the church, as soon as we lined up in double file. And the girls were wearing the same white dress, the same white imitation-lace mantilla, the same white shoes, knee-length stockings, and gloves that came halfway up their arms. They also had white plastic purses on leashes looped around their arms, white missals, and white rosaries, and instead of an arm ribbon they were holding a bouquet of artificial flowers. I thought they looked better than we did. They always did anyway, even when they were wearing hand-me-downs. Clean human beings — that's what they were — always neat. They took pains with themselves. They had better "characters" than the boys. ("Character" was a big word at our school.)

Every boy had a fresh haircut — standing room only at my

barber's the day before, and he had a couple of fast-working assist-
ants, too — slicked-back hair, most of it black except for some of
the Irish students, whose genes were different; some of them even
had freckles that matched their arm ribbons. I was wearing patent-
leather shoes. I wasn't the only one. Papi had insisted on that kind.
"So they won't lose their shine, Santos." Fine with me.

"Faggots," I had heard someone call us outside on the sidewalk
while we waited for the order to march inside the church. "Girls,"
someone else had called us. "Mama's boys," "bunch of punks." And
other put-downs of that kind. We knew who it was: the public
school barbarians. They were hiding in the crowd of parents, relatives, next-door neighbors, and people who just happened to be
passing by and wanted to see what this was all about.

Under orders from Sister Felicia, we had to ignore the barbarians. "Pretend they don't exist, boys," she told us. That wasn't easy.
They were always around somewhere, rubbing it in every chance
they got because we were their "betters," we were told, and we
believed it; and because they envied us and had to get back at us
somehow. The Sisters and our parents and other sympathizers tried
to shoo them away but didn't get anywhere. From behind parked
cars, from across the street (in front of the Good Neighbor Protestant Church), from the overflow mob gathered on the sidewalk
and spilling into the gutter, those P.S. Vandals, as Sister called them,
were giving it to us good. And as long as the Sisters had us in their
charge, as long as we were in a state of something called "grace,"
and fasting, too — starving for the Host — there was nothing we
could do about it. We were a bunch of "twats" in "pretty" outfits,
as our enemies called them. Envy. I couldn't wait to get inside the
church, and I hoped the priests would get it over with fast so I
could beat it back home in a hurry and change into normal human
pants and sneakers. This wasn't my idea of the greatest event in my
life since baptism.

Our parents and guardians felt differently, though. They were
actually enjoying this painful event. Otherwise why all the smiles?
And those cameras. At least one pair of parents had hired a professional photographer to immortalize the whole thing for their son
or daughter and for their old age. This pro, Mr. Taupiero, who had

his own storefront studio on Madison Avenue, between Rudi's *butchería* and Al Arentsky's *bodega*, specialized in weddings and funerals. He was always coming in and out of churches and funeral parlors with his equipment. He also made home visits for an extra fee and all the food and drink he could pack in. There was hardly a bride and groom in the neighborhood who hadn't been "shot" by him; he displayed his best portraits in his window, retouched out of recognition, looking embalmed, so that you could be staring at a member of your own family or at yourself and not know it. This Mr. Taupiero was a stout, well-dressed man with a perfect mustache (waxed, I think) and more photographic stuff than a movie set. He had brought his colossal tripod along, and after struggling for an open spot to set it up in, had seen it knocked over, with the camera mounted in place. Now he was almost in tears, cursing the public school *"bárbaros* and *bandoleros"* in two languages and threatening to call *la policía* on them if they didn't reimburse him for his broken camera. Just let him try catching them. He was still cursing when we marched in twos up the steps.

Another mob scene inside, except less noise and disorder. Every student's entire family must have been there, and some of those families were pretty big, from suckling babies to weak grandparents who had to be held by the hand and elbow and walked patiently up the high church steps, steered delicately through the mob, and squeezed carefully into the crowded pews. They had come to see their grandsons and granddaughters receive the Host for the first time; nothing would have kept them home. Then there were the next-door neighbors and friends, the curious snoopers and well-wishers, and a few hung-over crashers who were sneaking into the back pews for a free show and a nap. There was nothing the ushers could do with them.

"It's a free church," one of them told an usher when the usher told him to go home and sleep it off there.

"It's free for sober Christians, Tom," the usher said.

"Who's not sober?" the wino asked. And the usher just walked off, disgusted.

Way up at the top, over the main entrance, was the St. Misericordia Church Choir: twenty or more parishioners, about equally divided between single men and single women, some of them widows and widowers committed to long-term mourning, maybe addicted to it. The others were still looking around; they had a good view of the prospects from their loft way up there. And they were led by a man who called himself Maestro Padilla (he also rehearsed our entire school in choir practice every Friday). He was an organist, too, and (his real vocation, he insisted) a pianist. He was thin and nervous, a fastidious man with a tic in the right shoulder; it would jump up unexpectedly whenever things weren't going his way. He had been trying for years to make it as a concert pianist so he could quit the church-organ circuit. During choir practice he would tell us in a raised voice, while his right shoulder was ticcing away, that the only reason he was "stucked" with us in our basement auditorium (no heat, peeling walls, long benches for chairs) was because the concert halls were discriminating against him on account of his "national origins."

"On account of he's cracked, he means," one of the American Christian Brothers had told another ACB one afternoon during practice.

And the other Brother had said, seriously: "Bejesus, will you just listen to the man's playing?"

"What's wrong with it, Mick?" the other Brother had said.

"Arrah, it's not my idea of music, Jerry. I wouldn't pay him to grind me own organ on a street corner. Who does he think he is! Stuck with us in our basement, me foot."

Maestro Padilla, right or wrong, was also outspoken about his wages, which he called indecent. Our pastor, he said, was working him to the bone and paying him nothing for it. As we took our seats in the church pews, he was playing one of the four Puerto Rican national anthems, "La Borinqueña," on the huge organ, blasting the church with it, shaking statues on their pedestals. The pastor had warned him about playing unauthorized secular music there, and about pulling out all the stops except during rehearsals, when Our Lord was locked up in the tabernacle and the key safe in the sacristan's cabinet. But Padilla couldn't care less about these regulations and threats. He was both an artist and a diehard Puerto Rican patriot, and this organ racket was his way of both proclaiming his loyalty and protesting the wages he received from the "tied-fisted pastor." But Pastor Rooney's budget was so tight that, as he used to say, "all our saints are peeling off of the walls." Not only the painted saints but the statues, too, many of which were missing vital parts. The Christ Child on Saint Christopher's back had lost one of His hands and looked as though He might slip off the saint's back any day now, and another saint, Cecilia, I think, had lost her dulcimer, or harp, or whatever that strange-looking instrument she played was called.

"That's your problem," Maestro Padilla told Father Bardoni one day, when Bardoni, the pastor's right-hand man, tried to reason with him in the matter of wages. "You take care of the peeling saints, Father, I take care of the sacred music, and if I don't get a raise soon, I am going to complain to the Office of the Commonwealth of my country. I have connections with them." His cousin's sister-in-law was a secretary there, he once told Papi. "But keep it to yourself, Don Malánguez."

How could Papi keep it to himself? He told Mami and me right away. "I wish he *would* complain," Mami said. "I wish they'd raise his salary, so we can have some peace in that church."

"I don't think that connection of his is going to do him much good," Papi said. "Even Saint Anthony's better connected than that cousin of nobody."

"What do you mean *even* Saint Anthony?" She was a big fan of Saint Anthony's. Mami and Papi used to sit in one of the pews next to that saint's statue (the bunch of lilies he was holding in one hand needed replastering). That was where they were sitting now, in the back under the balcony, where Padilla's organ was less loud.

They were lost in a mob of well-groomed parents and others who looked as though they'd been put through the same dry-cleaning machine. The two of them had given me a quick kiss on the cheek and a couple of tight hand-squeezes when Sister Mary Principal flounced up to our group in her two-ton uniform and, putting her thumb to one of those metallic hand-crickets that every nun owned, signaled us with hand gestures and eye movements to proceed to our assigned seats. "With all due haste and decorum," she added, as if she needed to. Papi and Mami looked around them, bewildered, when the mob split up and scrambled for the best pews in the House.

I ended up sitting by the aisle, next to a spoiled classmate named Dom Silvestro Grippe, Jr. He was the only one in our class who called himself by three names, plus the Junior, as if his father were someone important. He got the "Dom" from his grandfather, a bricklayer who had come over from somewhere in Europe; and his late father, the original Silvestro, had been into something Grippe called "heavy construction." Dom Silvestro, Jr., was a pretty good example of heavy construction himself. He was so overweight that sometimes, just by looking at him, I'd lose my appetite. In our lunchroom the students called him cruel names, like Dom Grippe Leftovers or the Garbage Machine, and would offer him whatever leftovers they couldn't stomach themselves, preferring to fast till three. Sometimes they collected apple cores, dozens of them, and offered them to him on a platter. He'd throw them back in their faces. For all the heavy doses of religious instruction and discipline we received, we still had a pecking order; and Grippe, with all his weight and compulsive scrounging and scavenging, was our patsy, a martyr to his bottomless stomach.

He was sitting next to me in our packed pew, breathing heavily and staring straight up at the altar festooned with flowers and candles; and from the balcony, right above Mami and Papi and Saint Anthony, his mother was spying him and me out through a pair of heavyweight binoculars, as if this were the opera or the racetrack and we "first-timers" a troupe of overdressed midgets or jockeys. As a one-year widow, she was still dressed in black, head to toe, and the binoculars (also black) were looped around her neck, along with a huge gold medal that looked like a cymbal and flashed like a sunburst when the light caught it.

I don't think the Sisters were crazy about her. She pampered her son, overfed him, made all kinds of excuses for his absences, which were frequent and therefore, in Sister Felicia's opinion, "abusive"; he was always coming down with something, if his mother was telling Sister the truth. "And it can all be blamed on his stomach," I heard Sister tell one of the other nuns one day. "What that boy needs is a gag around his mouth."

"Or a zipper," said the other Sister.

I'd never heard that expression before, and spent a lot of time imagining zippers around Grippe's mouth. None of them fit. It was a capacious mouth, and sad-looking, when you came down to it. After all, he was a half-orphan already, with a mother who would probably go through life wearing those morbid-looking black dresses and dangling those heavyweight binoculars from her three-ring neck. And overfeeding her only son, her only flesh-and-blood possession, it looked like, because I don't think they had any relatives in this country. (Not that Papi and Mami and I had much to brag about on that score.)

But I wished she'd take those binoculars off my immediate area. I was feeling self-conscious enough to begin with, a semi–charity case in an outfit that the barbarians outside had called a "faggot fashion show." I didn't need in addition Mrs. Grippe's close-up inspection, or any comparisons with her dolled-up son, who was already sweating away to the left of me, sucking up all the scarce oxygen in our vicinity and expelling it in the form of what Sister had once labeled halitosis — one of those big words that stuck in my mind. I wrote it down in my spelling notebook as "holytoses." *Tos:* Spanish for cough. I thought she was referring to one of his frequent, "abusive" absences, and spelled it after my own misconception. But why the "holy" before "toses"? Mami and Papi said they hadn't the scarcest idea. They'd never heard of a cough like that; maybe it was some kind of Italian whooping cough, thought Papi. "Tos ferina, Santos."

Whatever it was, I didn't want to catch it, but since I was sitting next to the carrier in our assigned First Communion pews, I had no choice but to hold my breath as much as possible and not turn my mouth and nose his way, in the hope that whenever one of those holytoses germs happened to be coming in my direction, I'd be letting out my own breath, or holding it.

Dom Silvestro, Jr., wasn't what my family called a "considerate human being"; he was more like what Sister Felicia had once labeled a "regardless type," talking about another student who had coughed in a girl's face, and to whose parents she had written a special note: "Please buy Francisco a bottle of Father John's Cough

Syrup and a jar of Vick's Vapo-Rub. Put two tablespoons of this medicated ointment in a bowl of boiling water and have your son inhale it. (See the jar label for details on this.) It is effective. Otherwise Francisco may cause an epidemic in our class, and there will be many absences. And please teach him not to cough in other students' faces. It is not very polite." It was regardless.

Grippe's mother had received several such notes herself.

"Did Sister Felicia purchase that First Communion outfit for you, Malánguess?" Dom Silvestro asked me, just as I was inhaling. He had turned his mouth right up close to my nose.

I held my breath and kicked his fat foot, and told him, without exhaling, that it was none of his business. "What the hell's it to you, Grippe?"

"Hey, hey," he said, "you can't curse in here. This is the House of God. Now you can't receive, Malánguess."

"What you talking about, Grippe?" I kept my voice down to a whisper, beginning to feel the panic waking up somewhere in the tail of my spine. "Who says I can't receive?"

"I say," he said.

"Why not?"

"Because you just cursed."

"So mind your business."

"If you receive, I'm gonna tell Sister Felicha."

"Yeah? You tell her and I'm gonna get you right after this is over. Me and Almendras. We're gonna jump you outside. Kick your big ass, Grippe."

"Yeah?" he said, swarming my face with germs. "A whole bunch of my father's friends is in here. They're all over the place. And they got a piece in their pockets. With bullets, Malánguess. You and Almendras try anything with me, you ain't gonna receive no more Hosts in your life. You know what I'm talking about?"

Not quite, but I knew better than to mess with more than one Italian at a time, especially grown-up Italians, whose looks were always serious. So I cooled it with Grippe right there.

"Do me a big favor, Dom," I said, pulling out his first name for the first and last time in my life.

"Yeah? What you want now, Malánguess?" He wasn't about to return the familiarity.

"Don't squeal on me and I won't tell Sister you was talking in church."

"You're nobody to talk yourself, Malánguess."

"If I don't receive the Host," I said, "my father and mother's gonna kill me."

"Good," he said, to which I had nothing to add.

I was despising myself for coming on so abjectly, but this menace on my left wasn't giving me anything like a choice. He thought about it, with his face generously turned away from mine, and while his mother kept her binoculars trained on us.

"I'll give you a break this time, Malánguess," he finally told me, turning his germs loose on me again.

I thanked him, and actually felt grateful for a minute or two before going back to despising the "stoolie," as I put it to myself. A holytoses carrier, too. It figured. And now, through this degenerate specimen sitting on my left, they were trying to infect my people with it, through me. On top of committing the sin of cursing in church, I was committing the more serious one of self-righteousness. But I let it slide.

During this exchange, Maestro Padilla had been booming his idea of music down on us: a combination of sacred sounds, the strictly prescribed stuff, with intermezzos of all four Puerto Rican national anthems, which I had no doubt was endangering his immortal soul, and possibly the soul of his number one enemy, Pastor Rooney, who was officiating with two other priests up at the altar and probably cursing the choirmaster under his breath in between snatches of Latin. The choir of men and women who had lost their spouses, or who had still to find them, was doing its best to be heard above his irreligious blitz. But it was an unequal contest. Their own instruments were only vocal cords, many of them damaged from abuses of one sort or another, including, in at least three cases I knew of, chain-smoking.

And then, like something made for a pedestal, the looming apparition of Sister Felicia herself, staring down at me and Grippe, but mostly at me because I was closer to her.

She was standing there at right angles to me, with the metal cricket in her hand, thumb at the ready. If she squeezed its belly it would go off, *clic-cloc*, and attract everybody's attention, hundreds of eyes — possibly a thousand, the House was that packed.

She was huffing down at me, damning me through her nose, and ignoring Grippe, who had started it; and she was trying to make me dislike myself. It was working. As if on orders from her, sweat started working its way into the corners of my eyes and stinging them. She was close enough for me to smell her breath. A sweet odor. Pez. Papi used to chew the stuff himself, when he was off the Tums. I knew she carried a roll of them in her private placket. It wasn't all money in there.

She bent down in a swoop and said, right into my ear, "Ssantoss Malánguezzz!" At least four esses and three zees. "I am going to talk to you tomorrow morning, mark my word. For talking in church. Do you hear me?" I nodded at Father Rooney and his partners and the four altar boys who were helping them out. This was a fancy mass.

My nodding sprayed some sweat on Grippe's First Communion ribbon, a classy-looking one. His head jerked in my direction, caught itself halfway, and jerked back to starting position; then he wiped his sleeve and ribbon in a snobbish, show-off fashion, so Sister and his mother could both see what a slob I was. His father's associates must have seen it too. But at that point, whatever menace they represented couldn't have been as terrible as Sister, who had the whole Church behind her, right back to Saint Peter and his Rock. Though you could never tell how far Grippe's bodyguards went themselves. Heavy construction must have gone back a long ways.

Some of that same sweat had sprayed Sister's uniform; she either didn't notice or she was ignoring it for the time being. I'd find out first thing tomorrow morning. Right now I was self-consciously swiping a couple of telltale blotches off my missal. "If you ever talk in church again," she said, squinting down at me, "I myself will escort you outside in front of everyone, and —"

The end of her sentence was cut short by the altar boy in charge of the tintinnabulations. As if she had suddenly lost the lower half of her legs, she dropped to her knees — we all did — and bowed her covered head, joined her hands in the prescribed arch, tips of fingers touching chin, just like the rest of us, and kept that pose while Father Rooney up front held the chalice over his head and turned burgundy to blood with the magic of Latin. Then he repeated the razzle-dazzle with the "unlivened" wafers, and the tintinnabulator went into a fit of ring-a-lings, as if the spirit of Saint Vitus had entered him; and the rest of us in the pews, and Sister in the nave, stared down at the ground, having ourselves a good dose of awe and other important emotions. Even Padilla's organ was behaving itself during this mysterious thing called transubstantiation, another one of those big words that somehow seemed to illustrate the thing it was talking about.

Then Father Rooney lowered the cup called a ciborium, and the altar boy with the bells shook them again to inform us that the tasteless wafers had been turned by Padilla's number one enemy into Our Savior's flesh, fit for human consumption. Some of us cannibals back in the pews couldn't wait to get our teeth into Him.

"You're not supposed to chew It," Sister had told us repeatedly. Almendras had wanted to know why not. "Because you're supposed to let It dissolve. If It sticks to your palate, don't stick your fingers in your mouths. It's a sin to touch It. Just leave It alone." And other admonitions like that, plus a disappointing description of It as being tasteless, "so don't stick out your tongues expecting to taste jam on toast. It is unleavened."

And Almendras the curious had asked her, "What is unlivened, Sister?"

"You'll find out, Mr. Almendras," she said. "If you behave yourself and make a clean confession" — meaning by that a sincere one. No lies and no omissions. Every penny we'd stolen from our mothers had to come out, whispered in Father Confessor's neutral ear, in order to qualify ourselves for the Eucharist.

"The real presence," she had called it during our First Communion rehearsals, confusing every boy and girl in our classroom. She also called it "the Eucharistic banquet" (which Almendras later twisted into "You carry this blanket, man"), the "mystical body," the "sacrament of charity," the "central sacrament," the "source of grace," the "gift of His body," the "abiding presence," the "consecrated species," and the "sacramental dispensation." She told us, "His body broken and torn is why the priest breaks the bread into pieces," and other explanations and strange new Catholic words that had everyone in class confused. Our "spiritual vocabulary," as she sometimes called these new words, was catching up with our "profane" one, which I took to mean our dirty one.

She never got around to explaining the difference between a "real" presence and a fake one. We had to take her word for all sorts of things, so this mysterious presence was nothing new. "You have to take some things on faith" was one of her common injunctions.

We had to take a lot of things on faith, except for doubting types like Almendras, who wouldn't take his own mother's word for anything. "My mother, I don't think she know too good what she is always talking," he once told me. "Keep this secret to yourself, Malánguez." He didn't have to worry. It had something to do with his unvarying lunch of rice and beans, and why his mother wouldn't pack it up in a container for him, like some other mothers, so he could eat with the rest of us in our lunchroom.

He was sitting three pews behind mine, and when I snapped my head over my shoulder to see what he was up to, I was pinched hard just above the crook of my elbow, a tender spot without any muscle to speak of. It was Sister again; she had sneaked up to my right arm, which was dangling over the armrest, and brought me to painful attention in no time. I held back the scream I was entitled to, and fixed my eyes on the well-shaved neck in front of me.

"I'll talk to you in class tomorrow morning, Malánguezzz," she whispered. Right into my ear. Those three zees again: a bad omen. "Take-home punish lessons" coming up. A "castigation," it was called . . . something about my barbaric behavior in church . . . no defense from Papi and Mami, who also took some things on faith, so there was nothing to discuss. "Just do what she says, Santos. And don't do it again, whatever it was you did."

From that pinch on, the rest of the mass was a letdown. Things blurred: lights, flowers, linen altar cloth, priests' bright vestments, peeling murals and flaking statues of everybody's favorite saints, some of them dubious; and the entire community of faithfuls and hangers-on packed into those mahogany pews with scrollwork armrests. Sounds turned to stew. There was Father Rooney's falsetto Latin with a little sinus condition thrown in ("Hoc est my locos-pocus, my viva voce, my pro et con . . .") and Padilla's profane artillery shelling the place. Then the Sisters' crickets jumped in. About a dozen of them went off at the same time: *clic-cloc-clic-cloc*. An attack of grasshoppers, the signal for us to get off our knees and go get It, the "mystical body," the "unlivened Host" Almendras had been talking about.

With Dom Grippe breathing toses behind me ("Get up, Malánguess — this is it, man. Even though you cursed in church"), and his mother's binoculars trained on me, just in case I was thinking of pulling any "Portorican" stunts on her son, I got to my feet and faced the girl across the aisle — who was biting her lip, either out of nervousness or in expectation — and waited for the next *clic-cloc* of Sister's grasshopper. Every pew was a platoon of ten, and if you were one of the unluckies who had landed the aisle position, you were automatically the leader of nine others; no backing out. I'd never led anything in my life and I didn't like this, except for being ahead of Grippe, who was probably disliking me for my "luck."

The trouble was that you had to look good in front of all those "foreigners"; otherwise they'd start buzzing to each other about "that little P.R. over there who can't even walk a straight line to the abiding presence. He must have got grogged first thing he gets up this morning . . . can of six-pack in a little brown bag . . . keeps Rheingold and Schaefer in business . . . a sin to receive in that state . . . eighty-proof mouthwash . . . I hear they even wash their hair in it . . ." And my father and mother, sitting back there next to Saint Anthony and his lilies, would feel horrible about themselves, and about their son, the cause of it all.

So I watched my step; and when Sister let go with her cricket and gave me the nod (along with a menacing squint), I stepped out of my pew on tiptoes, looking (I hoped) like a self-important honors student going up to collect his big golden pin or plaque for straight A's and no absences.

I made it up to the Communion railing without tripping over myself. It was a long slow walk, halting half-steps all the way, as if we'd sprained our ankles to qualify for the You-carry-this-blanket.

I hit a bump when I got to where the central aisle of the nave ran into another aisle called the crossing (all these symbols of what this House was all about didn't help out my nerves). This happened a few feet from the railing, but it wasn't all my fault; I knew a loose floorboard when I stepped on one, even if it was hidden by a Catholic rug with symbolic designs all over it. A couple of other first-time receivers ahead of me had also stepped on it and had given a start as if the rug had teeth in it. It was like a trap set there to catch daydreamers, or anyone who'd cursed before receiving, or held back a couple of "grievous" sins at confession, cold-feet types who'd go through life lying to Fathers Confessor about how many pennies they'd really stolen from their mothers, while the poor woman was tied up in the kitchen, tending the pot of this and that with hacked codfish and oregano, unaware that she had given birth to a crook who was depleting the family's tight budget and stealing confiscated magnets from Sister's desk during lunch period: giving our people a bad name.

But I was doing it again, daydreaming. I had stopped when I got to the first line of pews at the crossing and waited there, inches from the trap, trying to make myself as stiff as possible so I wouldn't pee in my pants (we had rehearsed all this: "I don't want anyone passing water in his or her pants, whichever applies," Sister had told us during run-throughs), waiting for Sister to give me the go-ahead for the Host. You couldn't just walk up to the railing and kneel there with the others; you had to wait until you were told. Sister had been very strict about that for weeks. "Remember," she had told us, "you're not going up to a cafeteria for a frankfurter. Our church is not a luncheonette and the Host is not a hot dog. So just watch your *deportment*." (I wrote that new one down in my spelling notebook first chance I got, but I misspelled it as "department," and misused it for a long time.)

While I was waiting there, turning to stone, or salt, or liquid, someone grabbed my arm, the same spot where Sister had pinched it. It was still sore. "Don't move." It was her voice again, down low. It sounded like something out of a cowboy movie I'd seen with Papi. "Okay, Malánguezzz, don't move. This is a chodown."

She was only getting me ready for the walk to the railing. She held me there in a tight grip for about ten seconds, and as soon as one of the kneeling receivers, looking no better than before, had made a stiff about-face and started solemnly back to his pew with the Host in his mouth, Sister pointed a finger at the opening and told me to get It, before one of Sister Haughney's girls beat me to It. Then she let go my arm, and it was as if she had pressed a button or released a spring I didn't know I had: I took off for that railing like a hungry dog tearing ass for a bowl of chow. But there was a lot of "chow" for everyone. Father Rooney's ciborium was stacked, and there was plenty more Host back in the tabernacle. One of the assisting priests, Father Mooney, had already replaced Father Rooney's empty ciborium with a fresh ciborium and was standing by in front of the altar, waiting for another nod from the railing.

"Walk, Ssantoss Malánguezzz, don't run!" Sister hizzed behind me. Too late. I was already kneeling at the railing, hands joined under my chin. She'd get me tomorrow morning. Maybe in the auditorium. Special assembly for the execution. Organ music and chorus.

And then Father Rooney and his other assistant were on top of me with the ciborium. The assistant stuck a golden plate with a handle under my chin — a paten, it was called, a metallic bib just in case. Father Rooney was holding the Host between thumb and index finger and wagging It in front of my mouth, which suddenly wouldn't open. Lockjaw from fright. My punishment for cursing in church.

"Open your mouth, young man," Father Rooney suggested. We hadn't rehearsed this part.

I used both hands to do it: one hand under my nose, the other pushing down on my chin. But then my tongue wouldn't come out for the presence. The spit in my mouth had thickened and turned to glue, and my tongue was stuck to my palate.

"Stick out your tongue," the priest with the paten said.

I stuck two fingers in my mouth and unstuck my tongue.

"What's he doing, Matt?" Father Rooney asked his assistant.

"You got me, Mark. What are you doing, kid?"

"I am sorry, Father," I said. "The tongue got stuck to the —"

"Shh! You're not supposed to talk in here during mass," the pastor said. He wasn't looking too happy.

"I am sorry, Father," I said automatically, trying to get the spit going again.

"Out with the tongue, son," Father Matt repeated. "Or leave the railing."

I closed my eyes and did as he said. Then Father Rooney delivered his Latin lines: "Corpus Domini nostri Jesu Christi custodiat animam tuam, et cetera. Amen." Father Matt had his paten under my chin — cold metal — and I felt a familiar warm dribble working its way down my thigh, spoiling my fresh pair of First Communion shorts. The whole place was looking on, except possibly Papi and Mami, who must have been staring down at their hands in embarrassment. Then the worst of all possible things happened: the Host broke in half on my nose. I still had my eyes shut, so I didn't see just how Father Rooney managed to do it but I could figure it out. I must have made him nervous, and instead of slapping It down on the tip of my tongue, he caught the tip of my nose, and the presence broke in two. One half stayed in Father Rooney's fingers and the other floated past my tongue, bounced off the railing, missing Father Matt's paten altogether, and came to a stop on the symbol-crowded rug on their side of the railing, between Father Matt's shoes, which were barely visible under his alb, as Sister Felicia had called that fancy undergarment.

Both priests gasped at the same time and crossed themselves. Everyone in church, except for the sleeping winos in the back, must have done the same thing. Padilla's organ began playing "En Mi Viejo San Juan," a golden oldie, probably to distract everyone from the horrible accident I'd just caused at the railing. And my bladder was having itself a time with my new shorts. Father Matt stooped quickly, with his paten held tight to his heart, and started looking for the half Host. I remembered what Sister had said about "His body broken in pieces" is why something-something, and felt horrible. The people who had nailed Him to the cross couldn't have felt worse afterwards than I did just then.

Father Matt was still down on his knees looking for It. He was getting warm. I could have told him, but I was afraid to open my mouth. He was saying something under his breath, and Father

Rooney, all out of patience, said, "Just pick It up, Matt. We'll be here all day at this rate."

"Sorry, Mark," said Father Matt. "Here It is." He used his paten as a dustpan to scoop It up, nudging It with his index finger. It broke again during this delicate recovery, but that didn't matter. You could split It up into a couple of hundred pieces and It was still one. That was part of the mystery behind It. The "accidents" were one thing, Sister had told us; the "essence" was something else. You couldn't violate *that*. She had told us about an egg named Humpty Dumpty to illustrate the difference between a "material" object, in this case a talking egg, and the mysterious "indivisible Host." Just the same, I was having my doubts. One piece was in Father Rooney's chalice (he had slipped it back inside when no one was looking), and the other half was down there, getting scooped up by Father Matt; and I was having trouble understanding how both pieces were one and the same. Sister Felicia would tell me all about it first thing tomorrow morning, in front of everyone. I wanted to go back home. I wanted no part of this business; I was unfit, unworthy, un-everything, but I was frozen there on my knees, terrified.

Father Matt finally got back to his feet, the paten with the two extra pieces held against his chest, and the thumb and index finger of his other hand pinning Them down to prevent another accident. Then Father Rooney held out his ciborium, which looked like a fancy trophy to me — it had jewels in the middle and was made of gold, or something that resembled gold — and Father Matt nudged the two pieces into it. I thought Father Rooney was going to slap a fresh sample on my tongue, but he had nothing like that in mind. I didn't even get the three broken pieces. I had my tongue out again, but all I got was a piece of advice. "Go back to your pew, kid," he told me. "You're not ready to receive."

And Father Matt said, "Grow up, son. You're seven already." I was eight, already one year behind, and no end in sight. And then he turned to Father Rooney and said, in a whisper, "This whole neighborhood's going to the —"

But Father Rooney cut him short: "Not here, Matt. Later, in the rectory."

"You're the boss, Mark." And off they went to plant an intact presence on Grippe's tongue. The worst disgrace in my life to date; and once you started in with the disgraces, it was hard to stop. Some types couldn't do a thing right. They talked in church when they should have been praying in silence, they cursed before receiving, they didn't know their own neck size, or the size of their feet, and they conned their parents into paying for half their First Communion outfits, just to insult Sister. And now this. In public, too. Hundreds had seen it. Maybe a thousand. And my own parents sitting in the back, next to Saint Anthony and his lilies, pretending they didn't know who I was. At least I thought they were pretending. I wanted them to.

Sister Felicia helped me to my feet and turned me around toward the pews. She walked back there with me, slowly, because my knees seemed to have run out of the oil that makes knees work, and my shoes felt like something poured from cement. Heavy construction. She led me back to my pew by the arm she'd pinched, and as she was sitting me down, she put her mouth to my ear and said, "Ssantoss Malánguezzz, you are a disgrace to our school," bearing down on "disgrace." "You are not fit for First Communion, and maybe never will be. We have a lot to discuss tomorrow morning."

I nodded; but did she think I was going to show up at school next morning? Even as I sat there in my wet shorts, my mind was out in Central Park playing hooky next day. They were going to get me anyway, day after next, no way out of it; but in the meantime I thought I was entitled to a day of rest and I was going to take it. Maybe they'd send me to P.S. Genghis Khan, where I'd have no trouble blending in with the "barbarians," which might not be a bad idea.

Papi and Mami didn't bring it up on the way home — we left in a hurry — or in the house, where they insisted I sit down to eat after I changed out of my outfit, washed the pee off my thighs, and changed into normal clothes and sneakers.

Menu: fricasseed chicken (boneless), saffron rice, a hot loaf of unconsecrated garlic bread, a bottle of grape juice (full strength), and Humpty Dumpty egg custard. Not exactly my first post-

Communion meal, but no reason to throw it out, either. Mami reminded me that in the world at large a lot of people were going hungry right now. I knew she'd say that.

"You was nervous, Santos," Papi said in English while we were living it up in the dining room. I'd been expecting that one too. But he wasn't going to preach at me. "Next time," he added in Spanish, "no more accidents, okay?"

"Okay, Papi." But didn't he know it wasn't up to me?

ROLANDO HINOJOSA

Brother Imás

W ITNESSES, witnesses, witnesses. All six or seven thousand of them had seen the late Bruno Cano go under rich Valley loam (and in sacred ground, to boot), and it must have been riding close to nine o'clock (CDT) when Father Pedro Zamudio and I finally headed for the parish house. It'd been a long funeral, but more on that later.

Father Pedro looked depressed, saddened, beat down, even; but appearances are merely that, and nothing more. The man of the cloth was aboil, and the targets of his wrath were at hand: Belken County (Texas Mexican sector) generally, and specifically the Carmona brothers, Lisandro and Sabás. It was they, and no one else, who had led Don Pedro — and that's *led*, not *lied* — and then convinced him to bury Bruno Cano in sacred ground after Cano and Don Pedro had had a fatal but entertaining run-in the night before.

That night had started off with Bruno Cano and Melitón Burnias (that's Hard-luck Melitón) trying their hand and luck at coming up with some gold bullion said to be buried in Doña Panchita Zuárez's backyard, or near there. For the record again: Doña Panchita is a *curandera*, a healer. She also earns part of "my living," as she calls it, mending broken hearts and *virgos*.

Cano and Burnias were unsuccessful (as so many others before them), but it wasn't the failure that caused Bruno Cano's myocardial infarct; the man was a businessman and used to failure. No. The infarct was due to a helluva fright and to an even worse temper fit directed at Don Pedro Zamudio, who had refused (God's truth) to help Cano out of the ad hoc hole which he (Cano) and Burnias had dug.

Don Pedro and Cano came to hard words, and when Cano insulted Don Pedro's mother, the priest refused to bury his old friend. No, no, and not on sacred ground, either.

The Carmona brothers prevailed, however, and took charge of the funeral. To the point: less of a funeral, more of an entertainment — a foofaraw — and the damn thing took seven hours. Four choirs and everything . . .

And here we were, Don Pedro and I, seven hours later, heading for the parish house. Evening had come but the sun was visible still at nine o'clock, and it was hot, July-August hot. The first thing that came off was the collar.

"Here," he said. Then the soutane, and again, "Here, Jehu." And then his jacket, and since I was already carrying the ornamental funeral candles and candleholders and that big old Bible, well!, I couldn't keep up as he quickened his pace and that temper of his, too. The breathing was a fright, and the fury was now zeroed in on the one target of opportunity: the Carmona brothers . . .

Don Pedro was working on one of those sermons of his, and here I was, sweating, lagging behind, being yelled at, out of breath, hungry, and thinking of having to hear that fire and brimstone that night at supper and then for six regular masses, plus the evening mass at a ranch mission as well.

As acolyte, I was as much a prisoner as the Flora parishioners. And would they show on Sunday? Of course! Would the Carmonas show? Sure, it was Don Pedro's turn to get even, and while Flora people are many things (and one can convict 'em of being dull most of the time), they're not rude. They'd show, and they'd take their punishment, too. No need to say that they'd wait for another chance to get at the mission priest, who after all was Flora-born and -raised. (Oh, if Rome knew what went on in the outside world, away from the view and sight of *L'Osservatore* . . .)

The thought of old Chana's supper kept me afloat, but barely. To add to this, I'd have to bolt the food if I wanted to sneak out that night. The sneaking out would be easier this time, since Don Pedro's mind was on vengeance (Romans 12:19) and I wouldn't have to worry about Chana's tattling this time.

We walked in and Chana spoke first: "Supper's on the table, and the limeade is as cold as it's going to get."

I'd spotted her at the burial site, and she knew I had. I winked at the old fraud, but she pretended otherwise and turned the glasses upward and filled them. She busied about doing nothing, avoiding my stare at any cost, and then went out to the front porch.

Don Pedro ate in silence, but I noticed he ate well enough. I was on my firsts when he rose (without a word of thanks for the meal) and went to his room, slamming the door behind him. I waited for a few seconds, and then I heard his voice, a low rumble at first and then that clear baritone, and finally the words started coming out here and there, and choice ones, too. The parishioners were among the first casualties, then the town of Flora came under fire, after that the Valley went up in flames. At every inch of the way, though, the Carmona brothers and Bruno Cano were put to death, sent to hell, resurrected, and put to death again. Don Pedro was working on the sermon and enjoying it for once. "Seven hours! Seven! You sinners! No lunch, no merienda, and no supper either. No bathrooms! Prisoners all!"

I wanted to hear more, but I also wanted to go downtown, and I did. After all, I'd hear the sermon from first mass on, and by then the sermon would be polished to a high gloss and served to the cream of Flora society, which in turn would sit there and take it and love every minute of it. They're incorrigible.

But by the time that Sunday rolled around, I was no longer living in Flora. Between the time of the funeral and Sunday, a matter of four days, I was off and running again, this time with Brother Imás: a Preacher whose Persuasion was Protestant (*sicut*) and whose itinerary was variable and whose calling constant (*sicut, bis*).

The Brother was named Tomás, and thus answered to Tomás Imás. (Some parents have gone nose first and straight to hell for less.) According to him, he had abandoned His Humble Hearth to follow the Lord's Path, Preaching Precious Parables to Philistines and other livestock that had wandered, raced, or strayed from the Lord's Lovely Light. (We may as well stop right here; it could be because of his name or because of personal, peculiar, or particular preferences — and I believe it's catching — but Brother Imás was a card-carrying alliterationist.)

Brother Imás was keenly interested, first of all, in saving people from the Fiery Pits and, secondly, and on a dietary note, in eating at least one hot meal every day. Since he worked in the Valley and specialized in the *mexicano* branch of Christianity, the pickings were far from lean: The Valley *mexicanos* had already been stretched in the matters of credulity and belief and faith first in 1836, then in 1848, and subsequently as well. As for feeding one's fellow, well!, this is plain good manners and customs, isn't it? The Valley *mexicanos* solved Life's Great Problem years ago: deny neither food nor comfort to anyone, and when it comes to salvation, women and children first. After that, it's every man for himself.

It just so happens (so to speak) that on that Thursday after the funeral, I was on my way to Doña Panchita Zuárez's lot, shovel in hand, and ordered to cover up the hole dug up by Bruno Cano and Hard-luck Melitón. As you've read, this was the hole where Cano's heart collapsed on him. It was one of those days when it looks like rain and then it *doesn't*, and that may explain why the heat wouldn't let up for a minute. Since I had the entire day to carry out the chore, I'd stop here and there, greeting a friend here and a friend there when I spotted Edelmiro Pompa talking with a man, an outsider — a *fuereño*, as we say in the Valley. And there he was: black-suited, a white button-down shirt, no tie, wearing one a those hard, flat, wide-brimmed straw hats popular back in the thirties, and talking to Edelmiro.

When I walked up to them, they were talking in Spanish, and then I heard the *fuereño* say, "O bless-ed, when you growing up, you will be seeing how important are education and the benefits," or something like that. The words were in Spanish, all right, but that intonation! And the pronunciation! He *looked* Mexican, as Anglos say, but as soon as he opened his mouth and that Spanish came out . . . well, whatever it was, it was unique to a degree.

I looked at him a while longer, and I noticed that he stood with his hands behind his back, which was okay, too, but he didn't rock back and forth like a grown-up, and he didn't use his hands much either. He then crossed his arms and even *that* didn't look right. An outsider, then, no two ways about that. Edelmiro hadn't said a word for a while; he kept his eyes on the *fuereño*, making up his mind about something, it looked like.

Edelmiro'd shake his head just a bit and didn't even return my "howdy" when I came up to them. I finally got between them and Edelmiro pointed with his lips and said, "What do you think?"

The *fuereño* threw out his hand and I caught it as he said, "One of God's Good Guests, Tomás Imás. I Sing and Say Psalms for Salvation."

"Lo . . . (I got my hand back), Jehu Malacara; I just live here is all."

"And that shovel? You're a worker?"

"Oh . . . I'm on my way to cover up a hole, a big hole."

"A big hole? For a dead Christian?"

"Afraid so, yes. The thing is that the dead person isn't in the hole, though."

"There must be a logical explanation, youngster. A basis of historical reasoning for covering an empty hole?"

"It's a fairly long story, sir. I'm not sure I know where to begin . . . You weren't here yesterday, by any chance?"

"Oh yes, I, your newest friend, was present. But I was alone in this deserted town. Present and all alone, alone until night fell, when I see the townsmen late at night."

"The town was deserted because everyone from Flora was at the funeral. Isn't that right, Edelmiro?"

"Right. Jehu and I here are acolytes, and we were at the funeral."

"Funeral . . . And who is dying and getting buried, youngsters?"

"A man named Bruno Cano."

"He owns the Golden Fleece, the slaughterhouse."

"And his bereaved wife? Her whereabouts?"

"Aw, she's dead. Been dead, right, Jehu?"

"Ah-hah."

"Oh? And where do you do your work?"

"I work for Don Pedro Zamudio."

Edelmiro: "That's the priest I told you about."

"The village priest?"

"Well, sorta. The mission priest."

"Well now, I too toil the vineyards of the Creator."

"You mean you're a priest?" Edelmiro.

"Lutheran priest, a Preacher of Precious Parables."

"Are you a Holy Roller?"

(Softly) "Geez, Edelmiro, that's a dumb."

"Why? What's wrong with it?"

"I'm a priest. A Preacher of the Perpetual Pronouncements of Providence."

"He's a Roller, all right."

"And you are being an acolyte, you say?"

(Softly) "How do you like his Spanish, Jehu?"

"Yes. I . . . I . . . I help out in the mission . . . but I also run errands, sweep out stores, and once I worked in a carny troupe."

"You are having no parents, then?"

"That's right. I'm an orphan, but I'm Valley-born, and I've got friends and relatives here."

"Youngster, I am spending this Friday here, and tomorrow I am on my way to Klail City. You want to be my assistant? Want you, then, to Search for the Salvation of Souls and the Sweeping of Sins under the Soil? No, answer not as yet. You continue with your shovel work, and tomorrow you decide, for tomorrow is Friday, the Fairest Day of the Faithful."

"Well, I . . . Who's to know what will happen tomorrow?"

"Only God, that's true."

In the meantime, Edelmiro breaks in: "You want a ride to Doña Panchita's? We can ride double."

"Okay . . . Ah, Brother?"

"Please?"

"I gotta go now, ah, I'll see you."

"No doubt."

"What'd he say his name was? *Más y más*, more and more?"

"I dunno, Miro, that's what it sounded like to me, too."

"Lemme tell you this: old Don Pedro better not hear you been chinning with no Holy Roller, 'cause —"

"Ha! Two weeks ago, a week ago, yeah. Now? Forget it. Right now he's thinking about getting back at the Flora types come Sunday."

"On account of the funeral? Really?"

"Well, what did you expect?"

"Well . . . ha! That was quite a crowd out there, wadn't it?"

"I'll say. And I'll say this now: you-all from Flora don't miss a lick. And I'll tell you this, too: wait'll Sunday! Yessir. Come Sunday and Don Pedro's gonna . . . ah, which mass you want to work?"

"Oh, I don't care. Whacha got?"

"Well, I'm working the six, seven, and the eight o'clocks. I'll eat at nine and serve on the ten o'clock and the eleven high mass."

"Look! Over there . . . there's Doña Panchita. Let's see what she's up to. Ah, before I forget, put me down for the eight and nine and I'll work with you on the high."

"Good. We're gonna need two more for the high, now. Nice morning, Miz Panchita."

"Isn't it, though? And what brings you out to this neck a the woods?"

"That hole, and here's my shovel."

"And I see you've got yourself an assistant, too."

"Naw, he just gave me a ride is all."

"Well, if you want me to, I can help."

"And where're you off to, Miz Panchita?"

"To the herb store, kids. I need some balm gentle and some other stuff. I'll be back, and I'll leave you here with God."

"Yes, and a goodbye to you, Miz Panchita."

"Bye, Miz Panchita."

"Really, Jehu, I'll help, and then we can go to the river. Whadda ya say to that?"

"No, I better not, I really got to get to this, you know."

"I'll help. I'll spell you, really."

"Man! It's getting hot, you know."

"Okay, Miro, say no more. You're bushed, right?"

"Yeah. It's heavy going here."

"Well, we're about half done, I think."

"Come on, Jehu, let's leave it for now. Come on . . . let's hit that river."

"Okay, but we gotta come back to this."

"Sure, sure."

Sure, sure. Well, I didn't finish the job. What with going swimming with Edelmiro, stumbling across Señor Mata's watermelon patch, and sneaking a smoke, time just flew right on by. It's that daylight saving time; the sun finally went down, and when it did, so did Anacleta Villalobos, except she went down in the hole, and — wouldn't you just know it? — she broke her damn leg. Anacleta is like that. She's an only child (and that's just an expression); she's also the pride and joy, the apple of, etc., of her father, Don Jacobo, a k a Scorpio.

His child is nearing forty. She's a bit on the arid side, too, and minus a steady boyfriend (another expression). She didn't even live close to that neighborhood, but there she was, looking for Miz Panchita in the never-say-die hope of locating some good news via the tea leaves: a man, some hope of one, or perhaps going 0-for-4 again. Cleta must've been looking at the future, because what she didn't see was the hole. She plain missed it — and that *is* an expression — when down she went and there she stayed. For the count. That was some fall, that was.

I received the news faster'n fast. Edelmiro and I were finally on our way back from the Río Grande and we were tugging with the shovel when a grown-up said: "Don Pedro's hunting for you. Crazy Cleta got a broke leg; fell into Bruno Cano's hole, and . . ."

I remember extending my right arm and handing Edelmiro the shovel, and the next thing I knew I was running down to the Klail City–Flora Bridge. I must've run all the way, and as hungry as I was, I still fell asleep almost immediately.

God came through again: another glorious Valley sunrise, the gulf mist rising just high enough to form a rainbow that lasted an hour or more. When the sun drove the mist and the clouds away, I decided to cross the highway to sit under a chinaberry tree. If

Brother Imás was really going to Klail City, he'd have to pass through here; there wasn't any other way.

Around midday (and I'd missed three meals by then) I spotted him, and I waited for him under the chinaberry tree. When he drew up, I told him I was ready, and he didn't say a word. Instead, he looked at me for a while, reached for his knapsack, and produced two navel oranges from it. Again, without a word, he handed me the larger orange and we started out that clear, cloudless July day, leaving Flora and a trail of orange peels on our way to Klail City.

"Jehu?"

"Yes, brother."

"In the name of the Lord."

"Amen."

ALMA VILLANUEVA

Golden Glass

I T WAS his fourteenth summer. He was thinning out, becoming angular and clumsy, but the cautiousness, the old-man serious- ness he'd had as a baby, kept him contained, ageless and safe. His humor, always dry and to the bone since a small child, let you know he was watching everything.

He seemed always to be at the center of his own universe, so it was no surprise to his mother to hear Ted say: "I'm building a fort and sleeping out in it all summer, and I won't come in for anything, not even food. Okay?"

This had been their silent communion, the steady presence of love that flowed regularly, daily — food. The presence of his mother preparing it, his great appetite and obvious enjoyment of it — his nose smelling everything, seeing his mother more vividly than with his eyes.

He watched her now for signs of offense, alarm, and only saw interest. "Where will you put the fort?" Vida asked.

She trusted him to build well and not ruin things, but of course she had to know where. She looked at his dark, contained face and her eyes turned in and saw him when he was small, with curly golden hair, when he wrapped his arms around her neck. Their quiet times — undemanding — he could be let down, and a small toy could delight him for hours. She thought of the year he began kissing her elbow in passing, the way he preferred. Vida would touch his hair, his forehead, his shoulders — the body breathing out at the touch, his stillness. Then the explosion out the door told her he needed her touch, still.

"I'll build it by the redwoods, in the cypress trees. Okay?"

"Make sure you keep your nails together and don't dig into the trees. I'll be checking. If the trees get damaged, it'll have to come down."

"Jason already said he'd bring my food and stuff."

"Where do you plan to shower and go to the bathroom?" Vida wondered.

"With the hose when it's hot and I'll dig holes behind the barn," Ted said so quietly as to seem unspoken. He knew how to slither under her, smoothly, like silk.

"Sounds interesting, but it better stay clean — this place isn't that big. Also, on your dinner night, you can cook outdoors."

His eyes flashed, but he said, "Okay."

He began to gather wood from various stacks, drying it patiently from the long rains. He kept in his room one of the hammers and a supply of nails that he'd bought. It was early June and the seasonal creek was still running. It was pretty dark out there and he wondered if he'd meant what he'd said.

Ted hadn't seen his father in nearly four years, and he didn't miss him like you should a regular father, he thought. His father's image blurred with the memory of a football hitting him too hard, pointed (a bullet), right in the stomach, and the punishment for the penny candies — a test his father had set up for him to fail. His stomach hardened at the thought of his father, and he found he didn't miss him at all.

He began to look at the shapes of the trees, where the limbs were solid, where a space was provided (he knew his mother really would make him tear down the fort if he hurt the trees). The cypress was right next to the redwoods, making it seem very remote. Redwoods do that — they suck up sound and time and smell like another place. So he counted the footsteps, when no one was looking, from the fort to the house. He couldn't believe it was so close; it seemed so separate, alone — especially in the dark, when the only safe way of travel seemed flight (invisible at best).

Ted had seen his mother walk out to the bridge at night with a glass of wine, looking into the water, listening to it. He knew she loved to see the moon's reflection in the water. She'd pointed it out to him once by a river where they camped, her face full of longing — too naked somehow, he thought. Then, she swam out into the water, at night, as though trying to touch the moon. He wouldn't look at her. He sat and glared at the fire and roasted another marshmallow the way he liked it: bubbly, soft and brown (maybe six if he could get away with it). Then she'd be back, chilled and bright, and he was glad she went. Maybe I like the moon too, he thought, involuntarily, as though the thought weren't his own — but it was.

He built the ground floor directly on the earth, with a cover of old plywood, then scattered remnant rugs that he'd asked Vida to get for him. He concocted a latch and a door, with his hand ax over it, just in case. He brought his sleeping bag, some pillows, a transistor radio, some clothes, and moved in for the summer. The first week he slept with his buck knife open in his hand and his pellet gun loaded on the same side, his right. The second week Ted sheathed the knife and put it under his head, but kept the pellet gun loaded at all times. He missed no one in the house but the dog, so he brought him into the cramped little space, enduring dog breath and farts because he missed *someone*.

Ted thought of when his father left, when they lived in the city, with forty kids on one side of the block and forty on the other. He remembered that one little kid with the funny sores on his body who chose an apple over candy every time. He worried they would starve or something worse. That time he woke up screaming in his room (he forgot why), and his sister began crying at the same time, "Someone's in here," as though they were having the same terrible dream. Vida ran in with a chair in one hand and a kitchen knife in the other, which frightened them even more. But when their mother realized it was only their hysteria, she became angry and left. Later they all laughed about this till they cried, including Vida, and things felt safer.

He began to build the top floor now but he had to prune some limbs out of the way. Well, that was okay as long as he was careful. So he stacked them to one side for kindling and began to brace things in place. It felt weird going up into the tree, not as safe as his small, contained place on the ground. He began to build it, thinking of light. He could bring his comic books, new ones, sit up straight, and eat snacks in the daytime. He would put in a side window facing the house to watch them, if he wanted, and a tunnel from the bottom floor to the top. Also, a ladder he'd found and repaired — he could pull it up and place it on hooks, out of reach. A hatch at the top of the ceiling for leaving or entering, tied down inside with a rope. He began to sleep up here, without the dog, with the tunnel closed off.

Vida noticed Ted had become cheerful and would stand next to her, to her left side, talking sometimes. But she realized she mustn't face him or he'd become silent and wander away. So she stood listening, in the same even breath and heartbeat she kept when she spotted the wild pheasants with their long, lush tails trailing the grape arbor, picking delicately and greedily at the unpicked grapes in the early autumn light. So sharp, so perfect, so rare to see a wild thing at peace.

She knew he ate well — his brother brought out a half gallon of milk that never came back, waiting to be asked to join him, but never daring to ask. His sister made him an extra piece of ham for his four eggs; most always he ate cold cereal and fruit or got a hot chocolate on the way to summer school. They treated Ted somewhat like a stranger, because he was.

Ted was taking a makeup course and one in stained glass. There, he talked and acted relaxed, like a boy; no one expected any more or less. The colors of the stained glass were deep and beautiful, and special — you couldn't waste this glass. The sides were sharp, the cuts were slow and meticulous with a steady pressure. The design's plan had to be absolutely followed or the beautiful glass would go to waste, and he'd curse himself.

It was late August and Ted hadn't gone inside the house once. He liked waking up, hearing nothing but birds — not his mother's voice or his sister's or his brother's. He could tell the various bird calls and liked the soft brown quail call the best. He imagined their taste and wondered if their flesh was as soft as their song. Quail would've been okay to kill, as long as he ate it, his mother said. Instead, he killed jays because they irritated him so much with their shrill cries. Besides, a neighbor paid Ted per bird because he didn't want them in his garden. But that was last summer and he didn't do that anymore, and the quail were proud and plump and swift, and Ted was glad.

The stained glass was finished and he decided to place it in his fort facing the back fields. In fact, it looked like the back fields — trees and the sun in a dark sky. During the day the glass sun shimmered a beautiful yellow, the blue a much better color than the sky outside: deeper, like night.

He was so used to sleeping outside now he didn't wake up during the night, just like in the house. One night, toward the end when he'd have to move back with everyone (school was starting, frost was coming and the rains), Ted woke up to see the stained glass full of light. The little sun was a golden moon and the inside glass sky and the outside sky matched.

In a few days he'd be inside, and he wouldn't mind at all.

J. L. TORRES

My Father's Flag

L IKE IT'S the last thing on your mind: that your old man is gonna drop dead. Just like that. I mean, never in my mind could it've happened. Even when Moms took him to the hospital, I just thought he'd get better. People go to the hospital all the time, I used to tell her. Yeah, I was worried about how he was getting skinny, but I don't know; maybe I was trying to block it out. I had things to do. All my life my mother took care of him, and him of her. It wasn't about me. They took care of each other.

But it got worse. He couldn't do the work at the factory no more, so he took off from work, and they finally laid him off. That was bad news. But I figured my old man would bounce back. He always did. Back in '65 when he lost two of his fingers messing around with that shaky snow machine. We all panicked behind that one. But he got better and found the job at the plastics company. That was how he was. He worked his ass off, all the time. He loved to work too. I mean, he would get pissed if I stayed in bed past eight on a Saturday.

It killed me to see him losing weight. I mean, I figured it was the drinking, you know. He got into this thing where he just hung out with guys his age. They would get in a car, about six of 'em, and pass a bottle of rum. I used to tell Pops: "Hey, what's this? You used to slap me for shit like that." He would tell me to shut up and then run off his man-of-the-house trip.

It bugged me to come home from work and see him standing there with his boys. I was embarrassed. "His life," I used to say. But man, I still respected him. Because he worked hard all his life. Maybe that was it; he just couldn't make it click. He worked hard to buy this nice little house in Aibonito and it's been waiting for five years already. I kept asking him: "What's with the house? When you moving?" He never answered.

About that time, right before he started losing weight, he began the screaming. Every fuckin' night he'd come home drunk. My mother would be watching the *novelas*, and forget it: when she's watchin' those things nothing can shake her, not even an earthquake. He slobbered in, yelled for food, which was stupid 'cause he wasn't really hungry. But it was habit. You know, walk in through the door, ask for food. My mother kept cool. She would push him away when he tried to kiss her. I'd come in from my room and stand there in the hallway, arms crossed. I would kid him, telling him he couldn't hold his liquor, that after three months he should stop celebrating his return to P.R. And after a while he would laugh.

I think the *novelas* made him sad. I mean, he usually threw himself on our bowlegged sofa and would watch the television noddin'. Minutes later, he'd start talkin' to himself. He'd start with his last job, about how they treated him like *un inválido*, which he wasn't 'cause he's always been in good shape. And that's true. My father never missed a day of work on account of health. But he had this thing for his old bosses. All of 'em. He cursed them all out after a few *palitos*.

After getting off his cookies cursing 'em out, he'd keep quiet for some time, and then lookin' more ragged by the minute, he began with his P.R. stories. He'd go into this story about his brother and him when they were young dudes. It didn't matter what story, it always began with a relative or person he knew. They were funny stories. And they had a meaning to them, you know? But no matter if we were rollin' and fartin' from laughin', he'd always get depressed. That's when he looked up to the light and, raising his hands, would wish for death. "Please Lord, bring me death," he used to say. "I've lived long enough."

Moms would beg him to stop, but that never cooled him out. He'd get angry at the light bulb, like it was really supposed to bring death on him or something. He'd cursed at it in Spanish and English: "Carajo," "Puñeta," "Sonsabich." One time he even threw a shoe at it.

Those were some hard days. I'd bring in what little money I made, so I was always broke. But I dealt with it. Even with the classes after work. It wasn't fun, let me tell you. Right now, all I can do is sit back and relax. Go to work, come home, try to get me and Moms back to some type of real world. The only hard thing is fightin' them memories, the last times when everything was *so* crazy. Who could blame me? I held up good, man, all the way to the time when that jerk in the gray suit spread that flag over the coffin.

The phone call was nothing. It hurt; yeah, it stung me good. But the shock helped me get through it. Maybe it energized me, you know? It was a real nice May Saturday, I'll never forget. I was reading *Playboy*, looking at the cracks on the ceiling and thinking about Sonia's big ass. The phone rang, and I thought it was her. On the stove, some homemade soup was perkin'. My mother was gonna take it down to the hospital. She was gonna leave in half an hour. I picked up the phone on the third ring and a sandpaper voice asked for the Pérez residence. I said "Yeah?" And she hit me with the news. Just like that.

"Thank you" was all I said. The phone turned heavy, like a barbell, and it pulled my arm down toward my leg. I left it hanging off the hook and looked at my mother. She didn't speak English, but my voice gave me away. "Qué pasa?" she asked. And for the record, I said, "Mami, he's gone." She understood. I stroked her hair and held her tightly. "My love," she cried. "God, you've taken my love."

The neighbors heard my mother's screaming and came over. Moms didn't let 'em ask what happened. She yelled it at everyone that came in the door. Then Doña Gloria was crying, along with the two fat sisters from 3B, and even the old man, Don Pablo, he dropped a tear or two. People came from everywhere; it was like a fight had broken out on a corner. All of 'em snifflin' or cryin' because my old man had passed away.

I didn't know what to do. My head was down, my mouth tight. People came over and said how they were sorry, or they tapped me on my head. I felt like a dog. This went on for hours. The soup my mother made was still on the stove, cold now. My mother pointed to it from time to time and said how she was planning to take it to Pops. And people would say, "Ay bendito."

It was dinnertime by the time we decided to move on fixing the funeral. And my stomach was hitting 10 on the Richter scale. At one point all the neighbors left, so I decided to heat up some of the soup. Just as I sat down with a bowl and a chunk of Italian bread, the Dominican family from the fifth floor came in. I just couldn't feel comfortable eating, like it was a sin or something. I flushed the soup down the toilet.

After everybody left for good, I called my uncle Anselmo from Jersey, who we hadn't seen in years. We needed help. I didn't know a goddamn thing about funerals. I knew that we had to go to the VA hospital and get the body. But from there, what? So Tío Anselmo came over, fatter than ever, his goatee full of crumbs, looking around with them bug eyes. His old lady Miriam was lookin' as fine as ever, and the kids, Papo and Lourdes, were snottier and sat there like they never seen Ricans before. Anyway, Anselmo did help us. He made Moms cool down. A few calls and everything was cool. He kept saying, "It's good to have the family together."

It didn't take long to get to the hospital. We went to the administrative office, a little room full of banged-up cabinets and midget desks. We went down floors and through halls to finally get a pale-ass, wrinkle-faced woman with tinted, steel-rimmed glasses. She was the same one who called with the bad news. Sounding like John Wayne after two operations, I swear, she gave us the rundown. Then this doctor with a girl's face came down and signed some papers. He told us that Pops died because of his liver. That's when my mother started about the drinking, and telling me to take that as an example — like I drink that much, you know.

My mother started to cry and the woman held her hand and told us to sign a paper. My mother did, and then we were told about my father's benefits, on account he fought in World War II and Korea. We were lucky that he had these benefits, 'cause we had no money for bills. The hospital was good and all, but the times we visited always made me think about if he liked it there. All those old guys riding in wheelchairs, thinking about the good old days in the wars. It used to scare me shitless. That's why I only visited on Saturdays. I couldn't take a whole week of old men crying and shitting on themselves or rolling around without legs.

Maybe he was better off dying early. That's what everybody says, and maybe they're right. That's what I thought when we got outta the hospital, right after the vampire lady told us that my father had a right to a flag for his coffin. We didn't think about it then, it didn't seem important. So we told the VA people that some people from the Walter B. Cooke on Castle Hill would pick up the body. My uncle decided that was the best place. Who was gonna argue? The only thing that made sense was that my mother told him not to go to Vazquez Funeral Home because they were crooks. My father always said that they left bodies smelling bad. Not to use Vazquez; he used to tell us all the time. He used to tell us not to let anybody put an American flag on his coffin, too. He was a veteran, but he didn't think it was big shit. He made fun of all the politicians and called them *raqueteros*. After one election he got so pissed off that he tore up his registration card and swore never to vote again. And he kept his word. Pops was a man of his word, so when he told us these things about when he died, we used to listen, because deep down we knew he was serious.

The salesman at Cooke's was a young Italian guy with a five o'clock shadow and in need of a bad tan. You could tell he had done this for ages. He gave us the line about how we didn't want a cheap coffin for our beloved. And who's gonna say, "Hey, man, we wanna save money!" My mother bought a beautiful bronze coffin with a beige stain interior. She bought the little cards to hand out, with my father's name on them, and she was about to buy a head of Jesus with eyes that lit up, but Tío talked her out of it.

At first, the idea was to send my father straight to the Island, but he'd known a lot of people in the neighborhood, and they wanted to pay their respects. So for one day and night they had a chance to pay their respects. And let me tell you, they came. People who hadn't seen him for years. Even his sister from Poughkeepsie came down; so did his brother from Milwaukee, who we shouldn't have told. He's really into Jesus, and when he arrived he began preaching. He went on for about an hour, I swear, before someone told him he should rest.

Well, all these relatives and people came in, and by nighttime the small room had voices praying and talking, and the weepy sounds of old ladies, and I stood there, my eyes red from being tired. And I saw my father in his coffin. He looked so happy. I looked around the fancy wine-colored carpeted room, with the flowers, the folding chairs, the people standing around, and I wanted it to end. Then as I sat there, not paying attention to the pats on my shoulder and the sorry words, the mortician came over and put an American flag, folded in a triangle, by my father's head. I heard whispers: "Era veterano . . ." Nobody said anything else. My mother was busy with her crying. I felt a burning feeling inside, like I just had a shot of whiskey or something. I should have done something. I wanted to take the flag off, but I didn't. I didn't want trouble or to do something stupid. I didn't do nothing about it. I didn't do nothing. Just sat there. All day my father slept, a smile on his face and that triangle with stars sitting by his face. What was worse, they took pictures of him like that, too.

The next day, in the afternoon, Moms and me were on a plane headed for the Island. It was such a weird ride. Me, dressed in gray and black, my mother in black, her eyes red. I couldn't even think of P.R. the same way like those other times. I didn't think of the plane landing, or about how San Juan looked from a thousand feet. All I remembered was sitting and needing to go piss but not wanting to get up. And my mother also talked to this young chick across from us who said this was her first flight in years. My mother told her that she went all the time but that this time she was coming with her husband, who was riding down below in a coffin. God forgive me, but I wanted to laugh when she said that. I had to look out the window to stop from cracking up. It was just the way it sounded.

Anyway, we landed and the heat hit me like a blast from a furnace. I wanted to come to the Island all this year, but on what I made, forget it. But with my father dying, my mother took the money from her savings and there I was. But when I saw Tía Julia and her husband all droopy-faced, it hit me that, hey, this wasn't no vacation. Tía Julia hugged my mother, and they cried. My aunt cried all over my shirt. We went to get our bags, and with the weather and nobody talking, it felt like I was high; everything fuzzed out, my head buzzed.

The second day in Puerto Rico we waited for the body to come from the airport. We thought it was following us when we drove from San Juan to Aibonito, because we saw this hearse driving behind us on the highway. But that wasn't Pops. It got dark and cool and we waited in the funeral parlor.

Inside, in another room, people were praying for an old woman who they said died of a heart attack after she found out she won the lottery. Our group sat around talking and smoking. Flowers were everywhere. Wooden chairs were lined up in rows of fives, facing the fake marble stand where the coffin was supposed to be. I'm glad the place was modern; it had water fountains and clean bathrooms. They even had old-time pictures of the town on the walls.

The hearse came and some guys rolled the coffin in. My mother noticed a dent on the casket and started to yell. My aunt's husband went into the office and demanded money for the damages. I don't really know what happened next. Some guy took photographs and they promised to call up Cooke. We never received any money.

The next day we woke up early and got ready to bury the body. Friends and relatives took the coffin out to the hearse. As they did, the mortician unfolded the American flag. Now, the day before the same flag had been on the side of my father's face, just like in New York. But this guy decides to get real fancy and throw the flag over the coffin, like in those big-time funerals for Presidents. My heart started doing jumping jacks on that one. I went over to my mother and asked her if she was gonna let this dude spread the flag over

Pops. She told me it was tradition, that Pops used to say things he didn't mean.

I couldn't believe it. Moms knew exactly how Pops felt, but it was like she didn't want to argue. All she had to do was tell the guy. But she couldn't. She couldn't go up to the guy and tell him, "Hey, forget the flag."

I put my hands in my pockets and stared at the flag, now hanging over the coffin. My mother was heavy into praying, and no one knew what was happening. How could they? I looked at the flag, and the more I saw it, the madder I got. It got to the point that I went up to the main dude to tell him to get that fuckin' flag off my father. My old man deserved respect, deserved to die the way he wanted, even if he had fought in two wars. I went up to this fat motha, in his tight shiny suit, and parked right by his patent leathers. He was talking to another guy about who should be elected to some office in the neighborhood, some shit like that. Anyway, he didn't see me. He wasn't even paying attention to me, and I was so close to the asshole that I could see myself in his hair. He kept talking and talking and getting all excited about the bullshit he was laying out. I stood there thinking how I would explain to the man in my Spanish about my father's wishes. I wanted a joint. I wanted to clear my throat, but couldn't. Maybe I should've been loud or something. They must've thought I was a *pendejo*, 'cause they just kept talking like nothing was happening. The fat guy talked so fast that I couldn't get a word to him. The other guy was into it too, but he was worse 'cause he kept blowin' smoke my way. Ten minutes waiting there like a prick, and then I said, "Fuck it, what's the use."

I went outside. I walked across the town's main road. Across from all the shit in the funeral place. By the highway, I watched the few cars that went by. I wanted to hitchhike and just keep going. My chest felt like someone pushed a fist down my throat. Forgive me, Pops, I let you down, I thought. Then I broke down and cried like a little girl.

The next day we woke up early, drank a little coffee, ate crackers and cheese, and headed out to the funeral home, this time for the last time. Everything went so fast that morning. All I remember was squinting and just seeing a yellow fuzz; it was so fuckin' hot. I held my mother's hand, it was cold, and she held on to some flowers someone gave her. Friends and relatives put the coffin in the hearse and that started everyone and everything in motion.

My mother cried all the way to the cemetery, a block and a half away. We walked behind the hearse, in that sun that got hotter. I could feel nothing but the drops falling from under my arms. And all around, people praying. People stretched out windows to look. A woman with a scabby face and blond Brillo hair joined us; grabbing a rosary, she prayed like she knew my father all her life.

At the entrance to the cemetery, my mother met an old friend who was selling flowers to people going in. Moms said hello and then cried on her shoulder. The woman stroked her hair, told her to be strong and gave her a white carnation. I grabbed my mother and told her we had to go on. That entrance to the cemetery took forever. It was really long, with pillars on the sides. We got to the end and we made a right. Six men, who I didn't know, carried the coffin. I knew that it would be heavy, so I decided to stay with my mother and help her. I was feeling weak and didn't want to fall or trip or something.

We held each other as we climbed up the rocks and dirt piled up around the hole. We finally made it, and my mother began to cry loud. I looked down into it and my throat got dry. It was deep, man, really dark and deep. This is it, I thought. I held my mother tight. I heard stories about women jumping into these grief holes.

The priest said a few words, threw some holy water down the hole and nodded his head. One of the men folded the flag and gave it to my mother. My face turned red. Four big men tied the coffin with canvas ropes and let it down slowly to the bottom. The priest asked my mother to throw some dirt in and she did. The chunks of dirt hit the coffin and sounded like someone sat down on a car. On the way out, I turned around and saw those four men on top of that pile of dirt, digging away.

We went back a week later. Now it's been a month, and we're still figuring things out. Putting the pieces together. Moms goes around in black dresses, lighting candles and praying. She wears a rosary all the time. Me, I get the problems. The rent, gas or light bill, or telephone, she gives to me. I had to call Tío Anselmo a couple of times. And I can't keep calling him, 'cause he sounds pissed every time I do.

Sonia, my girl, tells me Moms is taking advantage. I told her the marriage had to wait, and that's all. I don't want it like that, but my mother comes first. I don't like it. I mean, sometimes Moms gets on my nerves and I walk out of the house. But everything will get back to normal. I know it will. I got my job; maybe I'll work a little overtime. I'll drop school for a while, until everything chills out. I have to do it. At least for Pops. At least for him.

GARY SOTO

Being Mean

W E WERE terrible kids, I think. My brother, sister, and I felt a general meanness begin to surface from our tiny souls while living on Braly Street, which was in the middle of industrial Fresno. Across the street was Coleman Pickles, while on the right of us was a junkyard that dealt in metals — aluminum, iron, sheet metal, and copper stripped from refrigerators. Down the street was Sun-Maid Raisin, where a concrete tower rose above the scraggly sycamores that lined Braly Street. Many of our family worked at Sun-Maid: Grandfather and Grandmother, Father, three uncles, an aunt, and even a dog, whose job was to accompany my grandfather, a security guard, on patrol. Then there was Challenge Milk, a printing shop, and the 7-Up Company, where we stole sodas. Down the alley was a broom factory and Western Book Distributor, a place where our future stepfather worked at packing books into cardboard boxes, something he would do for fifteen years before the company left town for Oregon.

This was 1957. My brother Rick was six, I was five, and Debra was four. Although we looked healthy, clean in the morning, and polite as only Mexicans can be polite, we had a streak of orneriness that we imagined to be normal play. That summer — and the summer previous — we played with the Molinas, who lived down the alley from us right across from the broom factory and its brutal *whack* of straw being tied into brooms. There were eight children on the block that year, ranging from twelve down to one, so there was much to do: wrestle, eat raw bacon, jump from the couch, sword fight with rolled-up newspapers, steal from neighbors, kick chickens, throw rocks at passing cars. While we played in the house, Mother Molina just watched us run around, a baby in her arms crying like a small piece of machinery turning at great speed. Now and then she would warn us with a smile, "Now you kids, you're going to hurt yourselves." We ignored her and went on pushing one another from an open window, yelling wildly when we hit the ground because we imagined that there was a school of sharks ready to snack on our skinny legs.

What we learned from the Molinas was how to have fun, and what we taught them was how to fight. It seemed that the Sotos were inherently violent. I remember, for instance, watching my aunts going at one another in my grandmother's backyard while the men looked on with beers in their hands and mumbled to one another, perhaps noting the beauty of a jab or a roundhouse punch. Another time the police arrived late at night in search of our Uncle Leonard, who had gotten into a fight at a neighborhood bar. Shortly thereafter, I recall driving with my mother to see him at what she said was a "soldiers' camp." She had a sack of goods with her, and after speaking softly to a uniformed man, we were permitted to enter. It was lunchtime and he sat on a felled log, laughing with other men. When he saw us coming, he laughed even harder.

In turn, I was edged with a meanness, and more often than not the object of my attacks was Rick. If upset, I chased him with rocks, pans, a hammer, whatever lay around in the yard. Once, when he kicked over a row of beans I had planted in the yard, I chased him down the alley with a bottle until, in range, I hurled it at him. The bottle hit him in the thigh and, to my surprise, showered open with blood. Screaming, his mouth open wide enough to saucer a hat inside, he hobbled home while I stood there, only slightly worried at his wound and the spanking that would follow, shouting that he had better never do that again. And he didn't.

I was also hurt by others who were equally as mean, and I am thinking particularly of an Okie kid who yelled that we were dirty Mexicans. Perhaps so, but why bring it up? I looked at my feet and was embarrassed, then mad. With a bottle I approached him slowly in spite of my brother's warnings that the kid was bigger and older. When I threw the bottle and missed, he swung his stick and my nose exploded blood for several feet. Frightened, though not crying, I ran home with Rick and Debra chasing me, and dabbed at my face and T-shirt, poked Mercurochrome at the tear that bubbled, and then lay on the couch, swallowing blood as I slowly grew faint and sleepy. Rick and Debra looked at me for a while, then got up to go outside to play.

Rick and I and the Molinas all enjoyed looking for trouble and often went to extremes to try to get into fights. One day we found ourselves staring at some new kids on the street — three of them about our age — and when they looked over their picket fence to see who we were, I thought one of them had sneered at us, so I called him a name. They called back at us, and that provocation was enough to send Rick to beat on one of them. Rick entered their yard and was punched in the ear, then in the back when he tried to hunch over to protect himself. Furious as a bee, I ran to fight the kid who had humbled Rick, but was punched in the stomach, which knocked the breath out of me so I couldn't tell anyone how much it had hurt. The Molinas grew scared and ran home, while Rick and I, slightly roughed up but sure that we had the guts to give them a good working over, walked slowly home trying to figure out how to do it. A small flame lit my brain, and I suggested that we stuff a couple of cats into potato sacks and beat the kids with them. An even smaller light flared in my brother's brain. "Yeah, that'll get them," he said, happy that we were going to get even. We called to our cat, Boots, and found another unfortunate cat that was strolling nonchalantly down our alley in search of prime garbage. I called to it and it came, purring. I carried it back to our yard, where Rick had already stuffed Boots into a sack, which was bumping about on the ground. Seeing this, the cat stiffened in my arms and I had trouble working the cat into the sack, for it had spread its feet and opened its claws. But once inside, the cat grew calm, resigning itself to fate, and meowed only once or twice. For good measure I threw a bottle into my sack, and the two of us — or, to be fair, the four of us — went down the alley in search of the new kids.

We looked for them, even calling them names at their back porch, but they failed to show themselves. Rick and I believed that they were scared, so in a way we were victors. Being mean, we kicked over their garbage cans and ran home, where we fought one another with the sacks, the cats all along whining and screaming to get out.

Perhaps the most enjoyable summer day was when Rick, Debra, and I decided to burn down our house. Earlier in the summer we had watched a television program on fire prevention at our grandmother's house, only three houses down from us on Sarah Street. The three of us sat transfixed in front of the gray light of the family's first TV. We sat on the couch with a bowl of grapes, and when the program ended the bowl was still in Rick's lap, untouched. TV was that powerful.

Just after that program Rick and I set fire to our first shoe box, in which we imagined were many people scurrying to get out. We hovered over the fire, and our eyes grew wild. Later, we got very good at burning shoe boxes. We crayoned windows, cut doors on the sides, and dropped ants into the boxes, imagining they were people wanting very badly to live. Once the fire got going, I wailed like a siren and Rick flicked water from a coffee can at the building leaping with flames. More often than not, it burned to ash and the ants shriveled to nothing — though a few would limp away, wiser by vision of death.

But we grew bored with the shoe boxes. We wanted something more exciting and daring, so Rick suggested that we brighten our lives with a house fire. "Yeah," Debra and I cried, leaping into the air, and proceeded to toss crumpled newspapers behind the doors, under the table, and in the middle of the living room. Rick struck a match, and we stood back laughing as the flames jumped wildly about and the newspaper collapsed into ash that floated to the ceiling. Once the fire got started we dragged in the garden hose and sprayed the house, the three of us laughing for the love of good times. We were in a frenzy to build fires and put them out with the hose. I looked at Rick and his eyes were wide with pleasure, his crazed laughter like the mad scientists of the movies we would see in the coming years. Debra was jumping up and down on the couch, a toy baby in her arms, and she was smiling her tiny teeth at the fire. I ran outside flapping my arms because I wanted to also burn the chinaberry that stood near our bedroom window. Just as I was ready to set a match to a balled newspaper I intended to hurl into the branches, our grandmother came walking slowly down the alley to check on us. (It was her responsibility to watch us during the day, because our father was working at Sun-Maid Raisin and our mother was peeling potatoes at Reddi-Spud.) Grandma stopped at the gate and stared at me as if she knew what we were up to, and I stared back so I could make a quick break if she should lunge at me. Finally she asked, "How are you, honey?" I stared at my dirty legs, then up to her: "Okay. I'm just playing." With the balled newspaper in my hand, I pointed to the house and told her that Rick and Debra were inside coloring. Hearing this, she said to behave myself, gave me a piece of gum, and returned to her house.

When I went back inside, Rick and Debra were playing war with cherry tomatoes. Debra was behind the table on which the telephone rested, while Rick crouched behind a chair making the sounds of bombs falling.

"Rick," I called, because I wanted to tell him that Grandma had come to see how we were doing, but he threw a tomato and it splashed my T-shirt like a bullet wound. I feigned being shot and fell to the floor. He rolled from behind the chair to hide behind a door. "Are you dead?" he asked. I lifted my head and responded: "Only a little bit."

Laughing, we hurled tomatoes at one another, and some of them hit their mark — an ear, a shoulder, a grinning face — while others skidded across the floor or became pasted to the wall. "You Jap," Debra screamed as she cocked her hand to throw, to which I screamed, "You damn German." We fought, laughing, until the tomatoes were gone. Breathing hard, we looked at the mess we had created, and then at each other, slightly concerned at what it might mean. Rick and I tried to clean up with a broom while Debra lay exhausted on the couch, thumb in her mouth and making a smacking sound. I can't recall falling asleep but that's what happened, because I awoke to Rick crying in the kitchen. Our mother had come home to an ash-darkened living room, a puddled kitchen, and tomato-stained walls. She yelled and spanked Rick, after which she dragged him to the stove where she heated a fork over a burner and threatened to burn his wrists. "Now are you going to play with fire?" she screamed. I peeked into the kitchen and her mouth was puckered into a dried fruit as Rick cried that she was hurting him, that he was sorry, that he would never do it again. Tears leaped from his face as he tried to wiggle free. She threw the fork into the sink, then let him go. She turned to me and yelled: "And you too, Chango!" She started after me, but I ran out the front door into the alley, where I hid behind a stack of boards. I stayed there until my breathing calmed and my fear disappeared like an ash picked up by the wind. I got up and, knowing that I couldn't return home immediately, I went to the Molinas. Just as I turned into their yard I caught sight of two of them climbing, hand over hand, on the telephone wires that stretched from above the back porch to the pole itself. A few of the younger Molinas looked on from an open window, readying for their turn, as the radio blared behind them. I threw a rock at the two hanging from the wires, and they laughed that I missed. The other kids laughed. Their mother, with a baby in her arms, came out to the back porch, laughed, and told us to behave ourselves.

GLORIA ANZALDÚA

People Should Not Die in June
in South Texas

Pᴿᴵᴱᵀᴵᵀᴬ squeezes through the crowd of mourners and finds a
place near the coffin. She stands there for hours watching
relatives and friends one after the other approach the coffin, kneel
beside it. They make the sign of the cross, bow slowly while
backing away. Even a few Anglos come to pay their respects to
Urbano, loved by all. But after two and a half days, her father has
begun to smell like a cow whose carcass has been gutted by
vultures. People should not die in June in south Texas.

Earlier that day Prietita and her mother had gone to the funeral
home, where in some hidden room someone was making a two-
inch incision in her father's throat. Someone was inserting a tube
in his jugular vein. In some hidden room *una envenenada abuja*
filled his *venas* with embalming fluid.

The white undertaker put his palm on the small of her mother's
back and propelled her toward the more expensive coffins. Her
mother couldn't stop crying. She held a handkerchief to her eyes
like a blindfold, knotting and unraveling it, knotting and unraveling
it. Prieta, forced to be the more practical of the two, said, "Let's
take that one or this one," pointing at the coffins midrange in price.
Though they would be in debt for three years, they chose *un cajón
de quinientos dólares*. The undertaker had shown them the back-

less suits whose prices ranged from seventy to several hundred dollars. *Compraron un traje negro y una camisa blanca con encaje color de rosa.* They bought a black suit and a white shirt with pink. "Why are we buying such an expensive suit? It doesn't even have a back. And besides, it's going to rot soon," she told her mother softly. Her mother looked at her and burst out crying again. Her mother was either hysterical or very quiet and withdrawn, so Prieta had to swallow her own tears. They had returned in the hearse with the coffin to a house filled with relatives and friends, with tables laden with *comida* and buckets overflowing with ice and *cerveza.*

Prietita stands against the living room wall watching the hundreds of people slowly milling around. *"Te acompaño en el pesar,"* dice la tía as she embraces her. The stench of alcohol enters her nostrils when male relatives pay their condolences to her. *Prieta se siente helada y asfixiada al mismo tiempo.* She feels cold, shocked, and suffocated. *"Qué guapa. Es la mayor y se parece mucho a su mamá,"* she hears a woman say, bursting into tears and clutching Prietita in a desperate embrace. Faint whiffs of perfume escape from the women's hair behind their thick black mantillas. The smells of roses and carnations, *carne guisada,* sweat and body heat mingle with the sweet smell of death and fill the house in Hargill.

Antes del cajón en medio de la sala aullando a la virgen su mamagrande Locha cae de rodillas persinándose. But Prieta does not cry, she is the only one at the *velorio* who is dry-eyed. Why can't she cry? *Le dan ganas, no de llorar, pero de reír a carcajadas.* Instead of crying she feels like laughing. It isn't natural. She felt the tightness in her throat give way. Her body trembled with fury. How dare he die? How dare he abandon her? How could he leave her mother all alone? Her mother was just twenty-eight. It wasn't fair. *Sale de la casa corriendo,* she runs out of the house, *Atravesó la calle,* she crosses the street, *tropezándose en las piedras,* while stumbling over rocks. *Llegó a la casa de Mamagrande Ramona en donde estaba su hermanito, Carito, el más chiquito.* She reached her grandmother's house, where her little brother was hiding out. His bewildered face asks questions she cannot answer.

Later Prietita slips back into the house and returns to her place by the coffin. Standing on her toes, she cocks her head over the casket. What if that sweet-putrid smell is perfume injected into his veins to fool them all into thinking he is dead? What if it's all a conspiracy? A lie? Under the overturned red truck someone else's face had lain broken, smashed beyond recognition. The blood on the highway had not been her father's blood.

For three days her father sleeps in his coffin. Her mother sits at his side every night and never sleeps. *Oliendo a muerte, Prietita duerme en su cama*, Prieta sleeps in her bed with the smell of death. *En sus sueños*, in her dreams, *su padre abre los ojos al mirarla*, her father his eyes. *Abre su boca a contestarle*, he opens his mouth to answer her. *Se levanta del cajón*, he rises out of the coffin. On the third day Prieta rises from her bed vacant-eyed, puts on her black blouse and skirt and black scarf, and walks to the living room. She stands before the coffin and waits for the hearse. In the car behind the hearse on the way to the church Prietita sits quietly beside her mother, sister, and brothers. Stiff-legged, she gets out of the car and walks to the hearse. She watches the pall bearers, *Tío David, Rafael, Goyo, el compadre Juan*, and others, lift the coffin out of the hearse, carry it inside the church, and set it down in the middle of the aisle.

El cuerpo de su padre está tendido en medio de la iglesia. Her father's corpse lies in the middle of the church. She watches one woman after another kneel before *la Virgen de Guadalupe* and light a candle. Soon hundreds of votive candles flicker their small flames and emit the smell of burning tallow.

"*Et Misericordia ejus a progenis timentibus eum*," intones the priest, flanked by altar boys on both sides. His purple gown rustles as he swings his censors over her father's body and face. Clouds of frankincense cover the length of the dark shiny coffin.

At last the pall bearers return to the coffin. Sporting mustaches and wearing black ties, *con bigote y corbata negra*, they stand stiffly in their somber suits. She had never seen these ranchers, farmers, and farm workers in suits before. In unison they take a deep breath and with a quick movement they lift the coffin. Her mother holds Carito's hands and follows the coffin while Prieta, her sister, and brother walk behind them.

Outside near the cars parked in the street, Prieta watches the church slowly emptying, watches the church becoming a hollowed-out thing. In their black cotton and rayon dresses, following the coffin with faces hidden under fine-woven mantillas, the women all look like *urracas prietas*, like black crows. Her own nickname was *Urraca Prieta*.

From her uncle's car en route to the cemetery, Prieta watches the billows of dust rise in the wake of the hearse. Her skin feels prickly with sweat and something else. As the landscape recedes, Prietita feels as though she is traveling backwards to yesterday, to the day before yesterday, to the day she last saw her father. Prieta imagines her father as he drives the red truck filled to the brim with cotton bales. One hand suddenly leaves the wheel to clutch his chest. His body arches, then his head and chest slump over the wheel, blood streaming out through his nose and mouth, his foot lies heavy on the gas pedal. The red ten-ton truck keeps going until it gets to the second curve on the east highway going toward Edinburg. "Wake up, Papi, turn the wheel," but the truck keeps on going off the highway. It turns over, the truck turns over and over, the doors flapping open then closing and the truck keeps turning over and over until Prieta makes it stop. Her father is thrown out. The edge of the back of the truck crushes his face. Six pairs of wheels spin in the air. White cotton bales are littered around him. The article in the newspaper said that according to the autopsy report, his aorta had burst. The largest artery to the heart, ruptured.

She had *not* seen the crows, *las urracas prietas*, gather on the *ébano* in the backyard the night before that bright day in June. If they had not announced his death then he couldn't be dead. It was a conspiracy, a lie.

Ya se acabó; ¿qué pasa? Contemplad su figura
la muerte le ha cubierto de pálidos azufres
y le ha puesto cabeza de oscuro minotauro.

Is it over? What's happening?
Reflect on his figure.
Death has covered him with pale sulfurs
and has given him a dark Minotaur head.

The *padrinas* place the coffin under the ebony tree. People pile flower wreaths at her father's feet. Prietita shuffles over to her father lying in the coffin. Her eyes trace the jagged lines running through his forehead, cheek, and chin, where the undertaker had sewn the skin together. The broken nose, the chalky skin with the tinge of green underneath is not her father's face, *no es la cara de su papi*. No. On that bright day, June 22, someone else had been driving his truck, someone else had been wearing his khaki pants, his gold wire-rimmed glasses — someone else had his gold front tooth.

Mr. Leidner, her history teacher, had said that the Nazis jerked the gold teeth out of the corpses of the Jews and melted them into rings. And made their skin into lampshades. She did not want anyone to take her *papi*'s gold tooth. Prieta steps back from the coffin.

The blood in the highway could not be her father's blood.

¡Qué no quiere verla!
Dile a la luna que venga,
que no quiero ver la sangre

I don't want to see it.
Tell the moon to come
that I don't want to see the blood

As she watches her father, a scream forms in her head: "No, no, no." She thinks she almost sees death creep into her father's unconscious body, kick out his soul and make his body stiff and still. She sees *la muerte*'s long pale fingers take possession of her father — sees death place its hands over what had been her father's heart. A fly buzzes by, brings her back to the present. She sees a fly crawl over one of her father's hands, then land on his cheek. She wants him to raise his hand and fan the fly away. He lies unmoving. She raises her hand to crush the fly then lets it fall back to the side. Swatting the fly would mean hitting her *papi*. Death, too, lets the fly crawl over itself. Maybe the fly and death are friends. Maybe death is unaware of so inconsequential a thing as an insect. She is like that fly trying to rouse her father, *es esa mosca*.

She stands looking by the coffin at her own small hands —

fleshy, ruddy hands — and forces herself to unclench her fists. A beat pulses in her thumb. When her hands are no longer ruddy nor pulsating she will lie like him. She will lie utterly still. Maggots will find her hands, will seek out her heart. Worms will crawl in and out of her vagina and the world will continue as usual. That is what shocks her the most about her father's death — that people still laugh, the wind continues to blow, the sun rises in the east and sets in the west.

Prieta walks away from the coffin and stands at the edge of the gaping hole under the ebony tree. The hole is so deep, *el pozo tan hondo,* the earth so black, *la tierra tan prieta.* She takes great gulps of air but can't get enough into her lungs. Nausea winds its way up from the pit of her stomach, fills her chest and becomes a knot when it reaches her throat. Her body sways slowly back and forth. Someone gently tugs her away. *Los hombres* push a metal apparatus over the hole and *los padrinos* place the coffin over it.

Under the *ébano,* around the hole, a procession forms. The small country cemetery, with Mexicans buried on one side and a few Anglos on the other, is now bulging with hundreds of cars *y miles de gente y miles de flores.*

Prieta hears the whir of the machine and looks back to see it lowering her father into the hole. Someone tosses in a handful of dirt, then the next person does the same, and soon a line of people forms, waiting their turn. Prietita listens to the thuds, the slow shuffle of feet as the line winds and unwinds like a giant serpent. Her turn comes, she bends to pick up a handful of dirt. She loosens her clenched fist over the hole and hears the thud of *terremotes* hit her father's coffin. Drops fall onto the dust-covered coffin. They make little craters on the *cajón's* smooth surface. She feels as though she is standing alone near the mouth of the abyss, near the mouth slowly swallowing her father. An unknown sweetness and a familiar anguish beckon her. As she rocks back and forth near the edge, she listens to Mamagrande's litany: *"Mi hijo, mi hijo, tan bueno. Diosito mío, ¿por qué se lo llevó? Ay mi hijo."*

Next Sunday the whole family has to go to mass, but Prieta doesn't want to attend. Heavily veiled women dressed in black kneel on the cement floor of the small church and recite the rosary in singsong monotones. *Llorosas rezaban el rosario*, hands moving slowly over the beads. "*Santa María, madre de Dios, ruega por nosotros* . . . Holy Mary, mother of God, pray for us now and at the hour of our death." Her mother and Mamagrande Locha dedicate Sunday masses to her father, promising *la Virgen* a mass a week for the coming year. They pay a small fee for each — all for a man who had never entered church except for the funeral mass of a friend or relative.

Her mother wears *luto*, vowing before a statue of *la Virgen de Guadalupe* to wear black for two years and gray for two more. In September when school resumes, her mother tells Prieta and her sister that they are to wear black for a year, then gray or brown for another two. At first her classmates stare at her. Prieta sees the curiosity and fascination in their eyes slowly turn to pity and disdain. But soon they get used to seeing her in black and drab-colored clothes and she feels invisible once more, and invincible.

After school and on weekends her mother shushes them when they speak loudly or laugh, forbids them to listen to the radio and covers the TV with a blanket. Prieta remembers when her father bought the TV. The other kids had been envious because hers had been the first Mexican family to have such an extravagant luxury. Her father had bought it for them saying it would help his *hijitos* learn to speak English without an accent. If they knew English they could get good jobs and not have to work themselves to death.

Pasa mucho tiempo. Days and weeks and years pass. *Prieta espera al muerto.* She waits for the dead. Every evening she waits for her father to walk into the house, tired after a day of hard work in the fields. She waits for him to rap his knuckles on the top of her head, the one gesture of intimacy he allowed himself with her. She waits for him to gaze at her with his green eyes. She waits for him to take off his shirt and sit bare-chested on the floor, back against the sofa watching TV, the black curly hair on the back of his head showing. Now she thinks she hears his footsteps on the front porch, and turns eagerly toward the door. For years she waits. *Four years* she waits for him to thrust open the sagging door, to return from the land of the dead. For her father is a great and good man and she is sure God will realize he has made a mistake and bring him back to them. *En el día de los muertos*, on the day of the dead, *el primero de noviembre*, on the first of November, *ella lo espera*, she waits for him. *Aunque no más viniera a visitarlos*, even if he only came to visit. *Aunque no se quedara*, even if he didn't stay — she wants to see him — *quiere verlo*. But one day, *four years* after his death, she knows that neither the One God nor her father will ever walk through her door again.

pero nadie querrá mirar tus ojos
porque te has muerto para siempre . . .
como todos los muertos de la Tierra.

but no one will want to look at your eyes
because you have died forever . . .
like all the dead on Earth.

SANDRA CISNEROS

The Monkey Garden

THE MONKEY doesn't live there anymore. The monkey moved — to Kentucky — and took his people with him. And I was glad because I couldn't listen anymore to his wild screaming at night, the twangy yakkety-yak of the people who owned him. The green metal cage, the porcelain tabletop, the family that spoke like guitars. Monkey, family, table. All gone.

And it was then we took over the garden we had been afraid to go into when the monkey screamed and showed its yellow teeth.

There were sunflowers big as flowers on Mars, and thick cockscombs bleeding the deep red fringe of theater curtains. There were dizzy bees and bow-tied fruit flies turning somersaults and humming in the air. Sweet sweet peach trees. Thorn roses and thistle and pears. Weeds like so many squinty-eyed stars, and brush that made your ankles itch and itch until you washed with soap and water. There were big green apples hard as knees. And everywhere the sleepy smell of rotting wood, damp earth and dusty hollyhocks thick and perfumy like the blue-blond hair of the dead.

Yellow spiders ran when we turned rocks over, and pale worms blind and afraid of light rolled over in their sleep. Poke a stick in the sandy soil and a few blue-skinned beetles would appear, an avenue of ants, so many crusty ladybugs. This was a garden, a wonderful thing to look at in the spring. But bit by bit, after the monkey left, the garden began to take over itself. Flowers stopped obeying the little bricks that kept them from growing beyond their paths. Weeds mixed in. Dead cars appeared overnight like mushrooms. First one and then another and then a pale blue pickup with the front windshield missing. Before you knew it, the monkey garden became filled with sleepy cars.

Things had a way of disappearing in the garden, as if the garden itself ate them, or, as if with its old-man memory, it put them away and forgot them. Nenny found a dollar and a dead mouse between two rocks in the stone wall where the morning glories climbed, and once when we were playing hide and seek, Eddie Vargas laid his head beneath a hibiscus tree and fell asleep there like a Rip Van Winkle until somebody remembered he was in the game and went back to look for him.

This, I suppose, was the reason why we went there. Far away from where our mothers could find us. We and a few old dogs who lived inside the empty cars. We made a clubhouse once on the back of that old blue pickup. And besides, we liked to jump from the roof of one car to another and pretend they were giant mushrooms.

Somebody started the lie that the monkey garden had been there before anything. We liked to think the garden could hide things for a thousand years. There beneath the roots of soggy flowers were the bones of murdered pirates and dinosaurs, the eye of a unicorn turned to coal.

This is where I wanted to die and where I tried one day, but not even the monkey garden would have me. It was the last day I would go there.

Who was it that said I was getting too old to play the games? Who was it I didn't listen to? I only remember that when the others ran, I wanted to run too, up and down and through the monkey garden, fast as the boys, not like Sally, who screamed if she got her stockings muddy.

I said, Sally, come on, but she wouldn't. She stayed by the curb talking to Tito and his friends. Play with the kids if you want, she said, I'm staying here. She could be stuck up like that if she wanted to, so I just left.

It was her own fault too. When I got back, Sally was pretending to be mad . . . something about the boys having stolen her keys. Please give them back to me, she said, punching the nearest one with a soft fist. They were laughing. She was too. It was a joke I didn't get.

I wanted to go back with the other kids who were still jumping on cars, still chasing each other through the garden, but Sally had her own game.

One of the boys invented the rules. One of Tito's friends said you can't get the keys back unless you kiss us, and Sally pretended to be mad at first but she said yes. It was that simple.

I don't know why, but something inside me wanted to throw a stick. Something wanted to say no when I watched Sally going into the garden with Tito's buddies all grinning. It was just a kiss, that's all. A kiss for each one. So what, she said.

Only how come I felt angry inside. Like something wasn't right. Sally went behind that old blue pickup to kiss the boys and get her keys back, and I ran up three flights of stairs to where Tito lived. His mother was ironing shirts. She was sprinkling water on them from an empty pop bottle and smoking a cigarette.

Your son and his friends stole Sally's keys and now they won't give them back unless she kisses them and right now they're making her kiss them, I said all out of breath from the three flights of stairs.

Those kids, she said, not looking up from her ironing.

That's all?

What do you want me to do, she said, call the cops? And kept on ironing.

I looked at her a long time, but couldn't think of anything to say, and ran back down the three flights to the garden, where Sally needed to be saved. I took three big sticks and a brick and figured this was enough.

But when I got there Sally said go home. Those boys said, leave us alone. I felt stupid with my brick. They all looked at me as if *I* was the one that was crazy and made me feel ashamed.

And then I don't know why but I had to run away. I had to hide myself at the other end of the garden, in the jungle part, under a tree that wouldn't mind if I lay down and cried a long time. I closed my eyes like tight stars so that I wouldn't, but I did. My face felt hot. Everything inside hiccupped.

I read somewhere that in India there are priests who can will their heart to stop beating. I wanted to will my blood to stop, my heart to quit its pumping. I wanted to be dead, to turn into the rain, my eyes melt into the ground like two black snails. I wished and wished. I closed my eyes and willed it, but when I got up my dress was green and I had a headache.

I looked at my feet in their white socks and ugly round shoes. They seemed far away. They didn't seem to be my feet anymore. And the garden that had been such a good place to play didn't seem mine either.

RUDOLFO A. ANAYA

The Apple Orchard

THE LAST WEEK of school and the warm spring weather made us restless. Pico and Chueco ditched every chance they got, and when they came to school it was only to bother the girls and upset the teachers, otherwise they played hooky in Durán's apple orchard, the large orchard which lay between the school and our small neighborhood. They smoked cigarettes and looked at *Playboy* magazines, which they stole from their older brothers.

I had stayed with them once, but my father had found out about it and he had been very angry. "It costs money to send you to school," he had said, "so go! Go and learn everything there is to learn! That's the only way to get ahead in this world! Don't play hooky with those tontos, they will never amount to anything!" So I dragged myself to school, which, in spite of the warm spring weather, had one consolation: Miss Brighton. She was the young substitute teacher who had come to replace Mr. Portales, who had had a nervous breakdown. I had her for first-period English and last-period study hall. The day she arrived I helped her move her supplies and books, so we formed a good friendship. I think I fell in love with her, because I looked forward to her class, and I was sad when she told me she would be with us only these few days until the end of school. Next year she would have a regular job in Santa Fe.

So for a few weeks I was happy, and my fascination with Miss Brighton grew. During study hall I would pretend to read, but most often I would sit and stare over my book at her. When she happened to glance up she would smile at me, and sometimes she came to my desk and asked me what I was reading. She loaned me a few books, and after I read them and told her what I had found in them she was very pleased. Her lips curled in a smile which almost laughed and her bright eyes shone with light. I began to memorize her features, and at night I began to dream of her.

Then on the last day of school Pico and Chueco came up with their crazy idea. It didn't interest me at first, but the truth is I was also filled with curiosity. So I gave in reluctantly.

"It's the only way to become a man," Pico said, as if he really knew what he was talking about.

"Yeah," Chueco agreed, "we've seen it in pictures, but you gotta see the real thing to know what it's like."

"Okay, okay," I said finally, "I'll do it."

That night I stole into my parents' bedroom. I had never done that before. Their bedroom was a place where they could go for privacy, and I was never to interrupt them when they were in there. My father had only told me that once. We were washing his car when unexpectedly he turned to me and said, "When your mother and me are in the bedroom you should never disturb us, understand?" I nodded. I knew that part of their life was shut off to me, and it was to remain a mystery.

Now I felt like a thief as I stood in the dark and saw their dark forms on the bed. My father's arm rested over my mother's hip. I heard his low, peaceful snore and I was relieved that he was asleep. I hurried quickly to her bureau and opened her small vanity box. I knew the small mirror we needed for our purpose lay among the bottles of perfume and nail polish. My hands trembled when I found it. I slipped it into my pocket and left the room quickly.

"Did you get it?" Pico asked the next morning.

We met in the apple orchard where we always met on the way to school. The flowering trees buzzed with honeybees as they swarmed over the thick clusters of white petals. The fragrance reminded me of my mother's vanity case, and for a moment I wondered if I should surrender the mirror to Pico. I had never stolen anything from her before. But it was too late to back out. I took the mirror from my pocket and held it out. For a moment it reflected the light which filtered through the canopy of apple blossoms, then Pico howled and we ran to school.

Miss Brighton was the kindest teacher we knew, so we decided to steal the glue from her room.

"Besides, she likes you," Pico said. "You keep her busy, I'll steal the glue." So we pushed our way past the mob which filled the hallway to her room.

"Isador," she smiled when she saw me at the door, "what are you doing at school so early?" She looked at Pico and Chueco, and a slight frown crossed her face.

"I came for the book," I reminded her. She was dressed in bright spring yellow, and the light which shone through the windows glistened on her dress and her soft hair.

"Of course . . . I have it ready." I walked with her to the desk and she handed me the book. I glanced at the title, *The Arabian Nights.* I shivered because out of the corner of my eye I saw Pico grab a bottle of glue and stick it under his shirt.

"Thank you," I mumbled. We turned and raced out of the room to the bathroom. A couple of eighth graders stood by the windows, looking out and smoking cigarettes. They usually paid little attention to us seventh graders, so we slipped unnoticed into one of the stalls. Pico closed the door. Even in the early morning the stall was already warm and the odor very bad.

"Okay, break the mirror," Pico whispered.

"Seven years bad luck," Chueco reminded me.

"Don't pay attention to him, break it!" Pico commanded.

I took the mirror from my pocket, recalled for a moment the warm, sweet fragrance which filled my parents' bedroom, the aroma of the vanity case, the sweet scent of the orchard, like Miss Brighton's cologne, and then I looked at Pico and Chueco's sweating faces and smelled the bad odor of the crowded stall and my hands broke out in a sweat.

"Break it!" Pico said sharply.

I looked at the mirror, briefly saw my face in it, saw my eyes which I knew would give everything away if we were caught, and

I thought of the disgrace I would bring my father if he knew what I was about to do.

I can't, I said, but there was no sound. There was only the rancid odor which rose from the toilet stool, Chueco's heavy breathing, and Pico's eyes glued to the mirror as I turned my hand and let it fall. It fell slowly, as if in slow motion, reflecting us, changing our sense of time, which had moved so fast that morning, into a time which moved so slowly I thought the mirror would never hit the floor and break. But it did. The sound exploded, the mirror broke and splintered, and each piece seemed to bounce up to reflect our dark, sweating faces again.

"Shhhhhhhh," Pico whispered, finger to lips.

We held our breath and waited. Nobody moved outside the stall. No one had heard the breaking of the mirror which for me had been like the sound of thunder.

Then Pico reached down and picked up three well-shaped pieces, about the size of silver dollars. "Just right!" He grinned and handed each of us a piece. Then he put his right foot on the toilet seat, opened the bottle of glue and smeared the white, sticky glue on the tip of his shoe. He placed the piece of mirror on the glue, looked down and saw his sharp, weasel face reflected in it and smiled. "Fits just right!"

We followed suit, first Chueco, then me.

"This is going to be fun!" Chueco giggled.

"Hot bloomers! Hot bloomers!" Pico slapped my back.

"Now what?"

"Wait for it to dry."

We stood with our feet on the toilet seat, pant legs up, waiting for the glue to dry.

"Whose panties are you going to see first?" Chueco asked Pico.

"Concha Panocha's," Pico leered. "She's got the biggest boobs!"

"If they have big boobs, does that mean they have it big downstairs?" Chueco asked.

"Damn right!"

"Zow-ee!" Chueco exclaimed, and spit all over me.

"Shhhh!" Pico whispered. Two boys had come in. They talked while they used the urinals, then they left.

"Ninth graders," Pico said.

"Those guys know everything," Chueco said.

"Yeah, they know how to get it, but after today we'll know too."

"Yeah," Chueco smiled.

I turned away to escape another shower and his bad breath. The wall of the bathroom stall was covered with drawings of naked men and women. Old Plácido, the janitor, worked hard to keep the walls clean, but the minute he finished scrubbing off the drawings in one stall, others appeared next door. The drawings were crude, hastily done diagrams. The one in front of me showed two legs spread apart. A swollen tool hung down from two giant balloons. Everything was always dripping. I wondered why. And why had I joined Pico and Chueco in this crazy plan?

Last year the girls didn't seem to matter to us. We played freely with them. But the summer seemed to change everything. When we came back to school the girls had changed. They had grown bigger. Some of them began to wear lipstick and nail polish. They carried their bodies differently, and I couldn't help but notice for the first time their small, swollen breasts. Pico explained about brassieres to me. An air of mystery began to surround the girls we had once known so well.

I began to listen closely to the stories the ninth-grade boys told about girls. They gathered in the bathroom to smoke before class and during lunch break, and they talked about cars or sports or girls. Some of them already dated girls, and a few bragged about girls they had gotten naked. I guessed those were the ones who drew the pictures on the bathroom walls. They knew.

But their stories were incomplete, half whispered, and the crude drawings only aroused more curiosity. The more I thought about the change which was coming over us, the more troubled I became, and at night my sweaty dreams were filled with the images of women, phantasmal creatures who danced in a mist and removed their veils as they swirled around me. But always I awoke before the last veil was removed. I knew nothing. That's why I gave in to Pico's idea. I wanted to know.

He had said that if we glued a small piece of mirror to our shoes, we could push our feet between the girls' legs when they weren't watching, then we could see everything.

"And they don't wear panties in the spring," he said. "Everybody knows that. So you can see everything!"

"Eehola!" Chueco whistled.

"And sometimes there's a little cherry there —"

"Really?" Chueco exclaimed. "Like a cherry from a cherry tree?"

"Sure," Pico said. "Watch for it, it's good luck." He reached down and tested the mirror on his shoe. "Hey, it's dry! Let's go!"

We piled out of the dirty stall and followed Pico toward the water fountain at the end of the hall. That's where the girls usually gathered, because it was right outside their bathroom.

"Watch me," he said daringly, then he worked his way carefully behind Concha Panocha, who stood talking to her friends. She wore a very loose skirt, perfect for Pico's plan. She was a big girl, and she wasn't very pretty, but Pico liked her. Now we watched as he slowly worked his foot between her feet until the mirror was in position. Then he looked down and we saw his eyes light up. He turned and looked at us and grinned. He had seen everything!

"Perfect! Perfect!" he shouted when he came back to us. "I could see everything! Panties! Nalgas! The spot!"

"Eee-heee-heeee," Chueco moaned. "Now it's my turn!"

They ran off to try Concha again, and I followed them. I felt the blood pounding in my head and a strange excitement ran through my body. If Pico could see everything, then I could too! I could solve the terrible mystery which had pulled me back and forth all year long. I slipped up behind a girl, not even knowing who she was, and with my heart pounding madly, I carefully pushed my foot between her feet. I worked cautiously, afraid to get caught, afraid of what I was about to see. Then I peered into the mirror, saw in a flash my guilty eyes, moved my foot to see more, but all I could see was darkness. I leaned closer to her, looked closely into the mirror, but there was nothing except the brief glimpse of her white panties and then the darkness.

I moved closer, accidentally bumped her, and she turned and looked puzzled and I said excuse me and pulled back and ran away. There was nothing to see; Pico had lied. I felt disappointed. So was Chueco when we met again at lunchtime.

"They all wear panties, you liar!" Chueco accused Pico.

"And most of them wear dirty panties," I added. That had been my only discovery.

"One girl caught me looking at her and she hit me with her purse," Chueco complained. His left eye was red. "What do we do now?" he asked.

"Let's forget the whole thing," I suggested. The excitement was gone, there was nothing to discover. The mystery which was changing the girls into women would remain unexplained. And not being responsible for the answer was even a relief. I reached down to pull the mirror from my foot. My leg was stiff from holding it between the girls' legs.

"No!" Pico exclaimed and grabbed my arm. "Let's try one more thing!"

"What?"

He looked at me and grinned. "Let's look at one of the teachers."

"What? You're crazy!"

"No I'm not! The teachers are more grown up than the girls! They're really women!"

"Bah, they're old hags," Chueco frowned.

"Not Miss Brighton!" Pico smiled.

"Yeah," Chueco's eyes lit up and he wiped the white spittle that gathered at the edges of his mouth. "She reminds me of Wonder Woman!" He laughed and made a big curve with his hands.

"And she doesn't wear a bra. I know, I've seen her," Pico said.

"No." I shook my head. No, it was crazy. It would be as bad as looking at my mother. Again I reached down to tear the mirror from my shoe and again Pico stopped me.

"You can't back out now!" he hissed.

"Yeah," Chueco agreed, "we're in this together."

"If you back out now, you're out of the gang," Pico warned me. He held my arm tightly, hard enough for it to hurt. Chueco nodded. I looked from one to the other, and I knew they meant it. I had grown up with them, known them even before we started school.

"This summer we'll be the kings of the apple orchard, and you won't be able to come in," Pico added to his threat.

"But I don't want to do it," I insisted.

"Who then?" Chueco asked, and looked at Pico. "We can't all do it, she'd know."

"So let's draw," Pico said, and drew three toothpicks out of his pocket. He always carried toothpicks and usually had one hanging from his lips. "Short man does it. Fair?"

Chueco nodded. "Fair." They looked at me. I nodded. Pico broke one toothpick in half, then he put one half with two whole ones in his hand, made a fist and held it out for us to draw. I lost.

"Eho, Isador, you're lucky," Chueco said.

"I, I can't," I mumbled.

"You have to!" Pico said. "That was the deal!"

"Yeah, and we never break our deals," Chueco reminded me, "as long as we've been playing together we never broke a deal."

"If you back out now, that's the end . . . no more gang," Pico said seriously. Then he added, "Look, I'll help you. It's the last day of school, right, so there's going to be a lot of noise during last period. I'll call her to my desk, and when she bends over it'll be easy! She won't know!" He slapped my back.

"Yeah, she won't know!" Chueco repeated.

I finally nodded. Why argue with them, I thought. I'll just put my foot out and fake it, and later I'll make up a big story to tell them in the apple orchard. I'll tell them I saw everything. I'll say it was like the drawing in the bathroom. But it wasn't that easy. The rest of the day my thoughts crashed into each other like wild goats. Fake it, one side said. Look and solve the mystery, others shouted. Now's your chance!

By the time I got to last period study hall I was very nervous. I slipped into my seat across the aisle from Pico and buried my head in the book Miss Brighton had lent me. I sat with my feet drawn in beneath my desk so the mirror wouldn't show. After a while my foot grew numb in its cramped position. I flipped through the pages and tried to read, but it was no use, my thoughts were on Miss Brighton. I wondered if she was the woman who danced in my dreams. And why did I always blush when I looked into her clear blue eyes, those eyes which even now seemed to be looking at me and waiting for me to dare to learn their secret.

"Ready," Pico whispered, and raised his hand. I felt my throat tighten and go dry. My hands broke out in a sweat. I slipped lower into my desk to try to hide as I heard her walk toward Pico's desk.

"I want to know this word," Pico pointed.

"Contradictory," she said. "Con-tra-dic-to-ry . . ."

"Cunt-try-dick-tory," Pico repeated.

I turned and looked at her. Beyond her, through the window, I could see the apple orchard. The buzz of the bees swarming over the blossoms filled my ears.

"It means 'to contradict.' Like if one thing is true, then the other is false," I heard her say.

I would have to confess, I thought . . . Forgive me, Father, but I have contradicted you. I stole from my mother. I looked in the mirror and saw the secret of the woman . . . And why shouldn't you, something screamed in my head. You have to know! It's the only way to become a man! Look now! See! Learn everything you can!

I took a deep breath and slipped my foot from beneath my desk. I looked down, saw my eyes reflected in the small mirror. I slid it quietly between her feet. I could almost touch her skirt, smell her perfume. Behind her the light of the window and the glow from the orchard were blinding. I will pull back now, won't go all the way, I thought.

"Con-tra . . ." she repeated.

"Cunt-ra . . ." Pico stuttered.

Then I looked, saw in a flash her long, tanned legs, leaned to get a better image, saw the white frill, then nothing. Nothing. The swirl of darkness and the secret. The mystery remained hidden in darkness.

I gasped as she turned. She saw me pull my leg back, caught my eyes before I could bury myself in the book again, and in that brief instant I knew she had seen me. A frown crossed her face. She started to say something, then she stood up very straight.

"Get your books ready, the bell's about to ring," was all she said. Then she walked quickly to her desk and sat down.

"Did you see?" Pico whispered. I said nothing, but stared at pages of the book, which were a blur. The last few minutes of the class ticked by very slowly. I thought I could even hear the clock ticking, and each stroke was like a bell.

Then seconds before the bell rang I heard her say, "Isador, I want you to stay after school."

My heart sank. She knew my crime. I felt sick in the pit of my stomach. I cursed Pico and Chueco for talking me into the awful thing. Better to have let everything remain as it was. Let them keep their secret. Whatever it was, it wasn't worth the love I knew would end between me and Miss Brighton. She would tell my parents, everyone would know. I wished that I could reach down and rip the cursed mirror from my shoe, undo everything and set it right again.

But I couldn't. The bell rang. The room quickly emptied. I remained sitting at my desk. Long after the noise had cleared on the school grounds, she called me to her desk. I got up slowly, my legs weak and trembling, and I went to her desk. The room felt very big and empty, bigger than I could ever remember it. And it was very quiet.

She stood and came around her desk. Then she reached down, grabbed the small mirror on my shoe and jerked it. It splintered when she pulled and cut her thumb, but she didn't cry out. She was trembling with anger. She let the pieces drop on the floor; I saw the blood as it smeared her skirt and formed red balls on the tip of her thumb.

"Why did you do it?" she asked. Her voice was angry. "I know that Pico and Chueco would do things like that, but not you, Isador, not you!"

I shook my head. "I wanted to know," I heard myself say, "I wanted to know . . ."

"To know what?" she asked.

"About women . . ."

"But what's there to know?" she said. "You saw the film the coach showed you . . . and later we talked in class when the nurse came. She showed you the diagrams, pictures!"

I could only shake my head. "It's not the same. I wanted to know how women are . . . why different? How?"

She stopped trembling. Her breathing became regular. She took my chin in her hand and made me look at her. Her eyes were clear, not angry, and the frown had left her face. I felt the blood wet my chin.

"There's stories . . . and drawings, everywhere . . . and at night I dream, but I still don't know, I don't know anything!" I cried.

She looked at me while my frustrations came pouring out, then she drew me close and put her arms around me and smoothed my hair. "I understand," she said, "I understand . . . but you don't need to hide and see through the mirror. That makes it dirty. There is no secret to hide . . . nothing to hide . . ."

She held me tight and I could hear her heart pounding, and I heard her sigh, as if she too was troubled by the same questions which hounded me. Then she let me go and went to the window and pulled shut all the venetian blinds. Except for a ray of light streaming through the top, the room grew dark. Then she went to the door and locked it. She turned and looked at me, smiled with a look I had never seen before, then she walked gracefully to the small elevated platform in the back of the room.

She stood in the center and very slowly and carefully she unbuttoned her blouse. She let it drop to her feet, then she undid her bra and let it fall. I held my breath and felt my heart pounding wildly. Never had I seen such beauty as I saw then in the pale light which bathed her naked shoulders and her small breasts. She unfastened her skirt and let it drop, then she lowered her panties and stepped out of them. When she was completely naked she called me.

"Come and see what a woman is like." She smiled.

I walked very slowly to the platform. Beneath me my legs trembled, and in my ears I began to hear a buzzing sound, the kind of sound the bees make when they are swarming around the new blossoms of the apple trees. I stood looking at her for a long time, and she stood very still, like a statue. Then I began to walk around the platform, still looking at her, noting every feature and every curve of her long, firm legs, her flat stomach with its dot of a navel, the small round behind that curved down between her legs then rose along her spine to her hair which fell over her shoulders . . . I walked around and I began to feel a swirling sensation, a very pleasant feeling, as if I was slowly getting drunk. And I continued to hear the humming sound, perhaps she was singing, or it was the sound of the bees in the orchard, I didn't know. But she was smiling, a distant, pleasant smile.

The glowing light of the afternoon slipped through the top of the blinds and rested on her hair. It was the color of honey, spun so fine I wanted to reach out and touch it. But I didn't. A part of her secret she would have to keep, I was content to look at the beauty of her soft curves. Once I had gone hunting with my uncles and I had seen a golden aspen forest which had entranced me with its beauty, but even it was not as beautiful as this. Not even the summer nights when I slept outside and watched the swirl of the Milky Way in the dark sky could compare to the soft curves of her body. Not even the brilliant sunsets of the summer when the light seemed painted on the glowing clouds could be as full of wonder as the light which fell on her naked body. I looked until I thought I had memorized every curve, every nook and shadow, the color of her hair, the flesh tone of her skin . . . and I breathed in, deep, to inhale the aroma of her body. Then when I could no longer stand the beauty of the mystery unraveling itself before my eyes, I turned and ran.

I ran out the door into the bright setting sun, a cry of joy exploded at my lips. I ran as hard as I could, and I felt I was turning and leaping in the air like a ballet dancer.

"Now I know!" I shouted to myself. "Now I know the secret and I'll keep it forever!"

I ran through the orchard, laughing with joy. All around me the bright white blossoms of the trees shimmered in the spring light. I heard music in the radiance which exploded around me; I thought I was dreaming.

I ran around the trees and then stopped to caress them, and the smooth trunks and branches reminded me of her body. Each curve developed a slope and shadow of its own, each twist was rich with the secret we now shared. The flowers smelled like her hair and reminded me of her smile. Then gasping for breath and still trembling with excitement, I fell exhausted on the ground.

It's a dream, I thought, and I'll soon wake. No, it had happened. For a few brief moments I had shared the secret of her body, her mystery. But even now as I tried to remember how she looked, her image was fading like a dream. I sat up straight and looked toward the school, tried to picture the room and the light which had fallen on her bare shoulders, but it was fuzzy, like a dream which fades as one awakens. Her smile, her golden hair and the soft curves of her body were already fading into the sunset light, dissolving into the graceful curves of the trees. The image of her body, which just a short time ago had been so vivid, was working itself into the apple orchard, becoming the shape of trunks and branches . . . and her sweet fragrance blended into the damp earth smell of the orchard and its nettles and wild alfalfa.

For a moment I reached out to keep it from fading away, and that's when I realized that this was the real mystery. That she should fade and grow softer in my memory was the real beauty! That's why she told me to look! It was like the mystery of the apple orchard, changing before my eyes even as the sun set. All the curves and shadows, the sounds and smells, were changing form! In a few days the flowers would wilt and drop, then I would have to wait until next spring to see them again, but the memory would linger, parts of it would keep turning in my mind. Then next spring I would come back to the apple orchard to see the blossoms again. I would always keep coming back, to rediscover, to feel the smoothness of flesh and bark, to smell hair and flower, to linger as I bathed in beauty . . . The mystery would always be there, and I would be exploring its form forever.

RICHARD RODRIGUEZ

Aria

1

I REMEMBER to start with that day in Sacramento — a California now nearly thirty years past — when I first entered a classroom, able to understand some fifty stray English words.

The third of four children, I had been preceded to a neighborhood Roman Catholic school by an older brother and sister. But neither of them had revealed very much about their classroom experiences. Each afternoon they returned, as they left in the morning, always together, speaking in Spanish as they climbed the five steps of the porch. And their mysterious books, wrapped in shopping-bag paper, remained on the table next to the door, closed firmly behind them.

An accident of geography sent me to a school where all my classmates were white, many the children of doctors and lawyers and business executives. All my classmates certainly must have been uneasy on that first day of school — as most children are uneasy — to find themselves apart from their families in the first institution of their lives. But I was astonished.

The nun said, in a friendly but oddly impersonal voice, "Boys and girls, this is Richard Rodriguez." (I heard her sound out: *Rich-heard*

Road-ree-guess.) It was the first time I had heard anyone name me in English. "Richard," the nun repeated more slowly, writing my name down in her black leather book. Quickly I turned to see my mother's face dissolve in a watery blur behind the pebbled glass door.

Many years later there is something called bilingual education — a scheme proposed in the late 1960s by Hispanic-American social activists, later endorsed by a congressional vote. It is a program that seeks to permit non-English-speaking children, many from lower-class homes, to use their family language as the language of school. (Such is the goal its supporters announce.) I hear them and am forced to say no: it is not possible for a child — any child — ever to use his family's language in school. Not to understand this is to misunderstand the public uses of schooling and to trivialize the nature of intimate life — a family's "language."

Memory teaches me what I know of these matters; the boy reminds the adult. I was a bilingual child, a certain kind — socially disadvantaged — the son of working-class parents, both Mexican immigrants.

In the early years of my boyhood, my parents coped very well in America. My father had steady work. My mother managed at home. They were nobody's victims. Optimism and ambition led them to a house (our home) many blocks from the Mexican south side of town. We lived among *gringos* and only a block from the biggest, whitest houses. It never occurred to my parents that they couldn't live wherever they chose. Nor was the Sacramento of the fifties bent on teaching them a contrary lesson. My mother and father were more annoyed than intimidated by those two or three neighbors who tried initially to make us unwelcome. ("Keep your brats away from my sidewalk!") But despite all they achieved, perhaps because they had so much to achieve, any deep feeling of ease, the confidence of "belonging" in public, was withheld from them both. They regarded the people at work, the faces in crowds, as very distant from us. They were the others, *los gringos*. That term was interchangeable in their speech with another, even more telling, *los americanos*.

I grew up in a house where the only regular guests were my relations. For one day, enormous families of relatives would visit, and there would be so many people that the noise and the bodies would spill out to the backyard and front porch. Then, for weeks, no one came by. (It was usually a salesman who rang the doorbell.) Our house stood apart. A gaudy yellow in a row of white bungalows. We were the people with the noisy dog. The people who raised pigeons and chickens. We were the foreigners on the block. A few neighbors smiled and waved. We waved back. But no one in the family knew the names of the old couple who lived next door; until I was seven years old, I did not know the names of the kids who lived across the street.

In public, my father and mother spoke a hesitant, accented, not always grammatical English. And they would have to strain — their bodies tense — to catch the sense of what was rapidly said by *los gringos*. At home they spoke Spanish. The language of their Mexican past sounded in counterpoint to the English of public society. The words would come quickly, with ease. Conveyed through those sounds was the pleasing, soothing, consoling reminder of being at home.

During those years when I was first conscious of hearing, my mother and father addressed me only in Spanish; in Spanish I learned to reply. By contrast, English (*inglés*), rarely heard in the house, was the language I came to associate with *gringos*. I learned my first words of English overhearing my parents speak to strangers. At five years of age, I knew just enough English for my mother to trust me on errands to stores one block away. No more.

I was a listening child, careful to hear the very different sounds of Spanish and English. Wide-eyed with hearing, I'd listen to sounds more than words. First, there were English (*gringo*) sounds. So many words were still unknown that when the butcher or the lady at the drugstore said something to me, exotic polysyllabic sounds would bloom in the midst of their sentences. Often, the speech of people in public seemed to me very loud, booming with confidence. The man behind the counter would literally ask, 'What can I do for you?' But by being so firm and so clear, the sound of his voice said that he was a *gringo*; he belonged in public society.

I would also hear then the high nasal notes of middle-class American speech. The air stirred with sound. Sometimes, even now, when I have been traveling abroad for several weeks, I will hear what I heard as a boy. In hotel lobbies or airports, in Turkey or Brazil, some Americans will pass, and suddenly I will hear it again — the high sound of American voices. For a few seconds I will hear it with pleasure, for it is now the sound of *my* society — a reminder of home. But inevitably — already on the flight headed for home — the sound fades with repetition. I will be unable to hear it anymore.

When I was a boy, things were different. The accent of *los gringos* was never pleasing nor was it hard to hear. Crowds at Safeway or at bus stops would be noisy with sound. And I would be forced to edge away from the chirping chatter above me.

I was unable to hear my own sounds, but I knew very well that I spoke English poorly. My words could not stretch far enough to form complete thoughts. And the words I did speak I didn't know well enough to make into distinct sounds. (Listeners would usually lower their heads, better to hear what I was trying to say.) But it was one thing for *me* to speak English with difficulty. It was more troubling for me to hear my parents speak in public: their high-whining vowels and guttural consonants; their sentences that got stuck with *eh* and *ah* sounds; the confused syntax; the hesitant rhythm of sounds so different from the way *gringos* spoke. I'd notice, moreover, that my parents' voices were softer than those of *gringos* we'd meet.

I am tempted now to say that none of this mattered. In adulthood I am embarrassed by childhood fears. And, in a way, it didn't matter very much that my parents could not speak English with ease. Their linguistic difficulties had no serious consequences. My mother and father made themselves understood at the county hospital clinic and at government offices. And yet, in another way, it mattered very much — it was unsettling to hear my parents struggle with English. Hearing them, I'd grow nervous, my clutching trust in their protection and power weakened.

There were many times like the night at a brightly lit gasoline station (a blaring white memory) when I stood uneasily, hearing

my father. He was talking to a teenage attendant. I do not recall
what they were saying, but I cannot forget the sounds my father
made as he spoke. At one point his words slid together to form one
word — sounds as confused as the threads of blue and green oil in
the puddle next to my shoes. His voice rushed through what he
had left to say. And, toward the end, reached falsetto notes, appeal-
ing to his listener's understanding. I looked away to the lights of
passing automobiles. I tried not to hear any more. But I heard only
too well the calm, easy tones in the attendant's reply. Shortly
afterward, walking toward home with my father, I shivered when
he put his hand on my shoulder. The very first chance that I got,
I evaded his grasp and ran on ahead into the dark, skipping with
feigned boyish exuberance.

But then there was Spanish. *Español:* my family's language. *Español:* the language that seemed to me a private language. I'd hear
strangers on the radio and in the Mexican Catholic church across
town speaking in Spanish, but I couldn't really believe that Spanish
was a public language, like English. Spanish speakers, rather,
seemed related to me, for I sensed that we shared — through our
language — the experience of feeling apart from *los gringos.* It was
thus a ghetto Spanish that I heard and I spoke. Like those whose
lives are bound by a barrio, I was reminded by Spanish of my
separateness from *los otros, los gringos* in power. But more intensely
than for most barrio children — because I did not live in a
barrio — Spanish seemed to me the language of home. (Most days
it was only at home that I'd hear it.) It became the language of
joyful return.

A family member would say something to me and I would feel
myself specially recognized. My parents would say something to
me and I would feel embraced by the sounds of their words. Those
sounds said: *I am speaking with ease in Spanish. I am addressing you
in words I never use with* los gringos. *I recognize you as someone
special, close, like no one outside. You belong with us. In the family.*

(*Ricardo.*)

At the age of five, six, well past the time when most other
children no longer easily notice the difference between sounds
uttered at home and words spoken in public, I had a different

experience. I lived in a world magically compounded of sounds. I remained a child longer than most; I lingered too long, poised at the edge of language — often frightened by the sounds of *los gringos*, delighted by the sounds of Spanish at home. I shared with my family a language that was startlingly different from that used in the great city around us.

For me there were none of the gradations between public and private society so normal to a maturing child. Outside the house was public society; inside the house was private. Just opening or closing the screen door behind me was an important experience. I'd rarely leave home all alone or without reluctance. Walking down the sidewalk, under the canopy of tall trees, I'd warily notice the — suddenly — silent neighborhood kids who stood warily watching me. Nervously, I'd arrive at the grocery store to hear there the sounds of the *gringo* — foreign to me — reminding me that in this world so big, I was a foreigner. But then I'd return. Walking back toward our house, climbing the steps from the sidewalk, when the front door was open in summer, I'd hear voices beyond the screen door talking in Spanish. For a second or two I'd stay, linger there, listening. Smiling, I'd hear my mother call out, saying in Spanish (words): "Is that you, Richard?" All the while her sounds would assure me: *You are home now; come closer; inside. With us.*

"*Sí,*" I'd reply.

Once more inside the house I would resume (assume) my place in the family. The sounds would dim, grow harder to hear. Once more at home, I would grow less aware of that fact. It required, however, no more than the blurt of the doorbell to alert me to listen to sounds all over again. The house would turn instantly still while my mother went to the door. I'd hear her hard English sounds. I'd wait to hear her voice return to soft-sounding Spanish, which assured me, as surely as did the clicking tongue of the lock on the door, that the stranger was gone.

Plainly, it is not healthy to hear such sounds so often. It is not healthy to distinguish public words from private sounds so easily. I remained cloistered by sounds, timid and shy in public, too dependent on voices at home. And yet it needs to be emphasized: I was an extremely happy child at home. I remember many nights when my father would come back from work, and I'd hear him call out to my mother in Spanish, sounding relieved. In Spanish, he'd sound light and free notes he never could manage in English. Some nights I'd jump up just at hearing his voice. With *mis hermanos* I would come running into the room where he was with my mother. Our laughing (so deep was the pleasure!) became screaming. Like others who know the pain of public alienation, we transformed the knowledge of our public separateness and made it consoling — the reminder of intimacy. Excited, we joined our voices in a celebration of sounds. *We are speaking now the way we never speak out in public. We are alone — together*, voices sounded, surrounded to tell me. Some nights, no one seemed willing to loosen the hold sounds had on us. At dinner, we invented new words. (Ours sounded Spanish, but made sense only to us.) We pieced together new words by taking, say, an English verb and giving it Spanish endings. My mother's instructions at bedtime would be lacquered with mock-urgent tones. Or a word like *sí* would become, in several notes, able to convey added measures of feeling. Tongues explored the edges of words, especially the fat vowels. And we happily sounded that military drum roll, the twirling roar of the Spanish *r*. Family language: my family's sounds. The voices of my parents and sisters and brother. Their voices insisting: *You belong here. We are family members. Related. Special to one another. Listen!* Voices singing and sighing, rising, straining, then surging, teeming with pleasure that burst syllables into fragments of laughter. At times it seemed there was steady quiet only when, from another room, the rustling whispers of my parents faded and I moved closer to sleep.

2

Supporters of bilingual education today imply that students like me miss a great deal by not being taught in their family's language. What they seem not to recognize is that, as a socially disadvantaged child, I considered Spanish to be a private language. What I needed to learn in school was that I had the right — and the obligation — to speak the public language of *los gringos*. The odd truth is that my first-grade classmates could have become bilingual, in the conventional sense of that word, more easily than I. Had they been taught (as upper-middle-class children are often taught early) a second language like Spanish or French, they could have regarded it simply as that: another public language. In my case such bilingualism could not have been so quickly achieved. What I did not believe was that I could speak a single public language.

Without question, it would have pleased me to hear my teachers address me in Spanish when I entered the classroom. I would have felt much less afraid. I would have trusted them and responded with ease. But I would have delayed — for how long postponed? — having to learn the language of public society. I would have evaded — and for how long could I have afforded to delay? — learning the great lesson of school, that I had a public identity.

Fortunately, my teachers were unsentimental about their responsibility. What they understood was that I needed to speak a public language. So their voices would search me out, asking me questions. Each time I'd hear them, I'd look up in surprise to see a nun's face frowning at me. I'd mumble, not really meaning to answer. The nun would persist, "Richard, stand up. Don't look at the floor. Speak up. Speak to the entire class, not just to me!" But I couldn't believe that the English language was mine to use. (In part, I did not want to believe it.) I continued to mumble. I resisted the teacher's demands. (Did I somehow suspect that once I learned public language, my pleasing family life would be changed?) Silent, waiting for the bell to sound, I remained dazed, diffident, afraid.

Because I wrongly imagined that English was intrinsically a public language and Spanish an intrinsically private one, I easily noted the difference between classroom language and the language of home. At school, words were directed to a general audience of listeners. ("Boys and girls.") Words were meaningfully ordered. And the point was not self-expression alone but to make oneself understood by many others. The teacher quizzed: "Boys and girls, why do we use that word in this sentence? Could we think of a better word to use there? Would the sentence change its meaning if the words were differently arranged? And wasn't there a better way of saying much the same thing?" (I couldn't say. I wouldn't try to say.)

Three months. Five. Half a year passed. Unsmiling, ever watchful, my teachers noted my silence. They began to connect my behavior with the difficult progress my older sister and brother were making. Until one Saturday morning three nuns arrived at the house to talk to our parents. Stiffly, they sat on the blue living room sofa. From the doorway of another room, spying the visitors, I noted the incongruity — the clash of two worlds, the faces and voices of school intruding upon the familiar setting of home. I overheard one voice gently wondering, "Do your children speak only Spanish at home, Mrs. Rodriguez?" While another voice added, "That Richard especially seems so timid and shy."

That Rich-heard!

With great tact the visitors continued, "Is it possible for you and your husband to encourage your children to practice their English when they are home?' Of course, my parents complied. What would they not do for their children's well-being? And how could they have questioned the Church's authority which those women represented? In an instant, they agreed to give up the language (the sounds) that had revealed and accentuated our family's closeness. The moment after the visitors left, the change was observed. "Ahora, speak to us en inglés," my father and mother united to tell us.

At first, it seemed a kind of game. After dinner each night, the family gathered to practice "our" English. (It was still then *inglés*, a language foreign to us, so we felt drawn as strangers to it.) Laughing, we would try to define words we could not pronounce. We played with strange English sounds, often over-anglicizing our pronunciations. And we filled the smiling gaps of our sentences with familiar Spanish sounds. But that was cheating, somebody shouted. Everyone laughed. In school, meanwhile, like my brother and sister, I was required to attend a daily tutoring session. I needed a full year of special attention. I also needed my teachers to keep my attention from straying in class by calling out, *Rich-heard* — their English voices slowly prying loose my ties to my other name, its three notes, *Ri-car-do*. Most of all I needed to hear my mother and father speak to me in a moment of seriousness in broken — suddenly heartbreaking — English. The scene was inevitable: one

Saturday morning I entered the kitchen where my parents were talking in Spanish. I did not realize that they were talking in Spanish however, until, at the moment they saw me, I heard their voices change to speak English. Those *gringo* sounds they uttered startled me. Pushed me away. In that moment of trivial misunderstanding and profound insight, I felt my throat twisted by unsounded grief. I turned quickly and left the room. But I had no place to escape to with Spanish. (The spell was broken.) My brother and sisters were speaking English in another part of the house.

Again and again in the days following, increasingly angry, I was obliged to hear my mother and father: "Speak to us en inglés." (*Speak.*) Only then did I determine to learn classroom English. Weeks after, it happened: one day in school I raised my hand to volunteer an answer. I spoke out in a loud voice. And I did not think it remarkable when the entire class understood. That day, I moved very far from the disadvantaged child I had been only days earlier. The belief, the calming assurance that I belonged in public, had at last taken hold.

Shortly after, I stopped hearing the high and loud sounds of *los gringos*. A more and more confident speaker of English, I didn't trouble to listen to *how* strangers sounded, speaking to me. And there simply were too many English-speaking people in my day for me to hear American accents anymore. Conversations quickened. Listening to persons who sounded eccentrically pitched voices, I usually noted their sounds for an initial few seconds before I concentrated on *what* they were saying. Conversations became content-full. Transparent. Hearing someone's *tone* of voice — angry or questioning or sarcastic or happy or sad — I didn't distinguish it from the words it expressed. Sound and word were thus tightly wedded. At the end of a day, I was often bemused, always relieved, to realize how "silent," though crowded with words, my day in public had been. (This public silence measured and quickened the change in my life.)

At last, seven years old, I came to believe what had been technically true since my birth: I was an American citizen.

But the special feeling of closeness at home was diminished by then. Gone was the desperate, urgent, intense feeling of being at home; rare was the experience of feeling myself individualized by family intimates. We remained a loving family, but one greatly changed. No longer so close; no longer bound tight by the pleasing and troubling knowledge of our public separateness. Neither my older brother nor sister rushed home after school anymore. Nor did I. When I arrived home there would often be neighborhood kids in the house. Or the house would be empty of sounds.

Following the dramatic Americanization of their children, even my parents grew more publicly confident. Especially my mother. She learned the names of all the people on our block. And she decided we needed to have a telephone installed in the house. My father continued to use the word *gringo*. But it was no longer charged with the old bitterness or distrust. (Stripped of any emotional content, the word simply became a name for those Americans not of Hispanic descent.) Hearing him, sometimes, I wasn't sure if he was pronouncing the Spanish word *gringo* or saying gringo in English.

Matching the silence I started hearing in public was a new quiet at home. The family's quiet was partly due to the fact that, as we children learned more and more English, we shared fewer and fewer words with our parents. Sentences needed to be spoken slowly when a child addressed his mother or father. (Often the parent wouldn't understand.) The child would need to repeat himself. (Still the parent misunderstood.) The young voice, frustrated, would end up saying, "Never mind" — the subject was closed. Dinners would be noisy with the clinking of knives and forks against dishes. My mother would smile softly between her remarks; my father at the other end of the table would chew and chew at his food while he stared over the heads of his children.

My *mother!* My *father!* After English became my primary language, I no longer knew what words to use in addressing my parents. The old Spanish words (those tender accents of sound) I had used earlier — *Mamá* and *Papá* — I couldn't use anymore. They would have been too painful reminders of how much had changed in my life. On the other hand, the words I heard neighborhood kids call *their* parents seemed equally unsatisfactory. *Mother* and *Father; Ma, Papa, Pa, Dad, Pop* (how I hated the all-American sound of that last word especially) — all these terms I felt were unsuitable, not really terms of address for *my* parents. As a result, I never used them at home. Whenever I'd speak to my parents, I would try to get their attention with eye contact alone. In public conversations, I'd refer to "my parents" or "my mother and father."

My mother and father, for their part, responded differently, as their children spoke to them less. She grew restless, seemed troubled and anxious at the scarcity of words exchanged in the house. It was she who would question me about my day when I came home from school. She smiled at small talk. She pried at the edges of my sentences to get me to say something more. (What?) She'd join conversations she overheard, but her intrusions often stopped her children's talking. By contrast, my father seemed reconciled to the new quiet. Though his English improved somewhat, he retired into silence. At dinner he spoke very little. One night his children and even his wife helplessly giggled at his garbled English pronunciation of the Catholic grace before meals. Thereafter he made his wife recite the prayer at the start of each meal, even on formal occasions, when there were guests in the house. Hers became the public voice of the family. On official business, it was she, not my father, one would usually hear on the phone or in stores, talking to strangers. His children grew so accustomed to his silence that, years later, they would speak routinely of his shyness. (My mother would often try to explain: both his parents died when he was eight. He was raised by an uncle who treated him like little more than a menial servant. He was never encouraged to speak. He grew up alone. A man of few words.) But my father was not shy, I realized, when I'd watch him speaking Spanish with relatives. Using Spanish, he was quickly effusive. Especially when talking with other men, his voice would spark, flicker, flare alive with sounds. In Spanish, he expressed ideas and feelings he rarely revealed in English. With firm Spanish sounds, he conveyed confidence and authority English would never allow him.

The silence at home, however, was finally more than a literal silence. Fewer words passed between parent and child, but more profound was the silence that resulted from my inattention to sounds. At about the time I no longer bothered to listen with care to the sounds of English in public, I grew careless about listening to the sounds family members made when they spoke. Most of the time I heard someone speaking at home and didn't distinguish his sounds from the words people uttered in public. I didn't even pay much attention to my parents' accented and ungrammatical speech. At least not at home. Only when I was with them in public would I grow alert to their accents. Though, even then, their sounds caused me less and less concern. For I was increasingly confident of my own public identity.

I would have been happier about my public success had I not sometimes recalled what it had been like earlier, when my family had conveyed its intimacy through a set of conveniently private sounds. Sometimes in public, hearing a stranger, I'd hark back to my past. A Mexican farm worker approached me downtown to ask directions to somewhere. "Hijito . . . ?" he said. And his voice summoned deep longing. Another time, standing beside my mother in the visiting room of a Carmelite convent, before the dense screen which rendered the nuns shadowy figures, I heard several Spanish-speaking nuns — their busy, singsong overlapping voices — assure us that yes, yes, we were remembered, all our family was remembered in their prayers. (Their voices echoed faraway family sounds.) Another day, a dark-faced old woman — her hand light on my shoulder — steadied herself against me as she boarded a bus. She murmured something I couldn't quite comprehend. Her Spanish voice came near, like the face of a never-before-seen relative in the instant before I was kissed. Her voice, like so many of the Spanish voices I'd hear in public, recalled the golden age of my youth. Hearing Spanish then, I continued to be a careful, if sad, listener to sounds. Hearing a Spanish-speaking family walking behind me, I turned to look. I smiled for an instant, before my glance found the Hispanic-looking faces of strangers in the crowd going by.

Today I hear bilingual educators say that children lose a degree of "individuality" by becoming assimilated into public society. (Bilingual schooling was popularized in the seventies, that decade when middle-class ethnics began to resist the process of assimilation —

the American melting pot.) But the bilingualists simplistically scorn the value and necessity of assimilation. They do not seem to realize that there are *two* ways a person is individualized. So they do not realize that while one suffers a diminished sense of *private* individuality by becoming assimilated into public society, such assimilation makes possible the achievement of *public* individuality.

The bilingualists insist that a student should be reminded of his difference from others in mass society, his heritage. But they equate mere separateness with individuality. The fact is that only in private — with intimates — is separateness from the crowd a prerequisite for individuality. (An intimate draws me apart, tells me that I am unique, unlike all others.) In public, by contrast, full individuality is achieved, paradoxically, by those who are able to consider themselves members of the crowd. Thus it happened for me: only when I was able to think of myself as an American, no longer an alien in *gringo* society, could I seek the rights and opportunities necessary for full public individuality. The social and political advantages I enjoy as a man result from the day that I came to believe that my name, indeed, is *Rich-heard Road-ree-guess*. It is true that my public society today is often impersonal. (My public society is usually mass society.) Yet despite the anonymity of the crowd and despite the fact that the individuality I achieve in public is often tenuous — because it depends on my being one in a crowd — I celebrate the day I acquired my new name. Those middle-class ethnics who scorn assimilation seem to me filled with decadent self-pity, obsessed by the burden of public life. Dangerously, they romanticize public separateness and they trivialize the dilemma of the socially disadvantaged.

My awkward childhood does not prove the necessity of bilingual education. My story discloses instead an essential myth of childhood — inevitable pain. If I rehearse here the changes in my private life after my Americanization, it is finally to emphasize the public gain. The loss implies the gain: the house I returned to each afternoon was quiet. Intimate sounds no longer rushed to the door to greet me. There were other noises inside. The telephone rang. Neighborhood kids ran past the door of the bedroom where I was reading my schoolbooks — covered with shopping-bag paper.

Once I learned public language, it would never again be easy for me to hear intimate family voices. More and more of my day was spent hearing words. But that may only be a way of saying that the day I raised my hand in class and spoke loudly to an entire roomful of faces, my childhood started to end.

3

I grew up victim to a disabling confusion. As I grew fluent in English, I no longer could speak Spanish with confidence. I continued to understand spoken Spanish. And in high school, I learned how to read and write Spanish. But for many years I could not pronounce it. A powerful guilt blocked my spoken words; an essential glue was missing whenever I'd try to connect words to form sentences. I would be unable to break a barrier of sound, to speak freely. I would speak, or try to speak, Spanish, and I would manage to utter halting, hiccupping sounds that betrayed my unease.

When relatives and Spanish-speaking friends of my parents came to the house, my brother and sisters seemed reticent to use Spanish, but at least they managed to say a few necessary words before being excused. I never managed so gracefully. I was cursed with guilt. Each time I'd hear myself addressed in Spanish, I would be unable to respond with any success. I'd know the words I wanted to say, but I couldn't manage to say them. I would try to speak, but everything I said seemed to me horribly anglicized. My mouth would not form the words right. My jaw would tremble. After a phrase or two, I'd cough up a warm, silvery sound. And stop.

It surprised my listeners to hear me. They'd lower their heads, better to grasp what I was trying to say. They would repeat their questions in gentle, affectionate voices. But by then I would answer in English. No, no, they would say, we want you to speak to us in Spanish. (". . . en español.") But I couldn't do it. *Pocho* then they called me. Sometimes playfully, teasingly, using the tender diminutive — *mi pochito*. Sometimes not so playfully, mockingly, *Pocho*. (A Spanish dictionary defines that word as an adjective meaning "colorless" or "bland." But I heard it as a noun, naming the Mexican-American who, in becoming an American, forgets his native society.) "¡Pocho!" the lady in the Mexican food store muttered, shaking her head. I looked up to the counter where red and green peppers were strung like Christmas tree lights and saw the frowning face of the stranger. My mother laughed somewhere behind me. (She said that her children didn't want to practice "our Spanish" after they started going to school.) My mother's smiling voice made me suspect that the lady who faced me was not really angry at me. But, searching her face, I couldn't find the hint of a smile.

Embarrassed, my parents would regularly need to explain their children's inability to speak flowing Spanish during those years. My mother met the wrath of her brother, her only brother, when he came up from Mexico one summer with his family. He saw his nieces and nephews for the very first time. After listening to me, he looked away and said what a disgrace it was that I couldn't speak Spanish, "su proprio idioma." He made that remark to my mother; I noticed, however, that he stared at my father.

I clearly remember one other visitor from those years. A long-time friend of my father from San Francisco would come to stay with us for several days in late August. He took great interest in me after he realized that I couldn't answer his questions in Spanish. He would grab me as I started to leave the kitchen. He would ask me something. Usually he wouldn't bother to wait for my mumbled response. Knowingly, he'd murmur: "¿Ay Pocho, Pocho, adónde vas?" And he would press his thumbs into the upper part of my arms, making me squirm with currents of pain. Dumbly, I'd stand there, waiting for his wife to notice us, for her to call him off with a benign smile. I'd giggle, hoping to deflate the tension between us, pretending that I hadn't seen the glittering scorn in his glance.

I remember that man now, but seek no revenge in this telling. I recount such incidents only because they suggest the fierce power Spanish had for many people I met at home; the way Spanish was associated with closeness. Most of those people who called me a *pocho* could have spoken English to me. But they would not. They seemed to think that Spanish was the only language we could use, that Spanish alone permitted our close association. (Such persons are vulnerable always to the ghetto merchant and the politician who have learned the value of speaking their clients' family language to gain immediate trust.) For my part, I felt that I had somehow committed a sin of betrayal by learning English. But betrayal against whom? Not against visitors to the house exactly. No, I felt that I had betrayed my immediate family. I *knew* that my parents had encouraged me to learn English. I *knew* that I had turned to English only with angry reluctance. But once I spoke English with ease, I came to *feel* guilty. (This guilt defied logic.) I felt that I had shattered the intimate bond that had once held the family close. This original sin against my family told whenever anyone addressed me in Spanish and I responded, confounded.

But even during those years of guilt, I was coming to sense certain consoling truths about language and intimacy. I remember playing with a friend in the backyard one day, when my grandmother appeared at the window. Her face was stern with suspicion when she saw the boy (the *gringo*) I was with. In Spanish she called out to me, sounding the whistle of her ancient breath. My companion looked up and watched her intently as she lowered the window and moved, still visible, behind the light curtain, watching us both. He wanted to know what she had said. I started to tell him, to say — to translate her Spanish words into English. The problem was, however, that though I knew how to translate exactly *what* she had told me, I realized that any translation would distort the deepest meaning of her message: it had been directed only to me. This message of intimacy could never be translated because it was not *in* the words she had used but passed *through* them. So any translation would have seemed wrong; her words would have been stripped of an essential meaning. Finally, I decided not to tell my friend anything. I told him that I didn't hear all she had said.

This insight unfolded in time. Making more and more friends outside my house, I began to distinguish intimate voices speaking through *English*. I'd listen at times to a close friend's confidential tone or secretive whisper. Even more remarkable were those instances when, for no special reason apparently, I'd become conscious of the fact that my companion was speaking only to me. I'd marvel just hearing his voice. It was a stunning event: to be able to break through his words, to be able to hear this voice of the other, to realize that it was directed only to me. After such moments of intimacy outside the house, I began to trust hearing intimacy conveyed through my family's English. Voices at home at last punctured sad confusion. I'd hear myself addressed as an intimate at home once again. Such moments were never as raucous with sound as past times had been when we had had "private" Spanish to use. (Our English-sounding house was never to be as noisy as our Spanish-speaking house had been.) Intimate moments were usually soft moments of sound. My mother was in the dining room while I did my homework nearby. And she looked over at me. Smiled. Said something — her words said nothing very important. But her voice sounded to tell me (*We are together*) I was her son.

(*Richard!*)

Intimacy thus continued at home; intimacy was not stilled by English. It is true that I would never forget the great change of my life, the diminished occasions of intimacy. But there would also be times when I sensed the deepest truth about language and intimacy: *intimacy is not created by a particular language; it is created by intimates.* The great change in my life was not linguistic but social. If, after becoming a successful student, I no longer heard intimate voices as often as I had earlier, it was not because I spoke English rather than Spanish. It was because I used public language for most of the day. I moved easily at last, a citizen in a crowded city of words.

4

This boy became a man. In private now, alone, I brood over language and intimacy — the great themes of my past. In public I expect most of the faces I meet to be the faces of strangers. (How do you do?) If meetings are quick and impersonal, they have been efficiently managed. I rush past the sounds of voices attending only to the words addressed to me. Voices seem planed to an even surface of sound, soundless. A business associate speaks in a deep baritone, but I pass through the timbre to attend to his words. The crazy man who sells me a newspaper every night mumbles something crazy, but I have time only to pretend that I have heard him say hello. Accented versions of English make little impression on me. In the rush-hour crowd a Japanese tourist asks me a question, and I inch past his accent to concentrate on what he is saying. The Eastern European immigrant in a neighborhood delicatessen speaks to me through a marinade of sounds, but I respond to his words. I note for only a second the Texas accent of the telephone operator or the Mississippi accent of the man who lives in the apartment below me.

My city seems silent until some ghetto black teenagers board the bus I am on. Because I do not take their presence for granted, I listen to the sounds of their voices. Of all the accented versions of English I hear in a day, I hear theirs most intently. They are *the* sounds of the outsider. They annoy me for being loud — so self-sufficient and unconcerned by my presence. Yet for the same reason they seem to me glamorous. (A romantic gesture against public acceptance.) Listening to their shouted laughter, I realize my own quiet. Their voices enclose my isolation. I feel envious, envious of their brazen intimacy.

I warn myself away from such envy, however. I remember the black political activists who have argued in favor of using black English in schools. (Their argument varies only slightly from that made by foreign-language bilingualists.) I have heard "radical" linguists make the point that black English is a complex and intricate version of English. And I do not doubt it. But neither do I think that black English should be a language of public instruction. What makes black English inappropriate in classrooms is not something *in* the language. It is rather what lower-class speakers make of it. Just as Spanish would have been a dangerous language for me to have used at the start of my education, so black English would be a dangerous language to use in the schooling of teenagers for whom it reenforces feelings of public separateness.

This seems to me an obvious point. But one that needs to be made. In recent years there have been attempts to make the language of the alien public language. "Bilingual education, two ways to understand . . . ," television and radio commercials glibly announce. Proponents of bilingual education are careful to say that they want students to acquire good schooling. Their argument goes something like this: children permitted to use their family language in school will not be so alienated and will be better able to match the progress of English-speaking children in the crucial first months of instruction. (Increasingly confident of their abilities, such children will be more inclined to apply themselves to their studies in the future.) But then the bilingualists claim another, very different goal. They say that children who use their family language in school will retain a sense of their individuality — their ethnic heritage and cultural ties. Supporters of bilingual education thus want it both ways. They propose bilingual schooling as a way of helping students acquire the skills of the classroom crucial for public success. But they likewise insist that bilingual instruction will give students a sense of their identity apart from the public.

Behind this screen there gleams an astonishing promise: one can become a public person while still remaining a private person. At the very same time one can be both! There need be no tension between the self in the crowd and the self apart from the crowd! Who would not want to believe such an idea? Who can be surprised that the scheme has won the support of many middle-class Americans? If the barrio or ghetto child can retain his separateness even while being publicly educated, then it is almost possible to believe that there is no private cost to be paid for public success. Such is the consolation offered by any of the current bilingual schemes. Consider, for example, the bilingual voters' ballot. In some American cities one can cast a ballot printed in several languages. Such a document implies that a person can exercise that most public of rights — the right to vote — while still keeping apart, unassimilated from public life.

It is not enough to say that these schemes are foolish and certainly doomed. Middle-class supporters of public bilingualism toy with the confusion of those Americans who cannot speak standard English as well as they can. Bilingual enthusiasts, moreover, sin against intimacy. A Hispanic-American writer tells me, "I will never give up my family language; I would as soon give up my soul." Thus he holds to his chest a skein of words, as though it were the source of his family ties. He credits to language what he should credit to family members. A convenient mistake. For as long as he holds on to words, he can ignore how much else has changed in his life.

It has happened before. In earlier decades, persons newly successful and ambitious for social mobility similarly seized upon certain "family words." Working-class men attempting political power took to calling one another "brother." By so doing they escaped oppressive public isolation and were able to unite with many others like themselves. But they paid a price for this union. It was a public union they forged. The word they coined to address one another could never be the sound *(brother)* exchanged by two in intimate greeting. In the union hall the word "brother" became a vague metaphor; with repetition a weak echo of the intimate sound. Context forced the change. Context could not be overruled. Context will always guard the realm of the intimate from public misuse.

Today nonwhite Americans call "brother" to strangers. And white feminists refer to their mass union of "sisters." And white middle-class teenagers continue to prove the importance of context as they try to ignore it. They seize upon the idioms of the black ghetto. But their attempt to appropriate such expressions invariably changes the words. As it becomes a public expression, the ghetto idiom loses its sound — its message of public separateness and strident intimacy. It becomes with public repetition a series of words, increasingly lifeless.

The mystery remains: intimate utterance. The communication of intimacy passes through the word to enliven its sound. But it cannot be held by the word. Cannot be clutched or ever quoted. It is too fluid. It depends not on word but on person.

My grandmother!

She stood among my other relations mocking me when I no longer spoke Spanish. "Pocho," she said. But then it made no difference. (She'd laugh.) Our relationship continued. Language was never its source. She was a woman in her eighties during the first decade of my life. A mysterious woman to me, my only living grandparent. A woman of Mexico. The woman in long black dresses that reached down to her shoes. My one relative who spoke no word of English. She had no interest in *gringo* society. She remained completely aloof from the public. Protected by her daughters. Protected even by me when we went to Safeway together and I acted as her translator. Eccentric woman. Soft. Hard.

When my family visited my aunt's house in San Francisco, my grandmother searched for me among my many cousins. She'd chase them away. Pinching her granddaughters, she'd warn them all away from me. Then she'd take me to her room, where she had prepared for my coming. There would be a chair next to the bed. A dusty jellied candy nearby. And a copy of *Life en Español* for me to examine. "There," she'd say. I'd sit there content. A boy of eight. *Pocho.* Her favorite. I'd sift through the pictures of earthquake-destroyed Latin American cities and blond-wigged Mexican movie stars. And all the while I'd listen to the sound of my grandmother's voice. She'd pace round the room, searching through closets and drawers, telling me stories of her life. Her past. They were stories so familiar to me that I couldn't remember the first time I'd heard them. I'd look up sometimes to listen. Other times she'd look over at me. But she never seemed to expect a response. Sometimes I'd smile or nod. (I understood exactly what she was saying.) But it never seemed to matter to her one way or another. It was enough I was there. The words she spoke were almost irrelevant to that fact — the sounds she made. Content.

The mystery remained: intimate utterance.

I learn little about language and intimacy listening to those social activists who propose using one's family language in public life. Listening to songs on the radio, or hearing a great voice at the opera, or overhearing the woman downstairs singing to herself at an open window, I learn much more. Singers celebrate the human voice. Their lyrics are words. But animated by voice those words are subsumed into sounds. I listen with excitement as the words yield their enormous power to sound — though the words are never totally obliterated. In most songs the drama or tension results from the fact that the singer moves between word (sense) and note (song). At one moment the song simply "says" something. At another moment the voice stretches out the words — the heart cannot contain! — and the voice moves toward pure sound. Words take flight.

Singing out words, the singer suggests an experience of sound most intensely mine at intimate moments. Literally, most songs are about love. (Lost love; celebrations of loving; pleas.) By simply being occasions when sound escapes word, however, songs put me in mind of the most intimate moments of my life.

Finally, among all types of song, it is the song created by lyric poets that I find most compelling. There is no other public occasion of sound so important for me. Written poems exist on a page, at first glance, as a mere collection of words. And yet, despite this, without musical accompaniment, the poet leads me to hear the sounds of the words that I read. As song, the poem passes between sound and sense, never belonging for long to one realm or the other. As public artifact, the poem can never duplicate intimate sound. But by imitating such sound, the poem helps me recall the intimate times of my life. I read in my room — alone — and grow conscious of being alone, sounding my voice, in search of another. The poem serves then as a memory device. It forces remembrance. And refreshes. It reminds me of the possibility of escaping public words, the possibility that awaits me in meeting the intimate.

The poems I read are not nonsense poems. But I read them for reasons which, I imagine, are similar to those that make children play with meaningless rhyme. I have watched them before: I have noticed the way children create private languages to keep away the adult; I have heard their chanting riddles that go nowhere in logic but hark back to some kingdom of sound; I have watched them listen to intricate nonsense rhymes, and I have noted their wonder. I was never such a child. Until I was six years old, I remained in a magical realm of sound. I didn't need to remember that realm because it was present to me. But then the screen door shut behind me as I left home for school. At last I began my movement toward words. On the other side of initial sadness would come the realization that intimacy cannot be held. With time would come the knowledge that intimacy must finally pass.

I would dishonor those I have loved and those I love now to

claim anything else. I would dishonor our closeness by holding on
to a particular language and calling it my family language. Intimacy
is not trapped within words. It passes through words. It passes. The
truth is that intimates leave the room. Doors close. Faces move
away from the window. Time passes. Voices recede into the dark.
Death finally quiets the voice. And there is no way to deny it. No
way to stand in the crowd, uttering one's family language.

The last time I saw my grandmother I was nine years old. I can
tell you some of the things she said to me as I stood by her bed.
I cannot, however, quote the message of intimacy she conveyed
with her voice. She laughed, holding my hand. Her voice illumined
disjointed memories as it passed them again. She remembered her
husband, his green eyes, the magic name of Narciso. His early
death. She remembered the farm in Mexico. The eucalyptus
nearby. (Its scent, she remembered, like incense.) She remembered
the family cow, the bell round its neck heard miles away. A
dog. She remembered working as a seamstress. How she'd leave
her daughters and son for long hours to go into Guadalajara
to work. And how my mother would come running toward
her in the sun — her bright yellow dress — to see her return.
"Mmmaaammmmááá," the old lady mimicked her daughter (my
mother) to her son. She laughed. There was the snap of a cough.
An aunt came into the room and told me it was time I should leave.
"You can see her tomorrow," she promised. And so I kissed my
grandmother's cracked face. And the last thing I saw was her thin,
oddly youthful thigh, as my aunt rearranged the sheet on the bed.

At the funeral parlor a few days after, I knelt with my relatives
during the rosary. Among their voices but silent, I traced, then lost,
the sounds of individual aunts in the surge of the common prayer.
And I heard at that moment what I have since heard often again —
the sounds the women in my family make when they are praying
in sadness. When I went up to look at my grandmother, I saw her
through the haze of a veil draped over the open lid of the casket.
Her face appeared calm — but distant and unyielding to love. It
was not the face I remembered seeing most often. It was the face
she made in public when the clerk at Safeway asked her some
question and I would have to respond. It was her public face the
mortician had designed with his dubious art.

SUGGESTIONS FOR
FURTHER READING

CONTRIBUTORS

SUGGESTIONS FOR
FURTHER READING

SELECTED WORKS BY AUTHORS
IN THIS ANTHOLOGY

Acosta, Oscar "Zeta." *The Autobiography of a Brown Buffalo*. San Francisco, Calif.: Straight Arrow Books, 1972. Reprint. New York: Vintage Books, 1989.

———. *The Revolt of the Cockroach People*. San Francisco, Calif.: Straight Arrow Books, 1973. Reprint. New York: Vintage Books, 1989.

Alvarez, Julia. *How the García Girls Lost Their Accents*. Chapel Hill, N.C.: Algonquin Books of Chapel Hill, 1991.

Anaya, Rudolfo A. *Bless Me, Ultima*. Berkeley, Calif.: Tonatiuh/Quinto Sol International, 1972.

———. *Heart of Aztlán*. Berkeley, Calif.: Editorial Justa Publications, 1976.

———. *Tortuga*. Berkeley, Calif.: Editorial Justa Publications, 1979.

———. *The Silence of the Llano*. Berkeley, Calif.: Tonatiuh/Quinto Sol International, 1982.

———. *The Legend of La Llorona*. Berkeley, Calif.: Tonatiuh/Quinto Sol International, 1984.

———. *Alburquerque*. Albuquerque, N.Mex.: University of New Mexico Press, 1992.

Anzaldúa, Gloria. *Borderlands / La Frontera: The New Mestiza*. San Francisco, Calif.: Spinsters/Aunt Lute Foundation Books, 1987.

Candelaria, Nash. *The Day the Cisco Kid Shot John Wayne*. Tempe, Ariz.: Bilingual Review Press, 1988.

———. *Memories of the Alhambra*. Palo Alto, Calif.: Cibola Press, 1977.

————. *Not by the Sword.* Ypsilanti, Mich.: Bilingual Review Press, 1982.

————. *Inheritance of Strangers.* Binghamton, N.Y.: Bilingual Review Press, 1985.

————. *Leonor Park.* Tempe, Ariz.: Bilingual Review Press, 1991.

Chávez, Denise. *The Last of the Menu Girls.* Houston, Tex.: Arte Público Press, 1986.

Cisneros, Sandra. *The House on Mango Street.* Houston, Tex.: Arte Público Press, 1984. Reprint. New York: Vintage Books, 1991.

————. *Woman Hollering Creek and Other Stories.* New York: Random House, 1991.

Colón, Jesús. *A Puerto Rican in New York and Other Sketches.* New York: Masses & Mainstream, 1961. Reprint. New York: International Publishers, 1982.

Gonzalez, Genaro. *Rainbow's End.* Houston, Tex.: Arte Público Press, 1988.

————. *Only Sons.* Houston, Tex.: Arte Público Press, 1991.

Hijuelos, Oscar. *Our House in the Last World.* New York: Persea Books, 1983.

————. *The Mambo Kings Play Songs of Love.* New York: Farrar, Straus & Giroux, 1989.

Hinojosa, Rolando. *Sketches of the Valley and Other Works.* Berkeley, Calif.: Tonatiuh/Quinto Sol International, 1972.

————. *Rites and Witnesses.* Houston, Tex.: Arte Público Press, 1982. ·

————. *The Valley.* Ypsilanti, Mich.: Bilingual Review Press, 1983.

————. *Partners in Crime: A Rafe Buenrostro Mystery.* Houston, Tex.: Arte Público Press, 1985.

————. *Dear Rafe.* Houston, Tex.: Arte Público Press, 1985.

————. *Claros Varones de Belken / Fair Gentlemen of Belken County.* Tempe, Ariz.: Bilingual Review Press, 1986.

————. *Klail City.* Houston, Tex.: Arte Público Press, 1987.

————. *Becky and Her Friends.* Houston, Tex.: Arte Público Press, 1989.

Martin, Patricia Preciado. *Days of Plenty, Days of Want.* Tempe, Ariz.: Bilingual Review Press, 1988.

Mohr, Nicholasa. *Nilda.* New York: Harper & Row, 1973. Reprint. Houston, Tex.: Arte Público Press, 1991.

————. *El Bronx Remembered: A Novella and Stories.* New York: Harper & Row, 1975. Reprint. Houston, Tex.: Arte Público Press, 1991.

————. *In Nueva York.* New York: The Dial Press, 1977.

————. *Felita.* New York: The Dial Press, 1979.

————. *Rituals of Survival: A Woman's Portfolio.* Houston, Tex.: Arte Público Press, 1985.

————. *Going Home.* New York: The Dial Press, 1986.

Ortiz-Cofer, Judith. *The Line of the Sun.* Athens, Ga.: University of Georgia Press, 1989.

————. *Silent Dancing: A Partial Remembrance of a Puerto Rican Childhood.* Houston, Tex.: Arte Público Press, 1990.

Paredes, Américo. *George Washington Gomez.* Houston, Tex.: Arte Público Press, 1990.

Rivera, Edward. *Family Installments: Memories of Growing Up Hispanic.* New York: Morrow, 1982.

Rivera, Tomás. *. . . y no se lo tragó la tierra / And the Earth Did Not Part.* Translated by Evangelina Vigil-Piñón. Houston, Tex.: Arte Público Press, 1987.

————. *The Harvest — La Cosecha.* Houston, Tex.: Arte Público Press, 1989.

————. *Tomás Rivera: The Complete Works.* Edited by Juan Olivares. Houston, Tex.: Arte Público Press, 1991.

Rodriguez, Richard. *Hunger of Memory: The Education of Richard Rodriguez.* Boston: David R. Godine, 1982.

Soto, Gary. *Living up the Street: Narrative Recollections.* San Francisco, Calif.: Strawberry Hill Press, 1985. Reprint. New York: Dell, 1992.

————. *Small Faces.* Houston, Tex.: Arte Público Press, 1986.

————. *Lesser Evils: Ten Quartets.* Houston, Tex.: Arte Público Press, 1988.

Thomas, Piri. *Down These Mean Streets.* New York: Knopf, 1967.

————. *Savior, Savior, Hold My Hand.* New York: Doubleday, 1972.

————. *Seven Long Times.* New York: Praeger, 1974.

————. *Stories from El Barrio.* New York: Knopf, 1974.

Vega, Ed. *The Comeback.* Houston, Tex.: Arte Público Press, 1985.

————. *Mendoza's Dreams.* Houston, Tex.: Arte Público Press, 1987.

————. *Casualty Report.* Houston, Tex.: Arte Público Press, 1991.

Villanueva, Alma. *The Ultraviolet Sky.* Tempe, Ariz.: Bilingual Review Press, 1988.

————. *Naked Ladies.* Tempe, Ariz.: Bilingual Review Press, 1992.

Villareal, José Antonio. *Pocho.* New York: Doubleday, 1959.

————. *The Fifth Horseman: A Novel of the Mexican Revolution.* New York: Doubleday, 1974. Reprint. Tempe, Ariz.: Bilingual Review Press, 1984.

————. *Clemente Chacón.* Tempe, Ariz.: Bilingual Review Press, 1984.

Viramontes, Helena María. *The Moths and Other Stories.* Houston, Tex.: Arte Público Press, 1988.

OTHER ANTHOLOGIES OF HISPANIC LITERATURE IN THE UNITED STATES

Albi, F. E., and Jesús G. Nieto, eds. *Sighs and Songs of Aztlán: New Anthology of Chicano Literature.* Bakersfield, Calif.: Universal Press, 1975.

Alurista, and Xilema Rojas-Urista, eds. *Southwest Tales: A Contemporary Collection in Memory of Tomás Rivera.* Colorado Springs, Colo.: Maize Press, 1986.

Anaya, Rudolfo A., ed. *Voces: An Anthology of Nuevo Mejicano Writers.* Albuquerque, N.Mex.: University of New Mexico Press, 1987.

————. *Tierra: Contemporary Fiction of New Mexico.* El Paso, Tex.: Cinco Puntos Press, 1989.

————, and Antonio Marquez, eds. *Cuentos Chicanos: A Short Story Anthology.* Albuquerque, N.Mex.: University of New Mexico Press, 1980.

————, and José Griego y Maestas, eds. *Cuentos: Tales from the Hispanic Southwest.* Santa Fe, N.Mex.: The Museum of New Mexico Press, 1980.

Anzaldúa, Gloria, ed. *Making Face, Making Soul / Haciendo Caras: Creative and Critical Perspectives by Feminists of Color.* San Francisco, Calif.: Spinsters/Aunt Lute Foundation Books, 1991.

————, and Cherríe Moraga, eds. *This Bridge Called My Back: Writings by Radical Women of Color.* New York: Persephone Press, 1981. Reprint. Latham, N.Y.: Kitchen Table/Women of Color Press, 1983.

Babín, Maria Teresa, and Stan Steiner, eds. *Borinquen: An Anthology of Puerto Rican Literature.* New York: Vintage, 1974.

Boza, Maria del Carmen, Beverly Silva, and Carmen Valle, eds. *Nosotras: Latina Literature Today.* Binghamton, N.Y.: Bilingual Review Press, 1986.

Cardenas de Dwyer, Carlota, ed. *Chicano Voices.* Boston: Houghton Mifflin, 1975.

Castaneda, Omar S., Chris Blackwell, and Jonathan Harrington, eds. *New Visions: Fiction by Florida Writers.* Orlando, Fla.: Arbiter Press, 1989.

Chávez, Albert, ed. *Yearnings: Mexican-American Literature.* West Haven, Conn.: Pendulum, 1972.

Fisher, Dexter, ed. *The Third Woman: Minority Women Writers of the United States.* Boston: Houghton Mifflin, 1980.

Flores, Joseph, ed. *Songs and Dreams: Mexican-American Literature.* West Haven, Conn.: Pendulum, 1972.

Gomez, Alma, Cherríe Moraga, and Mariana Romo-Carmona, eds. *Cuentos: Stories by Latinas.* Latham, N.Y.: Kitchen Table/Women of Color Press, 1983.

Harth, Dorothy E., and Lewis M. Baldwin, eds. *Voices of Aztlán: Chicano Literature of Today.* New York: New American Library, 1974.

Hayes, Joe, ed. *The Day It Snowed Tortillas: Tales from Spanish New Mexico.* Santa Fe, N.Mex.: Mariposa Publications, 1982.

Hospital, Carolina, ed. *Cuban American Writers: Los Atrevidos.* Princeton, N.J.: Linden Lane Press, 1988.

Kanellos, Nicolás, ed. *Los Tejanos: A Texas-Mexican Anthology.* Houston, Tex.: Arte Público Press, 1980.

————. *A Decade of Hispanic Literature: An Anniversary Anthology.* Houston, Tex.: Arte Público Press, 1982.

————. *Short Fiction by Hispanic Writers of the United States.* Houston, Tex.: Arte Público Press, 1992.

Keller, Gary, and Francisco Jimenez, eds. *Hispanics in the United States: An Anthology of Creative Literature, Volume 1.* Tempe, Ariz.: Bilingual Review Press, 1980.

————. *Hispanics in the United States: An Anthology of Creative Literature, Volume 2.* Tempe, Ariz.: Bilingual Review Press, 1982.

————, and Rose M. Beebee, eds. *¡Viva la lengua! A Contemporary Reader.* New York: Harcourt Brace Jovanovich, 1975.

Kopp, Karl and Jane, eds. *Southwest.* Albuquerque, N.Mex.: Red Earth, 1977.

Ludwig, Edward, and James Santibañez, eds. *The Chicanos: Mexican American Voices.* Baltimore, Md.: Penguin, 1971.

Ortego, Philip D., ed. *We Are Chicanos: An Anthology of Mexican-American Literature.* New York: Washington Square Press, 1972.

Paley, Julian, ed. *Best New Chicano Literature 1989.* Tempe, Ariz.: Bilingual Review Press, 1990.

Paredes, Américo, and Raymond Paredes, eds. *Mexican American Authors.* Boston: Houghton Mifflin, 1972.

Poey, Delia, and Virgil Suarez, eds. *Iguana Dreams: New Latino Fiction.* New York: HarperCollins, 1992.

Ramos, Juanita, ed. *Compañeras: Latina Lesbians.* Latham, N.Y.: Kitchen Table/Women of Color Press, 1988.

Rios-C., Herminio, and Octavio I. Romano-V., eds. *El Espejo — The Mirror: Selected Mexican-American Literature.* Berkeley, Calif.: Quinto Sol Publications, 1969.

Romano-V., Octavio I., ed. *The Grito del Sol Collection — Anthology.* Berkeley, Calif.: Tonatiuh/Quinto Sol International, 1988.

Simmen, Edward, ed. *New Voices in Literature: The Mexican American.* Edinburg, Tex.: Pan American University, 1971.

————. *The Chicano: From Caricature to Self-Portrait.* New York: New American Library, 1971.

————. *North of the Rio Grande: The Mexican-American Experience in Short Fiction.* New York: Mentor, 1992.

Simmons, Marc, ed. *Taos to Tome: True Tales of Hispanic New Mexico.* Albuquerque, N.Mex.: Adobe Press, 1978.

Steiner, Stan, and Luis Valdez, eds. *Aztlán: An Anthology of Mexican-American Literature.* New York: Knopf, 1972.

Tatum, Charles M., ed. *Mexican American Literature.* Orlando, Fla.: Harcourt Brace Jovanovich, 1990.

Turner, Faythe, ed. *Puerto Rican Writers at Home in the USA.* Seattle, Wash.: Open Hand Publishing, Inc., 1991.

Velez, Diana, ed. *Reclaiming Medusa: Short Stories by Contemporary Puerto Rican Women.* Latham, N.Y.: Kitchen Table/Women of Color Press, 1988.

Vigil-Piñon, Evangelina, ed. *Woman of Her Word: Hispanic Women Write.* Houston, Tex.: Arte Público Press, 1987.

Weigle, Marta, ed. *Two Guadalupes: Hispanic Legends and Magic Tales from Northern New Mexico*. Santa Fe, N.Mex.: Ancient City Press, 1987.

Zamora, Bernice, ed. *The Best of Chicano Fiction*. Albuquerque, N.Mex.: Pajarito Publications, 1981.

BOOKS ABOUT HISPANICS IN
THE UNITED STATES AND THEIR LITERATURE

Acosta-Belen, Edna. *The Puerto Rican Woman*. New York: Praeger, 1979.

Acuña, Rudolfo. *Occupied America: A History of Chicanos*. New York: Harper & Row, 1981.

———. *A Mexican-American Chronicle*. New York: American Book Co., 1971.

Anaya, Rudolfo A. *A Chicano in China*. Albuquerque, N.Mex.: University of New Mexico Press, 1986.

———, and Francisco Lomelí, eds. *Aztlán: Essays on the Chicano Homeland*. Albuquerque, N.Mex.: Academia / El Norte, 1989.

Arnold, Elliott. *The Time of the Gringo*. New York: Knopf, 1953.

Bruce-Novoa, Juan. *Chicano Authors: Inquiry by Interview*. Austin, Tex.: University of Texas Press, 1980.

———. *Retrospace: Collected Essays on Chicano Literature*. Houston, Tex.: Arte Público Press, 1990.

Calderón, Héctor, and José David Saldívar. *Chicano Criticism in a Social Context*. Durham, N.C.: Duke University Press, 1989.

Camarillo, Albert. *Chicanos in a Changing Society*. Cambridge, Mass.: Harvard University Press, 1979.

Castro, Tony. *Chicano Power*. New York: Dutton, 1974.

Chavez, John Richard. *The Lost Land: The Chicano Image of the Southwest*. Albuquerque, N.Mex.: University of New Mexico Press, 1984.

Chavez, Linda. *Out of the Barrio: Toward a New Politics of Hispanic Assimilation*. New York: Basic Books, 1991.

Elsasser, Nan, Kyle Mackenzie, and Yvonne Tixier. *Las Mujeres: Conversations from a Hispanic Community*. New York: McGraw-Hill, 1980.

Fabre, Genevieve, ed. *European Perspectives on Hispanic Literature in the United States*. Houston, Tex.: Arte Público Press, 1988.

Flores, Juan. *Divided Borders*. Houston, Tex.: Arte Público Press, 1991.

Galarza, Ernesto. *Barrio Boy: The Story of a Boy's Acculturation*. Notre Dame, Ind.: University of Notre Dame Press, 1971.

Gann, L. H., and Peter J. Duigan. *The Hispanics in the United States: A History*. Boulder, Colo.: Westview Press, 1986.

Herrera-Sobek, Maria. *Beyond Stereotypes: The Critical Analysis of Chicana Literature*. Binghamton, N.Y.: Bilingual Review Press, 1985.

———, and Helena María Viramontes, eds. *Chicana Creativity and Criticism: Charting New Frontiers in American Literature*. Houston, Tex.: Arte Público Press, 1988.

Horno-Delgado, Asunción, ed. *Breaking Boundaries: Latina Writings and Critical Readings.* Amherst, Mass.: University of Massachusetts Press, 1989.

Jiménez, Francisco, ed. *The Identification and Analysis of Chicano Literature.* Binghamton, N.Y.: Bilingual Review Press, 1979.

Kanellos, Nicolás. *Understanding the Chicano Experience Through Literature.* Houston, Tex.: University of Houston Press, 1981.

Lattin, Vernon E. *Contemporary Chicano Fiction: A Critical Survey.* Binghamton, N.Y.: Bilingual Review Press, 1986.

———, Rolando Hinojosa, and Gary Keller. *Tomás Rivera, 1935–1984: The Man and His Work.* Tempe, Ariz.: Bilingual Review Press, 1988.

Lomelí, Francisco A., and Carl A. Shirley, eds. *Dictionary of Literary Biography.* Volume 82: Chicano Writers. Detroit, Mich.: Gale Research, 1989.

Meier, Matt S., and Feliciano Rivera. *The Chicanos: A History of Mexican Americans.* New York: Hill, 1972.

———. *Readings on La Raza: The Twentieth Century.* New York: Hill, 1974.

Melville, Margarita. *Twice a Minority: Mexican American Women.* St. Louis, Mo.: Mosby Press, 1980.

Mirande, Alfredo, and Evangelina Enriquez. *La Chicana: The Mexican American Woman.* Chicago: University of Chicago Press, 1977.

Mohr, Eugene. *The Nuyorican Experience: Literature of the Puerto Rican Minority.* Westport, Conn.: Greenwood Press, 1982.

Moore, Joan W., and Harry Pachon. *Hispanics in the United States.* Englewood Cliffs, N.J.: Prentice-Hall, 1985.

Moquin, Wayne, and Charles Van Doren, eds. *A Documentary History of the Mexican Americans.* New York: Bantam, 1971.

Nava, Julian. *Mexican-Americans: Past, Present, and Future.* Millbrae, Calif.: American Book Co., 1969.

Olivares, Julian, ed. *International Studies in Honor of Tomás Rivera.* Houston, Tex.: Arte Público Press, 1986.

———. *U.S. Hispanic Autobiography.* Houston, Tex.: Arte Público Press, 1988.

Paredes, Américo. *With a Pistol in His Hand: A Border Ballad and Its Hero.* Austin, Tex.: University of Texas Press, 1958.

———. *Folktales of Mexico.* Chicago: University of Chicago Press, 1970.

———. *A Texas-Mexican "Cancionero": Folksongs of the Lower Border.* Urbana, Ill.: University of Illinois Press, 1976.

Perez-Firmat, Gustavo. *Do the Americas Have a Common Literature?* Durham, N.C.: Duke University Press, 1990.

Powell, Lawrence. *Southwest Classics: The Creative Literature of the Arid Lands — Essays on the Books and their Writers.* Tucson, Ariz.: The University of Arizona Press, 1974.

Robinson, Cecil. *Mexico and the Hispanic Southwest in American Literature.* Tucson, Ariz.: University of Arizona Press, 1977.

Rocard, Marcienne. *The Children of the Sun: The Mexican American in Litera-ture.* Translated from the French *Les fils du soleil* by Edward G. Brown. Tucson, Ariz.: University of Arizona Press, 1989.

Romo, Ricardo. *East Lost Angeles: History of a Barrio.* Austin, Tex.: University of Texas Press, 1983.

Ryan, Bryan, ed. *Hispanic Writers: A Selection of Sketches from Contemporary Authors.* Detroit, Mich.: Gale Research, 1991.

Salas, Floyd. *Buffalo Nickel.* Houston, Tex.: Arte Público Press, 1992.

Saldívar, José David, ed. *The Rolando Hinojosa Reader: Essays Historical and Critical.* Houston, Tex.: Arte Público Press, 1985.

Saldívar, Ramón. *Chicano Narrative: The Dialectics of Difference.* Madison, Wis.: University of Wisconsin Press, 1990.

Sanchez, Rosaura, and Rosa Martínez Cruz. *Essays on La Mujer.* Los Angeles: Chicano Studies Center Publications, University of California Press, 1977.

Shular, Antonia Cantaneda, Tomás Ybarra-Frausto, and Joseph Sommers, eds. *Literatura Chicana: Texto y Contexto / Chicano Literature: Text and Con-text.* Englewood Cliffs, N.J.: Prentice-Hall, 1972.

Sommers, Joseph, and Tomás Ybarra-Frausto, eds. *Modern Chicano Writers: A Collection of Critical Essays.* Englewood Cliffs, N.J.: Prentice-Hall, 1979.

Tatum, Charles M. *Chicano Literature.* Boston: Twayne Publishers, 1982.

Vega, Bernardo. *Memoirs of Bernardo Vega.* Translated from the Spanish *Memorias de Bernardo Vega* by Juan Flores. New York: Monthly Review Press, 1984.

Vento, Arnold C., Alurista, and José Flores Peregrino. *Portraits of the Chicano Artist as a Young Man: The Making of the "Author" in Three Chicano Novels.* Albuquerque, N.Mex.: Pajarito Publications, 1979.

Vidal, Marta. *Chicanas Speak Out.* New York: Pathfinder Press, 1971.

Villaseñor, Victor. *Jury: The People vs. Juan Corona.* Boston: Little, Brown, 1977.

Walker, Franklin. *A Literary History of Southern California.* Berkeley, Calif.: University of California Press, 1950.

CONTRIBUTORS

Oscar "Zeta" Acosta was born in El Paso, Texas, in 1936. After serving in the air force, Acosta attended college and graduated from law school. His semiautobiographical novels, *The Autobiography of a Brown Buffalo* and *The Revolt of the Cockroach People*, are written in a high-energy style and describe the adventures of a hard-living lawyer and writer seeking an identity among Chicanos and Anglos. In 1974, during a vacation in Mazatlán, Mexico, Acosta disappeared. Since then, rumors have circulated that he had worked for the CIA or that perhaps he was killed because of his political activities on behalf of Chicanos in Los Angeles.

Julia Alvarez was born in the Dominican Republic in 1951 and came to the United States in 1965. She received a B.A. from Middlebury College and an M.A. from Syracuse University. She has taught at Phillips Andover Academy, the University of Vermont, George Washington University, and the University of Illinois, and is currently assistant professor of English at Middlebury College. Alvarez has published two volumes of poetry and a novel, *How the García Girls Lost Their Accents*.

Rudolfo A. Anaya is one of the foremost Hispanic fiction writers of his generation. He was born in 1937 in Pastura, New Mexico, and received both his B.A. and M.A. in literature from the University of New Mexico, in addition to an M.A. in guidance and counseling. Among his literary awards are the Premio Quinto Sol for *Bless Me, Ultima*, published in 1972, which has sold more than 275,000 copies, and the Before Columbus Foundation American

Book Award for *Tortuga*. He has published five novels, several collections of short stories, anthologies, poetry, and criticism. Anaya is professor of English at the University of New Mexico.

GLORIA ANZALDÚA, a Chicana poet and fiction writer, is the editor of a number of anthologies, including *This Bridge Called My Back: Writings by Radical Women of Color*, which won the Before Columbus Foundation American Book Award, and *Borderlands / La Frontera: The New Mestiza*. She is also the author of a bilingual children's picture book, *Prietita Has a Friend / Prietita tiene un amigo*. Her stories have appeared in numerous magazines. She has taught at the University of Texas, San Francisco State University, Vermont College of Norwich University, and the University of California at Santa Cruz.

NASH CANDELARIA was born in Los Angeles in 1928, into a family that helped found Albuquerque, New Mexico, in 1706. He won an American Book Award for his novel *Not by the Sword*. Other works include *Memories of the Alhambra* and *Inheritance of Strangers* (a sequel to *Not by the Sword*), and a collection of short stories, *The Day the Cisco Kid Shot John Wayne*.

DENISE CHÁVEZ was born in Las Cruces, New Mexico, in 1948. She has a B.A. in theater from New Mexico State University, an M.F.A. in theater from Trinity University in San Antonio, Texas, and an M.A. in creative writing from the University of New Mexico. She is currently assistant professor of theater at the University of Houston. In 1990 an adaptation of her story cycle, *The Last of the Menu Girls* (1986), was produced as a play by Main Street Theater and the Teatro Bilingue de Houston.

SANDRA CISNEROS was born in 1954 in Chicago and first became known with her collection of poetry *My Wicked Wicked Ways*. She has worked in several colleges and universities as a writer-in-residence. In 1985 Cisneros's first work of fiction, *The House on Mango Street*, a novel about a young woman's coming of age told in a series of vignettes, was awarded the Before Columbus Foundation American Book Award. Her collection of short stories, *Woman Hollering Creek and Other Stories*, was chosen as a Noteworthy Book of 1991 by the *New York Times*.

JESÚS COLÓN is best known for his landmark work of essays and reminiscences, *A Puerto Rican in New York and Other Sketches*, which was first published in 1961. Colón was born in Cayey, Puerto Rico. At the age of seventeen he stowed away on the SS *Carolina* bound for New York. There he continued the socialist and communist activities he had begun in Puerto Rico and wrote a regular column for the *Daily Worker* (later the *Daily*

World), the city's communist newspaper. He was subpoenaed by the House Committee on Un-American Activities and later ran for the U.S. Senate on the American Labor Party ticket. In 1969 Colón ran for the office of comptroller of the city of New York but was defeated (this was the same election in which Norman Mailer ran for mayor). Colón died in 1974, and his ashes were scattered over his homeland.

GENARO GONZALEZ, born in McAllen, Texas, in 1949, holds a Ph.D. in social psychology from the University of California at Santa Cruz. He is the son of migrant workers, and throughout his childhood he traveled with his parents from farm to farm as they sought work. His first novel, *Rainbow's End*, was nominated for an American Book Award. His collection of short stories, *Only Sons*, was published by Arte Público Press in 1990. Gonzalez is associate professor of psychology at Pan American University in Edinburg, Texas.

OSCAR HIJUELOS was born in New York City in 1951 and received both his bachelor of arts and master's degrees from the City College of New York. He is the author of two novels: *Our House in the Last World* and *The Mambo Kings Play Songs of Love*. The latter was awarded the 1990 Pulitzer Prize in fiction and was made into a Warner Brothers movie. Hijuelos's other awards include the Rome Prize for literature from the American Academy and Institute of Arts and Letters, a Guggenheim Fellowship, and the Ingram Merrill Foundation Award.

ROLANDO HINOJOSA (SMITH) is the dean of Mexican-American writers. He was born in the border town of Mercedes, Texas, in 1929 of a Mexican-American father and an Anglo mother and grew up in a bilingual household. Hinojosa's major work is the Klail City Death Trip series of novels, which began in 1972 with the publication of *Estampas del Valle y otras obras*. The series follows the exploits of the inhabitants of Klail City and the surrounding area, told in their own voices, through anecdotes, dialogue, and interviews. The most recent installment is *Becky and Her Friends*, published by Arte Público Press in 1989. In 1972 Hinojosa was awarded the Premio Quinto Sol for best novel for *Estampas del Valle*, and, in 1976, the Casa de las Americas Prize for best novel for *Klail City y sus alrededores*. He holds a doctorate in Spanish from the University of Illinois and is currently the Ellen Clayton Garwood Professor at the University of Texas at Austin.

PATRICIA PRECIADO MARTIN was born in Prescott, Arizona, in 1939 and was graduated from the University of Arizona. In the early 1960s she served in the Peace Corps and later taught high school in California. She has done extensive field work in Mexican-American oral and folk history and has worked as a consultant and field historian for the Mexican Heritage Project at the Arizona

Historical Society in Tucson. In 1983 her collection of oral histories, *Images and Conversations: Mexican-Americans Recall a Southwestern Past* (University of Arizona Press, 1983), was presented the Virginia McCormick Scully Award for the best book published by a Chicano or Native American writer that year.

NICHOLASA MOHR is the foremost U.S.-based Puerto Rican writer of her generation. She was born in New York City in 1935 and was educated at the Art Students League, the Brooklyn Museum Art School, and the Pratt Center for Contemporary Printmaking. Among her books are *Nilda, El Bronx Remembered, In Nueva York, Felita, Rituals of Survival: A Woman's Portfolio,* and *Going Home.* Among her awards are the Jane Addams Children's Book Award and the *New York Times* Outstanding Book of the Year (for *Nilda*), the American Book Award, and an honorary doctor of letters degree from the State University of New York at Albany. In 1976 *El Bronx Remembered* was a finalist for the National Book Award. Mohr lives in Brooklyn, New York.

JUDITH ORTÍZ-COFER was born in 1952 in Hormigueros, Puerto Rico, spent much of her childhood in Paterson, New Jersey, and received an M.A. in English from Florida Atlantic University. She has published two books of poetry, the novel *The Line of the Sun*, which was the first new work of fiction ever published by the University of Georgia Press, and a collection of personal essays, *Silent Dancing.* Ortiz-Cofer teaches at the University of Georgia.

AMÉRICO PAREDES is a pivotal figure in the history of Hispanic letters in the United States. He was born in 1915 in Brownsville, on the Texas-Mexico border, and became interested in the border traditions. In 1934 one of his early poems won first place in the Texas state contest sponsored by Trinity College in San Antonio. The following year he began publishing poetry in *La Prensa* newspaper there. Paredes's interest in border folklore led to the 1958 publication of his University of Texas at Austin doctoral thesis, *With His Pistol in His Hand: A Border Ballad and Its Hero,* one of the first studies of the Mexican *corrido.* Paredes is professor emeritus of English at the University of Texas at Austin. In 1989 he was awarded the Charles Frankel Prize by the National Endowment for the Humanities, "for outstanding contributions to the public's understanding of the texts, themes, and ideas of the humanities."

EDWARD RIVERA was born in Puerto Rico in 1944 and came to New York City at the age of seven. He graduated from the City College of New York and received an M.A. from Columbia University. His major work is *Family Installments*, a semifictional memoir about a Puerto Rican family in New York's El Barrio. Rivera is an assistant professor of English at City College.

TOMÁS RIVERA was born in Crystal City, Texas, in 1935 and received a doctorate in romance languages and literatures from the University of Oklahoma. He was a poet, novelist, short story writer, literary critic, college administrator, and educational specialist. His novel . . . *y no se lo tragó la tierra (And the Earth Did Not Part)* is one of the most highly regarded Latino novels ever published. It was originally written in Spanish and has appeared in three English translations. Tomás Rivera died in 1984.

RICHARD RODRIGUEZ, a Chicano essayist and teacher born in San Francisco in 1947, is the author of *Hunger of Memory* (David R. Godine, 1982), an autobiographical account of his education and his search for identity and artistic style. He grew up in Sacramento, where he attended Catholic schools before going to Stanford University, Columbia University, the Warburg Institute in London, and the University of California at Berkeley, eventually completing a degree in the English literature of the Renaissance. His works have been published in *Harper's Magazine*, *The American Scholar*, *Saturday Review*, *Change*, and elsewhere. His second book, *Mexico's Children*, was published by Viking in 1992. A vocal critic of bilingual education, he has lectured extensively in colleges and universities across the country. He lives in San Francisco.

GARY SOTO has won many honors for his writing. He is the author of eight volumes of poetry, nine books of prose (both fiction and nonfiction), and scripts for short films. He has received the Before Columbus Foundation American Book Award, Guggenheim and NEA fellowships, the Bess Hokin Award for poetry, the "Discovery"/*The Nation* Prize, and the California Library Association's Patricia Beatty Award. He holds an M.F.A. degree in creative writing and teaches in the English department at the University of California at Berkeley.

PIRI THOMAS's autobiographical novel *Down These Mean Streets* is one of the best-known works about growing up Puerto Rican in New York City. Thomas was born in New York in 1928 and grew up on the Manhattan streets of El Barrio. He is also the author of the novels *Savior, Savior Hold My Hand* and *Seven Long Times*, in addition to the story collection *Stories from El Barrio* and the play *The Golden Streets*. He lives in Berkeley, California.

J. L. TORRES is a Puerto Rican writer. He was raised in New York City and has an M.F.A. degree from Columbia University. He teaches English at the University of Puerto Rico at Cayey.

ED VEGA was born in Ponce, Puerto Rico, in 1936 and came to New York City when he was twelve years old. He was raised in a devout Baptist home and grew up playing hockey. Vega is the author of three published works of fiction: the novel *The Comeback* and two collections of short fiction, *Mendoza's Dreams* and *Casualty Report*.

ALMA VILLANUEVA was born in California in 1944. She is the author of *Bloodroot*, a collection of poetry, and the long narrative poem *Mother, May I?* She holds an M.F.A. in creative writing.

JOSÉ ANTONIO VILLAREAL's novel *Pocho*, published in 1959, is widely considered to be the first Chicano novel. In addition to *Pocho*, Villareal is the author of *The Fifth Horseman* and *Clemente Chacón*. He was born in Los Angeles in 1924.

HELENA MARÍA VIRAMONTES was born in 1954 in East Los Angeles, California. She has a degree in English literature from Immaculate Heart College and an M.F.A. from the University of California at Irvine. She is the author of *The Moths and Other Stories* (Arte Público Press, 1988).

*   *   *

HAROLD AUGENBRAUM is director of the Mercantile Library of New York and former deputy director of the Museum of the City of New York. In 1992 he organized a project, funded by the National Endowment for the Humanities, on fiction writing by U.S. Hispanics, and edited *Latinos in English: A Selected Bibliography of Latino Fiction Writers of the United States* (The Mercantile Library of New York).

ILAN STAVANS is a Mexican novelist and critic, born in 1961. He holds a Ph.D. from Columbia University. Stavans is the author of a number of fiction and nonfiction books, written in Spanish and English, including *Imagining Columbus: The Literary Voyage* (Twayne), *Prontuario* (Joaquín Mortiz), and *Talia y el cielo* (Plaza & Valdés), which won the 1992 Latino Literature Prize. He has translated Felipe Alfau's poetry into English (*Sentimental Songs / La poesía cursi*, Dalkey Archive Press) and is the editor of *Tropical Synagogues: An Anthology of Jewish–Latin American Short Stories* (Holmes and Meier). His essays, stories, and reviews appear regularly in newspapers and journals in Europe, Latin America, and the United States.